BOOK OF THE KINGDOM

CATHOLIC BOOK
OF KNOWLEDGE

Volume Three

Behind the altar of the Church of Our Lady Queen of All Creation, Hemel Hempstead, is the artist
R. G. Lloyd's modern interpretation of the Dedication. He has painted a colourful mural depicting
Our Lady being crowned by Christ the Son and God the Father

BOOK OF THE KINGDOM

CATHOLIC BOOK
OF KNOWLEDGE

CATHOLIC LIFE and TEACHING:
Tradition, Doctrine, Church History

Over 1000 illustrations, 53 Color Plates, 13 Color Strips

Editor:

REVEREND LEONARD BOASE, S.J.

Assistant Editor: MABEL QUIN

Volume Three

THE KINGDOM
IN BEING

Contributors:
Rev. ISAIAS CAPALDI, S.J. · Rev. MOTHER CECILY
PETER CRABBE · G. PARISH
M. LANG · MABEL QUIN

Illustrators:
E. BLATTNER · FRANK M. LEA
ALFRED HACKNEY

CATHOLIC HOME PRESS, INC.,
6120 West North Avenue, Chicago 1, Illinois.

CONTENTS

COLOR PLATES

RELIGIOUS MASTERPIECES

BLACK AND WHITE REPRODUCTIONS

xiii

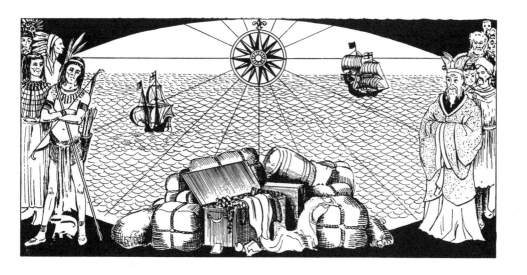

THE MODERN AGE

Galleons and guns, uncharted seas crashing on the bowsprits and lands unknown looming up out of the surge; Indians and Incas, Chinamen and negro slaves, gold and silver, silks and spices, and travellers' tales of pirates on the Spanish Main . . . what an exciting world it was for the men who lived with Drake and Shakespeare and good Queen Bess!

Perhaps you think it was a very long time ago, and your eyebrows go up when you look at the heading of this chapter and find us calling it "The Modern Age."

But it is. The Modern Age begins then. We have speeded up things dizzily since your grandfathers were boys, but the beginning of the exciting time was about four hundred years ago.

Let us try and see the Church of Christ, coming out of the Middle Ages and sailing like a towering galleon into the bright sunlight and the thundering waves of the Age of Discovery. What was happening in this new and exciting world in which the Church had to proclaim the message of God, the teaching of Jesus Christ? Six things we must keep in mind: it was the age of Discovery; it was the dawn of what we call Science; there was a great Revival of Learning; printing became widespread; there was a great revolt against the Church called the Protestant Reformation; the people of Europe grew very conscious of their own nations; and the spirit of nationalism came in.

These six things were all twisted together, like strands in a rope. They reacted on one another. Take the "lodestone" (magnet to you). There was a Franciscan Friar named Roger Bacon—he lived from 1214 to 1294, which is really earlier than our "Modern Age,"—who discovered a number of scientific facts, among others that a "leading stone," that is a lodestone or magnet, would always come to rest pointing north. There's your compass! With-

Edward Laning   Photo Mansell

Gutenberg at his press showing one of his patrons a page of his famous Bible

out the mariner's compass where would the great discoverers like Vasco de Gama and Columbus have been?

But what was Friar Bacon looking for when he found the lodestone? He himself was probably looking just for knowledge; but many of the "scientists" of his day were looking for the "Philosopher's Stone." They thought they could find something that would turn ordinary metals into precious gold and silver. Who wanted the gold and silver? Chiefly the kings and nobles, who wanted to pay soldiers to fight for them. And that fact pulls back a curtain and shows us a world in which powerful men were taken up with fighting, and were content to leave learning, and even reading and writing, to poor scholars or "clerks."

Incidentally, things are not so different now: just as in the old days it was the search for the philosopher's stone (to pay the soldiers) which led to many scientific discoveries; so now the race to make atom-bombs is leading to atoms-for-peace.

But why call it the "Philosopher's Stone"? Who was the Philosopher? That takes us back to something you can read about in Volume II of this book. In the chapter "The Northern Nations" you will read how for centuries Europe was in turmoil, learning was limited to the monks and the churchmen ("cleric" or "clerk" meant "learned man") and only gradually did the men of the West rediscover the ancient wisdom of Greece and Rome. They had been mainly concerned with the teaching of the Church, handing on the revelation of Jesus Christ; and this is what we call Theology. As they became once more interested in all that men can find out for themselves about the world they live in, they came to call this kind of knowledge Philosophy. Hence the "Philosopher's Stone."

At the time of which we are speaking, the beginning of the Modern Age, there was, we said, a great Revival of Learning. Something happened which accidentally gave a big thrust to that Revival. In 1453 the Ottoman Turks captured Constantinople. The City of Constantine, also called Byzantium, had inherited the ancient Greek traditions of learning and of art. When the Turks broke in, the scholars and artists fled. They fled to Europe. There they helped to enkindle the great enthusiasm for learning and art which was beginning.

At this time also something else happened. In 1454 Gutenburg of Mainz invented printing with movable type. This meant that from then books could easily be multiplied. Learning was being put within the reach of all.

Now another twist of the woven strands! The Turks had Constantinople. They blocked the way to the East by land. Was there another way? Sailors were now venturing far out to sea; they had the compass to sail by. Moreover, people were beginning to realise that the world was round. Long, long before, the ancient Greeks, such as Eratosthenes and Ptolemy, had worked this out, and now their ancient learning was spreading through Europe again. The brothers Marco and Nicolo Polo had travelled overland to the Far East, and came back with exciting stories of Cathay and Zipangu (China and Japan, you would say). If the Turks were barring the routes overland for silks and spices from the Orient, might there not be another way?

Vasco da Gama, the Portuguese adventurer, set sail in 1498. He rounded the Cape of Good Hope in Africa, and came to India by the sea. But already Christopher Columbus, a Genoese captain, with ships and money from Queen Isabella of Spain, had set out to reach the East Indies across the Atlantic

Photo Mansell
An engraving of Friar Roger Bacon who discovered the "lodestone"

The rulers and adventurers of Europe felt that new empires were theirs for the taking and the Church was roused to a burst of missionary zeal, the like of which had been unknown for centuries, unknown since the last of the pagan tribes of Europe had been baptised.

The consequence was something like a race. It was a race between the missionaries and the conquerors and traders. The missionaries learnt soon enough that when the traders and colonisers entered the new lands, their greed and cruelty blocked the way for preaching the Faith, and you will read later in this book how the Jesuits in South America tried to keep the natives safe from them; in North America, Franciscans did the same. But to begin with, the missionaries had to sail on the explorers' ships; there was no other way to get there. And although the seizing of the new lands by the men of Europe was befouled by untold avarice and violence, yet the Catholic kings of Europe did feel it was their duty as Christians to bring to the ignorant heathen the benefits of the Faith. The very names that were given to the newly-discovered lands are memorials to the Christian faith of the explorers and missionaries. San Francisco, San Domingo, Trinidad, Los Angeles, Vera Cruz, and countless more.

The early explorers gave the name "Indies" to the lands they were discovering. They mistook the West Indies for East Indies at first. For there had always been some contact between Europe and the dim distance beyond the deserts of Araby, and it was the search for ways of getting the silks and spices of the East which gave driving-force to the adventurous sailors. When full contact was made, the missionaries of the Church found themselves face to face with mighty paganisms of which they had never dreamed, with the Hinduism of India and with Buddhism. Greatest

Ocean, and on the way had found America. In 1520 Ferdinand Magellan sailed round the South of America—through the Straits which bear his name—and into the Pacific. Three years later his ship returned to Cadiz, though he himself had been killed. There could be no doubt now that the world was round!

Till then the men of Europe had felt that Europe was the world. They had been Christian men, and their world was one in faith. They had felt it to be a compact unity, surrounded by darkness out of which came their powerful enemies the Saracens, followers of Mohammed; but the darkness was like a thick wall, and about the unknown beyond it they thought little. Now they had suddenly come upon vast continents, wider than their own world, and upon teeming millions of pagans.

Two big results followed at once.

Columbus asking for bread and water at La Rabida in 1486.   From a painting in the convent at La Rabida

among the names of those who spent their lives and shed their blood to make Christ known to millions in the East, was the name of Francis Xavier. Of him you will read in another chapter.

Meanwhile the Europe from which these missionaries went forth was in a ferment. Christian unity was being split asunder by the rebellious movements called in general "Protestantism"; and the traces of political unity that remained from the ancient Roman

Cortes and his men look upon a vast continent stretching from the Pacific shores

Empire were vanishing as the new nations became increasingly conscious of themselves.

In Spain and France, and in England too, the power of the King was growing. The nobles, who had been so mighty in the old feudal days, were less mighty now. Jealousies between nations grew more intense. Rivalry in grasping at the trade and in seizing the lands which the discoverers had found, led to quarrelling even among Catholic nations; for instance Spain and Portugal quarrelled over South America, and laid their quarrel before the Pope, but neither side would accept his decision when he gave it.

Still more disastrous for the Church was the fact that kings and princes, like our own Henry VIII, claimed to be not only rulers but spiritual rulers. The Protestant princes found in Protestant-ism a very profitable means of increasing their power over their people. "He who rules the land sets the religion," they declared, and they set it to suit themselves.

But the deep feelings of patriotism, or love of country, that were aroused in the nations were good feelings in themselves. There was much that men could be justly proud of in the achievements of sailors and adventurers, of merchants and craftsmen, of poets and playwrights and painters, and of the brilliant men who were both artists and scientists.

It was a "brave, new world." Shake-speare's heroine, Miranda, in *The Tempest* cried out "O brave, new world, that has such people in it!" And you may remember that she had lived on an island with Prospero her father, and it was when the tempest threw on to the island a company of gallant gentlemen that she cried out excitedly. That was the feeling of the time. The great discoveries, the wealth pouring into Europe, the splendid buildings that were rising everywhere, the marble statues that seemed alive, the glorious paintings, the rich and lovely dresses of the women, the magnificent attire of the men, all these things stirred the heart and made men proud and glad to be alive.

But it was not all pomp and ceremony. To make their wonderful statues and paint their pictures that looked so real, the artists studied the human body. This led to a great increase of knowledge of the way we are made, which was of great value for the science and practice of medicine. In the early sixteenth century Andreas Vesalius published the first real account of the structure of the human body.

Yet Vesalius was only following in the footsteps of an artist. Leonardo da Vinci lived from 1451 to 1519, and we have his notebooks containing 750 sketches showing the way the body is made. Leonardo was a very great man: besides being a painter, he was a scientist. He realised the importance of what Friar Bacon had taught, about making experiments and observing facts. He pioneered in anatomy, but also in the art of war and in engineering. He studied the problems of flight, and imagined aeroplanes and submarines. He was a great mathematician and applied his mathematics to his feats of engineering.

So many are the great names of this age that we should write a catalogue if we wrote them all. Michaelangelo is one. The ceilings of the Sistine Chapel

Stradanus *Photo Mansell*

A Renaissance scientist at work in his study

Photo Mansell

Leonardo da Vinci

was born. He lived from 1564 to 1642.

The march of science was outpacing the minds of ordinary men, and it is well known that the great Galileo got into trouble with the Church authorities. It was partly due to his own aggressive attitude, but it was chiefly because the authorities felt he was putting new wine into old wine-skins, and upsetting the simple people who could not absorb quickly enough all the startling truths that were being discovered. What is not true, though you will constantly read it in books, even in your school text-books, is the statement that the Church is opposed to science, or that there is a conflict between science and religion.

In the "brave new world," the beginning of the modern age, when the spirit of revolt against the Church was in the

in Rome, with their amazingly powerful paintings, are a memorial to his genius, but perhaps more than anything else the great dome of St. Peter's tells us of the grandeur of the achievements of the men of those great days.

Astronomy was the science that made the most astonishing progress in that age. In the fifteenth century Nicholas de Cusa (1401–1464) had realised that our world is only one tiny planet of one small group in the midst of a universe so vast that there seems no end to it. After him came Nicholas Copernicus (1473–1543). He saw that it was not the heavens wheeling round the earth, but the earth spinning round its axis, that gave us night and day. And twenty-one years after his death, Galileo Galilei

Photo Mansell

Nicholas Copernicus, founder of modern astronomy

Galileo presenting his first telescope to the Doge of Venice

air, there was a great danger that man's discoveries would lead him into pride. The Church was anxious to prevent that. She did not quite succeed, and it is only, in our own times that men are coming back to a mood of humility, through their realisation of the greatness of God's creation. But the Church has always taught, as she teaches now, that true science is good, and is a great help to man in his reaching towards God.

Over the brilliant age which was the beginning of the modern world, there loomed a dark and menacing cloud. It was the cloud of the revolt against the Church which split Christendom asunder, and divided Protestants from Catholics.

Of that great disaster, of the mounting evils which led to it, and of the mighty reform which the Church achieved, you will read in other chapters of this book. It is the story of a storm, the swell of which is shaking us yet, but through it all, the Church sails on, battered but unsinkable, because She is the one, true Church of Christ, against whom the very gates of hell shall not prevail.

THE INVENTION OF PRINTING AND
THE POPULARISING OF THE BIBLE

If you had lived in England in the Middle Ages it would be by the greatest good luck that you would have been able to read or write, and if you had been able to read there would have been very few books for you to study.

Early Written Books

You see, books were not printed then as they are today. Every book had to be copied out by hand by one of the few men who knew how to write. He might have been a monk, sitting in the library of one of the great monasteries, writing out his manuscript and decorating it with beautiful illustrations, all with the utmost loving care, or he might have been a "scrivener," that is, a man who gained his living by copying books to the orders of rich patrons or of wealthy monasteries. There have been handed down to us in this way such wonderful treasures as the Luttrell Psalter, the Lindisfarne Gospels, the Exeter book, and many of the devotional works known

as "Books of Hours." This method of writing books often cost a lifetime of work on a single copy, and you would have searched in vain for anything resembling a library of today. For instance, in the library of King's Hall, Cambridge, there were, in 1397, only eighty-seven books and the library of the University itself possessed only 172 in the year 1424.

Invention of Printing

Britain, cut off from the mainland of Europe by rough, dangerous seas, was at this time self-supporting, needing very little from the Continent, and only gradually did news from across the Channel reach even the capital city of London. New discoveries, new inventions, new doctrines and theories of the "Age of Discovery" were all the work of foreigners. The mariner's compass, which made possible the great voyages of discovery; the telescope, without which the tremendous development of

Stradanus   *Courtesy St. Bride's Institute*

A printing shop showing the various processes, setting the type, using the press, drying the pages on lines,
in front a young apprentice and the master standing on the right

astronomy could not have happened; the invention of gunpowder, which brought about the end of the feudal period all were continental in origin. So too, was the greatest invention of the age— PRINTING, and by an amazing and lucky coincidence, almost at the same time, cheap paper was invented. This was of the greatest necessity for the success of printing as it replaced the expensive skin parchments of the earlier handwritten books. Early in the fifteenth century men had started to make block-books. To make a block-book each page was printed from a wooden block on which both illustration and print had been drawn and then all the background chiselled away, in exactly the same way as lino-cuttings are made in the art class in school today. The great drawback to this method was that for a book of sixty or seventy pages you needed that number of blocks, which could be used only for that book. On the other hand a great number of copies of the book could be printed once the blocks were cut.

Invention of Movable Type

Before long, someone saw that if the letters could be cut separately, they could be used over and over again to build up other words and other pages, and men began to experiment with the new idea. There has been a great deal of argument about the name of the first printer using the new movable type, but we do know that there is a fragment of a 74-page book printed in 1447 still in existence at Mainz, and that two indulgences were printed at Mainz in 1454. The printers were probably Johann Gutenberg and Johann Fust. Gutenberg was the actual inventor and printer, and Fust supplied the money. The letters were first cut in steel to form a punch, the punches being driven into brass to form a matrix. The matrix was placed at the bottom of a hand mould into which molten lead was poured to make a letter. The one mould was used for any number of matrices and each matrix was good for casting thousands of letters. Thus, when the required number of 'a's' had been cast, the 'a' matrix was replaced by the 'b' matrix, and so on. When the complete assortment of letters was cast, it was used to set up the pages to be printed. The new craft spread very quickly and by 1500 there were sixteen printers in Strasbourg, twenty-two in Cologne, seventeen in Nürnberg and twenty in Augsberg. Printing had also spread to Italy, France, and Switzerland.

William Caxton

Strangely enough, although printing was a German invention, the printing-press was first brought to England by an Englishman. William Caxton, who had been a wool merchant in Bruges, had translated the *Stories of Troy*. He was asked by so many people for a copy that the repeated copying became very wearisome. Then he heard about printing and set about learning the new craft. Before he left Bruges he had printed the *Stories of Troy*, and another book on *Chess*. About two years later, at the end of 1476, he came to England and set up his printing press close to Westminster Abbey, in a house he rented from the monks of Westminster.

The Printing Press

From the pictures we possess of the printing presses of the time we can tell what Caxton's must have been like. For example a printer of Amsterdam used a picture of his own press as his printer's mark. This he put on the title page of books printed by him. His earliest mark is dated 1511 and although this is

Photo Mansell

A page from the Lindisfarne Gospels showing St. Matthew writing his Gospel

some time after Caxton, yet Caxton's press must have been almost the same. At first, pages of books could be printed only one at a time, but before Caxton's death, two pages were being set up and printed at the same time.

The actual printing was a simple operation done entirely by hand. The letters were cast in the same way that Gutenberg had cast his, so there must have been a forge for melting the type metal. As the characters were taken from the moulds the backs were squared and levelled off. In another room, or perhaps in the same room, the "compositor," the man who built up the page to be printed, sat before a large tray just a little larger than the actual size of the page. The type was in drawers beside him and he built up the page line by line. When the page was finished the whole was held tight by driving in strips of wood and there it was ready for the press. First the ink was dabbed on by hand with sheepskin dabbers, then a

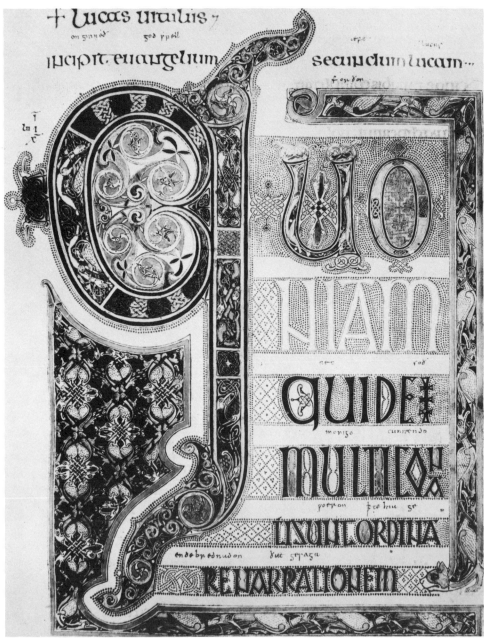

The first page of St. Luke's Gospel from the Lindisfarne Gospels   Photo Mansell

sheet of paper was laid over the inked type and the tray was slid under the press; the handles were turned until the paper was screwed tightly down against the type in its tray. When the press was unscrewed and the paper lifted, the page was taken away to the binder. Perhaps several hundred copies of one page would be made before the next page, for which the tray of type would be already set up, was touched. When the binder had all the pages, each of which had been numbered by hand by a "scrivener," he was able to set about binding the books.

Early Printed Books

Naturally, to us this would seem a slow and cumbersome process, but it was far in advance of the old method of copy-writing. Books were no longer as beautiful, but they were cheaper and more plentiful. Now, if we recall that the Fall of Constantinople took place in 1453 then we can see that printing came to England, and to France, and of course to Germany before the "new learning" had spread that far westwards and northwards. Because of that, the earliest books to be printed were in the language of the country where they were printed and not, as had been the rule, in Latin. Most of them were tales of chivalry, romantic stories, books on such pastimes as chess and hunting, and service books for clergy, as well as many devotional works. Later on, the classical works of the ancient Greeks and Romans were printed. These had been brought out of the Eastern Empire before the fall of Constantinople, and caused the "Revival of Learning." They became known in England through such men as Thomas Linacre, William Grocyn, William Latimer and John Colet.

Titles of Books

When men like Gutenberg, Fust, Schoeffer, Caxton, Pynson and de Worde began to print it must have been the natural thing for them to want to copy the work of monks who had turned out the beautiful books. These were still in the possession of the great nobles or the monasteries, and the printers took care that their letters should resemble as

nearly as possible the script of the most famous writers. And what of the books themselves? If we take any catalogue of a library of books of the period, whether that of a rich noble or a rich merchant, whether an Oxford or Cambridge college or a great church or monastery we shall find a large proportion of religious works. Often the most beautiful and most treasured were copies of the "Four Gospels", the "Bible," the "Psalter," the "Apocalypse" and, of course the "Missal" and the books of devotion known as "Books of Hours." When the new art of printing arrived what could be more natural than that printers should turn first of all to those books which were so well known? Even the common people who could not read knew them by heart.

We know that Gutenberg's first great effort was a Bible, an immense task which took him almost six years. It was published in 1456, the year before Fust and Schoeffer published their very lovely Psalter. Gutenberg's Bible, as it is known, consisted of two volumes and about 1300 pages. It was probably the first book printed in movable type in Europe. Two hundred copies were printed. The text itself was known as the Vulgate, the beautiful and majestic version which St. Jerome had translated into Latin. It dates from the fourth century, and has been the version in use in the Catholic Church all down the centuries. From it, the edition in English known as the Douai Bible was translated, the Old Testament in 1582 at Reims and the New Testament in 1609 at Douai. Within fifty years of the appearance of the Gutenberg or Mainz Bible more than one hundred editions of the Vulgate had been printed, and in less than fifty years from the invention of movable type, forty thousand editions of books numbering more than twenty million copies had been printed and it

Photo Mansell

Page of the Gutenberg Bible

first books were printed in the vernacular, that is the language of the country. As it happened, the first translation of the Bible into English had been made by John Wyclif (1320–1384) and was a quite orthodox translation from the Vulgate. What made it unacceptable to the Church was the heretical preface. About 170 copies of Wyclif's Bible are still in existence, so a great many copies must have been made, and we know that it was in general use, even by the nobility and religious, for the copies we have were once the property of Kings, nobles and religious houses. Although, therefore, it was the work of a heretic, yet the text itself was true to the Vulgate, and so the Church allowed it to be used without further hindrance. As a matter of fact, translations of the Bible into the vernacular had been in use for a long time. Some 104 editions of the Bible in the vernacular had been printed before the first Protestant Bible appeared. Twenty of these were Italian, twenty-six French, nineteen Flemish, two Spanish, six Bohemian and thirty German. The first German Bible had appeared as early as 1466, only ten years after Gutenberg's. All this speaks for itself of the demand for the Book of Books. Printing was, for good or evil, the greatest invention of the Middle Ages. Its effect upon the lives of ordinary people cannot be estimated. It carried far and wide the words and wisdom of great minds of the past and the present.

would be safe to say that the number of Bibles among these would be millions.

The Catholic Church and the Bible

The Church has often been charged with keeping the Bible from the faithful. We hear this said even today. I have myself had to deny the allegation many times, and I do so with the utmost vehemence. Particularly this charge has been made about the Church in Pre-Reformation times. Nothing could be further from the truth. Earlier in this article I explained that in England, in France, and of course, in Germany, the

CHRISTIAN ART FROM MANTEGNA TO RUBENS

In Volume II we wrote of the new discoveries made at the beginning of the fifteenth century by the artists in Italy and the northern countries which allowed them to draw in perspective and to paint real landscapes as backgrounds to their work. Not only did artists tell a sacred and beautiful story in a moving way, but they also showed us something of the real world they lived in. Something very new came into painting—a spirit of adventure which had not existed in the Middle Ages. Before the fifteenth century there was a style common to all countries of Europe. This was the style of the Gothic painters and sculptors which was generally the same among all leading artists of the period. There was an International style in art and in learning. All learned men spoke Latin and it was immaterial in what university they did their teaching.

Guilds of Artists

In the Middle Ages nationality did not matter. As we wrote in our chapters on Architecture and Painting in Volume II you might find a great Master working in France, England or Italy—having been recommended from one great cathedral to another. This internationalism belonged to the period when noblemen generally owed no special allegiance to any particular country. They were loyal to an overlord or king, but not to a nation. As cities grew more important, and merchants more powerful, jealousies and rivalries sprang up. The feeling of being separate nations became stronger. The various languages grew more and more unlike each other, and men from other countries were looked on as foreigners. They were not allowed to work or paint or do business.

This was the time when the Guilds developed. The Guilds were in some ways like Trade Unions, but they played a greater part in men's lives than Trade Unions do; they looked after their work and their pay, but they also took care of the cities and of their culture. Artists in consequence became members of

Mantegna

St. James on his way to execution

Photo Mansell

these wealthy companies, and worked for them rather than for the nobility. The Guilds, while ensuring a high standard of work, prevented artists from moving freely about, for no one except a famous master would be allowed to work except in his own Guild. From these conditions, what we call "schools" of painting developed. They were, in fact, the workshops of master-painters in which promising apprentices were trained.

The Young Apprentice

At first the young apprentice did all the odd jobs—running errands and cleaning palettes and brushes. Gradually he would advance to grinding the colours for his master and then one day, he might paint a background. If he would imitate his master well, he would get on very quickly and eventually would be allowed to paint a whole picture—supervised by the master. All this meant that each school had an individuality and it is not difficult to recognise from what town a picture of this period came.

Mantegna

One of the great artists of the fifteenth century was Mantegna, who had learnt a lot from the new art of Massacio. Mantegna worked in the beginning in the famous university town of Padua and then at the court in Mantua. In Padua, near the chapel where Giotto painted his famous frescoes, there is a church where Mantegna painted on the walls the legend of St. James. Unfortunately, most of these paintings have been destroyed by bombing. One of them is the famous picture of St. James being led to execution. To get the right clothes and the right atmosphere of the period Mantegna studied the habits and dress of the time from Roman classical monuments. This has made the picture almost like an ancient sculpture. You will remember that we mentioned how important perspective had become since Massacio. In this picture of St. James, Mantegna has used perspective to give him the real scene as it happened. The figures are solid human persons against a background of a Roman triumphal arch. The painting tells the whole human story of St. James. As the procession moves, a man suddenly holds it up by falling at the Saint's feet. The Saint turns round and blesses the man. The crowd stands by and the Roman soldier pauses and raises his hand as he watches St. James. At the end of Volume I we have a moving painting by Mantegna—the *Crucifixion* —and here too we can see the artist has used perspective to give us a picture of what must have happened on Calvary.

Piero della Francesca

Another great painter who lived about the same time as Mantegna was Piero della Francesca. He painted frescoes in Arezzo and Urbino. He had followed Giotto and Massacio in mastering the use of perspective and like Mantegna took great pains over the dress of his subjects, but he was also the first great painter to use light and shadow. Before this, artists had hardly used light at all and their figures were flat and without shadow. One famous wall-painting by Piero della Francesca shows us how effective Piero's use of light and shadow is in painting. The painting is called *Constantine's Dream* and tells us of the scene in the Emperor's camp before the great battle. Lying in the tent is the Emperor, with two soldiers standing outside and his own personal bodyguard sitting close to his bed. This is a night scene but it is illuminated by the light coming from the angel who is flying down holding the Symbol of the Cross in his hand. The whole scene is made real by the beam of light which makes the figures stand out clearly. The light also gives depth to the tent and we can feel that it is a round shape with a hollow inside. Light and perspective together have helped to give us a real picture of the event. The artist allows us to react to the situation in our own way. Piero's paintings are of subjects which are dignified and austere. His *Resurrection* is a solemn painting of a manly Christ rising out of the tomb in the grey light against the darkness of cypresses.

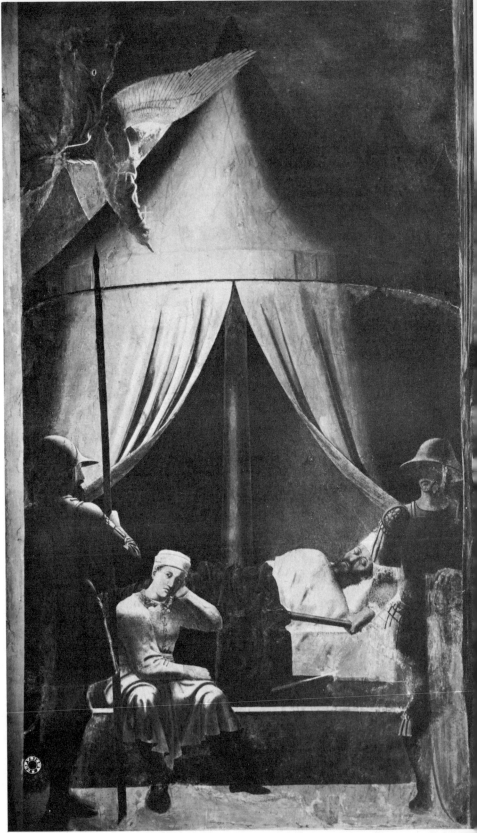

Piero della Francesca

Photo Mans

Constantine's Dream

Botticelli

Adoration of the Magi

Photo Mansell

Pollaiuolo

Now that perspective was being used by painters, the way they arranged their figures presented a different problem. In the Middle Ages, as we have said, painters knew nothing about perspective and they arranged their figures and backgrounds to form the most interesting pattern. At first it was difficult to paint a picture true to real life and keep a good pattern. One of the first attempts was Pollaiuolo's *Martyrdom of St. Sebastian*. This forms a kind of triangular pattern against a distant background in perspective. The artist has tried to balance the figures and at the same time has managed to give them different and natural positions.

Botticelli

Botticelli, who is perhaps most famous for his pagan picture *The Birth of Venus*, but who also painted some very beautiful Christian pictures, improved a great deal on Pollaiuolo. His paintings are full of harmony. One of these is his *Adoration of the Magi* where the centre group with the Madonna is surrounded by personages of the Medici Court and with the artist's self-portrait in the right-hand corner.

Fouquet

An interesting painter of the fifteenth century is the Frenchman Jean Fouquet who continued using light in the same way as Piero della Francesca had done.

Leonardo da Vinci   *Photo Mansell*

The Last Supper

Fouquet had been very much influenced by the Italian painters when he visited Rome in his youth, but he was influenced also by Jan Van Eyck who took so much interest in the texture of the things he painted. In his picture of *St. Stephen and Etienne Chevalier* we can see how he was influenced by the Italians in his use of light, but also the influence of Van Eyck can be seen in such things as the details of the rough stone—the symbol of St. Stephen's martyrdom. The detail of the deacon's dress is also there.

Engraving

When the new way of printing became known, it gave artists as well as printers something different to use in portraying their ideas. This was engraving. At first they used woodcuts, but they soon saw that this was not fine enough to give the details. Copper engraving gave much subtler effects and artists used it to give real life pictures. To do an engraving the artist used a special tool called a burin which he pressed into the copper plate to engrave a deep line. This line would hold any colour or printer's ink spread on the surface. To print the engraving the ink was wiped off the surface of the metal and the metal pressed against paper. The ink remaining in the engraved lines would then be squeezed on to the paper and form a print.

Schongauer

One of the most famous masters of the fifteenth-century engraving was Martin Schongauer who lived in the district we know today as Alsace. Like the great masters of Flanders whom he followed, Schongauer wanted to show ordinary people and things in his engravings. His *Holy Night* shows us just how much detail he was able to engrave—broken stones, flowers in the cracks and ivy on the walls. It is a beautiful scene—the ruins of a chapel used as a stable, the adoration of the Child, and St. Joseph lantern in hand, and in the right-hand corner the Heavenly Chorus with the shepherds at the back. Schongauer has filled the whole picture with interesting details giving us a real scene with the important figures standing out in life-like fashion.

Engravings played an important part in art development for they passed between the various countries and were the likeliest way in which artists learned from one another and many of the engravings were used by less famous artists to learn from the great masters.

Greatest Period of Italian Art

The beginning of the sixteenth century is the greatest period of Italian art. This was the famous period of Leonardo da Vinci and Michelangelo, of Raphael and Titian, of Coreggio and Giorgione, and in the north were Dürer and Holbein. There were many others, but these are names well known to most people who have looked at beautiful pictures.

This was the period when the artist had become something more than a craftsman in the world of other craftsmen. The process had been slow. Before this time painters and sculptors were considered only as craftsmen and were not on the same social level as the scholar who spoke Latin and knew philosophy. A painter had to accept a commission to do what the patron asked. Soon cities and churches were competing for the services of the great artists. So the process had become reversed and the great artist was now in a position to choose the kind of painting or sculpture he liked to do and not be forced to accept a commission he hated. This meant that art for the first time was free.

Leonardo da Vinci

The oldest of the great masters of this new period was Leonardo da Vinci who was born in a Tuscan village. Leonardo became the apprentice of the famous sculptor and painter Verrochio, who had his workshop in Florence. Verrochio was the sculptor of the famous monument in Venice erected to General Colleoni. This equestrian masterpiece shows just how great Verrochio was and we can believe that Leonardo learnt important technical methods from his master. Even an ordinary painter would have learnt a great deal but Leonardo was more than that—he was a genius. His great mind has been admired and wondered at by millions ever since. To Leonardo nothing seemed impossible. Throughout his life he was a great reader and made thousands of notes and sketches which have been handed down to us, preserved by his pupils. Anything that would perfect his work he felt compelled to learn. We still marvel at an artist who could have been so interested in and thoroughly studied so many fields of knowledge. Any problem that he was faced with he tried to solve himself and it is said that when he wanted to study the workings of the human body he dissected thirty corpses. His wide interests led him to the study of currents and waves. Because he believed that man could one day fly he spent years studying the flight of birds and insects. He was sure he would be able to invent a machine that could fly. It is amazing to think that in the fifteenth century he was already so sure of this. For his painting he studied everything in nature, trees, plants, clouds and even the effect that atmosphere has on objects at various distances.

Although Leonardo was a great scientist and his discoveries led later to Copernicus and to Galileo he did not think of himself as anything of the kind. It was his unlimited curiosity that led him to his discoveries, but his real desire was to bring his art, which he loved, to the highest possible level. For this he thought that a scientific basis was necessary. If he did not think a painting was finished he would never let it leave his shop. Unfortunately there were many unfinished paintings and even the ones handed down to us have been badly preserved. His most famous painting, *The Last Supper*, which covers a whole wall in the refectory of the monastery of Sta Maria della Grazie, Milan, is in a very bad state of preservation. We can perhaps visualise how it must have appeared to the monks in the first years. At first they must have been startled by the life-like quality of the scene which had happened so long before. They could see that it was somehow different from the usual painting of Jesus and his disciples at the Last Supper. Most painters had been content with a quiet row of men with Jesus sitting in the middle. This was not Leonardo's interpretation of the scene. He set about visualising the scene as it had really happened in the upper room and as it had been described in Matthew xxvi, 21–22 and in John xiii, 23–24. We can see the sorrowful disciples asking their questions, and Peter beckoning to Our Lord as in the Scripture. There is argument going on while Jesus sits calmly in the centre. Leonardo's wonderful art and understanding has given us a picture of the dramatic moment, exciting and real, and yet as a painting it is very harmonious.

We are told that on some days when Leonardo was working on his masterpiece he would spend hours just thinking and not painting one stroke. The thought and the painting together have given us one of the greatest masterpieces of all time.

Michelangelo

Another Florentine who came to fame at this time was Michelangelo. He was twenty-three years younger than Leonardo and like him was trained as a craftsman in his youth. His training began at the age of thirteen in the workshop of Ghirlandajo, another Florentine artist, whose *Adoration of the Magi* we reproduce in Volume I, page 4.

Ghirlandajo's paintings please us because the arrangement of the figures is so real and they are dressed as we would expect them to be in the sacred story he is telling. In his workshop Michelangelo learnt all about the technical part of painting as a trade, but he wanted more than that. He studied Giotto and Massacio. Like Leonardo, he did an immense amount of research into human anatomy, but unlike him he did not study nature as a whole. He mastered the art of painting the human form in every conceivable posture. Michelangelo was only thirty when he was accepted as one of the outstanding masters.

Michelangelo's great chance came when Pope Julius II invited him to Rome to ask him to erect a tomb for him. The artist, with the Pope's permission, spent months in the famous marble quarries at Carrara where he chose the marble for the work. Unfortunately when he returned to Rome the Pope was thinking of building a new St. Peter's and so the tomb was left for the time being. Michelangelo was very disappointed and he returned to Florence with all his great ideas for the mausoleum still in his mind. He developed the idea that there were people intriguing against him. At the Pope's request he reluctantly returned to Rome and very much against his will he accepted to paint the vault of a chapel in the Vatican built by Pope Sixtus IV— the Sistine Chapel. The walls had been decorated by Botticelli, Ghirlandajo and other artists, but the vault was bare of decoration. Michelangelo kept on

Michelangelo   *Photo Mansell*

Creation of Man

arguing that he was not a painter but a sculptor. He started on the work with a number of assistants. Soon he became enthralled and banished the assistants, shut himself in the chapel and worked alone. For four long years he carried on alone. As we look at the vault of the chapel today it is unbelievable that a man could single-handed have carried out such a thing in even twice as many years. Alone he planned and sketched and put in all the details before he transferred them on to the ceiling. Alone he lay on his back and worked on the scaffolding at that great height. The finished work is a thrilling spectacle as we look today. The grandeur of Michelangelo's conception leaves us awed as we realise the gigantic size of the images of the prophets. It was mighty men he

painted for us, and as you look through this book you will see some portions of the ceiling reproduced. There is an awe-inspiring vision of the creation. We see God calling forth the plants, the heavenly bodies, the animals and man. One of the most famous of these gestures of creation is the one in which we see God the Father carried by his angels approaching Adam and stretching out his hand to wake the first man. Here is omnipotence and beauty created by the artist. It is one painting that you must see if you go to Rome.

After completing this gigantic work Michelangelo went on to his beloved sculpture and among his famous ones are his *Dying Slave* in the Louvre, Paris; *David*, in Florence; and the most beautiful *Pietá* in St. Peter's, Rome. His

Raphael   *Photo Mansell*

Madonna and Child

last great work was the completion of Bramante's work on the new St. Peter's. He designed the crowning cupola. For this he refused payment, saying that he regarded this as a service to the Glory of God. Thus Michelangelo's cupola rises

Bellini

Virgin and Child with Saints

Photo Mansell

high in the Vatican City and forms an impressive monument to the great artist.

Raphael

From the greatest of all we move to another famous painter. Raffaello Sanzio arrived as a very young man in Florence. Raffaello (Raphael as we best know him) had learnt his trade in the workshops of Perugino at Urbino.

Titian

The Virgin and Child with members of the Pesaro family

Photo Mansell

Perugino, like Ghirlandajo and Verrochio, was a successful artist who kept a large number of assistants to work on his commissions. Raphael learned all Perugino could teach him and when he reached Florence he was unabashed by the new high standards set by Leonardo and Michelangelo. He knew he was not a great genius like the masters, but he was a kindly and popular young man and he was willing to work hard. He is famous for his beautiful Madonnas which generations of artists after him have taken as the standard to be aimed at. We see so many reproductions of his Madonnas that we are not always aware of the amount of work, of planning and designing, that Raphael put into his paintings. From Florence Raphael went to Rome where Pope Julius II commissioned him to decorate the walls of a number of rooms in the Vatican. These life-like figures have to be seen to be understood. It is difficult to realise what they are like from illustrations.

Unfortunately Raphael died when he was only thirty-seven, but during that short life he had produced a large number of building designs, of portraits and huge wall paintings.

The Venetians

We have written a great deal about Florence as the centre of Italian art, but it was not the only centre at the end of the fifteenth and beginning of the sixteenth century. There was a famous group in Venice whose approach to their art was somewhat different from the approach of the Florentines. One may say that the exquisite colour of their paintings was one of the main attractions of Venetian paintings. The Florentines were very busy with the reform of painting from the point of view of draughtmanship and perspective. Their colours too were beautiful, but colour seemed to be something added on, while this was never so with the Venetians. Colour to them was one of the most important ingredients in the actual forming of the picture. Even today after years of grime and actual dimming we feel awe-

inspired when looking at Giovanni Bellini's painting over the altar at the little church of San Zaccaria, Venice. The colour is what attracts us first and then we begin to see what the artist wants to tell us. The Virgin sits enthroned in a gilded niche with the Infant Child raising his hand to bless the people worshipping at the altar. St. Peter is there with his key and his book, St. Catherine with the broken wheel and St. Jerome the scholar reading.

The Church meant sacred painting to produce in the onlooker a mood of devotion, and these great paintings fulfil this desire. In the beginning, you will remember, art was intended by the Church to tell the legends and teach the dogmas to those who could neither read nor write. Now art had travelled a long way further. It had become the means of rousing deep emotion and sincere feelings of those educated to understand the beauty of painting and sculpture through colour and form.

Giorgione

Giovanni Bellini was the head of a very busy workshop and two of his famous pupils were Giorgione and Titian. Giorgione unfortunately had a short life and very few of his paintings remain, but what we still have show us the refinement of his work. Giorgione painted his pictures with a background of real life, indeed we feel that he did not paint a background but his figures and background were one in his mind. If you look at his painting *The Judgement of Solomon*, Volume I, page 212, you will see just how the figures and landscape are together parts of one whole idea.

Titian

As we mentioned, Giorgione died very young and it was left to Titian, who lived to be ninety-nine, to carry on his

Correggio   Photo Mansell

Holy Night

ideas. During his long life Titian worked on the same lines with the same joyous attitude to his work. In his wonderful painting of *The Assumption* there is a joyousness as the Virgin soars heavenwards with no support from the angels who are singing a victorious song. In the last thirty years of his life Titian painted with great vigour and his *Ecce Homo* shows the face of a god-like person with the marks of suffering. Titian is great because he managed to move with the times; his later pictures had more reality than his early work and he still combined light, air and colours to complete great masterpieces. There was a rule, generally accepted before Titian, that the main figure should be the centrepiece and it was thought that a painting would become unbalanced if any other way was used. It must have startled people when they first saw Titian's painting of the Madonna with members of the Pesaro family. The artist in this magnificent painting placed the Madonna to the side and it resulted in a gay and harmonious picture.

Correggio

There were other towns too who had painters of courage. One was Correggio who lived in the small town of Parma and led a very lonely life. Correggio painted his great works after the death of Leonardo and Raphael and at the time when Titian was already famous. He learned a great deal from these great artists, but he is great as a painter who used light and colour to give radiance to his paintings and he made his women more feminine than artists had before. One of his most famous paintings and one which gives us all the qualities of his work is *The Holy Night*. In this picture he uses the light radiating from the Child to give charm to the beautiful face of the Mother. Correggio painted many ceilings and throughout the ages

his way of treating such work was imitated. He painted them in such a way as to make those in the church, looking upwards, imagine that the ceiling was opening to show them the glory of heaven. His use of light enabled him to create an illusion which was breathtaking.

Dürer

Throughout the brilliant period of Italian painting there were in the north painters who studied the new approach of Italian artists. One of these was the greatest German artist Albrecht Dürer who was born just over ten years before Raphael. He lived in Nuremberg where he was apprenticed to a large workshop which produced altars and woodcut illustrations. After completing his apprenticeship he travelled to Alsace where he intended to work with the great master Schongauer, but he found when he got there that Schongauer had recently died. Dürer stayed a little while and then moved on to Switzerland and northern Italy and eventually returned to Nuremberg. Dürer was a wonderful engraver and his Nativity shows us the loving care with which he treated his subject. It is a scene of quiet and peace in a broken-down building, with the Mother adoring the Son and the shepherd kneeling in the background. The landscape in the background is engraved with infinite care and there is a tiny angel in the sky bringing the glad tidings.

Tintoretto

During the first quarter of the sixteenth century it was believed that the great masters like Leonardo, Michelangelo, Raphael and Titian had reached the peak of perfect art. There seemed nothing more for artists to learn. Many artists accepted this, but there was born in Venice in 1518 Jacopo Robusti (nick-

Dürer   Photo Mansell

The Nativity

named Tintoretto) who did not. He thought Titian's paintings beautiful, but he did not think they were the peak of achievement in art. He desired to give more power to his figures—a power which came from the new feeling for religion and poetry which was coming into being. He used light and shadow in the most impressive manner to show us the magnitude of the sacred event he was portraying. He gave it atmosphere of a different kind. If you look at the painting of *Christ carrying the Cross* on page 384, Volume I, you will see how Tintoretto gives us the feeling of gloom and oppressiveness of the atmosphere. His figures are often colossal, but they are not forbidding. There is drama in all their actions—they are alive.

El Greco

Tintoretto's methods were carried even further by a painter named Domenico Theotocopoulos who came from Crete and who was called "The Greek" for short. We know him as El Greco. He came to Venice and was fascinated by Tintoretto's paintings and, like the master, he was a devout man determined to tell the sacred stories with all his power and skill to stir the people. To us El Greco seems to have given up the idea of painting natural figures in ordinary colours. He dramatises every scene in a manner that stirs us with his elongated figures and vivid colours. From Venice El Greco went to Spain— to Toledo. In Spain perhaps religion was more fervent and El Greco's work-shop was very busy indeed. He was in fact very popular at this period, though a century later he was treated lightly and his work became unpopular. Since then we have learned that it does not follow that a painting is not great art because the painter chooses to tell his story in an unusual manner. Today El Greco has been rediscovered and is better understood.

Crisis from the North

From the south, from Italy and Spain where painters vied with one another in new methods of painting, we move now to the northern countries. Here a great crisis came into art with the Reforma-tion. The narrow Protestantism of the northern countries objected strenuously to the wonderful paintings and sculp-tures of Jesus, Madonna and the Saints. Everything that was beautiful and mystic was stripped in the name of "no idola-try." Strict Calvinists objected even to any decoration in private houses.

Holbein

We can best see how this affected painting if we give a brief sketch of the

The Wilton Diptych   *National Gallery*

St. John, St. Edward the Confessor and St. Edmund recommend Richard II to the Virgin

Possibly painted around 1400 by a French master for an English king, who is seen kneeling before the Virgin with the Holy Child bending forward as in a gesture of blessing

Facing p. 32

Siegfried Charoux   *The Grail, Pinner*

The Crucifixion

A fine sculpture in terra-cotta in the grounds of The Grail, Pinner

Siegfried Charoux   *The Grail, Pinner*

The Madonna and Child

This Madonna and Child, 6 feet high in terra-cotta, stands in the grounds of The Grail, Pinner

tained-glass window in the chapel at Quigley Seminary, Chicago, showing the Creation of the Fish and Fowl of the earth

A late sixteenth-century chalice in copper and gilt with silver-gilt bowl, an Italian processional cross of the second half of the fourteenth-century in copper-gilt; and a Spanish Standing Pyx, of about 1600, in silver-gilt

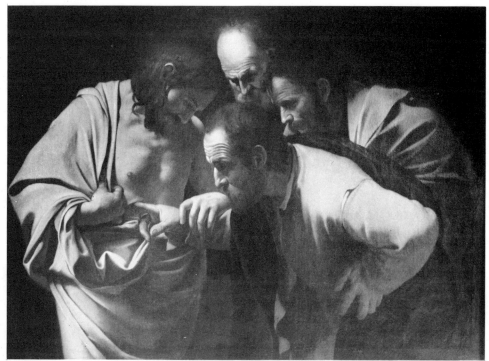

Caravaggio   Photo Mansell

The incredulity of Thomas

life of Holbein the great German painter. He was born at Augsburg in 1497 but moved to Basle. His father was a painter too and young Holbein had every opportunity to learn from artists of the north and the south. He was in his twenties when he painted the lovely altar painting of the Virgin with the family of the Burgomaster of Basle. The figures are arranged much like those in Bellini's *Madonna with Saints*, page 27). Holbein's painting is one of the most beautiful of this subject. There is great detail in the painting, which shows the influence of the north. The Reformation upheaval forced the artist to leave Basle and his religious painting. He arrived in England where he painted many portraits including the one of Sir Thomas More and family. Finally he became the court painter of Henry VIII's court. When Holbein died art

3—III

was in decline and the only form of painting which survived was portrait painting which he had introduced.

Caracci and Caravaggio

Going back to Italy, you will remember we mentioned two schools—Florence which concentrated on design, and Venice which made colour supremely important. There was constant controversy throughout the sixteenth century over these questions, but by the end of the century discussion went on about two painters who had come to Rome from northern Italy. One was Caracci from Bologna and the other Caravaggio from near Milan. Caracci was a great admirer of Raphael and he aimed to capture some of the beauty and simplicity of the master's work. Some of his altar-pieces are of classical beauty and he avoids showing any pain in his portrayal of such subjects as the dead Christ. In complete opposition to Caracci's avoidance of the painful and ugly are Caravaggio's realistic paintings. He believed that it was weak not to show ugliness and horror if it existed in life. He was determined to paint only the truth. He had no time for conventional beauty. He was a devout man who painted his figures as they really were. His *Doubting Thomas* (page 33) is an example of this. To him the apostles were real people with weather-beaten and wrinkled faces, as indeed they were in life. The whole gesture of Thomas pushing his finger into Jesus' side is just as we would imagine it from Jesus' words in the Bible. Caravaggio's figures are real people, and he makes full use of light and shadow to give us this feeling. His *Martyrdom of St. Peter* and the tortures of other apostles convey to us the stark horror of their suffering. The scenes stand out vividly and unforgettably before our eyes.

Rubens

Returning again to the northern countries we come to Peter Paul Rubens, who learned much from both Caracci and Caravaggio. He went to Rome for about eight years and admired Caracci's altar-pieces, but he also admired the extreme honesty of Caravaggio's work. Rubens did not produce small paintings like most other northern painters. He gave us large canvases. To the methods of Italian masters he brought more freedom and painted such pictures as *The Marriage of St. Catherine*, using many more people and with more light and movement. There is a grandeur about his whole conception, but he has not missed a single detail. He well knew that anything he painted came alive under his brush. The vitality and gaiety of his paintings brought him immense fame and success and he stood out above all others in the world he lived in, painting for churches, princes and kings.

So we leave the great masters of religious painting at the moment when the new discoveries of perspective, of the use of light and colour and of the painting of real people had brought harmony and freshness into the art of Catholic Europe.

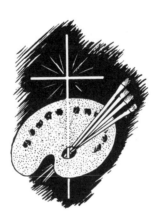

THE NEED FOR REFORMATION

"Now look here, Maisie," exclaimed Michael, almost exploding with indignation, "what do you know about it anyway?"

"Well, I like that!" cried Maisie as she glared at her brother across the table at which they were sitting. "What do I know about it? Why, you, you . . ." she failed to find the word she wanted and swept on, "I know as much about it as you do! So there!"

"But how can you?" asked Michael with what was meant to be an air of great patience. "How can a girl know anything worth knowing about these things? Girls don't understand history as men do!"

Mrs. Ashton, standing at the open door, blinked in astonishment. Her children had quarrelled, to her knowledge, about matters ranging from cricket (which Maisie considered to be fit only for cissies), to listening to Children's Hour (which for Michael was the last word in foolishness). But history? This was something different, something quite new!

Maisie's reaction was swift and sure. She picked up a hefty dictionary, which was lying open on the table, and with it smartly and determinedly rapped her loving brother over the head. Mrs. Ashton stepped into the play-room.

"Now, tell me what are you two quarrelling about?"

Michael, rubbing his head, looked at Maisie and she grimaced back at him.

"You tell Mums!" she said slyly. "You understand all about history!"

"We were not squabbling, Mummy," answered her son with an air of injured dignity. "We were talking about something that we both heard in school today."

"That's right, Mums!" interrupted Maisie. "It was about the Protestants. About the Protestant Reformation. We were discussing the Reformation!"

"Discussing the Reformation?" asked Mrs. Ashton in some astonishment.

"No, Mummy," said Michael, looking crossly at his sister, "not the Reformation exactly, but what my teacher called the causes of the Reformation, and . . ."

35

"And what Mother Simplicitas called the need for the Reformation, Mums!" broke in Maisie, once more interrupting her brother.

"I see. But you haven't yet told me why you were quarrelling, you know."

"It's like this, Mummy," volunteered Michael patiently. "Old Burton, my teacher, told me that at the time of the Protestant Reformation the Catholic Church was in such a bad way that She was on Her last legs."

"But Mother Simplicitas told us that although the Church was in a very bad way She was still very much alive and kicking. Who's right, Mums?"

The twins looked expectantly at their mother. Mrs. Ashton, however, was in no hurry to give her decision. Like the experienced teacher that she had been before she married Dr. John Ashton she knew that she would have to prepare the ground thoroughly before she could convince her children of the truth of her answer to their question.

"Tell me," she said as she pulled out a chair and sat down. "What did your teachers tell you about the cause, or the need," she hastened to add as she caught the pained look in Maisie's eyes, "of the Protestant Reformation?"

"My history teacher," said Michael who attended the only, non-Catholic, Secondary school in the little country town where the Ashtons lived, "told us that the causes of the Reformation went right back to the fourteenth century."

"And Mother Simplicitas told us the same thing," put in Maisie, who was a pupil at the local convent school.

Mrs. Ashton nodded her approval.

"That is quite correct," she said. "It is a mistake to imagine that the Reformation just happened. On the contrary it was a very long time preparing, more than two hundred years in fact. That

Francesco del Cossa   *Courtesy National Galler:*

St. Vincent Ferrer

is why, when the explosion came in 1517 it came with such terrible force. But g: on, Michael. What else did Mr. Burto:

have to say about the causes of the Reformation?"

"He said, Mummy, that there were a great number of them."

"And Mother Simplicitas told us, Mums, that while none of the reasons why the Reformation was needed was strong enough by itself to bring about a Reformation, all of them together were bound sooner or later to cause trouble."

"Yes, but what were those causes, or those reasons?" asked Mrs. Ashton, not without a touch of impatience in her voice.

"Oh, Mums!" protested Maisie in horror, "you don't expect us to remember all the reasons that Mother Simplicitas gave? Why, there must have been thousands of them!"

"Very well, Maisie, give me just one or two then. Perhaps between us, and Michael, we shall be able to remember them all."

"The first reason that Mother Simplicitas mentioned, Mums, was, I think the worldliness of the Cardinals and Bishops. Please, Mums, what did she mean by that?"

"She meant, my dear," said Mrs. Ashton, "that the Cardinals and Bishops, and many others of the higher clergy, had forgotten what they were priests for. The duty of a priest is to lead his people to Heaven by his own example and of his teaching. The Cardinals and Bishops, as well as a few of the Popes, that Mother Simplicitas had in mind, had lost sight of this duty, forgetting how to get their own souls and the souls of their flocks into Heaven."

"But, Mummy," protested Michael, "how did that happen? I mean how did all those Popes and Cardinals and Bishops get into such a muddle?"

"It was simple enough, Michael. The Church, you see, had gradually become more and more powerful. She had done wonderful work to save Europe during and after the invasions of the Barbarians, and was the most powerful organisation in existence. Those in authority in the Church began to look upon themselves as the political as well as the spiritual leaders of Europe. They found it more attractive to be political leaders than spiritual ones. It didn't demand any great spirit of sacrifice, and it opened wide the door to wealth, power and flattery. So many high-ranking prelates and priests decided that they were wasting their time and talents bothering about the souls of their flocks!

"But that's enough of that reason! Can you remember any more that Mother Simplicitas or Mr. Burton mentioned?"

Mrs. Ashton paused and looked first at Michael and then at Maisie. It was Michael who won this time.

"Yes, Mums," he said eagerly. "Old Burton did talk an awful lot about the bad lives of the priests and monks long before the Reformation. Were they really as bad and wicked as he said, Mums?"

Mrs. Ashton smiled.

"Since I don't know how bad and wicked Mr. Burton told you the priests and monks were before the Reformation I cannot say whether he was right or wrong, Michael."

"Oh, but he said that they were really bad, Mums!" protested her son.

"Very well then, Michael. The priests and the monks of those days were in such a bad state that they could hardly be worse. That's what many people say, even many Catholics. They were bad, a great number of them, really bad. There were wicked priests and monks, men who had only one desire, to enjoy the best of both worlds, this world and the next. There were also weak-kneed priests and monks who were only too ready to kow-tow to the wealthy ruling classes at the expense of the ordinary people. There were also badly trained priests and monks, ignorant and superstitious, who could no more guide their flock in the service of God than a blind man can lead another blind man. There were many priests and monks like this, it is true, but there were just as many others who were not a bit like this."

"That's just what Mother Simplicitas told us, Mums," put in Maisie.

"But then, Mummy," cried Michael in a tone of indignation, "Old Burton told us a pack of lies!"

"Not at all, Michael," said Mrs. Ashton. "You mustn't accuse your teachers of lying, you know! No, Mr. Burton told you what he honestly thought was the truth."

"But how can that be, Mummy?" protested Michael.

"Well, there are two points that you must never forget when you speak about the bad and wicked lives of the clergy before the Protestant Reformation," answered Mrs. Ashton. "The first of these is that evil things have a habit of making more noise than good things."

"Do you mean, Mummy, that there were good priests and monks as well as bad and wicked ones before the Reformation?" asked Michael.

"Gracious, yes!" replied Mrs. Ashton. "In every country of Europe, side by side with the bad priests and monks there were priests and monks who were famous for their holy lives and learning, and there were certainly many others who lived good and edifying lives without the world getting to know about them! Why, saints were almost as common as berries in autumn in those bad and wicked days! For instance there was St. Vincent Ferrer who was one of the great preachers of his time, and there was St. Bernardine of Siena who was every bit as good in getting people to love God. There was St. John Capistran who helped to drive the Turks out of Europe. There was St. Catherine of Siena who helped to bring the Popes back to Rome from Avignon where they had transferred the Papal Court and where they had remained for seventy years. There were hundreds of others of the clergy, Cardinals, Archbishops, Bishops, and ordinary common priests and monks who were all that they should be. The best proof of what I am saying is, I think, the fact that the masses of the people were not one half so bad as you might imagine. They were still very much attached to their religion. Many of them were members of guilds and confraternities. They helped to build wonderful churches. They helped to run many hospitals and hostels for the poor. And they were not slow in showing their Faith when they had occasion to do so. For example, when Pope Gregory XI laid an interdict on Florence, so that Mass could no longer be said there, the Florentines used to gather every evening before the statues of Our Lady at the street corners and pray and sing hymns together in her honour. So also when in 1450 Pope Nicholas V held a Jubilee Year such crowds of pilgrims flocked to Rome from all over Europe that eye-witnesses compared them to the flight of starlings or the march of millions of ants!"

"Well, I'm blessed!" exclaimed Michael breathlessly. "But Old Burton told us that we can read all about the awful things that priests and monks used to do in those days, in books written by men who lived then, and who knew what was going on."

"That," said his mother smiling at him, "brings us to the second point that you must never forget when you speak

Vivarini   *Photo Mansell*
St. John Capistran

about the bad lives of the clergy in the days before the Reformation. The point is this: you must not believe that something must be true just because you find it in a book. Now, a very great deal of what we know about the corruption and wickedness of the Catholic Church before the Reformation is to be found in books written by men who had axes of their own to grind. Take the case of the famous Italian poet, Petrarca. In his writings he paints the most awful picture of the corruption of the Church in his own times, the fourteenth century. But he exaggerated a great deal. Petrarca,

you see, was a very angry and disappointed man. He was angry because the Papal Court had left Rome for Avignon in France, and this, for a fiery Italian patriot like Petrarca, was just too much to swallow in silence. So he let fly against the Pope and the Cardinals. Although, mind you, he himself preferred to live in Avignon rather than in Rome! And he was a disappointed man also, because he felt that he wasn't making enough money out of the Church, and we know that he was a very greedy man where money was concerned."

"And that is Signor Petrarca put in his place, good and proper!" whispered Maisie.

"Or take the case of another well-known Italian writer," continued Mrs. Ashton as Michael muttered to Maisie to Sssh! "His full name was Gian Francesco Poggio Bracciolini, but he was known as Poggio for short. In his writings he accuses the priests and monks of his own days of all sorts of horrid things. He says that they were hypocrites, greedy, ignorant, proud, idle good-for-nothing, and many other unflattering things. Yet Poggio was one of the most vicious men of his century! It is quite clear that he himself didn't believe half the things he wrote about the poor priests and monks. He allowed his two sons to become priests, one of them a Dominican, and he himself wanted to be buried in the church of the Franciscans in Florence! Do you see what I am trying to get at?"

The twins nodded in unison.

"I don't want you to think for one moment," went on Mrs. Ashton, "that I am trying to prove that there was nothing wrong, or even not much wrong, with the clergy and the people in those days. There was on the contrary a very great deal that was wrong, in fact very, very wrong. But there was also a very great deal that was good, and in fact

Lorenzo Vecchietta   Photo Mansell

St. Catherine of Siena

very, very good. And if we want to have a true picture of those times we must never forget that in the midst of all the darkness of sin and vice there were, all the time, great shafts of light and sunshine. Is that clear?"

Again the twins nodded.

"Very well, then," said their mother, "and now let us see if you can remember anything else about the causes of the Protestant Reformation."

She looked at Michael who puckered his brow and thought hard.

"Yes, Mummy," he said at last, and his brow cleared like magic. "Old Burton told us all about the Great Schism."

"Oh yes, Mums," broke in Maisie determined not to be left out of such an important discussion. "So did Mother Simplicitas. And she told us also all about the Renaissance."

"And did Mr. Burton tell you all about the Renaissance, Michael?" asked Mrs. Ashton, turning to her son.

"Of course, Mummy," he replied.

"Good!" exclaimed Mrs. Ashton. "Well, let's take the Great Schism first, shall we? Do you know what it was, by the way?"

"I know what it was, Mums!" cried Maisie, thumping the table in her excitement. "It was the Schism that wasn't!"

Michael looked pityingly at his sister, but Maisie only made a face at him and went on excitedly:

"Yes, Mums, it wasn't really a schism at all. It was a fight between two and three sides in the Church."

"Quite right, Maisie," said Mrs. Ashton approvingly. "And what was the fight about?"

"About who was the real Pope, Mums. You see, there were two, and even three Popes at a time, all claiming to be the real one. And so the Church was divided into two, and then three sides."

"Can you add anything to that, Michael?" asked Mrs. Ashton of her son, who was clearly all agog to get a word in.

"Yes, Mummy, I can. The Great Schism started in 1378 and came to an end in 1417. It all started because the Cardinals who elected Pope Urban VI in 1378 soon got tired of him and tried to get him out of the way by saying that they had elected him out of fear of what the Romans would do to them if they didn't give them a Roman Pope."

"But Urban VI wasn't a Roman at all, was he, Michael?" protested Mrs. Ashton.

"No, Mummy, he was from Naples. But the Romans didn't really mind, so long as the new Pope wasn't a Frenchman."

"Was he a good man, Mums?" asked Maisie as her brother came to a stop.

"Yes, Maisie, he was a very good man. Everybody spoke of him as just the right person for the task of reforming the Church. But he didn't know how to be gentle and charitable, so that when he started to reform the higher clergy, who were the most to blame, he allowed himself to be carried away by his anger. This and his rough ways very soon got him into trouble with his own Cardinals, who resented being told by him that they were nothing better than foolish chatter-boxes, and even blockheads! St. Catherine of Siena tried her best to reason with him, but he wouldn't listen to her.

"To make matters worse," continued Mrs. Ashton after a slight pause to make sure that the twins were following her, "the French Cardinals, who were then in the majority, wanted him to transfer the Papal Court once more to France. Urban refused point-blank to do any such thing, and warned the French Cardinals that he was going to create a large

HIC SITA SVNT QVINTINICOLAI ANTISTITIS OSSA
AVREA QVIDE DEBAT SAECVLA ROMA TIBI
CONSILIO ILLVSTRIS VIRTVJEI ILLVSTRIO ROMNI
EXCOLVIT DOCTOS DOCTIOR IPSE VIROS
ABSTVLIT ERROREM QVO SCHISMA INFECERAT ORBEM
RESTITVIT MORES MOENIA TEMPLA DOMOS
TVM BERNARDINO STATVIT S VASA SACRA SENENSI
SANCTA IOBELE ITEMPORA DVM CELEBRAT
CINXIT HONORE CAPVT FRIDERICI ET CNIVGIS AVREO
BASITA LAS IGTO FOEDERE COMPOSVIT
ALTI CA ROMANAE C MPLVRA VOLVMINA LINGVAE
PRODIDIT ENTVMVLO FVNDITE THVRA SACRO

The tomb of Pope Nicholas V

number of Roman and Italian Cardinals. Then the French King, Charles V, stepped in and secretly encouraged the French Cardinals to break away from Urban, elect a new Pope, and return with him to Avignon."

"Did they agree, Mums?" asked Maisie, her eyes wide open.

"They did. On August 9, 1378, they publicly declared that Urban was not the Pope at all. And then, on September 20, they chose the French Cardinal, Robert of Geneva, to be the new Pope, with the name of Clement VII."

"And that's how the Great Schism started, isn't it, Mummy?" asked Michael.

"That's how it started," agreed Mrs. Ashton. "And it went on, as you told us a minute ago, for thirty-nine years, right up to 1417, when the Roman Cardinal, Colonna, was elected Pope in

the famous Merchant's Hall at Constance, and took the name of Martin V."

"Why at Constance, Mums?" "Why Martin, Mummy?" asked the twins together.

"At Constance, Maisie, because that is where the three Popes at the time, John XXIII, Gregory XII, and Benedict XIII, had agreed to submit their claims to a general assembly of the Church and try to put an end to the Schism. And Martin, Michael, because the new Pope was elected on the Feast of St. Martin of Tours, November 11, 1417. Both satisfied?"

Again the twins nodded their heads.

"But tell me, Michael," said his mother in a puzzled tone of voice, "what had the Great Schism to do with the Protestant Reformation? It ended in 1417, and the Reformation didn't start until exactly one hundred years later, in 1517. Where's the connection between the two?"

Michael was clearly clean bowled by the question. Mrs. Ashton therefore looked enquiringly at Maisie. She shrugged her shoulders, and shook her head violently.

"It's really very simple," said Mrs. Ashton. "The Great Schism made even worse, a hundred times worse in fact, all the bad things that were already crying out to be reformed or swept away. It held up all plans for reform. It also made the Christian religion a laughing-stock to Jews and Mohammedans, as well as to many lax Christians. Most serious of all, however, it lessened or completely destroyed in many Christians the respect and veneration that they had for the Pope and his authority. Simple, isn't it?"

The twins meekly nodded their agreement and managed to look sheepish.

Photo Mansell

Pope Martin V

"So much, then, for the Great Schism," continued Mrs. Ashton. "Now, what about the other cause you mentioned, the Renaissance? Let me explain. The word Renaissance means Rebirth, and it is used to describe what happened when the learned men of the fourteenth, fifteenth and sixteenth centuries threw themselves heart and soul into the study of the great artistic works of the ancient Greeks and Romans."

"What happened, Mummy?" asked Michael curiously.

"Their study led them to putting into practice what they found there."

"Was that very wrong, Mums?" asked Maisie, her chin cupped in her hands.

"It need not have been wrong at all, Maisie. There was a great deal in the works of the ancient pagan Greeks and Romans that the Christians of the fourteenth, fifteenth and sixteenth centuries could put to excellent use. But there was also a great deal that was bad and downright wicked, and it was these bad and wicked things that attracted many of those learned men of Europe. Little by little scholars like Lorenzo Valla, Antonio Beccadelli, and old Poggio came to despise Christianity as something fit only for ignorant and common people, and to hold up paganism as the only religion worthy of a cultured man, although, mind you, when it came to dying these men were usually only too glad to get a priest to put them right with God again!"

"But were they all like that, Mummy?"

"By no means, Michael. Other famous men of those times knew how to be good Christians and brilliant classical scholars, men for example like Cardinal Thomas Parentucelli, and Vittorino da Feltre. Cardinal Parentucelli became Pope Nicholas V in 1447, and it has been said that with him the Christian Renaissance ascended the papal throne. The other famous man I've mentioned, Vittorino da Feltre, was the greatest teacher of his age. He used to say that he wanted to teach his pupils to think, not to split hairs. But there were also many others who imagined that they could think and live like pagans and still be good Christians. A typical example of this class was your friend Signor Petrarca, and even more his bosom friend, Boccaccio.

"It isn't surprising, then, that bit by bit the new paganism got a strong hold on many of the ordinary people also in every country in Europe and caused fearful damage among them."

At this point Mrs. Ashton noticed that the twins' attention was beginning to wander.

"And that," she said with a smile, "will be enough for today! So let's see if we can now settle your argument."

The twins sat up with renewed interest at this, and looked at one another as much as to say: "Now we'll see who's right!"

"I'll tick off the main points on my fingers," continued Mrs. Ashton. "The clergy were full of worldliness. The clergy were so bad that they could hardly be worse. The Popes had forfeited the respect and reverence of the people mainly because of the Great Schism. Masses of the upper classes and also of the ordinary people were infected with the new paganism of the Renaissance. Therefore, says Mr. Burton, and Michael seems to agree with him, the Church was finished. But we have seen that not all the clergy, by any means, were worldly, or led evil lives; that not everybody, by any means, looked with contempt on the Papacy, and that not everybody, by a long way, lived like pagans. Therefore, says Mother Simplicitas backed up by Maisie, the Church was still very much alive and kicking, although badly in need of reform."

"I agree with Mother Simplicitas and Maisie," concluded Mrs. Ashton with a smile at her son's crestfallen face. "And so will you, my dear," she added, patting him on the cheek, "once you have had time to think it out."

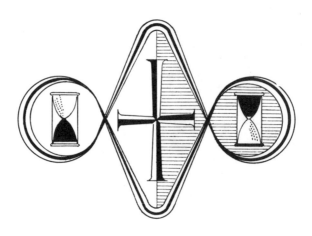

THE COUNCIL OF TRENT

"Timothy Smith," said Fr. Samson, "give me the name of the town where a famous General Council of the Church met in the sixteenth century."

Timothy Smith dragged himself back to reality from outer space in the pages of the book lying open on his knees under the desk. The voice of Fr. Samson had just managed to reach him across millions of miles, and he found it difficult to focus his attention on what the voice had asked him to do. "The name of the town," he muttered to himself as he rose reluctantly to his feet and slid the book under him.

"The name of the town," he asked looking at his teacher and blinking, "and a Council? Would it be London, Father? The London County Council?"

The class held its breath, waiting for the explosion. Fr. Samson, however, controlled his temper.

"No, Timothy, it is not London, and it is not a County Council that I asked you about. You were not paying attention to what I have been saying for the past ten minutes. You will stay behind after school and write out fifty times, neatly and with no blots, 'I must pay attention in class.' Now sit down and try to pay attention."

Crestfallen, Timothy sat down and tried to pay attention. But the call of outer space was too strong for him. Before Fr. Samson had succeeded in getting the right answer to his conundrum from Jeremias Flynn, the bright boy of the class, Timothy was once again speeding through space. Prudence, however, warned him to keep an ear cocked for any sounds that might come from the earth. And as he half-listened to his teacher he became more and more intrigued by what he heard. Until finally, almost unconsciously, he closed the book on his knees and listened attentively to what Fr. Samson was saying.

"And so, at long last, after years of squabbling and arguing between Popes and Emperor and Kings, after long-winded debates and discussions, after quarrels and wars, the Council of Trent

45

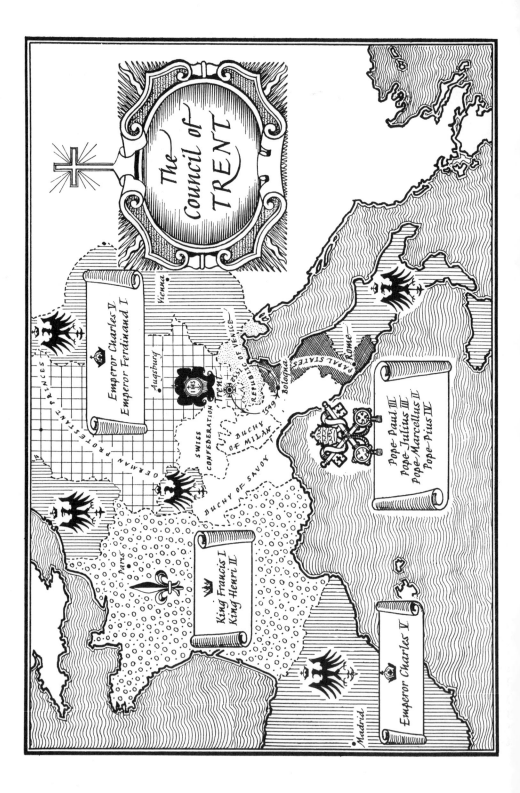

Hall   *Photo Mansell*

Pope Paul III

met for the first time on December 13, 1545." ("Oh!" thought Timothy, "so that was the town he wanted: Trent, the Council of Trent, the General Council of Trent!")

"Now," continued Fr. Samson, "before we go on to say something about what the Council of Trent did, will one of you tell us why the Council was needed, and what precisely it set out to do?"

There were no volunteers. It was clear that Fr. Samson's class had no illusions about themselves!

"Come now!" he snapped out. "I know that all your brains packed together wouldn't fill a thimble, but even that should be enough to help you to answer my question! You there in the back row, you trying to hide yourself, yes, you, Patrick O'Connor, stand up, please, and tell us in one word why the Council was needed, and what it meant to do."

Patrick rose to his feet, fixed a glassy

eye on a point above Fr. Samson's head, opened his mouth, and was silent.

"Well, Patrick," said Fr. Samson, "have you any idea at all why the Council of Trent was needed?"

Patrick gulped.

"Please, Father," he said at last, "it was because the Church was in a real mess. I mean," he hastened to correct himself as he saw the light in Fr. Samson's eyes, "I mean the Church was in such a bad way because of heretics and so on."

"Very well, that will do, thank you. The Church was in a very bad way. Now then, James Sinclair, you tell us what the Council set out to do."

James Sinclair groaned under his breath and dragged himself to his feet as Patrick O'Connor sat down with the air of a man who has done his duty and deserved well of his fellow men.

"Well, James?" asked Fr. Samson as James stood looking at him in silence. "What did the Council of Trent mean to do?"

"P . . . p . . . please, Father," stuttered James, "it—it—it wanted to re . . . re . . . form the Church. It wanted to reform everyone," he added with a rush, "and everything."

"And now, let us see what sort of a job the Council of Trent made of the tangle in which the Church and the nations of Europe found themselves twenty-eight years after the start of the Protestant Reformation. The best way to do that will be to follow the fortunes of the Council from its first meeting in December 1545, to its last meeting in December 1563."

"Please, Father!" the voice was that of Timothy's neighbour and crony, Robert Bruce, alias The Spider. "Did the Council of Trent last all those years?"

"No, not quite, Robert." Fr. Samson

Lizcano   *Photo Mansell*

Emperor Charles V interviewing the explorer Pizarro before he left for South America

seemed pleased at the question. "It started in 1545 and went on until 1549 under Pope Paul III. He was the Pope who was responsible for calling it and keeping it going against the continual opposition of the Emperor, Charles V, of the French King, Francis I, and of the Protestant Princes of Germany. The Council moved to Bologna in 1549, and was then suspended. It met again in Trent under the new Pope Julius III, but only for one year. Finally, after another ten years, it was summoned to meet for the last time under Pius IV. So you see the actual life of the Council was not very long at all, barely six years in fact."

"But was that not an awfully long time for a Council to meet, Father?" asked The Spider in surprise.

"Not really, when you consider the enormous amount of work it had to get through, and also the continual opposition and attempts at sabotage that went on during those years. As a matter of fact, the Council must have been on its toes and working at top pressure the whole of those six years to get through the work that it did."

"You see," continued Fr. Samson in the tone of voice that for his class was a sign that he was really coming to grips with what he wanted to say, "you see, the Protestant Reformation had already created so many problems in the whole of Europe that the Council's job was much bigger than you might think. It set out to examine very carefully the whole of the teaching of the Catholic Church. It had to find ways and means to bring order back into the lives of so many of the most important people in the Church. And it had also to put the Church in a position where She could defend Herself against Her new enemies as well as to carry the war into their territory."

"Please, Father, did the Council succeed in doing all this?" The question came from Timothy almost before he knew that he had spoken. Fr. Samson actually smiled at him.

"Yes, it did," he answered enthusiastically. "It succeeded in doing everything that it set out to do. But of course it was very heavy going all the time. Take, for instance, the first point that I've just mentioned, the one about the Council setting out to examine the whole teaching and belief of the Church. Almost right from the beginning of the Council, the Emperor tried his hardest to get it to shelve this point and to tackle the question of reform first. In fact he wanted the Council just to forget the first point and to pass on to the second and try to bring order into the lives of so many."

There was a murmur of surprise from the class. Several of the boys opened their mouths to speak, but Fr. Samson forestalled them.

"The reason for this," he said, "was simple enough from the Emperor's point of view. He did not want the Council to offend the Protestant Princes of Germany by condemning their new religion right from the beginning. There was another reason also. He did not believe that the Pope, Paul III, was really in earnest about reforming the Church."

4—III

Another murmur of surprise rose from the class.

"There were long and violent discussions in the Council between those who were on the Pope's side and those who were all for the Emperor. Finally it was agreed that the two questions should be dealt with at the same time, in the same sessions of the Council. That was nearly eight weeks after the opening of the Council."

"No wonder the Council lasted such a long time!" whispered Timothy to Robert.

"Indeed!" muttered The Spider out of the corner of his mouth. Luckily for them Fr. Samson was so wrapped up in what he was saying that he did not overhear them.

"When the Council really got started," he said, "that is, after the Third General Session or Meeting, it went on working at such high pressure that by the time it was suspended the first time, it had already carried out a great part of its task. Very briefly, this is what it managed to do in the first period of its existence. It settled the question whether all the books, or parts, of the Old and of the New Testaments, which were in common use in the Church, were to be regarded as Holy Scripture. At the same time it laid it down against the Protestants that the Bible does not contain everything that God wants us to believe and to do, but that some of it is contained in what is known as Tradition."

Fr. Samson paused and let his eyes wander over the class. The boys tried to avoid meeting his glance.

"Timothy," he said, "what is Tradition?"

"Tradition, Father?" said Timothy as he rose to his feet. "Oh, it's what the Church has always believed about God and so on, even though it isn't in the Bible. It's what has been handed down by word of mouth from the time of Our Lord and the Apostles."

"Good, that will do nicely. Now to return to the Council. In the next three general sessions it dealt with Original Sin, Justification, and the Sacraments. The discussions on Justification especially were very long ones, and it wasn't until the whole matter had been thrashed out down to the smallest detail by sixty-one general and forty-four particular committees that the Council published its decree on Justification on January 13, 1547."

"Please Father, what is Justification?" The question came from The Spider.

Fr. Samson looked rather surprised as he answered.

"Justification? Why, it's the problem of how men receive grace from God and become pleasing to him. The Council made it quite clear that when a man is justified by God he has his sins forgiven, really forgiven and not just covered over as the Protestants said, and that at the same time his soul is filled with what we call grace. Is that clear?"

"Yes, thank you, Father," answered The Spider.

"Soon after this," continued Fr. Samson, "and just when the Seventh Session was discussing the Sacraments, a plague broke out in Trent. It was known as the Spotted Fever, and as it was causing many deaths in the town the Council made it an excuse, at their Eighth Session, to leave Trent and go off to Bologna, to the great indignation of the Emperor who was already very angry with the Pope for various reasons, most of them political ones. Charles, by the way, was at this time cock-a-hoop because he had completely routed and defeated the German Protestant Princes of the so-called Schmalkaldic League at the Battle of Muhlberg on April 24,

1547, with the loss of only fifty of his own men!"

A gasp of astonishment from his class interrupted Fr. Samson at this point.

"Yes," he repeated, "fifty men. It sounds fantastic but it is true. What is more, the other side lost over two thousand men, and abandoned on the field of battle twenty-one guns, six hundred wagons of munitions and stores, and all its banners. So you can imagine how sure the Emperor was of himself just when the Council moved out of Trent and went to Bologna against his express wish. He did his best, or his worst, to get the Pope to order it back to Trent. But Paul III refused to listen to him. Things went from bad to worse with threats of one kind and another from the Emperor, until the Pope decided to adjourn the Council. He did this on September 17, 1549, and two months later he was dead. That was the end of the first part of the Council of Trent."

As Fr. Samson finished speaking Jeremias Flynn raised his hand to ask a question.

"Please, Father," he said as Fr. Samson nodded to him to speak, "did the Council not pass any decrees for the reform of the Church?"

"I was wondering if any of my brilliant class would ask that question," replied Fr. Samson with a smile. "Yes, Jeremias, the Council did pass certain very important decrees for the reform of the Church at the same time as it passed the decrees I've told you about, on the teaching of the Church. There was, for instance, a decree on the duty of bishops not to absent themselves for long periods from their own dioceses. Then there was another decree for bishops and other prelates of the Church reminding them of their duty to preach the Gospel to the people, and reminding parish priests of

Photo Mansell

A view of the city of Trent as it is today

their duty to teach the catechism to their congregation on Sundays and Feast Days. Most of the steps to be taken to bring about the reform of the Church were decided on in the Seventh Session. The reform of this Session dealt with, among other points, the qualifications that candidates to bishoprics must have, and with the duty of bishops to visit their dioceses regularly and to see that the churches in their dioceses were kept clean and in good repair. It also laid down the qualifications necessary in those who wanted to be priests. There were other regulations that the Council passed for the reform of the Church, but the ones I've mentioned were the most important ones. And so, as I've already said, we come to the end of the first stage of the Council of Trent's life.

"When the Council met again in 1551 it met once more in Trent. The new Pope considered that the old objections to Trent no longer held good, and so he ordered the Council to go back to Trent, much to the delight of the Emperor.

"This time it came to grips at once with its task, so that in the course of the next eight months it got through a prodigious amount of work. It brought out a famous decree on the Holy Eucharist. It prepared a detailed statement of the Catholic teaching on the Sacraments of Penance and of Extreme Unction. And it discussed for weeks on end the Sacrifice of the Mass, and the Ordination of Priests. At the same time the Council brought out various decrees of reform. These dealt mainly with matters concerning bishops and priests. And so," concluded Fr. Samson with a smile,. "they wouldn't hold much interest for you!"

A groan of protest broke from his class.

"Oh, Father!" they cried in unison. "We are interested!"

Tiziano Vecellio   Photo Mansell

The Council of Trent in Session

"Oh, you are, are you?" asked Fr. Samson, as if unable to believe his ears. "In that case I shall have to tell you what the reform decrees were that the Council passed in 1551 and 1552. Well, one of them told bishops how they could and should punish priests who didn't behave themselves, and what they must do to prevent bad priests from being in charge of souls. This same decree laid it down that priests must not go in for fashionable clothes. Another decree dealt mainly with the authority and the jurisdiction of bishops."

Fr. Samson paused as the sound of whispering reached him from the back benches. He was about to speak when a hand shot up.

"Yes, Laurence?" he asked. "What is it?"

"Please, Father," said Laurence Bright, the boy who had raised his hand and who now rose to his feet to ask his question, "is it true that the Council invited the Protestants to go to Trent?"

"Yes, quite true. The Council did invite the Protestants to send representatives to Trent to state their case there before the Council. The Council promised to give the Protestants a letter of safe-conduct if they came. And in fact, on October 22, 1551, two ambassadors of the Protestant Duke of Würtemberg arrived in Trent. Two other representatives, this time the ambassadors of the most powerful of the Protestant Princes of Germany, Maurice of Saxony, arrived at the beginning of 1552. But all these representatives soon made it quite clear that all they meant to do in Trent was to sabotage the Council. However, the Council decided to give them a fair hearing. And so on January 25, 1552, the Würtemberg ambassadors were received by the Council and asked to state their case. They demanded that all the decrees passed up to then by the Council should be scrapped because only one side, the Catholic side, had been heard. The other two ambassadors were received the same day at another meeting of the Council, and they had the nerve to tell the Council that the Pope had no authority in the government of the Church, and that the Council must start its work all over again! And then Maurice of Saxony showed his hand. He made an alliance with France and declared war on the Emperor. The city of Augsburg fell into his hands, and as this threatened the safety of Trent, the Pope, Julius III, decided in April 1552 to suspend the Council.

"That was the end of the second stage of the Council of Trent. The third and last stage did not start until 1562, ten years later.

"Emperor Charles was now dead but his brother, Ferdinand I, followed as Emperor, and his ideas on what the

Photo Mansell

Pope Julius III

Photo Mansell

Pope Paul IV

Church should do weren't much different from those of his brother. He wanted to make all sorts of concessions to the Protestants, who, by the way, were stronger than ever as a result of the Peace of Augsburg signed in September 1555. For example, he wanted the Pope to allow Communion under both kinds, and also to give priests permission to marry. He tried, like his dead brother, to prevent the Council from discussing matters of faith."

"Did he succeed, Father?" piped up The Spider.

"Not quite," said Fr. Samson. "At first the Council brought out various decrees of reform. It decided to revise the Index of Prohibited Books that Paul IV had brought out. It also made regulations for Holy Communion and Ordinations. And then it started once more to discuss matters of faith and doctrine. Thus, for example, it took up again the question of the Sacrament of Holy Orders, and at the same time it passed a decree that seminaries should be built for the education of candidates to the priesthood. Then, again, the Council discussed the Church's teaching on Purgatory, on the Invocation of Saints, and on the veneration of relics.

"And then, suddenly, a rumour reached Trent that the Pope was dying. That put an end to the Council, this time for good. It was closed for the last time on December 4, 1563.

"And there," added Fr. Samson, "goes the bell! Timothy Smith, you can forget about those lines."

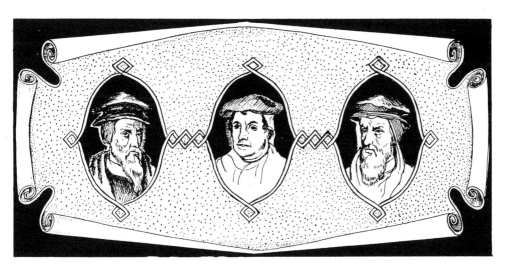

THREE REBELS

The three rebels of our title are Martin Luther, John Calvin and John Knox, the first a German, the second a Frenchman, and the third a Scot. They all died between three and four hundred years ago, but the rebellions they set in motion are still very much alive; and although their followers today do not always see eye to eye with them on many important points, they still look upon them with the admiration that we reserve for very great men and heroes.

We call them rebels because that is what they were, all three of them, rebels against the Catholic Church, which was the Church of their own Baptism.

They called themselves Reformers because they wanted to reform the Church, which was, according to them, riddled with superstition from top to bottom. It was so corrupt that it could no longer be the Church of Jesus Christ. Another name that was given to them was Protestants, after Martin Luther

and his followers had protested in 1529 against an edict, or order, of the Emperor, Charles V, and the Diet of Spiers condemning their efforts to "reform" the Catholic Church by substituting their own Church for it.

The first of our three rebels, then, was Martin Luther. He was born in the town of Eisleben in Saxony on November 10, 1483, just nine years before Christopher Columbus discovered a new world across the Atlantic. His father, Hans Luther, who was a miner, and his mother, Margaret, seem to have been very stern and heavy-handed parents. His mother once beat him until he was bleeding, just because he had stolen a nut! And his father gave him such a thrashing on one occasion that he ran away from home.

In spite of all this, however, Martin Luther seems to have had a pleasant time of it both as a boy and as a young lad. He was sent to school at an early age because his father wanted him to be

Martin Luther, in terror, fights his way through a raging storm of thunder and lightning

a lawyer, and even though he got more than his share of punishment from his teachers, he was happy. At eighteen he entered the University of Erfurt where he took his Master's degree. And then, less than seven months later, to the complete surprise of his father and his many friends, Martin Luther shut himself up in the monastery of the Augustinians in Erfurt!

Why he took such an unexpected step has always been something of a mystery. Some say that he was heart-broken over the sudden death of one of his friends who had been stabbed to death in a duel or a quarrel. Others say that he was scared almost out of his wits one day when he was caught out in the open country around Erfurt by a terrifying thunder-and-lightning storm, which threatened to reduce him to a cinder any minute. It was then that he made a vow to become a monk if his life was spared. He told his father that, as the lightning flickered around him, and the thunder rolled and boomed in the skies above him, he screamed out: "Help, St. Anne! I will be a monk!"

Less than two years after he had entered the monastery Martin Luther was ordained a priest. He went on studying with great diligence, and made such an impression on the rest of the monks that, three years later, he was chosen by them, and by the monks of six other monasteries of the same religious congregation of St. Augustine, to go to Rome as their spokesman.

One of their Superiors, named Staupitz, was trying to re-unite all the Augustinian monasteries of Germany, the strict and the not so strict ones, under one head, and the strict ones did not like the idea at all.

A great deal of nonsense has been written about the effect that Rome had on Martin Luther. It has been said that the wicked and superstitious things that he saw and heard in Rome convinced him that the only way for a man to save his soul was for him to believe in Jesus Christ: so long as he believed in Christ, no matter what he did, he would be saved. The Catholic Church, then, was quite wrong when she taught that in order to save his soul a man must try to live a good life with the help of God's grace.

What actually happened to Martin Luther while he was in Rome was something quite different. Five years after he had returned from the Eternal City he preached a sermon on the Pope. In this sermon he told his congregation that: "If Jesus Christ had not given all power to one man the Church would not have been perfect because there would have been no order, and each one would have been able to say that he was led by the Holy Spirit.

"This," Martin Luther went on to say, "is what the heretics did. . . . In this way as many Churches arose as there were heads! Christ therefore wills that his power should be in the hands of one man, to whom also he gives it, in order that all men may be gathered together in one unity. He has made this power so strong that he lets loose all the powers of hell against it, without injuring it. He says: 'The Gates of Hell shall not prevail against it,' as though he said: 'They will fight against it, but never overcome it.'"

Martin Luther preached that sermon at the beginning of August 1516. A year later he was about to join forces against the Pope with the heretics he had condemned in his sermon. What was the reason for this sudden change?

The change was not so sudden as one might easily imagine. When Martin Luther, or, as he was then, Fr. Augustine (his name in the monastery) returned from Rome, he was elected sub-prior of the monastery of Wittenberg. That was in 1512. Gradually he became more and more taken up with business of one kind and another in connection with the monastery. It came to the point when he had to have two secretaries to attend to his correspondence. He had also much preaching to do, for he was in great demand as a preacher; and besides

all this, he lectured on the Bible to the young students of the monastery. It is hardly surprising, therefore, that he had no time to attend to his own needs.

He neglected his studies, and began to be troubled with doubts about the teaching of the Church on the necessity of good works. Then he began to neglect his prayers and other religious duties in order to steal some time for his studies. The result was that he got himself into such a tangle of scruples and remorse that he became completely disheartened over the state of his own soul. After many months of this he suddenly saw, or imagined that he saw, where he had gone wrong.

Somehow he managed to convince himself that, as a result of original sin, no man has such a thing as free will, and that everything that a man does, thinks, or says, is bad and wicked, even when he imagines that it is good and virtuous. Martin Luther thus came to the conclusion that the only way for a man to save his soul was for him to believe in Jesus Christ, that, and no more. Bit by bit he developed this new doctrine of his (which became known as the doctrine of "justification by Faith alone"), and on it he built what he fondly imagined was the real Church of Christ.

Once he had reached this stage all that was required to cause an explosion between him and the Catholic Church was a match. The match fell into his hands when the Pope sent a Dominican Friar, the learned, brilliant and holy John Tetzel, to collect money in Germany for the construction of St. Peter's in Rome. Like many others, Martin Luther accused the Pope and Fr. Tetzel of making money out of indulgences. On October 31, 1517, therefore, he nailed to the door of the chapel of the castle of Wittenberg his now famous Ninety-five Theses. These pretended to be an attack on the abuse of indulgences.

Martin Luther nailing his thesis to the door of the chapel of the castle of Wittenberg

In reality they were an attack on the authority of the Pope, and of the Catholic Church.

Martin Luther was ordered by the Pope to go to Rome and give an account of himself, but he wriggled out of obeying the orders by pretending that he was too ill to face such a long journey. The Pope therefore had his case tried in Germany, at the Diet of Augsburg. The Diet found him guilty of heresy. He was excommunicated for heresy in July 1520.

A year later, at the Diet of Worms, he was found guilty of the same charge. There the young and newly crowned Emperor, Charles V, told him that he was not going to allow a mere monk to set himself up against the Faith that Christians had held for more than a thousand years. But Martin Luther had no intention of giving in, now that he had started his rebellion against the Pope.

"As for me," he said even before he was excommunicated, "the die is cast! I despise alike the favour and the fury of Rome. I do not wish to be reconciled with Her, or ever to hold any communion with Her!"

The die was indeed cast! With his furious and ferocious attacks against the Papacy and the Catholic Church he gradually won over to his side many of the German Princes, in spite of the fact that he spoke of them as "generally the biggest fools and worst scoundrels on earth"!

At the same time he won over many of the common people, even though he later abandoned them to their fate. This was when they had risen up against the tyranny of their rulers in the Peasants' War, for which he had been directly responsible with his sermons and writings. He did not, it is true, have everything his own way among his closest followers, for two of them especially, Carlstadt and Zwingli, were soon fighting him tooth and nail.

Long before his death on February 11, 1546, however, Martin Luther, the Rebel, the "Reformer," and the first Protestant, was one of the most powerful men in Germany. He died as he had lived for so many years, cursing the Papacy.

Our second rebel is a Frenchman, by the name of John Calvin, or the "Baldheaded" one. He was born at Noyon on July 10, 1509. His father, Gerard Calvin, was an advocate, a dishonest one, it seems, for when he died in 1533 he had been excommunicated for his shady practices. His mother, however, Jeanne Le Franc, was a very pious and devout woman, who saw to it that her four sons and two daughters grew up as good Catholics.

When John was fifteen his father sent him to live with his uncle Richard, a locksmith by trade, in Paris, there to continue his studies at the Collège de

Luther begins his revolt

la Marche. The following year John passed to the Collège de Montaigu. Ignatius Loyola, the founder of the Jesuits, joined the same College, but Calvin had left by then; the future saint and the future rebel never met.

It was not long before John Calvin had won for himself the nickname of "The Accusative," because of his constant habit of rebuking his friends. They liked him well enough, however, although his sharp tongue and even sharper reasoning over-awed them.

At the end of three years at the Collège de Montaigu John received marching orders from his father to go elsewhere.

Monsieur Calvin, the advocate, was no longer anxious for this clever son of his to study for the priesthood, like his elder brother, Charles. A much quicker way to wealth and fame was the way of the legal profession. In any case, one priest was quite enough for any family. So John must be an advocate, like his father.

He went, therefore, to study law, first at Orleans, and then at Bruges. But Monsieur Calvin's schemes for his younger son came to nothing, for as a result of his own shady conspiracies to cheat the Canons of Noyon, he was excommunicated. He died soon afterwards.

It was not long before John threw aside his legal studies and gave himself wholeheartedly to the study of the classics. In 1533 he made his way back to Paris as he was anxious to follow the lectures at the newly instituted Collège de France. It was here that he fell in with a group of would-be reformers, whose ideas about the Church were taken almost word for word from Martin Luther.

John Calvin very soon became infected with their enthusiasm, and for the time being was content to take them as he found them. Later on he put his own peculiar brand of Protestantism on the market.

Both Martin Luther and John Calvin held that God deliberately predestines every man, woman and child either to Heaven or to Hell, so that it makes no difference to a man's fate in the next world what he does in this world.

Calvin was to take this horrible doctrine and make it the pivot of his own

Nicholas Cop addressing the masters and students of La Sorbonne

religion, but with a difference. And what a difference! He was to claim that it was a most wonderful thing that God should act like this towards his own creatures! When people protested that such teaching was plainly against the goodness and justice of God, Calvin brushing them aside said it was "the grunting of pigs"!

Calvin was content to bide his time before he openly declared that he had broken with the Catholic Church. He was a clever, cautious, and calculating Frenchman, or so he thought until he took that false and fatal step on November 1, 1533.

An old school friend of his, Nicholas Cop, a medical student, was that year, in accordance with the custom of the times, elected Rector for three months of the University of Paris, La Sorbonne. One of his duties was to give an address to the masters and students of the university at the beginning of the new session, November 1. Desiring to cut as fine a figure as possible in this, he persuaded John Calvin to write his address for him.

Calvin, full of his newly acquired religious ideas on justification by faith alone, packed as many of these as he could into the address he composed for his friend and the new and very raw young Rector, all unsuspecting, read the address to the masters and students of La Sorbonne with drastic consequences. He was at once accused of heresy to the French Parliament. Before the authorities could lay hands on him, he fled to Basle.

What of John Calvin, the real cause of all the trouble and uproar? He too vanished from his usual haunts in Paris, and turned up in May 1534 in Saintonge, an out-and-out heretic now, whose one aim and desire was to crush and utterly destroy the Catholic Church. France, therefore, was no place for him, especially as the king, Francis I, enraged by a stupid and public insult paid to the Mass by some of the Protestants of Paris, had ordered them to be suppressed.

John Calvin decided to seek his fortune elsewhere. After a short visit to Salzburg and Basle, where, no doubt, he met poor Nicholas Cop, and then to Ferrara in Italy, he accepted an invitation from a certain Frenchman, William Farel, to make his home in Geneva.

Farel, himself a fanatical Protestant, had succeeded in getting the people of Geneva to follow his own example and change their religion. They abolished the Mass, emptied convents and monasteries, and drove the nuns and monks into exile. In May 1534 they officially declared themselves to be Protestants.

Three months later John Calvin appeared at the gates of their city and was persuaded by William Farel to throw in his lot with him and with the people of Geneva.

Before long, however, they woke up to the painful fact that John Calvin was a dangerous man to have in their city. He left them in no doubt at all that he looked on himself as a very important person indeed. He told them he was God's representative on earth. He had been sent by God to explain the Bible to them. He was the Prophet inspired by God to teach them the way to the truth, and therefore all his orders must be carried out at once, and no questions asked! He made it clear, also, that he was determined to get the people of Geneva to toe the line, ordering them to hand their city over to him so that he could then absorb it into the Church, his own new Church.

The leaders resented this, and told Calvin and Farel not to poke their noses into politics. Disappointed, the two would-be founders decided to shake the unworthy dust of Geneva off their feet and take themselves and their doctrines elsewhere.

Three years later, however, John Calvin returned, alone, but in triumph, to Geneva, at the earnest request of its inhabitants. They hailed him as a clever man of God and asked him to be their guide and pastor. He would lead them along a new road. Calvin returned on his own terms, and for the next twenty-three years the people of Geneva had plenty of time to wonder if

Calvin set upon by dogs

the old Pope in far-off Rome was not, after all, a much lesser evil than the new Pope in their midst!

For that is what John Calvin made himself, the Master and the Pope of Geneva. It is true that he called himself "the servant of the city of Geneva"; but there was never any doubt, either in his own mind or in the minds of the people of Geneva, who was the real master. No Pope ever ruled from Rome so despotically or ruthlessly as John Calvin ruled in Geneva. What is more, he ruled as he did because he was convinced, or said that he was, that he found all the severity and firmness of his rule clearly stated in the Bible, of which he claimed to understand every secret.

To help him to get the strangle-hold that he did over Geneva, and to hold it almost continuously until his death, Calvin made use of a Committee composed of six ministers and twelve elders. This committee, known as the Consistory, met every Thursday to examine very carefully the behaviour of every citizen, on the basis of information supplied to it by its own paid spies and informers. When the Consistory came across anything that, in its opinion, ought to be punished it passed the word to the City Council, which then went into action against the guilty party. It seems to have found plenty to do, for it is on record that the poor citizens of Geneva were punished for such "crimes" as having had too much to eat, or not having gone to hear a sermon! It did not spare anyone, no matter how popular or how powerful or rich. Thus it was responsible for having Clement Marot, the poet, thrown out of Geneva because he had been caught playing backgammon with another man, and drinking with him. Another well-known citizen, Ami Perrin, who was captain-in-general of the city, had to beg Calvin's pardon for having dared to hold a ball to celebrate a wedding.

The worm, however, turned at last. Perrin was elected Syndic of Geneva, and this encouraged the nobles to give John Calvin a taste of his own medicine. The common people followed their example, so that "the servant of the city of Geneva" could not appear in public and cross the streets without someone setting his dog at him. As he himself said many years later: "Anger and bitterness against me rose to such a pitch that whatever I said aroused suspicion. I had only to say that it was sunny at noon, and the people began at once to doubt it!"

That might have been the end of John Calvin's career as Pope of Geneva, had it not been for what happened on October 27, 1553. On that day, a Spanish doctor, known as Michael Servetus, was burned alive at the stake in Geneva as a heretic. He had denied that there was any proof of the Trinity in the Bible. This had been too much for Calvin. With Martin Luther he claimed that every man had the right to interpret the Bible as he felt inspired by God. Yet when anyone took him at his word, as poor Servetus did, and dared to interpret the Bible in a manner different from his own, he was immediately up in arms against the "blasphemer" and the "heretic." To get rid of Servetus he had hit upon the original plot of denouncing him to the Catholic Inquisition at Vienne, where Servetus happened to be at the time. Servetus, however, had managed to escape from the hands of the Inquisition, and decided for some unknown reason to return to Spain by way of Geneva. There Calvin was responsible for having him arrested and condemned to death as a heretic. Some months after the sentence had been carried out, Calvin published his Defence against Servetus, in which he stated that

Servetus, the Spanish doctor, burned on Calvin's denunciation

the Spanish heretic had deserved all he got, and denied, falsely, that he himself had denounced him to the Inquisition.

The death of Servetus brought Calvin back to power. Ami Perrin and his party had done their best to save the poor wretch from the flames, and for this act of mercy they were heavily defeated at the elections, while John Calvin became once again "the servant of the city of Geneva."

He continued to "serve" the city until his death on May 27, 1564, but long before he died he had wrested the tremendous power of excommunication, exercised by the City Council, from the hands of that body, and placed it in the hands of his own Consistory, so that the Church, his Church, dominated the State, and he was once more the absolute master over the lives of those he professed to serve.

For our third and last rebel and "reformer" we leave Switzerland for Scotland, and pass from Geneva to Edinburgh. As we shall see, this rebel spent a considerable part of his life in the city of John Calvin, and in his company.

John Knox was his name. We know very little about his early years, but we know a great deal about his later years, which were mostly the years of his rebellion. John Knox was born in Scotland, probably in or near the town of Haddington, some time between the year 1505 and the year 1515. His father, William Knox, was very likely one of the small peasant farmers of the district, for his son, speaking of himself, says: "I am a man of base estate and condition." Of his mother, as well as of his step-mother, nothing is known except that his mother's maiden name was Sinclair. William Knox had his son study for the priesthood, and a priest the boy became in due course, for in later years, when he was a fully fledged "reforming" preacher, he said of himself that he had been "one of

Cardinal Beaton is foully murdered by Wishart's men

Baal's shaven sort," which was his way of saying that he had been a Catholic priest.

John Knox really comes to life for us only in 1545. This is the date from which we get to know all about him from the pages of the *History of the Reformation*, which he wrote. It seems that he had begun to harbour doubts about his Catholic Faith as far back as 1540. But it was his friendship with a fellow Scot, George Wishart, who came home about this time from Germany full of Luther's new religion, that marked for John Knox the beginning of his break with the Catholic Church. George Wishart was the mortal enemy of Cardinal Beaton, the champion of the Catholic cause in Scotland, and in fact the champion and defender of Scotland against the English. Wishart knew that he could never hope to draw his fellow countrymen over to Protestantism so long as the Cardinal was alive, or at liberty, to resist him. So he began to

plot with Henry VIII of England to kidnap the Cardinal and hand him over to the English, or else to murder him. But Wishart was arrested, and condemned to death. His body was burned at St. Andrews after he had been strangled by the public executioner. That was in March 1546. In May Wishart's friends and followers burst into the Cardinal's private apartments in the castle of St. Andrews, and put him to a cruel and cowardly death. Then they shut themselves up in the castle to escape the vengeance of the Government. John Knox joined them and remained with them until the following year, when they surrendered to the Government, who had called in the help of their French allies. Together with several of his companions John Knox was sentenced to prison, not in Scotland, but in the galleys of the French.

For the next nineteen months John Knox was a busy man not only at the oars of his galley but also at his writing and preaching. He was allowed in fact to write a book on theology, and he was able to preach to his fellow-prisoners.

On his release he thought it would be more prudent for him to keep away from Scotland, where the foul assassination of Cardinal Beaton at the hands of his friends was still very fresh in the mind of the public and of the Government. There was always the danger that he might be arrested again, and given another dose of prison, and John Knox had no great desire, either at that time, or at any other time afterwards, to suffer for his new faith. It was safer for him to go to England, and so to England he went, and there he was given royal permission to preach at Berwick-on-Tweed. Five years later, after Mary Tudor, Edward VI's Catholic sister, had come to the English throne, and John Knox had married a young English girl, he thought it would be prudent if he made another change of climate, just in case Mary should get ideas into her Papist head about him and his peculiar behaviour. He took himself off to Dieppe, therefore, and then to Geneva to ask Calvin and other learned men of that city if it was lawful for him to rise up against Mary Tudor in England, or Mary of Guise, the new Regent, in Scotland. They refused to give him a straightforward answer to his dangerous questions, but John Knox was quite clear in his own mind what the answer was.

The following year his "mother-in-law" made him return, much against his will, to his young "wife," Marjorie Bowes. There was, however, nothing for him to fear now, even in Scotland, for the new religion was making steady progress in that country. He began, then, to preach openly in Edinburgh that it was the duty of every Christian (that is, Protestant) prince and magistrate (as well as of every true "believer" should the princes and the magistrates refuse to take action) to slaughter and wipe out all "idolaters." The "idolaters" were the Catholics, who, in Knox's eyes, were no better than those Jews who used to sacrifice their own children

Instigated by Knox the mob sets on fire a beautiful church

to the false God, Moloch. John Knox was encouraged to speak as he did by the support given him by many nobles, and many powerful Lowland lairds. So unbridled did he become in his preaching that in May 1556 he was summoned by the authorities to appear in the church of the Black Friars, and give an account of himself and of his novel doctrines. Needless to say he went to the church accompanied by some powerful nobles. Not surprisingly, he came away scot free! Another summons was issued against him a month or two later, but by that time John Knox had again gone back to Geneva.

He went back not because he was afraid of what might happen to him if he remained in Scotland, or even in England. What was there to fear, at least in Scotland, with such powerful supporters at his back? No, he left Scotland to go and attend to the spiritual needs of the English colony in Geneva, simply because he felt that the Scots were not yet ready to open their arms to him as to one sent by God to reform the Church in Scotland.

Two years passed before John Knox again set foot on Scottish soil. He did make a half-hearted effort to return earlier, got as far as Dieppe, dilly-dallied there for some time, and then retraced his steps back to Geneva and his family. But he was very active with his pen during these two years on behalf of the Protestants of Scotland and England, and produced, among other things, his famous "First Blast of the Trumpet against the Monstrous Regiment of Women," and his "Brief Exhortation to England." With his "Blast" Knox hoped to scatter to the winds the power of Mary Tudor in England, of Mary of Guise in Scotland, and of Catherine de Medici in France, and also to frighten the wits out of the young Mary Stuart even before she came to the Scottish throne. With his "Brief Exhortation" he tried to persuade the English to throw out "all dregs of Popery," and to bring in instead the "Kirk discipline" of John Calvin.

At last, however, John Knox tore himself away from Geneva, and made his way by sea back to Scotland, landing at the port of Leith, near Edinburgh. Elizabeth had succeeded her sister Mary in England, while in Scotland Mary of Guise was too ill to be able to do much about the ever-increasing activities of the "reformers." There was thus no danger to be feared, either north or south of the Border, and John Knox felt safe.

From the moment that he set foot again in Scotland he became responsible for the wholesale destruction of ancient churches, cathedrals and monasteries. This destruction was carried out at his instigation up and down the country by what he called the "rascal multitude." To speed on the "godly" work of the "reform" he started to plot with the ministers of Elizabeth of England against his own Government, until finally, Mary of Guise died, besieged in Edinburgh Castle, on June 10, 1560.

Then on August 1 Parliament met (illegally, because the new Queen, Mary Stuart, had not summoned it), and on August 17 forced upon the country the Confession of Faith drawn up by John Knox and his friends. The authority of the Pope was abolished. The Mass was thrown out as a piece of blasphemous idolatry. The Catholic Church was outlawed.

John Knox, the rebel, had triumphed with the help of a gang of treacherous and traitorous nobles, and of the "rascal multitude." But, had he been able to look into the future, and seen there the long years of strife, war, and bloodshed that were to follow upon his own death on November 24, 1572, John Knox might not have been so jubilant that day of August 1560, the day of his victory over the Catholic Church in Scotland.

ST. IGNATIUS LOYOLA

Too short by a foot to make an impression on the crowd, the red-haired little man with the burning eyes ran limping towards the nearest tree and climbed it.

Dwarf on the ground, he was a giant in the tree. Now he could make them listen, and if only one in that crowd got a glimmer of what he meant, then God be praised.

It was no new experience for Ignatius Loyola to climb a tree in order to preach, and if he ever regretted that he stood but 5 feet 2 inches in his stockinged feet, it was never recorded.

Small of stature, big of heart; courageous to the point of folly, impetuous, generous, proud at first to the point of touchiness, humble, with the humility of Christ, Ignatius was born in a castle in Spain. He was the son of the illustrious Don Betran of Onaz and Loyola, and had fine opportunities to get on in the world as he grew up. He lived at the

royal court, dressed in gay, fashionable clothes, and was fond of wearing not only sword, but dagger and cutlass too on his expeditions abroad.

At the end of the fifteenth century Spain was rich, powerful and aggressive. For long her king had eyed Navarre; when the opportunity came, he sent his soldiers into that country and captured it. Navarre accepted the situation until Ferdinand's death; only then did she dare to raise her head again. French troops laid siege to Pamplona, the garrison manned by Spaniards—among them Ignatius Loyola, now a swashbuckling soldier. The Spanish force was out-weaponed and out-numbered. They would have hoisted the white flag but for Ignatius who shamed them into fighting on. He took charge, was everywhere at once, and the soldiers rallied under such inspired leadership.

The whole course of history—one man's history—might have been different but for a cannon-ball. Fired by the enemy, it found its deadly mark. Ignatius fell to the ground, his leg shattered, blood staining the spot where he lay. At the sight of their fallen leader, the Spaniards once again lost heart. This time, Ignatius could not stop them from surrendering. What was left of the force became the prisoners of the French, who treated the gallant wounded captain with courtesy and even charity. They did their best to patch up the leg and then sent him home.

Ignatius was carried on a litter to the family castle at Azpeitia where his brother Don Martin and his wife lived. They received him kindly, but soon grew concerned when they saw the condition of his leg.

"These French surgeons have butchered you," his brother told him. "I shall send for a Spanish surgeon. He will put it right."

But the Spanish surgeon's efforts were no more skilful, and Ignatius when he looked down at his misshapen leg was in despair. He could bear pain with Basque-like courage and fortitude, but he did not know how to face life a cripple. Besides the unsightly piece of bone which protruded, the limb was much shorter than the other.

He demanded that something more be done.

"It could be broken and reset," the surgeons told him, "and a rack fixed to it so that it may be pulled out, but that will entail much additional suffering."

Ignatius did not hesitate. He would endure any amount of pain, if, at the end of it, he might be assured that he could take up his soldiering again. And so it was done, and for months he lay in bed, sometimes near to death, unable to fight off the fevers which took hold of him.

At last, when he was stronger, he asked for something to read.

"The days are so long and boring," he told his sister-in-law, "are there no books in the castle?" Magdalena promised to see what she could find, and when she returned carrying two heavy-looking volumes, Ignatius exclaimed in horror, "The Lives of the Saints and The Life of Our Saviour! These are not men's reading!"

He had been looking forward to romantic tales of knights in armour battling for their ladies.

"There is nothing else," Magdalena told him laying the books by his bed.

Out of sheer boredom, he started reading them. He read slowly at first, unwillingly, but gradually the soldier in him grew interested. The saints were real men, heroes. He could admire them, for they too had fought battles for their King, had suffered and died for him. Now he was reading steadily, and when he had turned over the last page, he started at the beginning again.

And then, in his beautiful handwriting of which he was justly proud, he set himself the task of copying into notebooks choice passages from The Lives of the Saints. It was a tremendous task and one which filled his days, and while he wrote, he determined that he too would serve under the banner of Christ the King.

By the spring of 1522 Ignatius was strong enough to leave the castle.

"I do not intend to go back to the army," he told his brother, "but first I shall go to Navarete to tell my Commander this. I shall then journey to Montserrat, to the shrine of Our Lady. Afterwards I shall make a pilgrimage to Jerusalem."

For days now, he had been able to think of nothing but this. To visit the Holy Land, to see and kiss the ground where Jesus had walked. It filled his thoughts. But first he must prepare.

St. Ignatius bestowing his cloak on a beggar

His kindly brother protested in vain. Had Ignatius thought of his future—that was assured if he returned either to the court or to the army. It was madness to entertain these wild thoughts of pilgrimages.

But neither his brother nor the Duke of Najera, his commanding officer, could turn him from his course, and one day Ignatius, still clad in his rich blue cloak and feathered hat, set out on a mule for Our Lady's shrine at Montserrat high up in the mountains where the Benedictines had their monastery.

The going was heavy, and Ignatius was not yet very strong; when he was forced to dismount, he limped, as he would always do for the rest of his life. He carried his beloved sword and dagger intending when the moment came to lay them at the feet of Our Lady. Stopping in one of the mountain villages, he bought for himself a coarse sackcloth, which he took immediately to a tailor asking that it might be fashioned into a loose robe which would reach to his ankles. He bought rope sandals and a pilgrim's staff. Then, as soon as the opportunity occurred, he bestowed upon a bewildered tramp his fine cloak and yellow stockings.

Ignatius did not go at once to the shrine. From the moment when he had decided to give his entire life to Christ, he had regretted bitterly the sins of his past life. He had been such a proud, swashbuckling cavalier, vain and hot-tempered; it had been all too easy to fall into the thoughtless ways of the court. There was, too, all the time spent in the army, when he had no thought of anything but winning glory for himself.

Ignatius wrote down all the sins of his life, even the smallest one. Then armed with this list, he made a general confession which lasted for three days, and at the end of it he received absolution. Now at last he was prepared to make the vigil of the armour before the shrine of Our Lady.

Ignatius lived in an age and in a country where knights were the brave

St. Ignatius praying in his cave at Manresa

knights of fairy-tale lore. It was the custom for a freshly dubbed knight before setting out on his brave adventuring to spend the whole of one night before the shrine of Our Lady dressed in his new armour.

Ignatius in his sackcloth and his hempen sandals would do the same, dedicating himself finally to God's service, and as a pledge leaving behind his sword and dagger.

Ignatius did just that, and then calm and peaceful, he attended Mass and received Holy Communion.

The Cave at Manresa

" I shall go to Jerusalem," Ignatius had told his brother, and that was his immediate intention, but much was to happen before he even reached Barcelona, the port from where he would sail.

The little town of Manresa lay below Montserrat, and it was there Ignatius stopped for shelter on his way to Barce-

lona. While there he learned that the newly elected Pope, Adrian VI, had not yet reached Rome and that there was, therefore, no need for haste, for without the Pope's permission no pilgrim could enter Jerusalem which was ruled by the Turks. The Holy Places themselves were in the custody of the Franciscans, and every precaution was taken to avoid upsetting the Turkish overlords.

Barcelona was only a few days' journey from Manresa; the delay in receiving permission was likely to extend into many months. And so Ignatius stayed on at Manresa, and discovered the cave; it was a large cave outside the town, isolated and ideal for his purpose. Here he could give himself up to prayer and meditation.

Father James Brodrick, S.J., in his book called *The Origin of the Jesuits* says that there " he went through the dread, mysterious Dark Night of the Soul known to the great mystics, and there too he was caught up into Paradise and heard secret words which it is not granted to man to utter . . ."

During the ten months that Ignatius stayed at Manresa, and while he was alone in his cave he began to think out exercises which would help to bring God closer to men. Later he wrote them down. The book is called *Spiritual Exercises*. He also had a vision of the Holy Trinity which filled him with such joy that "he wept for the remainder of the day." He was to have other visions too before he set out for Barcelona— there was one in which he was bathed in a bright light so dazzlingly bright that he was almost blinded. God appeared to him and told him that he would get together a company of men who would help to bring souls closer to him.

Much was to happen before this came true, but Ignatius was now spiritually grown up. Whatever hardship and suffering came his way, he accepted it as a mark of God's love. Long hours of prayer and severe fasts and little sleep had weakened his health. He was ill before he set out for Barcelona, dangerously so, but he recovered, and when he arrived at the city, he set about finding a ship which would take him to Italy, to Rome where he intended to ask the Pope personally for permission to go to the Holy Land.

He had no money when he at last reached the Holy City, and he begged in the streets, keeping for himself only the barest necessity for life, and giving everything else away to the poor around him. All his life Ignatius observed most strictly this rule of poverty. A man who had nothing of his own had freedom of heart to love God wholeheartedly. Ignatius was a joyful beggar as he roamed the streets of the great city and visited its churches.

There, as everywhere else, his days were spent in prayer, and his nights too, more often than not, as he lay under the stars. When at last permission to go to Jerusalem was granted, Ignatius set out for Venice where he was given a free passage to the Holy Land, and in August of the year 1523 landed at Jaffa, the port for Jerusalem.

Never in all his life had Ignatius known such happiness, as he wandered from one hallowed spot to another. He kissed the ground on arriving at the Garden of Gethsemane, his eyes blinded with tears, but they were tears of joy, not sadness, for the love of Christ filled his heart to overflowing.

He determined to stay in Jerusalem for the rest of his life, but when he asked permission from the Provincial of Franciscans, he was told he must leave with the other pilgrims. The Turks, the Father Provincial told him, would never permit him to remain and preach. They despised Christians, and the present situation was difficult enough.

For Ignatius it was the end of a dream, and when in January 1524 he reached Venice it seemed that he had failed. He was ill and destitute, having long since given away any useful possessions. His clothes were in rags; he had no money. Once more he begged in the streets. A rich Spanish merchant who had known him previously offered him clothing and shelter, at the same time telling him that "begging" would not get him very far towards his goal.

Ignatius considered his words, humbly. Perhaps he was right. There were some men who would not be attracted to God simply through love; they would want to argue and reason about him. Then and there he decided that the best way to serve God was to study so that he might be ready to draw many different kinds of men into his net. But it was to Barcelona he must go.

"I am going to school again," he told

Rubens

Photo Mansell

St. Ignatius

his good friend Isabel Roser. And how she laughed at him. "A man of thirty-three sitting down to his lessons with children!"

But that is just what Ignatius did, and though the boys mocked him sometimes, his teachers were understanding and after two years' hard study, for to begin with he learned very slowly, his masters said that he might enter one of the universities.

Ignatius went to the university at Alcala. He was delighted when he found the chance of giving the Spiritual Exercises. Until the university opened in October, he was to be found, either staggering along with a load of goods on his back for the poor, or preaching. Young men were coming to him, too, about this time asking that they might follow him and wear the grey robe made of coarse material which was the dress Ignatius had adopted.

To understand what happened next you would have to realise the unhappy state of Spain just around the beginning of the sixteenth century. It was a country divided against itself.

The Church was divided, and the country a mass of rumour and intrigues. To safeguard the Faith, King Ferdinand called in the Inquisition.

Rumours of the strange little man who limped and who spent his time working among the poor and preaching, and yet who was neither priest nor brother, had reached the Inquisition. Briefly, Ignatius found himself arrested and thrown into prison. He was tried and released after questioning, but he did not attempt to return to the university, and finally, after again being arrested, decided that he must leave Spain and study in Paris where the long arm of the Inquisition could not reach out to him.

It was raining when Ignatius arrived in Paris; it was cold too, for it was the month of February 1528, but Ignatius was too happy to care. The gold which friends had insisted he must take to pay for his keep was a burden to him, and he gave it to a fellow countryman to care for. The man promptly spent it, and Ignatius was forced to find work between his classes in order to keep himself. Later, when he heard the thief was ill, he walked for three days to visit him and gave him all he had to tide him over until he got well, then found him a ship for Spain.

Despite all manner of difficulties Ignatius went on giving the Spiritual Exercises. The next year at the university saw him starting on his philosophy, and sharing a room with two students; one was Pierre Favre, the other a Spaniard, Francis Xavier.

Both were to become Jesuits, Peter Favre was the first priest of the Company, Francis one of its greatest, and most difficult to catch!

Ignatius, as soon as he met them, knew that they were going to be members of his Company, and the gentle Peter Favre was not long in joining. Francis Xavier was proud and independent, however, and resisted Ignatius for a long time, but finally he too was won over.

The little Company was growing, Ignatius had now finished his studies, Peter Favre had been ordained. But others were still students. One day their leader called a meeting at the Church of Our Lady of Montmartre. It was decided that when they had all become priests they would make for the Holy Land and try to convert the Turks. If, however, after trying their best to get a passage to Jerusalem, they failed, then they would go to Rome and offer themselves to the Pope. They were seven: Favre and Francis Xavier, Lainez, Salmeron, Bobadilla, Rodriguez.

Laying the foundation stone of the Society of Jesus

The little band of seven, as Father Brodrick writes, then "decided to bind themselves by vows of poverty and chastity as well as to go to Jerusalem. On the feast of the Assumption, 1534, they repaired together at dawn to a little, unused chapel half-way up the slopes of Montmartre, and there, unobserved except by God, burned their boats behind them during a Mass celebrated by Favre. It was the quietest ceremony, that laying of the Foundation stone of the Society of Jesus. . . ."

By the following year, Ignatius was ill again, and his doctors sent him back to Spain. He went to his own village, to Azpeitia, where so long ago the French soldiers had carried him through the streets on a litter to his brother's castle. But this time, he did not go to the castle. He lived in the village, determined to spend his vacation preaching to the villagers. And when they did not listen, he climbed a tree to attract their attention.

He stayed three months in Azpeitia, visiting his brother Don Martin, but refusing himself the luxury of staying at the castle. Then he returned to Venice, where he studied and prayed and gave the Spiritual Exercises, and waited for the others. It was a long wait—nearly a whole year—for Ignatius was actually twelve months ahead of his appointment with the rest of his Company.

For practical reasons it had been decided at that momentous meeting at Montmartre in 1534 that three years should elapse before they all met again in Venice. January 1537 was the date fixed, and how Ignatius' thoughts must have dwelt on the reunion. He would see Francis again and Peter, and there would be eleven not seven wearing the grey tunic.

And then at last the moment came, and they were all there and all of one heart. It was to be Jerusalem! But Venice was in the grip of winter, and no ship could be found to take them to Jaffa.

"We shall work in the hospitals and preach and be the servants of the poor," Ignatius told them, "and when the spring comes, you must go to the Holy Father and ask his blessing, but I shall remain here until you return."

The months passed, and the grey-robed men were well known in the poorest districts of the city, before it was time once again for them to say "good-bye" to their leader and set off for Rome. And how happy Ignatius was to see them on their return and to hear the good news that the Pope had given them his blessing.

"We were welcomed everywhere," they told him, "but we cannot go to Jerusalem, for the Turks are at war, and we cannot hope to be permitted to land."

"I shall go to Jerusalem," Ignatius had told his brother long ago. Not only would he go, but he would live out his life close to where his Beloved King had preached and died. Now it seemed that God was asking him to give up his cherished dream for ever. And he no longer pursued it. "We shall go to Rome, to the Holy Father and put ourselves at his disposal," Ignatius told his followers, and that same night Jesus appeared to him in a vision. He was carrying his cross, and he said: "I shall be favourable to you in Rome."

And so to Rome they went, and were favourably received. The Holy Father asked some of them to teach in schools and colleges; others he sent to distant countries. The little Company was scattered far and wide, until, without warning, the Inquisition pounced, and once again Ignatius found himself arrested for questioning. Just as on all other occasions, no fault could be found with his teaching, and he was released, but now Ignatius was justly angry.

"Tell them publicly," he begged the Holy Father, "there is no fault in our lives and teachings," and this the Pope agreed to do.

Ignatius had never intended to found an Order, but as the months passed and more and more of his Company were being sent hither and thither it was decided after much prayer to ask the Holy Father to approve their Company as a new Order. On September 27, 1554, the Papal Bull appeared which marked the foundation of the Order of the Company of Jesus.

Until he was utterly convinced that it was God's will, Ignatius could not bring himself to accept the role of Superior, but the vote was unanimous. And Superior he remained until the hour of

Photo Mansell

Exterior view of the Church of St. Ignatius, Rome

Interior of the Church of St. Ignatius

his death, despite his efforts, to begin with, to hand over the control of his Order to a younger and fitter man.

He was now permanently "stationed" in Rome, his days and nights taken up with the writing of the Constitution of the Order, and with organising. He lived to see Jesuit colleges established in Spain, Portugal, Germany and France. He watched his best friends, men like Francis Xavier and Peter Favre, striving in heathen countries and at home no less valiantly than the saints whose lives he had so patiently and lovingly recorded long years ago.

Of his own life and endeavours he thought little, of his health nothing at all. Ill through overwork and lack of sleep (he spent much of each night in prayer), he foretold his own death. He died on July 31, 1556, without the consolation of the last Sacraments, because his secretary could not believe that he was so desperately ill. But Ignatius knew, and recalling as he must have done the joy of the saints when they went to meet their Master, his great heart must have throbbed with happiness as he too surrendered his soul to God.

SAINTS OF PRAYER

In the sixteenth century the great disaster called the "Reformation" took place. The Reformation happened because there were so many evil things which had to be changed. For long years there had been corruption, injustice, greed, worldliness, even among the most highly-placed in the Church. Then came a movement to sweep away the wickedness and bring about reform. That in itself was good. But the disaster of the Reformation was that large groups of people broke away from the Church, and as a result, peoples of the Christian world were no longer united under one spiritual head.

The Church, like the world, was in need of reforming. Its priests, some of them, had become politicians, and others had grown lazy and lax in the discharge of their duties. But it would be wrong to think that she did not have saints. Indeed, one of the most wonderful things about the time when the great disaster happened was the number of saints God raised up to meet the need. Especially he raised up many who by their lives of prayer restored the strength of the Church.

The saints you are going to read about have been especially chosen because, above all, they were saints of prayer, and had therefore a most powerful influence on the spiritual life of the whole world.

St. Catherine of Genoa

"St. Benedict, pray to God that he make me stay three months sick in bed." What a strange prayer for a young and beautiful lady to make! And she had chosen, too, to make it in the little church which stood close to the sea, just outside her own city of Genoa and which was specially dedicated to Benedict.

But it did not seem strange to Catherine. The desire to make God the centre of her life had been growing and growing over the past ten years. If Benedict interceded for her with God, and her prayer was granted, three months' sickness would take her out of the worldly life she had been living; she would have time to think—to make fresh resolutions. There would be time to remember herself as a child when she longed to become a nun. Her ten years of marriage had not been happy. Julian, her husband, was a spendthrift, a weak, irresponsible young man. They had married because their parents had desired it, and children of the fifteenth century did not dream of defying their parents in such matters.

It was the eve of St. Benedict's feast and the year was 1473. Catherine had come to the church, tired of the world and its pleasures, knowing in her heart that her true happiness was to be found only in service to God. But it was hard to break away from old friends and old habits . . . and so she prayed. Two days later, while visiting her sister who had become a nun, her prayer was answered, though not in the way she expected. She just knew that God filled her, had taken possession of her heart, and from that moment she was filled with sorrow for her past life, and filled also with the desire to give herself to him.

Catherine returned to her husband knowing that her life was changed, determined to begin again, and to try if possible to save her husband from himself.

They were, by now, deeply in debt, for Julian spent money as fast as it came to hand. They could no longer afford their big house. Nothing dismayed, Catherine persuaded Julian to move with her to a small house in a poor part of the city. And Julian, at last able to see himself for what he was, repented of his ways, and became all that Catherine had prayed he might become.

Together they offered themselves as helpers in the hospital near their house, and during the plague which now struck the city, Catherine nearly died from the disease because of her devotion to the sick. She became matron of the hospital and kept the accounts so accurately that she was never a farthing out!

But it was not because of that she was beatified; it was because of her wonderful, steadfast love of God. Her fasts and her long night-watches spent in prayer united her to her beloved Lord in a very special way. Her work, because of her prayer, became an offering, the finest she could make to God. And when she died on September 15, 1510, after months of suffering, she was mourned by all Genoa. She never became a nun, but her whole life has been an inspiration to men and women living in the world down the centuries.

St. Peter of Alcantara

Do you think the old man who sits guard by his glowing fire knows that he too has a patron saint? As he leaves his hut to light the lantern which will warn motorists that the road is under repair, St. Peter of Alcantara no doubt blesses his labour, and gives him protection against unseen dangers.

St. Peter was named the Patron Saint of Night-watchmen because of his own watchings through the night. Great Saints of prayer habitually spent some part of their night in prayer, but Peter's watchings were so exceptional that much has been written about them. For one thing he never lay down. When he slept, it was in a sitting position, with his head against the wall. *When* he slept, that is, for as the years passed, the hours he permitted himself for rest grew shorter and shorter.

And yet he was a most active, energetic young man in the daytime, and so lovable that men willingly accepted all the strict rules he laid down for them.

He was born in a small town in Spain called Alcantara in the year 1499. His father was a lawyer and Peter too thought he might become one, until one day when he was sixteen, he deliberately chose to become something quite different, a Franciscan—a member of the Discalced Franciscans which was one of the strictest Orders in Spain.

Sometimes Peter's habit of always having his mind on spiritual matters got him into trouble. It made him somewhat absent-minded, and once when he was put in charge of feeding the friars, there was a complaint that he never gave them any fruit.

"But," says Peter, "I have never seen any fruit to give them." And then his superiors were obliged to point out that the fruit was there in plenty hanging in bunches from the ceiling. So preoccupied had Peter been, that he had never once raised his eyes upwards, and so had missed seeing the grapes.

He had no worldly belongings; his solitary habit, worn and patched, was his only protection against wind and rain, and when it was being washed, Peter had to hide himself away until it was dry enough to wear again. And because he was so poor himself he loved and understood the poor around him. He loved to preach to them, and they would say that even if he had not uttered a single word, his presence among them was enough to bring God into their hearts.

The missions given by the saint, and his book on prayer, brought him recognition from John III, King of Portugal, and Peter was sent by his Provincial to Lisbon to talk with the king. The king would have liked to keep Peter at his court, but the saint desired solitude more than anything else, and although they gave him a cell and an oratory all to himself, Peter found an excuse to return to Alcantara.

Throughout Europe there was much false teaching and heresy which was taking people away from the true Church. He determined to oppose all these false doctrines, and he decided that what he must do was to found a congregation of friars which would have stricter rules than any yet known.

To get permission from the Holy Father he set out for Rome. The journey took Peter a long time; he walked every mile of the way, barefooted, his shabby old habit giving him not the slightest protection against sun and rain. Yet somehow, we can't imagine Peter complaining. God had given him the most precious of all his gifts, the gift of prayer, and Peter was so filled with the divine grace that nothing could disturb his thoughts once centred on God.

Peter obtained papal permission for his plan, though it met with strong disapproval in every other quarter, and when he returned, a friend helped him to build the first convent according to his own specifications. The cells were so small that the three boards placed in each to serve as a bed took up half the space. The friars went barefoot and lived in extreme poverty. Long hours of prayer, and severe fasting regulations, made the life almost unbearably hard. And yet men came willingly to put themselves under the direction of the saint.

In 1560, Peter went to Avila, and there met for the first time St. Teresa, who was still at the Incarnation convent. And it is from Teresa's own autobiography that we learn something of Peter's life.

Photo Mansell

Statue of St. Peter of Alcantara in St. Peter's

St. Teresa of Avila

The mules pulled and strained as their drivers urged them forward—up the steep mountain track. Dislodged boulders rolled away to crash hundreds of feet below in the ravine.

Inside the roughly fashioned wooden carts which they pulled behind them sat Mother Teresa and some of her nuns. They were on their way to found another convent, and it seemed to Ana and the others too, that in a moment they would fall to death. Panic was written on the faces of the muleteers; this track over the Spanish mountains was a death-trap. The only serene person among the party was Mother Teresa herself, who hushed her nuns into silence, telling them to pray; to ask the good St. Joseph to guide them.

And as they prayed, all at once a voice came to them, a voice which sounded from a great distance, from the very pit of the ravine itself.

"Stop! Stop!" cried the voice. "There is danger if you continue. That way leads to the precipice!"

The muleteers tugged on the ropes, the carts creaked to a protesting standstill. Fear was in the eyes of the drivers as they consulted together. How could they go back; the track was too narrow for turning. And yet how could they proceed? They cupped their hands and shouted down the ravine to the unseen friend. "What can we do?"

And the voice answered: "There is nothing to fear if you go backwards—quietly backwards. Then you will find the proper road."

One of the men ran back a little way, and found that what "the voice" had said was true. There was another way, and they had missed it. And so, with infinite care, the muleteers backed along the track, and took the right road.

Full of gratitude, they made a search for their unseen saviour, but although they peered down the sloping sides of the ravine, there was no sign of him.

Only Teresa knew they would never find him. She knew the secret of "the voice." St. Joseph had come to their rescue, and he was with them so that it seemed their mules had wings, all the rest of the long weary road to Segovia on the Spanish border, the place of the new Carmelite Convent.

Teresa, one of the greatest women in the whole history of the world, was born at Avila in Castile on March 28, 1515. She grew into a beautiful girl, gay, witty,

6—III

and so charming that visitors to her lovely home found it difficult to leave. Among the aristocratic Spanish girls, it was quite a custom to decide to enter a convent, and the convents of that time were sometimes far more like fashionable finishing schools than places of retreat and penance. The nuns wore jewelry and saw all their friends almost daily in the parlour.

Teresa's father, Don Alonzo Sanchezy Cepeda, sent his high-spirited, pleasure-loving young daughter to the Convent of the Augustine nuns in Avila, hoping that she world sober down. Five years later, aged twenty, Teresa had finally made up her mind. She would become a nun, and she offered herself to the Convent of the Incarnation of the Carmelite nuns. Her father, good holy man that he was, grieved over this new turn of events, for he had no wish to lose his daughter to an Order, and indeed refused his consent, so that Teresa was forced to go secretly to the convent.

Not very long afterwards she became so dangerously ill that she was taken home—to die, and it was during this stage in her long, adventurous life in God's service, that the saint began to practise mental prayer. She suffered intensely for nearly three years, but all the time her love for God was growing. One day, though it was to come twenty years later, Teresa was to shout her love of God from the roof-tops. That was the day, when after many wonderful graces in mystical prayer, she was to say: "The desire of serving God which comes to me is so intense that I should like to shout out and tell everybody how important it is not to be satisfied with giving only a little."

Teresa received a direct command from God to start a reform in the Carmelite Order. It would be strict to the point of austerity. It would make Lady Poverty its mistress as St.

Cignaroli   Photo Mansell
The ecstasy of St. Teresa of Avila

Francis had made her his mistress. There would be no parlours, no visitors. The nuns' lives would be devoted to prayer, and the convent dedicated to St. Joseph.

After God had spoken to her, Teresa was transported with joy—and fear. All over Spain, new Orders were springing up in reply to laxity of the Old Orders, but she was middle-aged, single-handed, and attached to her own convent.

It was a challenge, and the fighting spirit in this grand saint rose to meet it. His Majesty was always with her, and she also had the friendship of St. Peter of Alcantara, a saint of prayer, who had strengthened her during the times she had suffered persecution because of her visions. She had humour, and intelligence and a gay sparkling wit. They were all valuable weapons in the fray. And what a fray it was!

As Prioress of her own convent, all her movements were watched with the keenest interest by the gossip-loving townsfolk of Avila. She had no money; she knew no house that would be suitable; she would lose the love of her community.

But still she made her plans, and at last she got a house with the help of her sister's husband. It was only a small house, but Teresa set workmen to adapt it, and though it seemed the devil himself interfered causing walls to crash, all was ready at last, and St. Joseph's of Avila became the mother house of the newly reformed Carmelite Order.

Teresa became Prioress, her community consisted of just four nuns. They wore coarse habits, and sandals instead of shoes (which explains why they were called "discalced"), and they observed the strictest rules as regards silence and abstinence.

The saint spent five of the happiest years of her life at St. Joseph's. Then in 1567 she left to found a second convent at Medina del Campo. There she met two Carmelite friars, Antony-of-Jesus and John-of-the-Cross, and to them she gave the task of becoming the first of the Discalced Friars. John-of-the-Cross was already fired with the love of God. Their souls met and fused, and he became Teresa's confessor and partner in all her future foundations.

Not one book but many would be needed if all this great saint did for Spain and for the whole world were to be faithfully recorded. Her autobiography, her writings on prayer, and her discourses to her beloved nuns have guided souls over the centuries. Her courage in the face of intrigue, persecution, even violence, never failed her. There were crushing disappointments, cruel setbacks, treachery, physical hardship, but she accepted them all. From the age of forty, her life was one of intense activity, and yet His Majesty grasped her so firmly by the hand, that in the midst of it all, she was never without thought of him.

She died in the arms of her beloved Ana, the little peasant lay-sister, who became her secretary and closest friend. The day was October 4, 1582.

St. Catherine dei Ricci

At fourteen most of us don't yet know what we are going to be. Catherine did. And at fourteen her wish came true. She received the veil in a convent near Florence. But the year was 1535, and then it was not uncommon for girls to enter convents.

In her Dominican convent, Catherine united herself quite perfectly with God's Will, and the wisdom which comes to those who pray perfectly was hers even at an early age.

So great became her reputation for sanctity that cardinals and princes came

Sodoma   *Photo Chauffourier*

St. Catherine receiving the ring

to the convent to ask her advice, and the Pope himself, Pope Gregory XV, met and talked with her.

Catherine is one of the few saints who received the grace of the stigmata, but the best-known and loved story about this wonderful mystic is the story of the ring. It happened on Easter Day, 1542, and the ring which she received was given to her by Our Lord himself with these wonderful words: "My daughter, receive this ring as pledge and proof that thou dost now, and ever shalt, belong to me." Then we are told, Jesus drew from his finger, a shining ring, and placed it on the forefinger of Catherine's hand.

Though often ill and nearly always in pain, Catherine went about her task in the convent quietly and humbly, and was especially pleased when she was given charge of the sick. She lived until she was sixty-eight years old, dying in the year 1590.

St. Paschal Baylon

They called him "The Holy Shepherd," this simple peasant of the open spaces, and though he is perhaps not very familiar to us, he has his place among the great saints of prayer of the sixteenth century.

For some years he tended the flock of his master near the little countr town of Torre-Hermosa in Aragon where he was born. But rarely can sheep have been cared for by such a holy shepherd, for Paschal used to pray and meditate while they grazed.

Determined at last to become a lay-brother, he journeyed into the kingdom of Valencia, to Montfort, where in a desert region outside the town stood a lonely convent of reformed Franciscans, and where, after study and further preparation, he was finally accepted by the fathers as a lay-brother.

But Paschal's journeys were not yet over, for he was sent on a mission to Paris. France at that time was hostile to Catholics for the Huguenots had gained control of the cities. To travel bare-foot and in a friar's habit was courting death. Paschal was not killed, but many a time he was chased and beaten, and once so cruelly that he remained lame for the rest of his life as a result of the blows.

Once again in his convent, he thought so little of his hardship that he did not even mention it. A greater part of this kindly saint's life was spent in adoration at the foot of the altar, and God after his death in 1592, permitted many miracles to take place at his tomb.

St. Joseph of Cupertino

It has been said and repeated over and over again that no matter what a man's occupation may be he has it within him to be a saint.

Joseph's first job in life was as an apprentice shoemaker and at this he was far from being successful. His childhood had been unhappy. His mother, widowed and very poor, had little patience with her dreamy, forgetful son. And in the village he was mocked because of his forgetful ways, and his indifferent health. Who would have thought in these early days that Joseph of Cupertino had the makings of a saint, and yet it was true that absent-minded and stupid as he appeared to be, he was neither the one nor the other when it came to the matter of going to church.

As a shoemaker he was a dismal failure, but his heart was not set on cobbling shoes. He wanted to become a lay-brother. At seventeen he offered himself to the Franciscans and was rejected. Some months later, he tried again, this time with the Capuchins at Martino, near Taranto. He was accepted, but the good friars soon had reason to regret it, for Joseph made almost as bad a lay-brother as he had a shoemaker.

Never were so many plates broken, never did the kettle boil dry so often, and as for the fires, they were rarely lit. It wasn't that Joseph didn't try—he did, but he was so clumsy, so forgetful that finally the friars despaired of teaching him anything, and he was sent home in disgrace.

Cupertino is a village lying six miles from the coast of the gulf of Taranto, and it was there he was born on June 17, 1603. When he returned to it, there seemed little he could do, and had not an uncle, a Conventual Franciscan, persuaded his Order to give him a trial, Joseph might have remained there in obscurity as the village idiot.

But finding himself once more in the friar's habit, Joseph at last mended his ways. It was an extraordinary change, and so perfect was his spirit of mortification and his desire to serve that the friars soon resolved to admit him to the religious of the choir.

From the moment of his ordination in 1628 St. Joseph united himself perfectly with God's will. Then followed miracles and ecstasies which were quite exceptional in number.

Stranger still was the wonderful power which he had over animals—sheep and sparrows obeyed his word—and Joseph, it is recorded, actually preached to them.

One of the outstanding indications that God has particularly singled out a soul is the gift of Levitation.

St. Joseph of Cupertino was favoured in this way, and it was not unusual to see him leave the ground; sometimes he would be lifted off his feet and "soar" away like an eagle above the heads of the people. Little wonder, then, that pilgrims in their thousands began to flock to his convent, and the humble friar became, to his distress, an object of curiosity, and sometimes of persecution. But never did he relax his efforts to become perfect in his spirit of prayer, and when he died at the age of sixty his reputation for sanctity had spread throughout the whole of Italy.

These are but a few of the great saints of prayer. There were many others who lived during the time of the Reformation, but they did other great things besides leading lives of prayer, and they have their place in another section of this volume.

THE ENGLISH MARTYRS

This name, the English Martyrs, is given to those men and women who were put to death for the Catholic religion, in England, between the year 1535 and the year 1683.

There had been other martyrs who had died for our Faith, before this time. Look in your Missals for St. Alban (June 22) for St. Oswald (August 9) and add to them an Englishman who was killed by the Frisian people, St. Boniface (June 5) apostle of Central Europe. The difference between these three and the English Martyrs is that while the early martyrs were trying to live as Christians in a pagan world, the English martyrs were holding to their Faith against a new state religion.

When the new religion was made law, many Catholics felt that they could not obey that law, because they were bound to keep to their own true religion. Then it grew very hard for them, indeed. They were fined, imprisoned, left to die in prison, or killed outright because they would not practise the new religion that had been made law, nor would they give up their own beliefs, or betray their priests.

You will find in the stories of the English Martyrs the most high and exciting adventures, and astonishing happenings, as well as a noble courage and sterling character, that will never fail to show you how true to Our Lord the English people could be, in the teeth of cruel persecution.

Of all those who suffered loss of life for the Faith, the Church has named special lists of martyrs to be honoured in different ways. The chief of these are:

1. Saint John Fisher and Saint Thomas More, who died in 1535, and were solemnly declared saints by Pope Pius XI on May 19, 1935.

2. Sixty-one Blessed Martyrs of the years 1535 to 1583, given this title by Pope Leo XIII on December 29, 1886 and May 13, 1895.

3. One hundred and thirty-six Blessed Martyrs proclaimed so by Pope Pius XI on December 15, 1929. Because these martyrs died in the years 1537 to 1680, we add to them the Scottish martyr Blessed John Ogilvie, who was given his title on December 22, 1929, and one Irish Martyr, Blessed Oliver Plunket, who had been given his rank by Pope Benedict XV, on May 23, 1920. The cause of canonisation of forty of these one hundred and thirty-six martyrs is being considered in Rome. They are now known as "The Forty Martyrs of England and Wales."

4. The hundred and sixteen Venerable Martyrs, listed by Pope Leo XIII in 1886, whose lives and deaths are still being examined by the Church.

The accounts of the martyrs have to be examined in this way, very closely, because of the difficulties of times of persecution. Then, it is necessary to keep many things secret and to hide, so that sometimes even those who loved and honoured the martyrs in life could not be sure where or how they died. Nor was it always known where they were buried. There might be doubt about relics said to belong to them. Again, it is important that the Church should not honour as martyrs men who were too deeply busy with affairs of the state, or too eager for their own profit. That is why many of those known to have lived and died good Catholics, and staunchly true to their religion, have not been placed in the number of those to be publicly honoured. Such were some of the men put to death after the Rising called the Pilgrimage of Grace, and again after the Rising in the North, in 1569, and yet again after the Gunpowder Plot of 1605.

In the stories of the martyrs, you may read of those claimed by the different counties and towns of England; by Lancashire, Yorkshire, the counties of Durham and Northumberland, the broad lands of Hampshire and the Sussex Downs, the great cities of London and of York. You may read too of the kind of men and women these martyrs were, not at all dull or foolish people, but full of life and interest and a spirit no torment could break.

Foremost among the heroes that you are sure to read about and love when you study the English Martyrs, is the great St. Thomas More. He was so great a lawyer that he became Lord Chancellor of England, and one of the most important men in the court of King Henry VIII. He was rich and happy, in a lovely home in Chelsea, with his family all around him; but he lost his life because although he was "the King's good servant" he was "God's first." He was beheaded after some months of imprisonment because he would not sign a paper which said that the king had more right over English Catholics than the Pope had. The saint who had laughed and jested all his life, was to show the same happy spirit at his death. "Let me put my beard aside," he said jokingly, "for it at least hath never committed treason." His very executioners were almost in tears at the bright courage of the man about to die for his religion.

Early in the list you will meet one of the four recognised women martyrs, the Blessed Margaret Pole. She was the last of the line of the Plantagenet family, and was beheaded at the age of 72 because she was the mother of the exiled Cardinal Pole, and would not deny her son or her religion. Early in the lists also, you will find that grave and dignified Sir Adrian Fortescue, Knight of Malta, and kinsman of the Stonor family, who still live in Oxfordshire and still keep the Catholic Faith.

Later martyrs were put to death for other reasons, most of them on account

Photo Mansell

Saint Thomas More and his daughter in prison

of the Mass and the priesthood. Many names then that you meet are those of priests or of layfolk who sheltered and helped the priests, so that the Sacraments might be given to Catholics, and the Faith so kept alive. The other three women martyrs were all of this later time. Mistress Ann Lyne, put to death for "harbouring" priests, said bravely that she had "indeed done this thing," and only wished she had more lives to lose if it meant that she could do more for the cause of God. As this work had cost her imprisonment and death, you may judge how strong was her faith.

Mistress Margaret Ward helped a hunted priest to escape, and for doing this, was put to death. With her died a young Irishman, John Roche, who was a Thames water-man. He had the clever idea of changing clothes with the priest, and so was caught and died in his stead, while the real priest escaped.

Mistress Margaret Clitherow is the last of the four brave women on our list. She was the wife of a well-known citizen of York, and used to have Mass said in her house as often as she dared. She was for long suspected of this, but nothing could be proved against her. Then one day a fresh search was made, and a frightened boy, a foreigner, told the searchers all about the priests and their visits. The vestment-press used for the Masses came to light, and Margaret was arrested, in her husband's absence. She refused to plead at her trial. She did not wish her husband and children to suffer the ordeal of having to give evidence against her. For refusing to plead she suffered the worst penalty

John Roche, the Thames waterman, is helped by Margaret Ward to change clothes with the priest

possible. She was pressed to death between oaken doors weighted with stones, sharp stones put to her back. This most cruel death, of a much-loved and valued wife, shocked the people of York very much, but they could not change the law. It is good to know that Margaret's three children lived to keep their mother's faith alive, and were always faithful to it. She had been a lovely, laughing mother, and was still young when she died.

We must of course remember that the times of which these things are written were not like ours. They were rough and coarse times, when sport was often cruel and jokes could often hurt. Still, men loved life, success and happiness, just as they do today, and many of them found it hard to give up all that was so dear. Some of the martyrs showed this, and were not ashamed to say it. Swithin Wells, a gentleman of means, was put to death for allowing Father Edmund Genings (another martyr) to say Mass in his house. On the way to execution, Master Wells said firmly: "Farewell, hunting and hawking and all good life. Much as I have loved you, I go from you to better things."

Again, Thomas Percy, Seventh Earl of Northumberland, was more than once offered his life if he would follow the new religion. Each time he refused, and once when someone asked if he did not value his own life, he answered: "On the contrary, I think life is good, and I would willingly save mine if I could save my soul as well. But that I cannot. As for this new religion, I do not recognise it. I die in the belief of the Holy Catholic Church." He owned all the land in most parts of the North of England, from the Humber to the Tweed, yet he was put to death in a York street, in public, on a market day, and died bravely like the great gentleman he was.

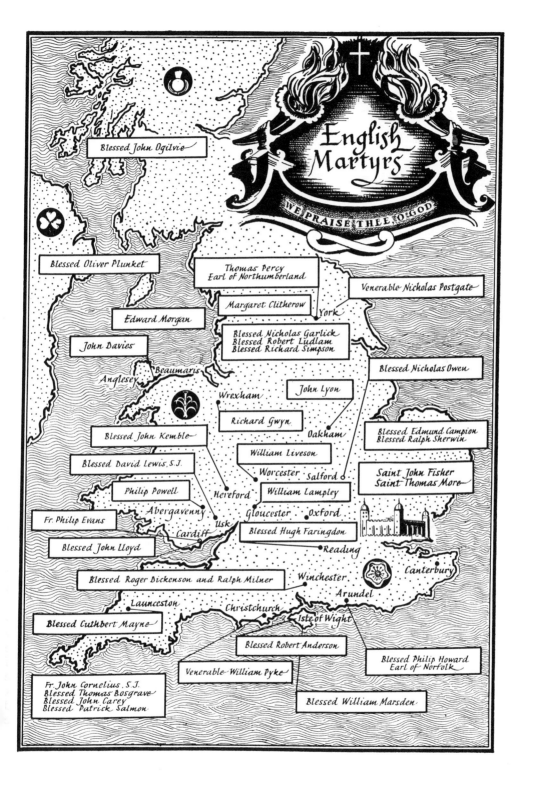

English Martyrs

WE PRAISE THEE O GOD

Blessed John Ogilvie

Blessed Oliver Plunket

Thomas Percy
Earl of Northumberland

Venerable Nicholas Postgate

Margaret Clitherow

York

Edward Morgan

Blessed Nicholas Garlick
Blessed Robert Ludlam
Blessed Richard Simpson

John Davies

Beaumaris

Anglesey

Blessed Nicholas Owen

Wrexham

John Lyon

Richard Gwyn

Oakham

Blessed John Kemble

Blessed Edmund Campion
Blessed Ralph Sherwin

William Liveson

Blessed David Lewis, S.J.

Worcester

Salford

Saint John Fisher
Saint Thomas More

Philip Powell

Hereford

William Lampley

Abergavenny

Gloucester

Oxford

Fr. Philip Evans

Usk

Cardiff

Blessed Hugh Faringdon

Blessed John Lloyd

Reading

Canterbury

Blessed Roger Dickenson and Ralph Milner

Winchester

Arundel

Launceston

Christchurch

Isle of Wight

Blessed Cuthbert Mayne

Blessed Robert Anderson

Blessed Philip Howard
Earl of Norfolk

Venerable William Pyke

Fr. John Cornelius, S.J.
Blessed Thomas Bosgrave
Blessed John Carey
Blessed Patrick Salmon

Blessed William Marsden

Courtesy Catholic Times

Carthusians after sentence leaving the Tower of London, to be dragged on a hurdle to Tyburn and there hanged

There were those among the martyrs who were given no such chances, to whom such offers were not made. Some of them were so long in prison that they could have answered as Father Philip Evans did his jailor. When the news was brought that he was soon to die, the priest said with a smile: "Why, what haste is there? We have waited so long that you may as well let me finish my game of bowls." You will agree that this is even more heroic than the similar reply made by Drake when he received the news of the Armada.

As people came to see that the Faith could be kept only by secret means, there came the time of changing names, of having different disguises, of going to Masses said in the night, or just before the dawn of day. At the same time there came the dreadful fear of being sold to the Government, who now offered large sums of money to people who would tell them of Catholics, and especially of priests. There are many sad and terrible stories of these times. But there is one joyful tale about a priest who is said to be the only person who ever made good his escape from the Tower of London. He was Father John Gerard, S.J. (born in Lancashire). His book will tell you of many devices for avoiding arrest, including the exciting one of using orange-juice for letters, to make writing invisible until held to the fire! Again, the well-known and well-loved Edmund Campion (called Blessed in the lists of the Church) had so many disguises that he could walk through the streets of London undetected, and at one time was said to lodge in the house of the chief man appointed to hunt out Catholics! But he was taken at last, and put into the cruel cell called Little Ease, which you may still see in the Tower of London. He argued with his judges at their request, but although he got the better of the argument, he was tortured by the rack and put to death with the greatest suffering. He was hanged, drawn and quartered, at Tyburn gallows. Yet at one time Campion had been a great favourite of the Queen (Elizabeth) and of the Earl of Leicester, and met his death for no reason but that of being a priest.

With Campion died Ralph Sherwin (also Blessed now) the first priest of the English College in Rome who was put to death in England. When the judge pronounced the sentence of death on him, Sherwin called out TE DEUM LAUDA-MUS (which means WE PRAISE THEE, O GOD) to show how proud he was to die for his Faith. When he was being led out to die, he looked up at the sun and laughed. "I shall shortly be above yonder fellow!" he said. Many of the martyrs were happy and proud at the last, but whenever anyone tried to make them say that they were guilty of anything punishable by death except religion, then they were firm and stern as they denied this.

One story about this kind of denial is that of Venerable Nicholas Postgate, a learned and holy old priest who had worked for fifty years on the moors of North Yorkshire before he was arrested and tried. An officer tried to make him say that he was being hanged for a plot hatched in London (afterwards called the Titus Oates Plot). The martyr could not agree. "No, no, Master Sheriff,"

Edmund Campion on the way to Tyburn

he said, "be you pleased to state that I die for my holy religion. Of the plot I have no knowledge nor could have, but I die for the holy religion in which I believe." He was hanged at York Castle, in August, as late as 1679, but the Sheriff did not and could not contradict him.

Although they could not obey the laws about the new religion, all the martyrs were greatly devoted to the Queen and the country of England. Blessed John Felton publicly prayed for the Queen as he was being put to death, and sent her a valuable ring to show that he was still her loyal and true subject. Other martyrs sent her messages, and used their last moments to beg God's blessing on her, on her reign and on their beloved country.

For those of you who like finding places on maps, as most of us do, it is a good plan to learn more about the martyrs by following up their stories as you go on imaginary journeys. If you start at Canterbury, in Kent, where St. Augustine landed when he came to bring Christianity to England in the year A.D. 596, it will remind you that in 1588 four priests were put to death there for holding to the same religion that St. Augustine came to teach. Then if you go along the Sussex coast and eleven miles inland, you will come to the great castle of Arundel, the home of the present Duke of Norfolk. That will remind you that another Earl of Arundel, Blessed Philip Howard, was for nearly twelve years kept a prisoner in the Tower of London and died there, because he would not give up that same religion which the Duke of Norfolk has now. You can still see on the wall of the Bell Tower a prayer which that young and brilliant courtier wrote when he was there.

As you look at the Isle of Wight, you can think of two priests born in far-off Lancashire, who were put to death on the Island in 1586, merely for being priests. These were Robert Anderton from Chorley, and William Marsden (both Blessed now) whose surnames are well-known still in Chipping and Goosnargh and other parts of their native county.

On the mainland, near Christchurch in Hampshire, you can think of the heroic joiner who worked on the Moors district, and was put to a cruel death five days before Christmas in 1591, only for saying that he would live and die a Catholic. His name was William Pyke, and he is called Venerable in the lists of the Church.

Near Winchester, in the same county, were hanged and butchered together the priest Roger Dickenson and the layman Ralph Milner, who had fed and helped the priest in his hiding and captivity (both Blessed now). Notice how these names, both Christian and surname, are thoroughly English, and might be those of any of your friends today.

Going further west, in Cornwall you meet the traces of the great martyr Cuthbert Mayne, also called Blessed, of the town of Launceston, where you may see his relics and his tomb. (Holidays are good times for following up the traces of the martyrs.) In Cornwall too are memories of the good Fr. John Cornelius, S.J., and those who were put to death with him, for being kind to him. These were the gentlemen, Blessed Thomas Bosgrave, who tried to reverence the priest before his death, and the two Irish serving-men, Blessed John Carey and Patrick Salmon, put to death for helping him.

Crossing over into Wales, you meet the sadder story of a land starved of its religion for lack of priests, but here was once no lack of martyrs. In the town of Usk, there is the church and special altar of Blessed David Lewis, S.J. In

Roger Dickenson and Ralph Milner at the gallows

the fine city of Cardiff, you learn of the Fr. Philip Evans, whose story we have mentioned. He was a Jesuit, but his companion, Blessed John Lloyd, was a secular priest. The gentle martyr Philip Powell belonged to Abergavenny, and Edward Morgan to Flintshire, while the Welsh layman (for the others so far have been priests) Richard Gwyn of Wrexham, was a schoolmaster. Such men were put to death because they tried to teach their pupils to hold fast to the Catholic Faith which was theirs.

Going back into England from Wales, you come to the borders called the Welsh Marches, and there find the town of Hereford. In it, you may still hear the people speak of "Kemble's pipe" when they mean weighing a thing well before doing it. This saying comes from the martyr Blessed John Kemble who was coaxed by a kind-hearted jailer to deny his Faith and so put off his death. "There lies the town," said the man, "here you will suffer if you do not heed my words." "Well, well," said the

martyr, "let us sit down in sight of it and smoke a pipe over the matter." Yes, that was in England after the days of Sir Walter Raleigh and the introduction of the tobacco plant and the habit of smoking. It will show you what a hero the martyr was.

Gloucester can boast of more than one martyr, and among them is the glove-maker William Lampley, who dared to tell his friends that his Faith "was worth a little salt to one's supper," which is how he described his death. Worcester too has its share of glory, in the Franciscan martyr William Leveson, and off the coast, the Isle of Anglesey even has its faithful martyr, John Davies of Beaumaris town.

Many other places in England can speak of the martyrs, too, as the city of Oxford and the town of Reading, with its once great Abbey and its Abbot (Blessed Hugh Faringdon) put to death outside the gates. In the high roads of Derbyshire, you can come across the names of families and traces of their homes, who can claim martyrs too. Such are the three Padley priests who were put to death on Derby Bridge. There were Blessed Nicholas Garlick, Robert Ludlam and Richard Simpson, and you can find their names in what remains of Padley Chapel, a few miles beyond Sheffield, in Yorkshire. Even the tiniest county of England, little Rutland with its town of Oakham, can boast from that town the martyr John Lyon, well named! . . . who was put to death for being loyal to the Pope.

In the lists of the English Martyrs, these are only a few of all the stories you can read about the martyrs, and a few of all the places that can claim them. Some indeed belong to no one place, but were at the service of any community, like the Jesuit lay-brother Nicholas Owen, who died under torture, but without betraying a single name or place, although he had travelled up and down among the Catholics of England for years. It was his work to make hiding-holes for priests, and so well did he do this, working secretly by night, that even now these places can be found only by those who know where they are. (Do you know of any of them, in your neighbourhood?) Perhaps you will see the one in the Manor House at Stoke Poges, or at Prior Hall, near Salford, at Evesham. Then you will remember Blessed Nicholas, the clever carpenter.

In this article, you have been told a little about the English Martyrs, in the hope that you will read and learn more about them for yourselves; that you will follow up the clues in names and places, in your families, your schools, your neighbourhood and perhaps a church called after one of the martyrs. You will find much more than a lesson or a task, and you will be able to see what these great and good people did to keep our Faith alive in England, so that we can have it today.

Sydney Nolan

The Flight into Egypt

A modern Australian artist's interpretation of the flight into Egypt against the background of the Australian desert

Facing p. 96

Madonna and Child

European artists naturally portray Christ as a white man, but here you see an Asiatic painter showing the child Jesus and the Virgin Mary as Eastern people and wearing Eastern clothes

Smith and Walton Ltd.

Interior of the Church of St. Osmund, Barnes, Surrey

Joseph Nuttgens   *St. Ethelreda's, Ely Place, London*

East Window of the church of St. Ethelreda's, Ely Place, London

THE OLD MONASTERIES OF ENGLAND

The Monastery Scene

Let us take a look at the countryside of this England of ours about the year 1500. Where shall we go? North to the Abbey of Rievaulx; west to the Abbey of Tewkesbury; west again to the Abbey at Cirencester; or to Sherborne Abbey in Dorset in the south-west. I don't suppose it would matter one little bit which way we went, the scene would be very much the same. Outside the monastery buildings we should see the black or white robes and tonsured heads of the monks as they busied themselves with their daily tasks, for although the bell of the monastery would ring seven times a day for service in the monastery church yet in between times the monks were busy men. There were wide cornfields to be ploughed, tilled and reaped; the herb gardens to be cared for; the fish ponds to be kept filled for Friday meals and the vines to

be tended so that the cellars should not lack wine. That may sound strange, but during the Middle Ages there were plenty of vineyards and much wine was made in the southern part of England.

Suddenly a cloud of dust rises along the road to the Abbey and we see rich robes and gay colours as the horses canter by. Some rich travellers who have come to seek the hospitality of the abbey, we say to ourselves, and then, as the dust clears we see more travellers, poor this time and on foot, but hurrying along, just as certain as the others that they too will find food and rest inside the monastery walls. As we draw close to the gates we hear the voices of the monks rising above the hum and noise, as they sing for lauds, or matins, or compline. If we should happen to arrive around mid-day we shall find a crowd of poor people and beggars all

Monastery of Rievaulx

Photo Mansell

eagerly awaiting the free meal which is issued daily to those in need.

We pass through the gateway and inside we wander round, fascinated by the varied scene. In the quiet of the cloister-garth, the square of grass surrounded by the cloisters, we see a group of young boys, obviously the sons of nobles, doing their lessons under the watchful eye of an elderly Brother, while others of his Brethren pace slowly up and down in the shade of the cloisters themselves. In the library there is stillness and shade, save for two or three monks who are reading quietly and for the bright colours in the pots of paint which another monk is using to colour the bindings of some of these new-fangled printed books which are being turned out in their hundreds from the printing presses of William Caxton or Robert Pynson or Wynken de Worde. What a pity the beautiful written work and illustrations of the old monks is a thing of the past. We move quietly out of the library and into the kitchens. Here, there is plenty of activity. Brethren and servants hurry here and there, bringing in game, partridges, pheasants, geese, ducks, hens, venison and beef to be cooked for the Brethren, their visitors, and the servants, a task which several red-faced cooks are tackling under the direction of a stout Brother, while the Sub-prior gives orders for the guest rooms to be prepared for the important guests.

Coming Clouds

This, then, could be a picture of life at any one of the great abbeys or monasteries with which this country was dotted. The community gave alms to the poor, hospitality to the traveller, and said prayers for the living and the dead; administered wide lands and much property and made a living for numbers of people whom it employed as servants. We shall hear more of the services it rendered to both poor and rich later in this article.

Dark Clouds

What we have described has made a pleasant enough picture, but the dark clouds of trouble were soon to cast their shadows over the scene. The wide estates of the abbeys, left to them in gratitude and in payment for perpetual prayers by past generations: the riches of the shrines where the devout had offered their gifts were being coveted by the nobles, who saw in them a way of repairing their fortunes, depleted through civil war and royal taxes. Even the king himself saw in the wealth of the monasteries a means of paying for his extravagances and of increasing the royal power. His opportunity came in 1531, when his petition to His Holiness the Pope for a divorce from his wife, Queen Catherine, was categorically rejected. This was the excuse for which he had been waiting and he forced Convocation to split with the Church of Rome and henceforward to recognise him as "Supreme Head of the Church". Having persuaded Parliament into the split with Rome, Henry had next to persuade the people that the monasteries, convents and abbeys were full of useless, lazy, good-for-nothing monks and nuns lead-

ing wicked, immoral lives, and that the money and estates which belonged to the different communities would be better used if it were spent on schools, colleges and universities, all of which was, as we well know, merely an excuse for seizing most of it for himself.

The Visitation

To do this, the country was divided into regions, and men sent by Thomas Cromwell, the king's secretary, visited each abbey in turn, making a list of all the property it owned, even down to the plate on the altars, and reporting on the behaviour of the monks or nuns. Cromwell had boasted that he would make his master the richest monarch in Christendom, and he saw to it that, except where he had been bribed largely enough, the reports were as he wanted them. And so the way was paved for the suppression of the communities. The small ones were the first to go. On April 14, 1536, the king sent commissioners to make a survey of two hundred and twenty of the smaller monasteries

Giving alms at a monastery

Aylesford Priory from the air

and convents which were to be dissolved. This was to make sure that all the spoils were still there, that no properties had been sold or leased, that no monies or valuables had been given away. When this was done, then the monks and nuns were either transferred to larger communities or driven out to face the world. Then the commissioners put everything up for sale: the gold and silver vessels from the altar, the furniture; the vestments; the service books; the cattle; the ploughs; the kitchen utensils. The bells were melted down; so was the lead from the roofs and the metal sent off to London. The buildings were pulled down or sold for dwelling houses and farm-buildings, while the lands around were taken over by the rich burgess or noble to whom they had been granted by Henry, often as a payment for his debts.

Henry, however, had not entirely realised the love and respect which the monasteries had commanded among the people. In the north, on the lonely uplands, the people missed the hospitality of the monks, and they were filled with bitter hate at the wanton destruction of the shrines they loved and at which they worshipped so devoutly. In the autumn rebellion broke out and Henry was forced to put it down with great severity. In nine great abbeys the Abbots were executed and all their property forfeited. Five other abbeys were confiscated on the excuse that they had resisted the king's armies. So much land, jewels, lead, copper, deeds and leases fell into the hands of Henry from the suppression and the confiscations that it took three or four generations before it was all sold.

The End of the Monasteries

By the end of 1537, only about one hundred and fifty large monasteries remained out of some five hundred and fifty and these too found it impossible to continue the struggle. Henry had rea-

rightly the temper of the common people, and though he was still determined to suppress all the monasteries, he announced that he would accept only voluntary surrenders. But the executions of 1539 had been a stern reminder that no mercy could be expected from a greedy king. One by one the Abbots and brethren surrendered their possessions and by the end of 1539 only six communities remained. Westminster Abbey gave itself up on January 16, 1540, and last of all, Waltham Abbey, in March 1540.

So the monasteries in this country came to an end, and nothing remained but crumbling walls. What, then, shall we ask ourselves, had been lost with the monasteries that men had thought it worth while to fight for and to give their lives for? In the main, three things: prayers, hospitality and charity.

The Duties of the Monasteries

The most important duty of the monks had been to "pray for the dead and for the living." In the abbey church there were continual prayers of intercession for the dead, for the founders of the house and for all those benefactors who had made bequests to that end. Many of the lands held by the abbeys had been left to them by wealthy patrons on condition that perpetual masses and prayers should be offered for their souls and for the souls of those in Purgatory. When the dissolution of the monasteries became inevitable many of the great families of the land refused to accept estates at the expense of the spiritual welfare of their forefathers. Nor were the living neglected, prayers were said for all Christian souls; seven times a day the prayers went up to Heaven.

These were the prayers of the monks themselves, but the people too had their prayers to offer. You may have seen recently a map which was published during the "Marian" year and which showed all the shrines of Our Lady

Photo Markiewicz

Aylesford Cloisters today

Boys at lessons in a monastery many years ago

which existed during the Middle Ages. Add to these the shrines such as that of St. Thomas of Canterbury and the Holy Blood of Hayles and countless others to which pilgrimages could be made for spiritual and physical solace and we can realise how people felt their loss.

Hospitality was the second duty laid down by the founders of the monasteries. In the days when roads were only rough tracks journeys between towns often took days or even weeks. Hospitality then meant a great deal to the traveller, whether he be rich or poor. The inns of the time were usually little more than drinking-houses so the good food and comfortable beds to be found in the monasteries were much better than the rough comfort of the inn. The service was free for rich and poor alike, but the rich travellers usually left some gift of sufficient value to pay for their entertainment. The loss of this hospitality was felt much more severely in the north than in the south. Imagine what the thought of good food and a warm bed at Shap Abbey meant to travellers crossing lonely Shap Fell, or Rievaulx Abbey to the traveller high up on the Yorkshire moors. The rebellion of 1536 took place round the northern abbeys or Jervaulx, Salley and Whalley, away in the wild country of the Pennines between Lancashire and Yorkshire. Their loss was irrecoverable.

The regular giving of alms and the care of the sick and feeble was laid down as the third duty which was expected of the monastery. The monks must give to the poor according to the wishes of their benefactors; the fragments from their meals were the perquisite of the poor who flocked to the gate to receive them. Many bequests too were made for the distribution of clothing. Founders and benefactors usually laid down the conditions under which these doles were to be administered. In Exeter there was a Priory of St. Nicholas, some of whose buildings have recently been rescued from misuse and decay. At the Priory, every day, seven poor men were given a twopenny loaf, a bottle of ale, and a piece of meat, except on Fridays, when all the poor among the Priory tenants came, and received the loaf, the ale, a piece of fish and a penny. On St. Nicholas' day bread was distributed and on Good Friday every poor person received a penny, including the twelve poor men at Furness; the five aged men at Cockersand; these were the people who suffered most when the alms were no longer given.

Other Services Lost to the Country

We could call prayers, hospitality and the giving of alms the duties of the monasteries because they were a condition of the bequests by founders and benefactors, the usual clause in the will saying "where sick and feeble men may be maintained, hospitality, almsgiving and other charitable deeds might be done, and that in them prayers may be said for the souls of the said founders and their heirs."

Beyond this, though, there were many other ways in which the monasteries were missed by the people. In the Abbey of Exeter boys were being taught by one of the brethren. The sons of rich men were sent to the monks; there were poor boys who received their education as alms; there were the young monks, seminarists as we should call them today, all of whom were instructed in Latin, grammar, logic and philosophy. When the houses were suppressed not only did the education of so many young people cease, but there was a wholesale loss of books and manuscripts. This was because the great monastic libraries also were destroyed or broken up. Not only were books lost, but church and choir music and painting too suffered the same fate.

During the time when feudalism had barely died out, when the Wars of the Roses were still in people's memories, when baron fought baron, and the land

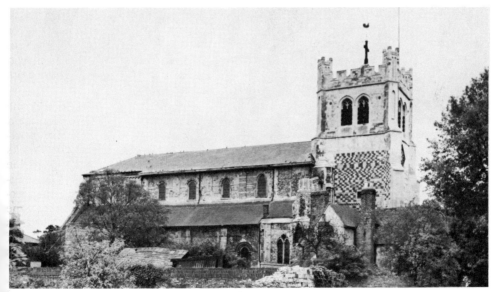

Waltham Abbey

Photo Mansell

was despoiled, the monasteries with, the power of the Church behind them, had been safe from interference. Men sent their valuables to the monasteries for safety, and the custom had arisen for the great abbeys to act as bankers for the gentry and nobility and even for the king himself. From now on that service could not be maintained. Many people had always depended on the monasteries for a living. When the dissolution came, the sons of gentlemen and of nobles who acted as land agents, as bailiffs, as lawyers, or who held large farms as tenants, all found themselves out of home and living, together with the servants of the household, the farm-workers, the carpenters and the masons. The glorious abbey churches, many of them as beautiful as any in Europe, were the victims of a destruction which appalled many of the men who had made no effort to support the monks against the king.

All this was material loss. But the greatest loss of all to the people was the old, familiar, devout life in the monasteries. A new, strange Church, under a Head who had no claim to priesthood, and whose hold could be maintained only with the threat of the gallows and the block, could never be a substitute for this.

SAINTS IN HOSPITALS

The most frightening thing about going to hospital is that you don't know what it will be like. Once you are there and tucked up comfortably in a small white bed it doesn't seem so bad after all.

How lucky to be a patient in a modern hospital where there are skilful doctors and trained nurses to look after you! Imagine what it was like in the early days. Jesus while he was on earth showed compassion and tenderness towards the sick, but it was a very long time before men came to see the suffering as their own responsibility.

We have to remember, too, that the early Christians were persecuted by the Romans, and that they dared not openly organise relief for their poor and suffering brethren. It was not, in fact, until Constantine became a Christian himself, that Christians attempted to carry out the second of Our Lord's Commandments " *Thou shalt love thy neighbour as thyself,*" by setting up hospitals.

The First Move

Then it fell upon the bishops to try and organise help for the sick and dying. They threw open the doors of their palaces and took in as many ailing people as their accommodation would permit. But this was not always successful; rooms, even corridors, became overcrowded, and many a poor woman died through lack of care. The bishops meant very well, but they needed assistance, and at last the Great Council of Nicea in 325 laid down that it was the duty of bishops to provide adequate accommodation for the sick—in other words, hospitals.

But who was there to run such hospitals? The bishops to begin with turned to the pious ladies of their dioceses; later they called in the religious orders, when these were formed, and so monks and nuns became the nurses of the sick.

Before we tell the stories of just a few of the great saints who devoted their lives to the service of the poor, we must banish from our minds the picture of a modern city with its well-run hospitals and skilled medical staff, its ambulances and its out-patient departments.

During these early centuries, only the rich were able to buy the services of people to care for them. A poor man suddenly afflicted by some terrible and perhaps loathsome disease was forced sometimes by his own relatives to wander about the countryside until he became too weak to move; then he died, often by the roadside.

Hordes of beggars in a big city like Rome lined the streets, sometimes exposing gaping, horrible wounds. Children died every day because there was nobody to care for them, and old people, too feeble to beg and too weak to fend for themselves, lingered on in terrible pain until death released them.

The First Hospital City

Men like St. Basil and St. Ephraem could think of no better way of pleasing God than to try and relieve the suffering all about them.

St. Basil, who like St. Ephraem was a saint of the fourth century, founded his "hospital city" at Caesarea in A.D. 350. To begin with he organised it to take care of the lepers, for until his "hospital city" came into being, the fate of lepers was terrible indeed. If a man found that he had contracted this dreaded disease he knew that soon he would be made an outcast. He must leave forever his home, his family and his friends. He was given a bell which he must ring should anyone be in danger of crossing his path. There was a special ceremony which the Church performed in order to comfort him in his banishment to his solitary hut in the woods.

The lepers who found their way to St. Basil's hospital were cared for in the best sense of the word. They were given work to do, so that their self-respect might not be destroyed. Their "hos-pital" was not exactly a hospital but more a settlement of homes, which the doctors and nurses visited every day.

Later this magnificent "hospital city" expanded, and the saint started a school for orphans and for children whose parents had died from plague or famine.

The First Wards

The fame of this first Christian hospital spread all over the world, and perhaps it was from hearing about it that twenty years later St. Ephraem was inspired to build his own hospital at Edessa in Western Mesopotamia. This, he ruled, should be for the exclusive use of the sick and dying. And the building, for the first time in history, was actually divided into sections, which could be called "wards." The beds were decently spaced out, and the nurses trained and compassionate.

But there was behind all this the inspiration of the saint himself, who had vision enough to see that his patients could never hope to survive the scourge of the plague unless they were given undivided attention.

During these early centuries, the hospitals were, for the most part, built on to the churches, and were usually supported by good men and women who saw nursing the sick as their vocation.

Then, and much later, the religious and monastic Orders gradually assumed responsibility for them.

Later still, in France and Spain, in Italy and in Jerusalem, groups of saintly men and women vowed their lives to the service of the sick, but in the small space of this article it is not possible to list all the men and women whose efforts to relieve pain and suffering raised their own lives to sanctity.

We have chosen four: St. Elizabeth of Hungary, St. John of God, St. Camillus de Lellis and St. Vincent de Paul.

St. Elizabeth tries to find shelter but is turned away

St. Elizabeth of Hungary

A young woman, beautiful in spite of her coarse dress and shabby cloak, is trying to find shelter in the town. She knocks at the doors, begging in gentle voice for a place where she might sleep.

Above the town, on a great rocky hill, stands the castle—the king's castle—black against the sky. From door to door she moves—and the answer is always the same. "No room here. We cannot help you," and the young woman notes their fearful glances towards the castle. She knows that they are afraid to help her; afraid of the wicked Henry who now sits on her dead husband's throne.

For the young woman is a Queen, and like a beautiful Princess in a fairytale she has been banished by the wicked younger brother of her husband.

At last she finds a cottage—poorer than the rest—and a cottager braver than the rest, who opens his door and bids her welcome to stay the night; and

so the night passes, and Elizabeth, for that is her name, does not sleep, but spends the hours in prayer.

The story of Elizabeth of Hungary is one of the most beautiful, and perhaps the saddest of all stories, because she was such a very little girl when she was sent away from her mother and father, Queen Gertrude and King Alexander II of Hungary. Most children grow up with their parents, but Elizabeth, because she was a king's daughter, was sent away at four years old to the royal court at Thuringia, where she must live until she was old enough to marry the King's son, Louis.

The Castle of Wartburg must have been a gloomy place for a child, and though at first her foster-parents were kind to her, they quickly grew to hate her because she was so different. She did not ask for beautiful dresses, and when they said that she must wear them, she obeyed only when she knew

St. Elizabeth handing grain to the poor during the great famine

that important people were visiting the Castle.

Nobody gave a thought to the poor. Elizabeth as a little girl used to beg the scraps from the servants so that she might take them to the beggars crowding round the castle gates.

Harshly treated at Court, Elizabeth made no complaint, and then at thirteen with great pomp and ceremony she was married to Louis. Louis understood his gentle wife. He stood between her and all his jealous relatives who tried to send her away. Elizabeth loved her fine husband too, and they were very happy.

Now that she was Queen, she could do much more for the sick and poor, and soon all her time and thought was given to how to help them best. She became known as the Patroness of the Poor, and soon, every day, nine hundred poor people climbed the rocky path up to the castle for food and alms, which Elizabeth herself gave to each one. But food and money were not enough, and at last Elizabeth turned part of the castle into

a hospital, and when she heard that large numbers of old people could not climb all the way to the top of the hill, she built another hospital half-way up for them.

Daily, she visited the hospital, taking her turn at nursing the patients, and always being very careful to see that those with the most horrible diseases received her special attention.

Just like our own matrons of today, Elizabeth took upon herself the duty of inspecting and improving the wards. The patients grew to count on her visits, and no matter how tired she was, or how many demands her own small family made upon her, she never let them down. Louis was frequently called away, which meant she was responsible for the whole management of the province, and all too soon she was forced to use her powers.

A great famine struck Germany and Thuringia was hit worst of all. In a short time, the people were starving. In mobs they went out into the woods to dig up and eat the roots. They killed their horses and ate the flesh, and many robbed and killed their neighbours if they thought there was food hidden in the house.

Elizabeth, after a night of prayer, opened the castle granaries. That day and for many days after no poor person was turned away without a handful of grain to stave off hunger. The castle became a kind of Food Dispensary. Elizabeth kept nothing back for herself. She sold her lands, her precious jewels, her clothes in order to find enough money to help her stricken people.

Starvation brought illness and death in its train; and Elizabeth in an effort to save her subjects' lives, opened two more hospitals, visiting them every day.

The plight of the lepers was desperate for in the early thirteenth century even less was done for them than in the centuries which followed. Elizabeth nursed them herself, kissing them tenderly, never showing fear of infection, and there is a beautiful story, which may be no more than legend, that once she placed a leper in her own bed, and that when even the long-suffering Louis protested, they were suddenly granted a vision of Christ lying on the bed in place of the beggar.

It is certain, however, that many miracles of healing did take place both during Elizabeth's lifetime, and afterwards at her shrine.

But what of Elizabeth the young Queen and mother of three children? What of Louis, her husband, who when he returned was met by a storm of protests from his own relatives, especially from his jealous brother, Henry.

"Look what she has done. She is ruining us." You can just imagine how they would proceed to malign the young Queen. But Louis knew his Elizabeth and he sent his brother packing, saying he was well content with what she had done.

Gradually, the country recovered from the famine and Elizabeth spent more and more time in her hospitals, though wisely she saw to it that she was always there when Louis wanted her to attend State banquets. Few would have recognised in the tall gorgeously robed young Queen, the shabby young woman who liked to slip out of the castle early in the morning and visit her hospital half-way down the hill.

One day in 1227, Louis came to tell her that he was going away to Palestine to fight in a holy war against the Saracens. Such wars are referred to in history books as Crusades, and were fought by Christians in an endeavour to win back the Holy Places from the infidels.

Elizabeth did not attempt to dissuade her young husband from leaving her yet again, but there was a heavy sadness tugging at her heart as she watched him ride away.

By September, Elizabeth heard that Louis was dead, and weeping bitterly, she vowed that she would never again wear any dress but that of the widow, and that she would die to herself. At twenty her life it seemed was over, and could have no meaning for her if she did not devote every moment to God's service.

No sooner was the news spread abroad that Louis was dead than the wicked Henry stepped in. He seized the throne for himself, and expelled Elizabeth from the castle.

And so it was that one night, separated from her three small children, Elizabeth fled from the castle, and sought shelter in the town, and found it that night in the cottager's home.

For a time she lived by her spinning, until one day her relatives in Hungary heard of her plight, and coaches were sent to the town to take her and her family back to Hungary.

Elizabeth refused to marry again; in Hungary she increased her austere way of living; wearing only the coarsest of dresses, and fasting and praying long hours. Her father would have had her at court; she was still young and very beautiful; the widowed Emperor himself wished to marry her, but Elizabeth spent her days among the sick, and nursing the lepers.

In 1228 the wicked Henry was overthrown, and Elizabeth and her family invited back to Thuringia. Elizabeth by now had become a member of the Third Order of St. Francis, and had given all the revenues from her lands to the poor and sick, but for her son's sake she agreed to return.

She lived only three years longer; dying at the age of twenty-four on November 19, 1231. As she requested, her body was buried in the chapel near the first hospital which she had founded, and almost at once, sick people visiting her tomb were miraculously cured.

For all eternity, the name of this gentle saint, queen and mother, will be linked up with the sick and poor, for whom she did so much in her own short life.

St. John of God

The little boy of eight who in 1503 ran away from his home in Portugal came at last to rest with a kindly farmer across the Spanish border. And there he stayed, helping on the farm, as he grew older and stronger. But there was a strong adventurous streak in John's nature, and when the chance came to join the Spanish army which was at war with France, he took it.

As a soldier, John was not a great success, but the desire to defend the Faith had grown very strong. He fought in the Crusaders' war against the Turks; and then later, no longer a soldier, made a pilgrimage to the shrine of St. James of Compostella.

Whilst on this pilgrimage, John determined to devote his life to God's service. And instead of going home, as he had originally intended, he set out for Africa with the noble idea that in some way he might be able to come to the rescue of the Christian slaves who had fallen into Moorish hands. But as so often happened with John, no sooner had he determined on one course, than another one appeared. The ship put in at Gibraltar, and there for the first time, he found himself in close contact with the sick, and offered to help in the hospital there.

He might after all have continued on his way to Africa had he not stumbled across a little family in exile from his own country. They were noble and kind, but, it seemed to John, quite unable to look after themselves. He suggested that he became their servant, and they were relieved and willing to accept him. So John went with them to Ceuta, and cared for them until they were able to return to their own country.

By now, John was middle-aged. But he had all the energy of a young man. He made up his mind not to return with them to Portugal but to make for Granada, and there in Granada he decided to become a bookseller. No ordinary bookseller; the books he would sell would be books about God which would teach the people to lead better lives. Still not quite clear in his mind what his vocation was to be, John spent his spare time in the hospitals, and then one day, perhaps after a visit to one of

St. John collecting blankets for his hospital

the countless shrines to Our Lady, John knew!

Henceforward he would devote his life to the service of the poor and sick, and he would begin in Granada, for it was there that there seemed to be the greatest need. John had been a farmer, a soldier and a bookseller. All his life he had been active, and so now, he did not sit down and just wait for things to happen.

First of all, he would need a house, and he found one almost immediately— a great, empty, warren of a house in a poor district.

But an empty house needs furniture; John went out and bought beds and mattresses and blankets; and when they were all set up and placed in order, above each bed he hung a crucifix.

So far so good, but a house now furnished, even sparsely so, was useless unless it was filled with people; and the kind of people John sought for his house were the sick, the unwanted. He found them as easily as he had found his house. He found them in the gutters, in the church porches, at street corners. Some of these beggars were so hideous from their infections and their wounds, that ordinary decent people could not bring themselves to go near them. Not so John. He positively ran up to them, embraced them, and led them back to his house.

And so his house at last began to look like a hospital. But the poor and sick had to be fed; money did not flow in, although the good people of Granada were mildly interested, and John found that the only way to get funds was to beg himself. He went round everywhere, begging, and the funds came in, and the house grew—grew until it could expand its walls no more, and so John moved into a larger building. And all this time, the ex-soldier was hoping passionately not only that his poor sick children should get well, but that they should turn to God in their new strength. and learn to love him.

After a time, John found that he needed other men to help him, and at last the Bishop said that John must wear a habit and organise his community into a religious Order. The Bishop said too that from now onwards John should bear the title of John of God.

The wonder of John of God's hospital touched at last the hearts of the people of Granada; where else could the lepers go; where else could the dying find such comfort; where else could they place the city's lost and homeless orphans?

John and his Brothers worked without ceasing to provide an answer to all these questions. He went on a journey—it was really a kind of grand begging expedition—all the way through Spain, to get more funds for his poor. But though this was successful, John's own health broke down. Although he reached home safely, he lived for only another two years, dying on the same date as he was born, March 8, at the age of fifty-five.

St. Camillus of Lellis

When Camillus was born his parents were already old, and he was only thirteen when his mother died; a few years later his father also died, and the boy was left an orphan.

There was soldiering in the young man's blood, and as soon as he could, he enlisted. Camillus loved fighting for fighting's sake. He enjoyed the rough life of the army, and he quickly adapted himself to its ways. Life went on merrily enough. It was fun to fight, and fun to gamble; fun to boast and live from one unthinking day to the next.

That was Camillus, the young soldier. Then one day, all was changed. On the battle-field, he was wounded in the leg; the wound was serious enough for Camillus to realise that his soldiering days were over.

Perhaps the suffering and disappointment contributed as much as anything to Camillus' sudden change of heart. He began to wish to fight, not in some great king's army, but in the army of Christ. But his leg showed not a sign of healing, and at last he made his way to Rome, to the Hospital for the Incurables, where after a spell of treatment, he felt strong enough to offer himself as a nurse.

But although Camillus had said "good-bye" to his life of soldiering, he found he could not change his habits so easily; he still had a fierce temper; he still loved gambling, and he was still very fond of breaking rules. The hospital cured his leg, but it could not cure his temper or disposition, and at last when Camillus decided to leave Rome, the hospital authorities sighed with relief.

Over and over again Camillus reminded himself of the vow he had taken to give himself to God, but the memory of it grew fainter and fainter.

Then something unexpected happened. On his way to Naples, his ship was nearly sunk by a great storm. Camillus, faced as he thought with almost certain death, vowed that if he survived he would never again turn his back on his vocation. In the storm, he lost everything but his life and his will to carry out his vow, and for a time he wandered about Naples, destitute, glad to accept any kind of labouring work, sometimes even begging, until at last the Franciscans took pity on him, and allowed him to stay with them.

His leg, once cured, now became troublesome again, and little wonder, for it had had small chance to rest. In desperation, Camillus thought once more of the hospital in Rome. He would return there; even if he was unwelcome,

Camillus clinging for dear life as a great storm rages

they would surely do something for his leg. Perhaps he might there at last find his true vocation. And find it he did, in that great hospital.

A meeting with the great saint, Philip Neri, strengthened and helped Camillus to see where his vocation surely lay. The hospital was badly organised; its thousands of patients suffered unnecessarily from bad nursing, and often complete indifference to their pain.

In his heart, Camillus believed that he could lead men, but he knew too that he was ignorant; he was thirty-two, yet he knew scarcely more about ordinary school subjects than a lad of ten. He now began urgently to desire to become a priest, but he was so badly educated he did not dare offer himself.

At last, his mind made up, he decided to go back to school. He sat in the benches among small boys, patiently ignoring their inquisitive glances.

If he was slow at learning, he was stubborn enough to refuse to accept defeat. Slowly he began to learn, and when it seemed that he knew enough, his

preparation for the priesthood commenced, until the day came when he was ordained.

Camillus wasted no time in drawing up the rules of the Order which he desired to found. Already he had five men in mind who had worked in the hospital; he decided their habit should bear the Red Cross, and that they should devote their lives to the sick. They must, he said, be well trained; they must be skilled hospital nurses, and they must, above all else, put their patients before themselves.

It must have seemed to Camillus that his life had been just a preparation for the disaster that suddenly descended upon Rome. In 1590, the whole city was laid low by plague. Sixty thousand people died, and the number would have been higher if it had not been for Camillus and his devoted band of followers. They were everything; and everywhere. To the desperately sick, they were the tenderest of nurses; to the dying and despairing they brought the comfort of the sacraments; to the

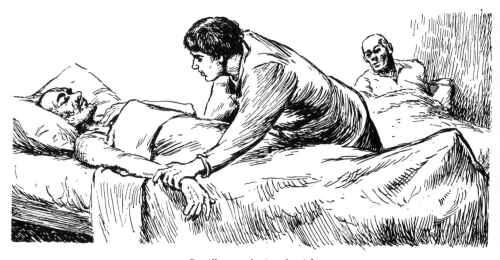

Camillus comforting the sick

orphaned children they were father and mother. From the gutters, they carried the stricken to the hospitals; no home, however dirty or plague-infested, was bad enough to drive them away.

When the plague had subsided, some of the Camillans joined up with the army, and there, just as they had done in Rome, they put themselves in the front line, tending the wounded soldiers under fire, organising base hospitals, and introducing hygienic methods of nursing. Countless soldiers' lives were saved by their skill. Now it seemed their services were demanded everywhere, and Camillus, in spite of ill-health and lack of funds, opened houses in Italy, in Hungary, Spain, Portugal, Peru, France, Holland and Belgium.

Many of his Brothers were killed on the battle-field, others died from plague or from overwork, but still the work of this magnificent soldier-saint continued. He refused to be discouraged, even when he himself could well have shared the bed of some of his patients. He was sixty-four, this saint of the Red Cross, when he died on July 14, 1614, having carried on to the very end.

St. Vincent de Paul

A small boy in brown cap and gaiters, a striped sheepskin over his shoulders, and bread and cheese in his linen wallet, sets out for the hills round Pouy. He drives before him his father's sheep, and when he reaches the pasture land, he eats his bread and cheese, and in the stillness of an early morning, his thoughts reach upwards . . . into the blue, cloudless sky.

In his village, bordering on the sea, there is much talk, and in the evening, round his father's fireside, the villagers meet and discuss in whispers the horrors of war. Poor France, torn by wars which ceaselessly rage between Catholic and Protestant! Even the very part of Gascony where stands his village—that too is divided against itself.

At seven, Vincent had already learned much, and he was well-instructed in the holy scriptures—his parents had seen to that. They had found him once solemnly and earnestly teaching himself to say Mass before a toy altar which he had made and placed in the hollow trunk of a tree. But still, he was only a little boy, and the dreams he had of being a priest were only dreams. Many were the adventures—some more thrilling than any fiction hero's—that he would have before the longed-for day when he would celebrate Mass as a priest of God.

He was born on April 24, 1581. From tending his father's flock, he became a pupil under the care of the Franciscans. At twelve he was more clever than most boys of his own age, and his thirst for learning continually delighted the good friars. What more natural than that after his schooling days, they should find him a good living tutoring the sons of a local lawyer. The boys were just as sorry to lose their brilliant young tutor as Vincent himself was to leave, but he was impelled by the urge to become a priest, and at the same time to pursue learning.

From the time he left Pouy, Vincent found himself almost constantly "on the move." On foot, he visited Spain and France, and while in Toulouse he embarked on one of his strangest adventures, though he could not foresee it. A chance acquaintance offered him a passage on his ship, which was bound for Marseilles, the very port Vincent, for private reasons, was anxious to reach in some haste.

Gratefully, Vincent accepted, but no sooner was the ship in the Gulf (of Lyons) than it was attacked by pirates. Here is how Vincent described the whole incident, which he recorded in a letter written two years later.

"... They chased and attacked us so smartly that two or three of our men were killed and all the rest wounded, and even I received an arrow wound which will serve me as a clock for the rest of my life. And we were forced to surrender to these ruffians who are worse than tigers.

"In the fury of their rage they cut our captain into a hundred thousand pieces because he had killed one of their leaders. . . . They put us in chains and finally, laden with merchandise, after seven or eight days, they headed for Barbary. . . . On arrival they exposed us for sale. . . ."

Vincent setting out to the hills with his father's flock

St. Vincent taken captive by pirates

In this letter, Vincent goes on to tell how his captors stripped him and dressed him in a "pair of breeches, a linen jacket and a cap," and marched him through the city of Tunis with chains round his neck. He and his companions were then sold to merchants. These merchants treated them just like cattle, examining their teeth and pinching them to see how fit they were, before making an offer to buy.

Vincent, however, was more fortunate than some of the other poor captives. He was bought by a fisherman. The fisherman found quickly enough that he had made an uncommonly bad bargain, for his new slave was a hopeless sailor and absolutely no use to him. Very soon he got rid of him to a strange and rather frightening old man, an alchemist, who apparently grew quite fond of his French slave, and did not treat him over-harshly. At any rate, on his deathbed he left Vincent to his nephew.

The nephew was never in two minds about the slave; he did not want him, and sold him at once to a man who had once been a Christian.

This man had three wives, and so sweetly did Vincent talk about his own faith, that the women began to persuade their lord and master to release Vincent and send him home. Their master listened to their pleadings in such good heart that not only did he give Vincent his freedom, but resolved that he would return with him to a Christian country.

So Vincent finally returned to France, and by 1609 was in Paris, and on friendly terms with the nobility. Madame Gondi, in particular, influential wife of a high official, conceived a great admiration for the saint, and persuaded him to accept an appointment in her household as her children's tutor.

As a small boy, Vincent had once saved all his pocket money in order to have something to give to a beggar. In the midst of plenty, his thoughts turned again and again to the poor. The small boy peeped out of Vincent's eyes, urging him to devote himself entirely to Christ's poor.

In Paris he met Francis de Sales who further strengthened him in his resolve to follow his true vocation. But release from his duties in the capital was not yet in sight.

Through the influence of Madame Gondi, who was quite determined that her children should not be deprived of their saintly tutor, he was appointed Chaplain General of the Galleys. In some ways, this phase of his life was a preparation for the work, his true work, which lay ahead of him.

Vincent realised immediately that the plight of the slaves was desperate. He visited the galleys. He saw with his own eyes how the slaves were treated; that they were chained to heavy cannon balls, that they had to sleep between benches—when sleep was permitted. Sometimes they were driven on by the whip of the lash for twenty-four hours at a stretch, with nothing but a biscuit to keep them from starvation.

He saw too that each slave had a cord hung round his neck. At the end of it was a cork gag. They told him that when the slaves were driven on even beyond their strength, the guards forced these gags into their mouths so that their agonised screams would be stifled.

No slave was ever questioned as to his religion, none were given the chance of going to Confession or the Sacraments. If they died, their bodies were pitched overboard as though they had been so much flotsam.

Vincent was horrified, and angry, furiously so. As their chaplain, he laboured to improve conditions on the galley ships, and time and time again he went down amongst them, with Christ's message of hope and comfort on his lips. That took courage, for the slaves were embittered, desperate men who had long ago abandoned all hope in humanity. Vincent showed himself utterly fearless, and some at least of the slaves were grateful and died peacefully when their time came.

When at last the opportunity came for the saint to undertake parish work, he grasped it with both hands. There was nothing inspiring about the little town of Chatillion. Its church had long fallen into disrepair; its people had had no priest for a hundred years, and his reception was a hostile one. The people had no wish to have their consciences

St. Vincent among the galley slaves

stirred, and to begin with they did everything they could to drive him away.

Vincent, with patient and gentle words, gradually won their confidence. He repaired their church, buried their dead, cared for their poor, comforted their sick. And slowly, his wonderful example and his sermons won their hearts. When Vincent was recalled to Paris, no sadder parish was there in the whole of France.

Once more in the great city, where there was more misery, more want, than anywhere else, Vincent realised that if he was going to lighten the burden of his beloved poor, he must enlist the help of the rich. There were plenty of noble ladies, many of them very charitably inclined, but until Vincent went among them, their charity had consisted of giving a sum of money from their substantial incomes. This, as Vincent told them, was not true charity at all. It was not enough merely to give money to the poor.

"What an honour it is to visit Jesus Christ," he told them. "If you look only at the poor they will inspire you with disgust. See Jesus Christ in them, and you will be attracted and charmed."

One of these noble ladies, Louise de Marillac (now canonised) helped him to found the Ladies of Charity, but it was a simple peasant girl, Margaret Naseau, who got the idea first. She came to him and offered her services. True, she could neither read nor write, but she could teach herself, and this she did by means of a simple alphabet which she bought.

Margaret nursed the sick devotedly under Vincent's direction. The sights which horrified the high-born French ladies, in no way horrified Margaret. She brought to her tasks the plain, commonsense of a practical country girl—ready for anything.

Vincent's first Margaret gave him the idea of the enlisting the help of these country girls who were so strong and so willing and so calm. Unfortunately, Margaret herself did not live to see how the Movement spread. While still young, she died . . . from the plague. Absolutely indifferent to the risk of infection, Margaret, the story goes, shared her own bed with a plague-stricken patient, and as a consequence caught the plague herself.

Already, the saint had many "Margarets," who were willing to work anywhere and nurse even the most terrifying diseases. He had, too, many "Ladies," who now no longer shrank away from the poor or refused to nurse them. And these he called his "Ladies of Charity."

His "Margarets" were his "Sisters of Charity," and they undertook to go anywhere he sent them. In 1638 some of his Sisters took charge of a small house in Paris which had as its inmates —babies!

For some time Vincent had been well aware that in Paris there was a home run by unscrupulous women. It was supposed to be a home for foundlings, but in actual practice the woman sold the babies—sometimes to cruel circus folk who intended to make such babies grow up deformed.

Little wonder the saint set up in competition! And of course the babies just "poured in." The saint himself was always stumbling across them in his church porch, or even in the church itself or among the gravestones. His Sisters found them in doorways, in deserted buildings, anywhere and everywhere, and by 1643 they had rescued well over a thousand children.

Two years later, King Louis XIII gave Vincent money to build thirteen small houses—which he immediately staffed with his Sisters and then threw open the

St. Vincent's Ladies of Charity visiting the sick

doors to welcome in children who had lost their parents through war or pestilence or just desertion. Vincent never enquired too closely as to how the children came to him. It was enough that they had arrived and that above all they needed love and understanding.

Although we have talked much about Vincent and his activities we have not seen him walking between the beds of some great hospital. Always, he has been penetrating the slums, teaching, preaching, and for ever looking on to fresh horizons in his efforts to help the poor and suffering.

Four years before he started his Foundling Home, that is in 1634, Vincent was charged by the Archbishop of Paris to take over the running of the Hôtel Dieu, the great hospital in Paris, which in a year tended 25,000 patients.

The hospital was badly run; the patients frequently dying from neglect. Vincent asked his high-born Ladies of Charity to help him, and they did, with splendid courage—for they disdained all the ordinary precautions which the nurses of that time employed when nursing plague victims. Gay, beautiful and poised, their very appearance in the overcrowded wards must have given the patients fresh hope.

Behind every scene was Vincent, organising, planning, extending. Working night and day, and yet somehow praying at all hours too, for without his deep and wonderful trust in God's love and mercy, he would have been utterly discouraged by all the misery around him.

Then he achieved so much—and in so many different directions—was proof of his abiding confidence in God.

"If persons of the world consider themselves honoured by serving the children of the Government, how much more should you who are called to serve the children of God."

The children of God? Who else but his beloved poor? St. Vincent de Paul died in September 1659; he died in harness, as he would have wished, sitting in his chair, and wearing his cassock.

These are but four great names among

the countless men and women who have devoted themselves to the service of the sick. There are nowadays not only individuals but whole religious congregations who follow this great vocation, there are Brothers and nuns, so many that we could not even give a list of the congregations. They work among the sick, the mentally afflicted, the dying and all whom disease and weakness bring low.

In our own country and century the State has undertaken the main burden of caring for the sick, and we have grown accustomed to the idea of public hospitals. Let us never forget that it was the love of Christ that inspired the long early history of nursing.

MISSIONARY ENDEAVOUR

St. Francis Xavier

"If I get into China I fancy you will probably find me in one of two places—a prisoner in chains or at the royal palace in Peking."

The Portuguese merchants knew better than anyone the danger that awaited any man who dared to enter China, ruled as it was by an Emperor who hated foreigners. Capture meant imprisonment, torture, death. Yet here was Francis with only two companions contemplating a meeting with the Emperor himself.

They could not dissuade him, this tall frail man with the burning eyes and captivating smile, but none believed that it would be the "royal palace."

The story of Francis Xavier, the Basque nobleman who, riding forth from his castle in Navarre, came at last as a student to Paris, is packed with almost incredible adventure.

In Paris, the gay, fascinating Francis shared a room with Ignatius Loyola, another Basque, and founder of the Company of Jesus. Ignatius loved the high-spirited irresistible Francis almost from the beginning, but Francis would have none of his friendship, until Ignatius conquered him with one oft-repeated question: "What does it profit a man if he gain the whole world and lose his own soul?"

With a handful of others, Francis, by the beginning of 1534, was ready to sacrifice everything to follow after Christ. Spreading his Master's teaching, he was destined to traverse continents; to starve and sweat in the heat of India; to face torture and death in Japan. But for the moment we see him as a tall, slender man, wearing the black gown and leather belt of the University student. He completed his course brilliantly, but by 1536 France was once again at war with Spain, and parts of France were ravaged by the invading Spaniards. Francis with eight companions started out for Venice where Ignatius awaited them.

Their journey was filled with hard-

Poussin   *Photo Mansell*

St. Francis Xavier brings the young girl back to life

St. Francis Xavier is held up by French troops on the way to Venice

ships and danger, but the spirit of the little company was such that it welcomed every hazard. Confronted by the French troops one or two members of the party replied in French; attacked by Spaniards, those among the nine who knew Spanish answered they were pilgrims, while the others remained dumb. The subterfuge worked, and the band eventually reached Venice.

From Venice, according to their vows, it had originally been intended that they should make for Jerusalem; this was now seen to be impossible. "Jerusalem," Ignatius told them, "is now out of the question: God wants us surely for other work."

Francis and another Jesuit, called Bobadilla, were sent to Bologna, and there we find him, not lecturing, but preaching his simple sermons with heart-burning intensity, praying long hours in the night, working in the hospitals, hearing confessions, constantly at the service of the people, so that when at last he

was recalled to Rome, his brethren thought he would surely die, so thin and worn he looked. They little knew; perhaps only Ignatius realised the unquenchable fire and courage of his most dear friend and disciple.

The little Company of Jesus in five years had grown, despite persecution and suffering, indeed perhaps because of it. Now came the call for Jesuit missionaries to the East. Portugal controlled vast territories outside her country. Goa in the East was under her rule, and Vasco da Gama in 1502 had opened up for Portuguese traders the route to the Calicut coast. In these early days the crusading spirit against the Moors was strong, but greed for the new-found wealth overcame all that was best in man. The Portuguese in the Indies abused their privileges shamefully. Many of them had openly broken away from the Church and were living vicious, sinful lives.

As early as 1500 the Franciscans had

established a mission in Calicut, which was almost immediately wiped out by the Mohammedans. The Dominicans a few years later suffered a similar fate.

Goa might be declared the capital by her Portuguese overlords, mosques might be altered overnight into chapels, a cathedral, magnificent in its conception, might be erected, but still the pagan spirit of the place prevailed. What good could a handful of priests do in a diocese so large that it extended across practically the whole of India.

In 1540 the King appealed to the Pope for more missionaries, and the Pope asked the Jesuits to undertake the work. Ignatius chose Bobadilla and Simon Rodriguez. Bobadilla fell ill, and Francis was chosen in his place. For years he had dreamed of serving Christ in the mission field; but as he gazed down upon his beloved Superior who was himself ill with fever and in bed, he did not declare his dreams. "Good! I am here and ready!" was all he answered when Ignatius told him the news.

There was little time to prepare, only a few short hours, but Francis was soon ready; his worldly possessions—just a crucifix, his breviary and a religious manual.

Two years after he left Rome and thirteen months after he set sail for India from Lisbon, Francis reached Goa. In his heart he knew that never again would he see the face of Ignatius Loyola or walk the dusty roads of his beloved Spain.

The Bishop of Goa welcomed him eagerly; the state of his spiritual children could not be worse. Many of the Portuguese traders had themselves taken to worshipping idols; others thought nothing of murder, robbery and every other kind of violence. The plight of the Indians was desperate, exploited as they were by the white man.

Francis must of course stay at the palace. But Francis replied: "My home is in the hospital beside the suffering poor," and the generous, charming smile and tender, eager voice robbed his words of reproach or offence.

If we could step on to a magical carpet which would carry us across the seas to the Goa of the sixteenth century, in the early summer of 1542, in all probability as we landed we would hear the sound of a bell. And then when our eyes grew accustomed to the strong light, we would make out a strange sight; in the narrow street, striding towards us, comes the tall, slightly stooping figure of a man, dressed in a shabby cotton gown without sleeves or belt. He is ringing a bell and calling to the people to come out of their houses and listen.

The children come running first, fat little Indians, white children too, all eager to hear the words of this strange priest who lives in the hospital, and who eats the food of slaves; who thinks nothing of spending the whole night beside some leper, or kissing the sores of a beggar.

And Francis talks to them of the love of Jesus, his own face lit up with love, his voice gentle. He teaches them how to pray; with the magic of the Pied Piper he gradually leads them towards the church, draws them inside, and there slowly and patiently explains and instructs them in the faith.

In five short months the face of the city has changed; the traders deal fairly, there is justice in the courts, vice and brutality disappear from the homes. The sick are cared for, children baptised, churches crowded. Then comes the day when Francis hears of the plight of the pearl fishers, where "the land is so desolate and the heat so terrible that no priest can stay among them."

The land of the pearl-fishers stretched

The sound of his bell draws the pearl-fishers to listen

along the east coast of India—from Cape Comorin to the island of Manaar; Portuguese traders visited it only when the pearl season was on; the people worshipped idols, knew no other language except their own; and were sunk in every kind of sin.

Francis could hardly wait to accept the new pair of shoes which one of his friends insisted he must take to protect his feet from the burning sands, before he was on his way. He went by sea, landing on Cape Comorin in the September of 1542. At Goa he was understood by the majority of those who listened. In the land of the pearl-fishers he was faced with a people who ran away at the sight of him, who did not understand his language or his intentions; who were completely in the power of their Indian priests, called Brahmins.

By means of an interpreter, Francis talked in village after village until one day he came across a young woman who was dying in childbirth. The Indian

priest had failed to comfort her; Francis was allowed to enter the mud hut where she lay. He told her of the wonderful love of Jesus and His power. The woman asked to be baptised, and then miraculously she began to recover. News of this miracle spread from village to village and at last the success of his mission seemed assured.

The noise of his bell drew the people into the streets, and Francis, with characteristic enterprise and courage, laboriously translated the Our Father, the Creed and the Hail Mary into the Malabar tongue. All along the East coast he journeyed, living as the natives lived, on the poorest of food, a handful of rice, sleeping on the mud floors, enduring the torrid heat and drenching rains with that wonderful cheerful courage which impressed itself even upon the Brahmins, whose way of life was itself extraordinary.

These Brahmins, who were priests, used to receive absolute veneration

Villagers fleeing in terror as the Badages throw firebrands on their huts

from the people. Some of the priests, at certain times, went into solitude, living in a lonely cave or in the hollow of a tree, fasting for months at a time.

The power they held over the pearl-fishers was complete, and the poor people would do anything they told them to do, like throwing themselves over a cliff edge, or plunging into a blazing furnace. The priests lived wicked, sinful lives between their spells of solitude, extorting from the people all manner of goods and threatening them with the vengeance of Brahma if they did not obey. Francis found that the priests of a village were always comfortable and well fed, while the villagers went in desperate want.

Francis spent a year among the pearl-fishers giving instructions and administering the sacraments, then he determined to return to Goa in order to find more priests to take back on the mission. Francis left the coastal villages to penetrate into the country beyond. On his

return from Goa with several companions he found that while he was gone the pearl-fishers had been suddenly attacked by the Badages, a terrible race of people, who hated Christians.

The attack was swift and furious. On their fleet Arab horses, the marauders thundered through the villages, throwing firebrands on the huts. In complete panic, the villagers rushed to their canoes, leaving everything behind. They made for the isolated little islands lying off the coast which would be safe from their enemy. But although many escaped, their plight soon became desperate for in their fear they had taken neither food nor clothing. Days passed, and then one morning, boats were sighted, and in the leading one, to their utter relief and joy, was Francis, with his crucifix held high for all to see.

Like the Good Shepherd seeking his lost sheep, the missionary did not rest until he had visited all the desert islands round the coast, rounding up his poor frightened flock, and then with boats of provisions which he obtained from the Portuguese Government, he fed them and comforted them and brought them safely back to their own land after the Badages had left.

Francis helped them to build their homes again and to restore the ravages of the enemy, and then he left them in the care of the missionaries he had brought from Goa. He had won the pearl-fishers for Christ; but there were vast territories where no missionary had penetrated and to these he must go.

In Southern India, the wonder of his mission, so often accompanied by miracles, had spread like a forest fire, but sometimes he was saddened by the lack of missionary priests. . . .

". . . So great is the multitude of those who are converted to the faith of Christ in the country where I am that often my arms are aching from baptising and my voice is gone from having so often recited the Creed and the Commandments in their language. . . . Some days I baptise a whole village, on the coast where I am there are thirty Christian villages" . . . thus he wrote in a letter from Cochin in 1544.

"So great is the multitude" . . . Francis could not, would not rest. He turned his steps towards the coast of Travancore. There, among people who had never heard the name of Jesus, he built nearly fifty churches, despite the plots of the Brahmins who schemed to take his life, sometimes by lying in wait for him at night with poisoned arrows, or causing the hut where he slept to be set on fire. But Francis always escaped.

In 1549 Francis Xavier is back once more in Goa, this time his mind and heart burning with only one idea; he will go to Japan. "India," he cried, "is not the boundary of my mission."

Going to Japan involved a sea voyage of four thousand miles; there were, besides dangers from pirates, the great typhoons which tossed ships on to black, murderous rocks. Even if he reached Japan, what chance had he? The Japanese hated and distrusted foreigners; it was also a country at war with itself, divided into many small kingdoms each one governed by force. What chance had a lone white missioner in such a land where superstition and paganism had existed for centuries?

But none could reason with the man in the patched old cassock and bare feet who was never seen without his wooden crucifix.

At last it was arranged. To his joy, Francis encountered a Japanese in Malacca who wished to become a Christian—and furthermore, he offered his services and that of his two servants in the enterprise. Two others, Father Cosmo de Torres and John Fernandez, also accompanied Francis, and on June 24, 1549, all six embarked in a Chinese junk owned by a pirate. The voyage was as strange as it was terrible, for all the crew worshipped idols, and despite the presence of the missioners, proceeded to set up images of their gods and make sacrifices to them as soon as the ship set sail.

Threatened shipwreck and the open hostility of the pirate captain added to the terrors of the voyage. When they eventually sailed into the bay of Kagoshima, the date was the Feast of the Assumption, August 15, 1549.

Who can say what Francis thought about this strange country where the standards of beauty and culture were just the opposite to his own country, where black teeth were thought to be a sign of beauty, and where the mourners in a funeral procession wore white instead of black, where men squatted on the floor eating rice with chopsticks and women were considered of no account?

But it was the priests of the pagan temples who openly declared themselves the enemy of Jesuits, despite the friendliness of the king of the province Kagoshima.

Towards the end of October, Francis set out for the capital of the Empire. His mission had so far been fairly successful, but there were still only little pockets of Christians. From the capital Francis hoped to set the torch alight that would burn throughout the length and breadth of the island. Misfortunes dogged his footsteps. He was often soaked through by drenching rain; he lost his way in the forests, was sometimes in danger of being drowned by the torrents of flood water which cascaded down the valleys. Worst of all, when he tried to preach God's word in the villages, the people laughed at him and turned away. In the capital, finding that the people jeered at his patched old cassock and bare feet, Francis realised he would gain their attention more quickly if he abandoned his beggar's robe, and so for the first time he wore a new and respectable gown.

Now the pagan priests were openly stirring up the people, and often the Jesuits were pelted with stones and mud as they walked through the streets of Kyoto. Worse, the "king" would not see them. The guards stared at them contemptuously as they approached the palace; if they persisted in their desire to be given audience, they were driven away with sticks.

After only eleven days, Francis left Kyoto. He went back to Hirado where Father de Torres was waiting for him. How eagerly they greeted each other, and how glad Francis was to be able to say Mass again. His mission to Kyoto had been a failure but he had learned that it was folly to attempt to convert the haughty Chinese nobles without rich presents and a display of importance.

In their eyes a man humbly dressed could not be the ambassador of a King. Francis, who was the servant of the King of Kings, resolved to meet them on their own ground.

He replaced his worn gown by an impressive robe, he obtained presents from Goa, and this time took with him all the rich vestments of the Mass. And the subterfuge worked; the nobles listened to him, and some were converted, but in the two years he remained in Japan he had none of the sweeping conversions which characterised his work in Southern India. Still, he had opened the way, and now his thoughts turned insistently to China.

"If I get into China . . ." But foreigners, they told him, when at last he returned to Goa, were forbidden to enter. Death or imprisonment was the certain fate of any who tried. When it seemed that his dream would come to nothing, a rich merchant put all his wealth at the saint's disposal with the suggestion that the expedition should take the form of a trade deputation! In the name of the king of Portugal the Emperor should be asked to allow his subjects to trade with Portuguese merchants.

Francis gladly accepted the proposal, and on April 14, 1552, the ship named the *Santa Cruz*, richly appointed, set sail from Goa.

A month later the *Santa Cruz* entered the Straits of Malacca. Malacca was laid low by a terrible plague; and Francis at once went to the assistance of the sick and dying, working tirelessly in the scorching heat to save lives. While he laboured, his enemies, the enemies of Christ, intrigued against him. The *Santa Cruz* was forbidden to leave the harbour; the whole idea of approaching the Emperor had to be abandoned.

Francis, however, could not abandon his own dreams, and at last the saint

Pelted with mud and stones in the streets of Kyoto

was promised a passage. But his heart was nearly breaking at the sudden flood of hate which so unexpectedly had burst upon him.

The crew of the ship turned against him, scarcely giving him enough to eat. All were afraid of what the Chinese would do to them if their ship were captured. Many were for turning back, and Francis found himself without any human comfort. Yet his resolve to go on remained unshaken. They put him ashore on a lonely little island called Sanchian within sight of the shores of China.

His half-starved body was shaken with fever, his hair white, and while he waited for the Chinese merchant to take him to Canton, he did what he could for the miserable occupants of the few wooden huts along the shore. He was not alone. His companions were a Jesuit lay brother, a Chinese, and the other a Portuguese merchant. Weeks passed. The date on which it had been promised the merchant from Canton would appear and take him to China came and went.

Francis grew weaker. He lay "in a hut open to the cold and wind, without any comfort but that which came from God. . . ." Seeing that he was dying, Antonio placed his crucifix between his hands. The saint fixed it with a look of adoration, and then shortly afterwards the spirit of this great missionary saint fled. It was Friday, December 2, 1552. No missionary saint earned the name of Apostle—Apostle of the Indies —more worthily than Francis Xavier.

Jesuits in S. America

The Early Days of South America

If you have an atlas handy, let me suggest that you turn to the map of South America. This great continent is so vast, 4800 miles from north to south, and 3300 miles from east to west, that there are parts of it today of which white men have no knowledge, although

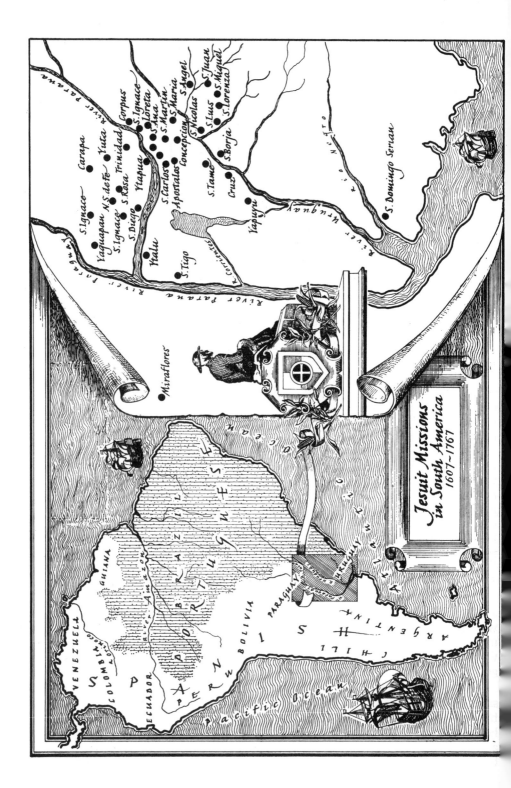

Jesuit Missions in South America 1607–1767

Christopher Columbus discovered it in 1498, four hundred and sixty years ago.

In the depths of the tropical forest which covers the basin of the river Amazon and its tributaries there exist Indian tribes who have never seen a white man. Some of you may have read about the disappearance of Colonel Fawcett, the explorer, and of the search which his son made for him. Colonel Fawcett vanished without trace only some twenty years ago, and although rumours of his existence have reached the outside world from time to time, his disappearance remains a complete mystery.

If then, with all the resources of modern invention: the steamer, the railroad, the aeroplane, the motor-car, so much of South America has remained unknown, what can we say of those men who set out almost five centuries ago to carry the Christian faith to the Indian tribes? Some of the tribes are as uncivilised today as they were then, and the early records are full of the martyrdom of the missionaries who set out, full of enthusiasm, to convert them. The most famous of all these missionaries were the Jesuits, and in this article I want to try to tell you of a wonderful experiment in colonisation which this Order carried out in South America and which lasted for one hundred and sixty years, from 1607 to 1767.

The First Missions

To understand just how and why the Jesuits set out to do something which was quite unheard of, that is, to run a number of missions in which everything was done on commercial lines, we must go back some years.

In the year 1526 Sebastian Cabot sailed from Spain for the Spice Islands by way of the Straits of Magellan, but he ran short of supplies and so sailed up a broad estuary which he thought might be a short cut to the Pacific. This was the estuary of the River Plate. He returned to Spain with the news of this new country and in 1535 another expedition entered the estuary of the Plate and sailed up the river Paraguay. It was here that the town of Asuncion was founded in 1537, and it was here too that the Spaniards first met the Guarani Indians, who later on were to be converted by the Jesuits, and to be the subjects of the experiment which I have mentioned.

If you look at the country of Paraguay on your map you will see that it is a comparatively small country, but in those days Paraguay meant most of what is marked on your maps as Argentina, some of Uruguay, and a great part of Brazil as well as Paraguay itself. The first missionaries to arrive here were the Franciscans, two of whom reached Asuncion about the year 1540. Within ten years of the founding of their Order, the Jesuits landed in Brazil and gradually penetrated the entire area which was then known as Paraguay. Their college in Asuncion was founded and later a conference of Jesuit missionaries was held to decide on a common policy.

I expect you have read in your history books about the behaviour of the Spaniards in their American colonies. Their first aim was to set about making their fortunes. Where there was gold or silver they worked the mines by Indian slave labour. There were no mines in Paraguay, but the Jesuits found that they were still expected to help in making slaves of the Indians. This they refused to do, and sent a protest to King Philip III of Spain, who issued letters patent to the Society of Jesus for the conversion of the Guarani Indians. This gave the Jesuits their first official status in the country. It was on the banks of the Parana river that in 1610 the Reduction of Loreto was founded. "Reduction" comes from the Spanish

Indians marching as slaves into Brazil

word "reduccion," meaning "missionary settlement."

Early Troubles

This Reduction was the foundation stone of a system which was to last for nearly two hundred years. It proved a wonderful success, and one mission after another was formed, all of them far away from the Spanish settlements. This was a deliberate policy, designed to gain the confidence of the Indians, and to isolate them from those people who would enslave and exploit them. It was this very policy of isolation which was to form one of the chief charges against the Jesuits in later years. Meanwhile the Spanish colonists grew to hate the Jesuits who persisted in treating the Indians as men, instead of looking upon them as potential slaves. The Order grew in influence and in numbers and by 1614 there were one hundred and nineteen Jesuits in Paraguay and about forty thousand Indians lived in the six or seven main Reductions, and the several smaller ones which had been founded.

So far, everything had gone well, but dark days were soon to arrive. The Missions were attacked by slave-raiders, called Mamelucos. They came from Brazil, where there was a constant demand for labour on the plantations. Within twelve months, six of the reductions were raided and destroyed. Fifteen thousand of their Indians were marched back to Brazil as slaves, while most of those who escaped fled back to the forests. Everywhere was confusion, as mission after mission was ruined.

Yet at the very same time as these events were taking place in Paraguay, new missions were being set up on the banks of the river Uruguay and these proved most successful. It was this successful foundation that induced the Jesuits finally to abandon their ruined missions in the province of Guayra. Only three of these missions now remained intact, so they set out for the new Reductions in Uruguay with as many Indians as were left in the missions.

Move to the Banks of the Uruguay

Imagine for yourself some of the difficulties of this "exodus" as it might well be called. Out of one hundred thousand Indians in the first Reductions some twelve thousand assembled to make the journey to their new homes. The leader of the expedition was Antonio Ruiz de Montoya, a Jesuit who had arrived in the mission field about 1612, and who had risen to the rank of Provincial of the Order in Paraguay. He gathered a fleet of seven hundred boats, but they could go only part of the way by water, because of a great cataract or fall on the river. From then on it meant a journey on foot through tangled forest, where paths had to be cut through the dense vegetation, and where fever and starvation were rife. We may well be amazed that any survived, but Montoya, by his own example and tremendous energy, brought nearly twelve thousand people a distance of five hundred miles, and settled them safely, far from their enemies.

Later, the people of the three remaining Reductions were also to be evacuated, and the Jesuits finally settled with their Indians in the land between the rivers Parana and Uruguay.

Extent of the Missions

On a visit to Spain in 1637 Montoya received permission for the Indians to use firearms in self-defence. The Jesuits then raised a militia and this practically put an end to the slave raids by the Mamelucos, as well as serving to protect the missions from the inroads of the Spanish colonists.

The missions themselves gradually extended till they ranged from Brazil to Paraguay and from the river Parana to the river Uruguay. Most of the country was open plains, with numerous streams alongside which were woods. The plains were covered with fine short grass, especially suitable for the rearing of cattle. How suitable we can easily tell, for when the Jesuits were finally

expelled from South America the cattle numbered seven hundred and twenty thousand, while there were forty-four thousand oxen, twenty-seven thousand horses, and one hundred and forty thousand sheep.

Almost all the missions were built to one plan. When sufficient Indians had been gathered together then the township was laid out, and although the Jesuits left in 1767, yet from the remains and from accounts written at the time we may easily describe what they must have been like during their occupation by the Jesuits. The whole township was built around a square. At one end stood the church and storehouses, and the houses of the Indians formed the other three sides, built in long lines, and separated by lath and plaster walls, but all under one long roof.

The Mission and Mission-life

Each of the houses might shelter one hundred or more families. The Churches, built of stone where possible, or else of the hardwood with which the country abounded, were splendid buildings. An account written at the time describes the church at Los Apostoles as having three aisles, rich altars, high altars, and statues brought all the way from Italy and Spain.

The priests' house, too, was built in the form of a square and in its storehouses were kept the arms for the militia, together with corn, flour, wool, seeds and provisions. In the smaller missions there were only two Jesuits to manage all the affairs of the township, Church and Indians. The magnitude of the work and the devotedness of the Jesuits can be imagined when we find that a small mission such as San Miguer had 1353 families and 6635 people in 1750.

The greatest difficulty in dealing with the Indians was to overcome their natural indifference to work. Normally, the various tribes wandered about, never

Leaving the boats and disappearing into the forest

settling for any length of time, and only cultivating sufficient for their needs. They required very careful handling, for regular work either drove them back to the woods, or more remarkable still, killed them off in hundreds. In order to overcome these difficulties the Jesuits took advantage of the natural love of music shown by the Indians. So, every day, priests and Indians set off for the fields in procession, headed by the figure of a saint, to the singing of hymns. At wayside shrines, prayers were said and more hymns were sung, until the last group of workers reached the fields where they were to labour. Then the priest with his choir returned to the town. The mid-day break gave further opportunity for singing, and at sundown they returned from the fields, gathering the parties of labourers, and singing and praying as they went. After a rest they all went to church and then to supper. If the weather prevented them from working in the fields, they worked indoors at various industries and went to church for their singing.

Apart from their great ranches, on which anything up to fifty thousand head of cattle might roam, the Jesuits taught the Indians the arts and trades of Europe. They learned how to weave cotton, and one township produced eight thousand five hundred yards of cotton cloth in three months. They had tanneries, carpenters' shops, tailors, coopers, rope-makers, boat-builders, cartwrights, joiners, and every other useful trade. They made arms and gunpowder, their own musical instruments, silver ware for the churches, and printed their own books.

Communal Life

All this was worked by the community in common, and the produce fed and maintained them. The cattle and horses too were used in common, and the money from the sale of any surplus was used to buy necessities from the nearest large towns or from Europe. The only condition laid down was that of good conduct and work. As long as the family did its fair share it received enough supplies upon which to live, but any slacking was punished by withdrawal of the supplies.

By the example of their unceasing devotion to work, to teaching and to preaching, by their continual watchfulness over their flocks, the Jesuits tried to induce the habit of work among the Indians. They taught them to plant vegetables in their gardens, and gave such things as knives, scissors, cloth and looking-glasses in exchange for any surplus.

The clothing, both for men and women, was simple, and was issued by the Jesuits who themselves wore rough homespun. In this way, both food and clothing cost very little, and the Indians lived in the midst of simple plenty. Their one luxury was *yerba maté* or Paraguayan tea. This was made from the leaves of a shrub beaten into a fine powder. The shrubs were cultivated in plantations known as yerbales, and these plantations brought in quite a large revenue to the Jesuits every year.

All this, you will notice, was done without compulsion or force of any kind. Indeed, what force could two Jesuits employ against several thousand Indians?

I mentioned the Indians' love of music, and their custom of singing on their way to and from work. Like most simple people, they also had a great liking for what we would call "show," and the Jesuits used music and show to celebrate the frequent feast days of the Church's calendar: rockets, fireworks and the ringing of the church bells would usher in the day. Everybody flocked to Mass, and those who could not get inside the church stood listening outside the doors, which were left wide open that they might hear. Then the ceremonies and processions began and the Jesuits took care that, as far as possible, everybody had some share in the celebrations of the day. The long proces-sions were formed and the image of the saint was borne round the town and then into Church where Mass was celebrated with music from all the instruments which the Indians had been taught to use. Then the procession was formed once more and after parading the town again, feasting and dancing ended the day.

Indian Militia

The government of the mission lay in the hands of the Jesuits, who chose certain of the men to act as police, and who also trained the militia for defence. There was always the danger of attack, not only from slave-raiders but also from the Spaniards of the settlements, and the militia carried their weapons everywhere, even to Mass. Many of the Jesuits had been soldiers, like their famous founder, Ignatius of Loyola, and they were well able to plan the defence of the townships. We must still remember, though, that all this work fell upon a very small number of priests. Indeed, in 1767, when the Jesuits were forced to leave, there were only seventy-eight of them in the whole of Paraguay.

The Indians were allowed to keep their own caciques, or chiefs. To give them a feeling of their own importance, and so keep them content, these chiefs were given special privileges—a guard of honour round their houses and extra food. In return they organised their subjects into labour companies and from time to time called them together for training in defence. It was this system of an ever-ready armed militia that made the Jesuits so unpopular with the ordinary Spaniards. They were continually asking why the priests should maintain a private army, quite ignoring the fact that without this same army the missions would again be overrun and their inhabitants carried off as slaves. They showed no gratitude for the help which this same militia had often given

Rancho Paraguay

Courtesy Royal Geographical Society

against the Portuguese, who were continually attacking the Spanish settlements.

Between the missions, trade was carried on by means of barter, cattle for cotton, sugar for rice, wheat for iron or tools and so on, but outside the missions the Jesuits proved good business men. Tobacco, hides, cotton cloth, linen, hardwood and maté were all sent to Buenos Aires for export or sale. The money was sent to the Superior of the missions, who decided how to lay it out to the best advantage. When we realise that sixty thousand hides a year were sent, about two million pounds weight of maté, a hundred thousand pounds of tobacco, four hundred barrels of honey, and about thirty thousand dollars' worth of hard woods, giving a yearly income of more than a million dollars; and that

out of this sum only eighty-four dollars a year was set aside for the maintenance of each priest, we can see that these communities were quite well-to-do.

The Spanish-Portuguese Treaty

If then, the missions were so successful, why were the Jesuits expelled and the missions abandoned? To begin with, two things had always been held against the Jesuits. For a long time rumours had been fostered that the Jesuits were merely using the missions as a pretext to cover up rich mines which they were working in secret and that they had accumulated tremendous wealth. The other thing was their attitude towards slavery. Long, long ago, Montoya had obtained a decree from Philip III that all the Indians were free, and it was this second reason that made the Jesuits so unpopular with the Spanish settlers, who saw in an Indian nothing more than a potential slave. It was, however, the covetousness of the Portuguese, who firmly believed the rumour about gold mines, that finally brought about the expulsion of the Jesuits from their missions.

For many years the colony of Sacramento on the River Plate had been a bone of contention between the Spaniards and the Portuguese, and in 1748 the Portuguese, who were then in possession of it, signed a treaty by which it should be exchanged for the seven Reductions of Uruguay, and the Jesuits were notified that they must prepare their Indians to leave their townships and march into the woods, where they could found new towns. Full of grief, the Jesuits had to break the news to their people, while at the same time they made every effort to have the treaty annulled. All was in vain, and in 1752 the Jesuits were ordered to help in the evacuation of the seven towns. The Indians, however, were not willing to leave the lands which they had possessed for so many years and in the end they decided to defend their possessions by force of arms. War broke out in 1754, but the Indians stood little chance against the well-armed Spanish troops, and they were defeated with heavy loss of life. After that the war dragged on for several years, with the Indians using guerilla tactics, ambushing small parties, or cutting off small convoys, but finally the Portuguese and Spaniards became allies and took possession of the seven towns. By this time, of course, the Indians had fled into the woods and the once flourishing towns were deserted, the fields had become desolate wastes and of the fourteen thousand Indians who had inhabited them only a handful were left.

The End of Jesuit Rule

After all this long struggle and the ruin of the missions it seems sad to think that in four years Spain signed

At the mission church

A ruined church in **Paraguay**

another treaty revoking the former and declaring that the seven towns should remain in Spanish hands. Although their efforts to keep the missions intact appeared to have been successful, the beginning of the end for the Jesuit missions and for the Jesuits themselves in South America was in sight. The rumours of wealth from their hidden mines had spread all over the Americas, and their attitude towards slavery and their protection for the Indians had set every Spanish colonist against them. The regular clergy and the Jesuits had been at loggerheads for years, and the success of the latter in the struggle only served to increase their unpopularity.

Suddenly the storm broke. Saying that his reasons were reserved "to God and himself" Charles III of Spain signed a decree expelling the Jesuits from Spain and the Spanish dominions. This was in June 1767.

There have been many guesses as to the reason for this sudden decision on the part of the Spanish King, but no one has been able to point with any certainty to the power which influenced the king to make the decision. It may have been jealousy of the power of the Order in Spain itself: it may have been its outspoken opinion on the Inquisition, which it had denounced as "having its roots in hell."

Whatever it was, the decree was final. In the large towns of South America the expulsion went forward quietly, greatly to the astonishment of the military Governor, who expected the Jesuits, with their trained and armed militia, to put up a fierce resistance. His surprise and disgust must have been far greater when, having taken possession of the buildings and property belonging to the Jesuits, he found no treasure and no evidence of any wealth.

And so it was in the missions also. The priests quietly gave up the keys to all their possessions and they themselves were carried off as prisoners to Buenos Aires. In less than four months the Jesuits, after two hundred years of devoted work, were driven from Paraguay. It would have been an easy matter to resist; a few words and the whole Indian population would have been in arms, but no such thought entered a Jesuit mind. Seventy-eight of them were put on board ship and sent back to Europe, taking with them all their possessions: a couple of shirts, a pair of sandals, a pound or two of snuff.

The missions were handed over to members of other Orders, who had little conception of the system by which the Jesuits had ruled and no thought for those over whom they had been put in charge. As a result, within the space of two years, everything was lost. The great ranches, which had pastured more than a million head of cattle, had reverted to scrub; the fields were masses of weeds; the yerba plantations gone to decay, and the fruit trees cut down for firewood. The churches were no longer served and Mass was no longer said. The Indians disappeared gradually, and were absorbed into the woods. Within a quarter of a century there remained of the hundred and fifty thousand who had lived in the Reductions only a few who lingered about the ruined buildings. Of the Jesuits who had laboured so devotedly and who had struggled so unceasingly to protect their charges from slave-raiding, Mamelucos and rapacious Spanish colonists, the only remains were the glorious churches of the townships and the rough wooden crosses over their graves.

For nearly two hundred years they had succeeded in creating and maintaining a community where every man laboured for the common good, where money was unknown and where happi-

Courtesy Royal Geographical Society
An Indian of the Tobo tribe

ness reigned. If men are remembered by their deeds, then the Jesuits of Paraguay can have no greater memorial.

The Franciscans of Mexico

It might be as well to mention here the work of the Franciscans in Mexico. The Franciscans, whom I mentioned early in this article as having been the first missionaries to arrive in Paraguay, were invited to Mexico by the conqueror Cortes in 1523. They discovered that the natives were being exploited under a system of "encomiendas," a system by which so many slaves were allotted or given in trust (se os encomiendau) under a chief, to the encomendero (trustee) to make use of in his fields and mines; and he was to teach them the things of the Holy Catholic Faith. These early missionaries, humble, devoted men, tried in vain to check the cruelty of these trustees, appealing to the king, preaching against them in the pulpit, even refusing absolution to those Spaniards who held Indians in slavery.

It was in the diocese of Michoacán, in an area which had gained the nickname of "land of hell," that a community of Indians was first set up. There the native crafts were developed; weaving, wood-carving, work in gold and silver, painting and pottery. There, among so much cruelty, the Indians became happy and self-supporting; and it was the knowledge of this experiment that probably induced the Jesuits in Paraguay to isolate their missions from the colonists. Only in this way could the faith and trust of the Indians be gained.

Chinese Heart-break

Francis Xavier died at the gateway to China. Thus far and no farther, and still the gate remained barred against all foreigners.

China kept her ancient civilisation, her idols and her marvels a closely guarded secret. Her frontiers were impregnable; there was no country in the whole world more effectively sealed off from outside contacts.

In the eyes of the western world China was a land of mystery; fabulous legends about her Emperor, her wealth and her customs multiplied with the centuries.

The Portuguese and the Spaniards who had conquered much of the East dreamed of the day when there would be free trade. Saints like Francis Xavier saw the Empire Christianised, its millions of souls won for Christ.

Francis died within seven miles of China's coast in 1552, the first Christian missionary to get so close. These seven miles, however, might have been seven thousand, so far was he from crossing that barrier, breaking that seal. China's hatred of the white man, and in particular the missionary, was so deep-rooted that even the Missionary Orders had abandoned hope of sending members there.

And yet within thirty years of the death of Francis Xavier, a white man, a Jesuit, set out for China.

All his life Matthew Ricci had been preparing for just that moment. He was born at Macerata in Italy in the year Francis died. Exceptionally gifted both in looks and personality, he grew up determined to serve Christ in one of the great missionary Orders. He chose the Society of Jesus, and soon his outstanding gift for languages, his diplomacy, and above all his burning desire to work in the mission-field resulted in his being sent to India.

At Goa he completed his theological studies, and then once again he was on the move—this time crossing the China Sea bound for Macao, a small peninsula in the Canton estuary.

Matthew began to learn Chinese, for everything about China fascinated him. He talked with Chinese sailors and traders who were permitted by their Emperor twice a year to trade with the Portuguese. He studied ancient documents, and learned something of the Empire's customs, its Bonzes (priests) and its idol-worshipping.

With the encouragement of his Superior, Matthew directed all his natural gifts to one end. His wonderful memory enabled him to master some-

Matthew Ricci and his companion boarding a junk to Canton

thing of the Chinese signs and symbols, a most difficult feat and one which no western had yet managed to do.

His genius for mechanics and especially his skill in making and mending clocks soon became known among the natives who began to look upon him as something of a magician.

Macao's population was a mixture of Portuguese and Chinese, Macao having once been part of the Chinese Empire. Matthew seized every opportunity to identify himself with the oriental mind; he saw that the gulf between the Orient and the West was almost too wide to be bridged unless he could find some way to build upon what was already there. Like the great Saint Gregory centuries before, he resolved that if he were ever permitted to enter China he would try to turn to account whatever was good in the Chinese customs.

But first he had to have a permit, for it was death to any foreigner who attempted to break through the barrier without official permission. This came

one day so unexpectedly that it seemed like a miracle.

Wang P'an, the mandarin of the province of Shiuhing, had heard tell of Matthew's skill with clocks. No longer able to control his overwhelming curiosity about such strange objects, what they looked like, how they worked, he at last sent word that Matthew might visit him in his province, and he sent his official permit which would ensure Matthew's safe arrival.

Matthew set out with one companion. In his heart he had said "goodbye" for ever to his old way of life for he meant, if possible, to remain in China for the rest of his days.

The Jesuits took little personal luggage, but there were clocks and prisms and maps all calculated to fascinate and attract the mandarins.

They boarded the junk which was to take them to Canton, dressed in long grey tunics similar to those worn by the bonzes—the Buddhist priests or holy men—knowing that this was the best

Matthew Ricci showing a painting of Our Lady to the frightened mandarin

way to show the Chinese that their aims were religious. They also shaved their heads and beards. And because Matthew had not yet mastered the language, they took with them, as interpreter, Philip, a Chinese Christian.

When at last Shiuhing was reached, after many delays, even Ricci, who was prepared to find strange things in a strange land, was bewildered by the countless differences between China and the world he had known.

Their first and most urgent problem was to find a way of making themselves understood. Not only were there hundreds of different ways of speaking Chinese, each locality having its own dialect, but the way in which it was spoken by officials and men of culture was different from any that Ricci or his companion, Father Ruggieri, had ever heard. This was called "Mandarin." Moreover, they soon found that the same sound had different meanings, according to the pitch or note on which it was spoken, and it was nearly im-

possible for them to distinguish the five notes or pitches used.

Wang P'an was friendly and intensely interested in the clocks, despite the barrier of language, but very soon after their arrival he told them that the Laws of the Middle Kingdom, that is China, did not allow foreigners to live in the country. This was a death blow to all Ricci's hopes, but then the wily old mandarin went on to say that according to an ancient privilege permission might be given if they fulfilled one condition. In everything they must become Chinese.

The colour of their skins and the shape of their bodies they could not change, but in all else they must change; they must be quiet, humble and useful to the country. They must obey Chinese laws and wear Chinese dress. Should they wish to marry they must marry Chinese women, and they must promise never to invite other foreigners to join them.

It was a hard choice to make, but Matthew and his fellow Jesuit made it; they accepted what we would now call "naturalisation," and they asked for and were given a small piece of land on which to build their house.

When Ricci protested that it was too small to allow them to build a "pagoda," meaning a chapel of their own, Wang P'an pointed to the Buddhist temples indicating that there was room enough in them for the missionaries to worship.

"We cannot worship there, Your Excellency," Ruggieri answered. "We do not adore idols, but only the King of Heaven."

The mandarin's surprise was understandable, but all the same he generously doubled the amount of land, and gave them permission to build their own "pagoda," and to place in it whatever images they chose.

His delight at their presents was unaffected. In particular, he was startled and delighted by the prism, for the Chinese had never seen glass before, and the breaking up of light into the colours of the spectrum seemed to them very powerful magic. The prism they called "The Jewel Beyond Price."

The painting of Our Lady which Ricci next presented to Wang P'an frightened him; the Chinese had never seen a picture painted in perspective, and so Our Lady appeared as a living person, real and yet not real, but again it was a marvel the mandarin was proud to possess.

Now the missionaries were at liberty to set about the building of their house; it was to have two storeys, a thing unknown in China, and the workmen they were given had to be shown step by step how to proceed.

Ricci and his companion found themselves doing many of the jobs themselves; they grew accustomed to the crowds which came to stare at them; to the hostility of the bonzes and graduates, and to the new names which Wang P'an insisted they must take. Ricci was

called Ma-tou Li, and Ruggieri was named Lu.

Gradually Ricci, unlike Ruggieri, began to master something of the language, but he could not overcome the hostility of those around him. Only Wang P'an's powerful patronage saved them from imprisonment and death. Their number of converts was heartbreakingly small—in two years only twenty.

Ruggieri returned to Macao to try and get funds without which the missionaries could not hope to complete their house, and Ricci was alone, the only white man in China. Some of the time he spent in constructing models of clocks and making maps in order to keep level with the custom of giving presents when visiting, for he was too poor to buy anything.

He began to translate the Ten Commandments into Chinese, and had them printed locally from wooden blocks.

His friend's return with funds enabled them to proceed with their building, but now Wang P'an was turning against them, fearing that his friendship with the foreigners was losing him his chances of promotion. When promotion did come, he generously accredited it to their influence and for a time Ricci found himself in favour.

Translations were made of the Creed and the Our Father and these were well received, but still progress was almost unbearably slow. Their friend and protector was sent to another province; promotion for Wang P'an spelt disaster for the Jesuits. For although the next governor of the province was friendly his successor was not and they were ordered to return to Macao.

Protestations were useless. Packing up their few belongings they departed, only to get as far as Canton before being recalled. The mandarin, fearing that he had gone too far, recalled them on a

Presenting the great clock with Chinese characters and huge weights to the Emperor

pretext that he wished to make them a present of money for their journey westwards. Ricci refused the money, insisted that they desired to stay in the Middle Kingdom permanently, and the mandarin at length gave them permits to travel further inland, out of his province.

At the end of ten years, Ricci reviewed the position. Ruggieri on a second journey to Macao had not returned; the Provincial had decided that he was never likely to make headway with the language. Instead, a young Portuguese, Antonio de Almeida, was sent to replace him. He accompanied Ricci to Shuichow; but died from malaria in their second year there. Almeida's death was a severe blow to Ricci, but he carried on, more determined than ever to find a way to reach the heart of China.

As bonzes, holy men, they had been treated almost invariably with scorn and suspicion. He began to realise that the guise of the humble grey robe of the Bonze was not one likely to win him

success. Daringly he resolved to become a graduate, to meet the mandarins on their terms.

The graduates were the élite of China; they were accepted everywhere, and on receiving approval from his Provincial, Ricci threw away his rags; he dressed himself in the purple silk robe of a graduate and put on his head the square black hat which all graduates wore.

Now his ambition to reach the Emperor himself seemed more likely to be realised. His feats of memory impressed the officials so much that they were willing to further his petitions. Gifts suitable to present at the Imperial Palace arrived. Magnificent clocks, prisms and paintings reached Nanchang where he was now stationed.

Months passed, months when Ricci himself was on the point of death from fever, when he was imprisoned by a greedy, unscrupulous Minister who hoped to keep for himself the magnificent presents. Peking, the Forbidden City, seemed as out of reach as the stars which shone down on the pagodas, the paddy fields and the canals.

Surrounded by intrigue, Ricci almost despaired; to enter the Forbidden City the Emperor himself must give permission. The Emperor, however, could be as curious as a mandarin; news of the striking clocks had stirred his imagination. He ordered the foreigners to come to Peking. Ricci was jubilant, a jubilation which Lazzaro Cattaneo, successor to Antonio, shared. Only when they realised that the Emperor was surrounded by an army of eunuchs numbering ten thousand, did they begin to see that to gain access to the palace would require more than diplomacy and patience; only the intervention of Divine Providence would make it possible.

Contrary to the gloomy predictions of their friends, the Emperor received the gifts and with them the Petition which Ricci had composed. In particular the large clock with its huge weights and Chinese characters had merited imperial approval; the little clock the Emperor kept close to him ordering that two of his eunuchs should wind it daily lest it run down.

But still, the missionaries were no closer to entering the palace itself, and what they heard of Wan Li the Emperor was discouraging; cruel, lustful, swollen by pride and bloated with over-indulgence in eating, he was more monster than man.

And then . . . the big clock stopped; it would not strike, and none of the court officials, the mathematicians and craftsmen imperially summoned, could mend it. Ricci was sent for. Once again his spirits rose, and fell again when although he mended the clock he was not permitted to speak on the subject close to his heart, religion.

But the Emperor's passion for the clocks ensured at last that they received deferential treatment and were allowed access to the palace.

The Emperor still refused to see them, but he ordered their portraits to be painted so that he might see what they

Before the empty throne of the invisible Emperor

The Catechism is printed in Chinese

looked like, and he asked questions about the Western world which the missionaries answered by sending pictures and engravings.

Nothing compares with the stark drama of the moment when at last Ricci was summoned to appear before the Emperor, only to find himself addressing an empty throne. "The Son of Heaven," as the Emperor was called, had chosen to remain invisible.

To remain in Peking became increasingly dangerous and difficult. As long as the clocks were working, the Emperor no longer desired the missionaries to visit the palace. On the other hand, the Ministers, jealous of the foreigners, were constantly conspiring to bring them into disrepute. It required all Ricci's faith and courage to accept what was virtually imprisonment. He appealed once again directly to the Emperor for a permit to stay permanently in Peking. There was no answer, but fortunately the clock once

again went wrong, and Ricci after repairing it, was ordered to regulate it four times a year.

With the help of Diego Pantoja, a young Spaniard who had joined him at the beginning of the century, and who was already fluent in Chinese, Ricci at last began to make some headway among the scholars and men of influence. Their first and most brilliant convert was Li Yingshih, a soldier and mathematician. But as their converts increased, the Buddhists marshalled their forces against them. When it seemed likely that the Buddhists would succeed in getting them expelled from the capital, one of their leading members fell into disgrace with the Emperor, and the whole religion was discredited.

Ricci chose that moment to print his Catechism which had taken him nine years to prepare. In compiling it, he had identified himself with the Chinese mind, using images which would be readily understandable, and yet never for a moment disguising the purity of his Faith. The graduates accepted it, and it was widely read and appreciated by the mandarins.

During the next few years Ricci published a number of books all setting forth the Christian doctrine; he met the finest scholars of the country on their own ground, matching argument for argument. His learning, his indomitable courage and industry can scarcely be appreciated.

The mission house in Peking became a permanency, with three missionary priests, and two Chinese novices. The number of converts in Peking was two hundred, in China well over a thousand. Compared to the numbers Francis Xavier had brought to Christ in Japan the result was small, but Ricci had been faced with obstacles which had been considered by the whole Western world as insurmountable.

The year 1604 was memorable for two things. In the summer the River Pai Ho, no longer a river, but a seething mass of turbulent water, swept into the capital. When the floods subsided there was little left to feed the stricken people. Hundreds had been drowned, thousands were now dying from famine and plague. The missionaries spent most of that summer nursing the plague victims, and caring for children and old people deserted by their families.

That summer too, when the worst of the floods were over, there arrived an eight-volume Bible from Rome so magnificently conceived and bound that to gaze upon it was to receive conviction! That at least was how Ricci's converts felt, and Ricci himself was no less pleased.

In the years which followed Ricci became more and more respected and honoured in Peking. His influence directly affected the lives of many of the graduates and intellectuals. His tall figure, in its purple robe, his impressive height and even more impressive curling

Working among the flood victims of the River Pai Ho

beard were a familiar sight in the streets. As Doctor Li, Matthew won the affections not only of the intellectuals but of the poor peasants.

And yet there were times when he saw himself as little better than a prisoner; an exalted prisoner it is true, high in favour with the Emperor whose face he had not yet seen, but trapped in the capital as securely as if he had been placed behind iron bars.

In 1609, though still comparatively young (he was fifty-six) he realised with something like dismay that his span was running out. Already his hair was snow-white, he suffered from terrible headaches; he felt old and tired. And so he set himself to record the happenings over the past twenty-seven years. Methodically and without exaggeration he set down in diary form an exact account of all that had happened to him. His writings filled five books, and on their completion Matthew began to make preparations for his death.

Sick and tired as he was, he refused to make his illness an excuse for not receiving visitors, and they crowded in on him—many thousands over the next few months, and to them all Ricci gave the same kindly rapt attention so endearing to them and so exhausting to himself.

The end came swiftly. On May 3 the following year he was too ill to leave the mission house. On May 11, after receiving Extreme Unction the evening before, he died.

Astonishing was the manner of his life, no less astonishing was the manner of his death and last resting place, for the Emperor, contrary to every expectation, approved the burial of Ricci by the missionaries on land which he gave them outside Peking. And it was done as the Emperor decreed and on the plaque were engraved the words: "To one who loved righteousness and wrote books."

Years passed; a hundred years. . . . China was made accessible to missionaries, but Ricci's methods and advice were forgotten; the Emperor and mandarins were angered and offended by the direct approach. For many, many years the doors were closed again.

Compelled by threat of invasion and humiliated by one overwhelming defeat, China at the beginning of the present century turned to the West, at the same time lifting her ban against missionaries.

The first half of the present century has gone, and so fiercely has the pendulum swung in the other direction, that China is closed to the Gospel of Christ more violently than ever.

Father Ricci would be strangely out of place in the new Communist-controlled country of today; he would look in vain for the bonzes, the mandarins, the graduates.

All is changed. But the writings of one Doctor Li, the Western, have not changed, and the spirit of the Chinese Christian convert does not differ from other martyrs of the Church, nor does the manner of his death.

Ricci himself never saw his mission as a heart-breaking failure; he believed that after his death, the seed sown would blossom and bear fruit. And in China today there are men and women who are living testimonies to this belief. In God's good time they will be justified.

Explorers and priests arriving in North America

Blackrobes and Redskins

The wagon train is making its last stand. In ever narrowing circles the Redskins on their wiry mustangs draw closer and closer, shooting their deadly arrows as they gallop. The air is shrill with their war-cries—and then, when all, it seems, is lost, and the palefaces have fired the last of their bullets, a solitary scout, mounted on a magnificent horse, appears on the horizon. Behind him—white troops.

Now the Redskins change their cries; the covered wagons are alight, but the paleface scalps are safe. Wheeling their ponies about they scatter across the plains, making for the safety of their villages where only the women and the old men and the fat brown babies are waiting to welcome them. . . .

Yes, it's all strangely exciting and even romantic—in a film or a book, but we don't often ask ourselves—do we—

what were they really like, these Redskins? What was life in a wigwam like? Who were the white men, the palefaces, who first made close contact with these bloodthirsty savages?

In the days when Cavaliers and Roundheads were fighting the Civil War in England, the vast prairies of North America were still the hunting-ground of the Indians. It was in those days that eight courageous men from France lived and died among those Indians. They were missionaries of the Church—with only one idea in their hearts—to take the knowledge of Jesus Christ to the Redskins.

There are not any descriptions of martyrdoms written by the martyrs themselves. The reason is clear: dead men tell no tales. But Saint Isaac Jogues did write an account of his earlier sufferings, because he survived them.

When you have read what he wrote, you will be amazed that he did not die; you will be even more amazed that having got away, he had the courage to return to face it all again. You will agree that if ever a man deserved the martyr's crown it was he. You will be almost glad to know that he was killed by the Redskins in the end, and is fully and truly a martyr-saint.

Here is a passage from his letter:

". . . What I suffered, is known to One for Whose Love and cause it is a pleasant and glorious thing to suffer. Finally, moved by a cruel mercy—wishing to conduct me alive to their country, they ceased beating me and conducted me, half dead, to the stage . . . all bleeding from the blows they had given me, especially in the face . . . then they loaded me with a thousand insults and with new blows. They burned one of my fingers and crushed another with their teeth. . . ."

Impossible to believe that a man who had suffered so much—many of his tortures were too terrible to repeat here —could have gone back.

Saint Isaac Jogues was canonised by Pope Pius XI in 1930 with seven fellow-martyrs. All of them were killed by Redskins, Indians of North America. Six of them were "Blackrobes," as the Indians called them; they were Jesuit priests. Two of them were laymen, one of them a doctor: all had devoted themselves to the work of helping the Jesuits to win the Indians for Jesus Christ.

These eight men, all Frenchmen, were in at the very beginnings of the exploration of North America, and rightly are they looked upon now by Catholics as patron saints of that new land.

Some of them were martyred in what is now Canada, some in places that are now in the United States. Their story is one of stark and glorious heroism. It is a shining proof of the truly apostolic and missionary Spirit of the Church. Not for any earthly gain, hardly with any hope of even spiritual success, they spent their lives on the Indians. Every day was a living martyrdom, and even the frightful deaths they died were only the final anguish of a long-drawn-out agony.

Their stories have no chapters. There were no great events to make chapters. They simply lived, day by day, in imminent peril of death, and at length were killed. Their achievements were that they baptised dying babies and some grown-ups, who were on the point of death. They built nothing, established nothing. They only shed their blood to be the seed of the Church.

These Jesuit Martyrs were not the first white men to land in North America. A hundred years before this, Jacques Cartier, a Frenchman and a brave explorer, had planted the Cross (in 1535) where Quebec now stands. Although his real business was exploring, he said that he wished "to make known the sacred name of God and our Holy Mother the Catholic Church." Though Cartier made four voyages to North America and suffered many hardships, no colony was founded until sixty years after his death.

Hardy fishermen and fur-traders from Brittany and Normandy sailed to North America, but they did not settle, and it was not until 1603 that France made serious efforts to found a colony in the "new France." In 1607 the English settled in Virginia. In 1609 Hudson was in New York Bay. In 1614 the Dutch were on Manhattan. During these early years of the century nothing, it seemed, could hold back the explorers who were for ever seeking fresh lands to discover, and encouraged by their nations, they included priests and chaplains in their ships' crews.

The French colony with which we are

Teaching the Love of God to the Huron Indians

concerned was at Port Royal, in Acadia, and there in 1608 two Jesuit priests were sent, and two more followed in 1613.

This early party of Jesuits were hindered in their work, even by their fellow Frenchmen, and the English from Virginia broke up the French colony in Acadia.

Nevertheless the work went on. This was largely due to a great man, whose name is linked with the birth of the Canadian nation. This was Samuel Champlain. He had gone with the first colonisers in 1603, had seen how much religion is hampered when missionary work is made to serve the purposes of trade, and yet—though not a priest—he still longed to bring the Faith to the Indians.

He urged that missionaries should be sent to New France—and that they should be provided with enough money to set up a mission station which would be independent of the traders.

In 1618 three Franciscan Friars, Friars Jamet, Le Caron and Dolbeau set out for Montreal; they were going to work among the Algonquin Indians. These Indians were a roving people, ranging over the land from the coast to what we now call the Middle West, and as far north as Hudson Bay. Further away lived the Hurons, and they were, by comparison, a stay-at-home tribe living in their villages, and going abroad simply for hunting or making war on neighbouring tribes.

The Indians, including tribes like the Iroquois and Hurons, numbered over three hundred thousand, and of these about thirty thousand were settled. The missionaries pinned all their hopes on the settled tribes, realising how difficult it would be to attempt to teach nomadic tribes.

Friar Le Caron decided that he would try to teach the Hurons something of the love of God. Day in and day out he endeavoured to show them by reason and example what the faith meant, but the Hurons were a wicked, thieving and brutally cruel tribe; they worshipped a demon and made sacrifices to it, and they believed in black magic and were under the influence of sorcerers or witch doctors.

Friar Le Caron made no progress among them even although he had the help of Samuel Champlain for some months. He did not despair, but returned to France to persuade more Franciscan Friars to join the mission, and then in 1625 they called on the Jesuits to help them.

Three Jesuits came, just in time to meet the Indian traders who had murdered Friar Viel at Sault-au-Recollet. One of these three Jesuits was John de Brébeuf. He was a Norman, from near Lisieux, where the Little Flower lived. One of his ancestors had fought with William the Conqueror at Hastings, and probably through him St. John de Brébeuf is connected with the noble English family of whom Philip Howard, Duke of Norfolk, the martyr, was one.

John de Brébeuf when he became a Jesuit at the age of twenty-four was almost an invalid; then the most wonderful thing happened; once out on the mission he began to grow. He grew so big and strong that he was given the name "the Giant of God." He was so massive that the Indians were afraid to carry him in their canoes in case his great weight should sink them.

He could carry heavier loads even than the Indians and outstrip them in endurance tests and soon he became known as the lion of the Huron mission.

About ninety miles north of Toronto, there is a Shrine called the Martyrs' Shrine; nearby is the place where the Jesuit Fathers built their mission station in 1639. In the church itself you can see a picture showing the terrible tortures which the Indians inflicted on Father Brébeuf and Father Lalemant.

You can see too a little cabin which is built exactly as Father Brébeuf described it when he wrote about his life among the Indians. Here are his own words:

". . . Imagine a great ring or square in the snow, two, three or four feet deep according to the weather . . . the depth of snow makes a white wall for us, which surrounds us on all sides, except the end where it is broken through to form the door. The framework . . . twenty or thirty poles is planted upon the snow, then they throw upon these poles, which converge a little at the top, two or three rolls of bark sewed together beginning at the bottom . . . and behold, the house is made. You cannot stand upright as much on account of the low roof as the suffocating smoke and you must always lie down, or sit flat upon the ground. . . . A little place like their cabins is easily heated by a good fire, which sometimes roasted and broiled me on all sides. . . . But, as to the smoke I confess to you that it almost killed me and made me weep continually . . . I sometimes thought I was going blind; my eyes burned like fire. . . ."

And besides this terrible torture of the wigwams, there was hunger. The Indian food was so filthy that Brébeuf could not touch it; and ended up by eating the skins of eels which he had used to patch his cloth gown. In order to keep alive he tells us: "I even ate old moose skins, . . . and I went about through the woods biting the ends of the branches and gnawing the more tender bark. . . ."

The missionaries found the savages unbelievably cruel, greedy and conceited. Cheating and stealing were natural to them, and they were proud of their wicked ways. Their greed, too, was a frightening thing because it revealed how little they were prepared to discipline themselves.

One day a small group of Indians had

A Huron village burnt down by the savage Iroquois

a feast. Here is what they consumed, all at one sitting too: 30 mallard; 20 teal duck and other game; 50 Canada geese; 2 barrels of peas; 1 barrel of sea-biscuits; 20 lb. of prunes; 6 baskets of Indian corn. They gorged themselves until they collapsed. No wonder the missionaries viewed their task of converting the Redskins as likely to be a long and difficult one. But they had no thought of giving up.

The Fathers failed almost entirely to win the confidence of the Hurons. Terrified most of the time by the threat of their bitterest enemy, the Iroquois, who hated them and who would swoop down on their villages without warning, the Hurons were ready to sacrifice the Blackrobes at a moment's notice in order to save their own skins.

Almost daily the missionaries expected death, and prepared for it with fearless, cheerful courage. The first of the group to die was René Goupil, the devoted surgeon, who was murdered by the Iroquois in 1642.

Four years later, in 1646, Father Isaac Jogues, the missionary who had once been tortured and mutilated beyond description and yet went back to the mission, was finally martyred with his lay companion.

At the very beginning of this story of the Jesuit Martyrs of North America, we used Father Jogues' own words to describe some of the tortures he endured. In another of his earlier letters which bears the name of a Mohawk village, he describes his life among one of the fiercest Indian tribes in the east, the Iroquois, whose hatred of the Hurons was equalled only by their hatred for the French and the Blackrobes.

Father Jogues wrote his letter in Latin. In it he told of his capture, how the Iroquois, seventy of them, in twelve canoes which they had concealed in the long grass and woods, "suddenly surrounded us and fired their arquebuses. . . ." Terrified, the Huron guides abandoned their canoes and fled, leaving the white men, with a handful of

Insensible to the horrors heaped upon them Brébeuf and Lalemant are burned by the Indians

baptised Indians and catechumens, to their fate.

The savages took the priest back to their village. They made him their slave, and in time Jogues was given a certain amount of licence. He was able to build himself an oratory where he spent time in prayer. He was able to comfort the prisoners whom the Mohawks brought back with them from their raiding expeditions; sometimes he was permitted to baptise them before they were killed.

It was almost with reluctance that Father Jogues at last accepted an opportunity to escape. Once safely back in France he was acclaimed a martyr, but he could not forget his Hurons or his Iroquois and Mohawks, and so he returned . . . to final martyrdom.

In 1648 Father Anthony Daniel was tortured and murdered at the mission station of St. Joseph in Huronia. It was Daniel who had first taught the Indian children the Our Father, and who had for the Hurons a kind of fatherly affection which made him hope great things

for their future . . . especially as he counted among his friends the small children.

That year and the next, the Iroquois were on the warpath. The Fathers knew that nothing could stop the scalp-hungry Redskins. They knew what awaited them if they stayed on, and yet not one of them dreamed of going back.

On March 16, 1649, the Iroquois swooped down on the village where Fathers Brébeuf and Lalemant were stationed.

Here is an account of how these two brave men met their end: it was written very shortly afterwards by another missionary Jesuit, who sent it to the Superior of his Order in Quebec:

". . . having had certain news, through some escaped captives, of the deaths of Father Jean de Brébeuf and of Father Gabriel Lalemant, we sent one of our Fathers and seven other Frenchmen to seek their bodies at the place of their torture. They found there a spectacle of horror—the remains of cruelty itself or rather the relics of the love of God, which alone triumphs in the death of martyrs. . . . As soon as they were taken captive, they were stripped naked, and some of their nails torn out; and the welcome which they received upon entering the village of St. Ignace was a hailstorm of blows with sticks . . . no part of their bodies which did not then endure its torment. . . ."

Then follows a wonderfully moving account of the great giant of a man, Brébeuf who "being overwhelmed under the burden of these blows," and yet still conscious enough to see that among the prisoners were some Christians, Indians of his village whom he had only lately baptised, called out to them: "Let us lift our eyes to heaven. Let us die in this faith . . . I have more pity for you than for myself. . . ."

And the response of his few faithful converts so incensed the Iroquois that they attacked them afresh. New tortures were quickly devised; a necklet of red hot hatchets was slung about their necks; their hands were cut off . . . and Father Brébeuf "suffered like a rock, insensible to the fires and flames, without uttering any cry . . . which astonished his executioners." Both Fathers died asking God to forgive their murderers.

Father Charles Garnier, one of the last of the missionaries to die, was alone in his mission village that same year, when a band of raiding Iroquois appeared at its gates. The savages put to death immediately all they encountered. They threw the babies on the fire, murdered their mothers. Some of the Christian Indians begged their priest to escape with them if he could. But Father Garnier refused to save himself. Instead he remained in the village, baptising, giving absolution, comforting the children. A bullet fired from a musket brought him to the ground, another fatally wounded him. Dying, he struggled somehow to his feet in an effort to reach one of his flock. Then

As he struggles to get up Father Garnier is finally struck down by hatchet blows

two blows from a hatchet brought the end.

Absent from the village at the time of the raid, Father Noel Chabanel, the missionary companion of Father Garnier, escaped the murderous attack of the Iroquois only to be killed by a Huron apostate. Father Chabanel had made a vow to remain until death among the Hurons, and perhaps life for him among them was harder than for the other missionaries. For one thing, he never managed to master the language; he could not make himself understood even over the most everyday subjects. And unlike Father Daniel and Brébeuf and the others, he saw nothing in the Indians to attract him. He could not get used to the food they ate, and suffered agonies in trying to adapt himself to their wigwams. God, it seemed, gave him no comfort—only the unswerving determination to stay for ever on the Cross until death released him.

A story without chapters, without headlines; a story of eight brave men who gave their lives to bring Jesus to the Indians; a story as thrilling as any Western. The story of a failure also it seemed. But the blood of the martyrs is the seed of the Church, and today a hundred thousand pilgrims come each year to the Martyrs' Shrine, the living witness of their triumph.

SAINTS OF THE NEW WORLD

Rose of Lima, Martin de Porres, and Mother Seton

A land of gold—desperately in need of saints—and within the span of a man's lifetime, it was granted two. The conquest of the New World by Spain is paralleled by the conquest of the Indies by Portugal.

Both countries at the instigation of their rulers sent missionaries with the first invading parties. Prince Henry of Navarre, whose passion was the sea and the discovery of uncharted lands, insisted always that his ships should carry missionaries, and the first white men to land on the coast of Gambia in 1438 were missionaries from Portugal.

A generation later we find Vasco da Gama, one of the greatest of Portuguese explorers, setting out for the East, and taking with him, as a matter of course, missionaries. Conquest of the East brought both shame and glory to Portugal. Conquest of the New World by Spain tarnished practically all those who took part in it, for few men could resist the lure of gold. In both Mexico and Peru there was gold for the asking. Little wonder that the New World was called the "land of gold." Little wonder too that saints were needed to turn men's thoughts away from the sins of avarice and cruelty into which their greed for it led them.

Two saints of the New World were born within ten years of each other, in the same city, Lima, capital of Peru. Isabella de Flores, afterwards named Rose because of her beauty, was born in 1585. Martin de Porres, whose father was a high-born Spaniard, and his mother a negro freed woman, was born in 1579.

There is nothing to tell us if they ever met, but Rose may have seen Brother Martin going into one of the hospitals where he worked. They may have passed each other in the street when Rose on rare occasions was almost forcibly "taken out" by her family, on a round of social calls.

As children, both suffered scoldings and blows from their mothers, but we

Rose of Lima at her embroidery

must not blame the mothers too much. It could not have been easy to be the mother of Rose, for what normal, pretty little girl wants to spend half the day and night talking to God in a tiny wooden shelter at the bottom of the garden? And it was certainly not easy for Martin's mother. For one thing her merry little son with his light-coloured skin and bright eyes reminded her all too often of the gay Spaniard nobleman who had come into her life for a short time, and then disappeared leaving her almost penniless and with children to feed and clothe. For another thing, the boy was so generous. Every penny he managed to earn or save, he wanted to give away to the first beggar he met. And why did he keep on and on about the poor people he saw in the streets; why didn't he play and tease and fight like other boys. . . . All the same—sometimes Martin's mother would smile to herself over her wash-tub—he was a good little boy, and quick at his lessons—there was no denying.

Martin had a sister; Rose had several brothers, one of whom, called Ferdinando, was her favourite, and perhaps he understood her best. At any rate, it was he who helped her to build a kind of cell in the garden so that she could talk to Jesus.

But sometimes, even the best of brothers can tease, and one never-to-be-forgotten day, Ferdinando managed to make his little sister furiously angry; he rubbed sand into her beautiful long hair, and the gentle Rose losing all her calm, struck out wildly. Any little girl who was proud of the beauty of her long glossy curls would have done just the same. Ferdinando made matters worse by suddenly, after the storm had passed, asking her why she minded so much. If you are going to be so very holy, he as good as said, you shouldn't bother about your hair, which is just going to attract a lot of attention and make people admire you. . . .

Rose reacted quickly and violently.

She grabbed her mother's scissors and before Ferdinando could stop her, sheared off all her lovely curls.

She was only a very little girl then! Even so, she knew just exactly what she was going to do, and be. For fifteen years or more she endured a great many taunts and much harsh treatment from those nearest to her, who might have been expected to understand. Yet when we read about the kind of life Rose deliberately set out to lead, we can sympathise with her mother and friends who found her so puzzling.

Martin's young life was divided into two almost equal parts. The first part was spent with his mother at home. They lived in the poorest part of Lima, and how to feed and clothe her children from day to day, was a problem which his mother (her name was Anna Velasquez) solved in part by taking in washing. But they were always desperately poor, and often hungry.

The second part belonged to the realms of fairy princes and magic wands. Into Martin's life suddenly stepped his handsome, rich father—the Spanish lord.

Anna must have been glad that he should take an interest in the children and when he said he was going to take Martin and his sister back with him to Ecuador, and see that Martin was taught to read and write, she would not try to stop him. Perhaps he did not even ask her consent. She would not expect him to; she had only to look around and see the pitiful state of the Negroes and Indians everywhere.

Hundreds of thousands had been forced into slavery by the white man. Mulattoes, like Martin himself, boys of mixed blood, were sold in the market places, and then sometimes worked so hard that they died when still young. Even the missionaries, the Jesuits and the Dominicans, could not stem the flood of wickedness which was drowning all that was good in life.

And so she let the children go, and Martin was with his father for two years until he was ten. He was apprenticed then to a barber-surgeon in Lima; a man who was both haircutter and doctor. There was plenty of work; plenty of chances of helping the poor; plenty of opportunities for revealing that wonderful tender humility and charity, which conquered the heart of Lima, as it finally conquered the world.

But if Martin plunged himself into the throbbing heart of Lima, Rose did just the opposite. For her, solitude was everything. This desire to be alone, never to have visitors or go visiting, was quite disastrous from her poor mother's point of view. The family fortunes were getting very low; Rose could save them all, if only she would consent to see and be seen. There were dozens of eligible, well-to-do young men only too willing to ask for her hand in marriage. But if Rose would not even glance at them; if indeed, she even went so far as to rub pepper in her eyes in order to disfigure herself, and plunge her fine white hands into lime, in case they were too much admired, what then?

What then indeed!

Determined that her family should not suffer because she rejected the rich suitors, Rose worked long hours at embroidery; her work fetched a good price from the society ladies of Lima, for it was most exquisitely executed. While she worked she prayed, and work and prayer became one; a perfect offering to lay at the feet of her Lord.

Finally, Rose joined the Third Order of the Dominicans, adopting, as many pious women of the day adopted, the rough brown robe of the tertiary. On her head she wore a thin circle of silver. This band was studded on the inside with sharp nails which would recall, in case

Martin among the slum dwellers of Lima

she should ever forget, the sufferings of Jesus when he wore his crown of thorns.

Up to three years of her death at the age of thirty-one, Rose lived in a little cell at the bottom of her parents' garden. Finding that neither entreaties nor threats nor ill-treatment were of any avail, her mother grew resigned, and Rose, whose face would light up as if she were consumed by an inward fire when in the presence of the Blessed Sacrament, was left almost entirely alone.

Her last three years on earth were spent under the roof of a kindly well-to-do couple who gave her the hospitality of their home, but many of her visions came to her while she was alone in her cell. There, her thirst for suffering led her to undertake penances which startled and horrified those who heard about them, and some of them may have contributed to her last mysterious illness which brought her great pain, a pain which she welcomed with the prayer: "Lord, increase my sufferings, and with them increase thy love in my heart."

It was a prayer which Martin de Porres would well have understood, one, indeed, which he understood with the humility of a saint. By the age of fifteen he had given himself, quite literally, to God. There was no bitterness in his great, generous heart that he was the son of a slave, a mulatto, one of the despised.

He did not become a Dominican friar, but a tertiary, eager to be at the service not only of the friars, but the whole of the sick and suffering humanity of Lima.

The Dominican Priory of the Holy Rosary at Lima was magnificent in its spaciousness, for it was one of the finest and biggest in the New World, and there was ample opportunity for Martin to put his ideal of service and love into practice. Most of the priories of the New World were rich, and many of the friars were influenced by the power of gold. They had come with the conquering army, and if, to begin with, their missionary zeal was uppermost, all too soon it began to fade amidst the luxury and easy living which the Spaniards in America regarded as their right.

Some of the priories maintained large groups of slaves, all of them enjoyed the revenues from land given to the priories by the Spanish Government. Many of the friars themselves were seen abroad in the rich, colourful dress of the Spanish nobility.

Martin changed the priory. To begin with the friars could not believe in him; his charity, his sweetness, his utter obedience and humility all seemed too good to be true. Could a mulatto love almost like Christ himself? It seemed that he could. Martin never for a moment saw himself as sent there to revolutionise the lives of the friars or the people he served in the hospitals. He said he was the least and most unimportant of men, and he believed it so sincerely that he did not even consider himself worthy to wear the white tunic of the Dominican tertiary.

Officially his work was in the Infirmary of the priory; Negroes, Indians, Spaniards—all types and conditions of men came under his care. Martin loved them all equally and with a passionate tenderness. Every minute of his day was filled, and yet he found time to do more. He knew better than anyone where to find suffering and terrible poverty, and he found it in Lima's slums . . . homeless children came to him and he found them homes; mothers begged him for food and clothes for their babies, and somehow Martin obtained them.

Night after night he sat beside some man or woman in pain, and his very presence brought them comfort and hope in God's mercy.

High-born Spaniards came to him seeking advice, down-and-out negroes and mulattoes talked freely to him. He had a strange and wonderful power over animals, and there are accounts of

how miraculously he appeared in two places at once.

He shared with Rose that thirst for penance which drew from his Prior something like remonstrance. He hardly slept at all, and when he did lie down to rest it was on the stone floor of his bare cell; he fasted continuously, wore a hair shirt, and nightly scourged himself. Yet, though he treated himself as the cruellest of slave owners would treat his slaves, he was the most gentle of nurses, the most tender of friends.

The wonder of his life in that "land of gold" was not the frequency of the miracles which occurred at his intervention, but the power it had to unite all men, no matter what caste or creed, under the banner of Christ, his King.

He died on November 3, 1639, at the Holy Rosary Priory. Twenty-two years before, in the August of 1617, Rose, the first canonised saint of the New World and patroness of South America, had died, and the streets of Lima were crowded then with sorrowing, devoted citizens, as her body was taken to the church. And so it was with Martin. Beggars and slaves mingled with Spanish nobles and the highest dignitaries of the Church to give honour to Martin, the humble, smiling Dominican lay brother whom in life they knew as their friend, and in death as a friend of God.

Martin was canonised by Pope John XXIII in 1962. A few months later in March 1963 the Vatican Basilica was thronged once more, when the same Pope enrolled among the Blessed a third person of the New World, Elizabeth Ann Bayley Seton, who is the first native-born citizen of the United States of America to be declared Blessed. Elizabeth Bayley was born in New York in 1774. Her father was a doctor, and the Bayley family was related to some of the great Dutch pioneer families which

11—III

had left Europe and settled in New York. Betty and her family belonged to the Episcopalian Church. She was a gay and pretty girl and loved dances and parties. At one of these parties she met a young man, William Seton; they fell in love, and in 1794, when Betty was nineteen years old, their marriage was the biggest social event of the year. After their marriage, William and Betty settled down in a fashionable house in New York. As the nineteenth century began, however, tragedy struck the happy family, because William's business failed and he fell seriously ill. His doctor advised him to go to Italy in 1803, as it was thought that the Italian climate would restore his health.

William and Betty went to Italy, but William's health grew rapidly worse, and he died, leaving Betty almost penniless and with five young children to care for. She was helped by a kindly Italian Catholic family, and the strength of their faith so impressed her that she, too, resolved to become a Catholic, and she was received into the Church in 1805. But when she returned to New York, her friends and relations would have nothing to do with her, because she was now a Catholic. In order to support herself and her children, Betty opened a boarding-house for schoolboys in New York, but it was not a success, and so she moved in 1808 to the more Catholic city of Baltimore, and set up a school for girls.

In the following year, Betty formed a religious community of women in Emmitsburg, Maryland, and gave it the name of the Sisters of Charity of St. Joseph. The community which she founded cared for the needs of orphans and destitute children, and also gave them a good Catholic education, so that Betty—who was now known as Mother Seton—was one of the founders of the great system of parochial schools which provide Catholic education for children throughout the length and breadth of America. Mother Seton had founded nine more houses of her Society by the time she died of tuberculosis in 1821. Before she died, she expressed a wish that her Society should be united with the other branches of the Sisters of Charity of St. Vincent de Paul, and this was done in 1850. In addition to the community which Mother Seton founded in Emmitsburg, five other religious congregations of Sisters of Charity in the United States look to her as their Mother and their Foundress. With eleven thousand members, they form the largest of the American orders of nuns. Their colleges and high schools for girls have earned great praise throughout the United States, and everywhere little Betty Seton is now honoured as the Blessed Elizabeth Ann Seton.

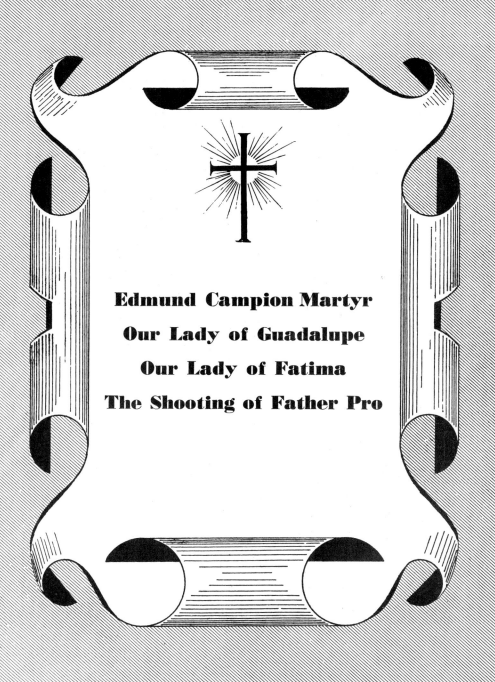

Edmund Campion Martyr

Our Lady of Guadalupe

Our Lady of Fatima

The Shooting of Father Pro

EDMUND CAMPION MARTYR

1. Edmund Campion lived when Elizabeth I was Queen of England. When he was at Oxford University the Queen came. He spoke before her and pleased her very much, Edmund, however, was unhappy, because Elizabeth had changed the religion of England from Catholic to Protestant, and he saw that this was wrong.

2. Campion fled, and in Rome joined the Society of Jesus. He wished to return to England to show the people that the old religion was the true one. So when the Pope asked for two Jesuits for this dangerous mission, Campion was chosen as one. Dressed as a merchant selling jewels, he landed once more in England.

3. The country was full of spies who were trying to catch the Jesuits, and arrest people who held to the Catholic Faith. Father Campion rode from one Catholic house to another, saying Mass secretly and preaching to little groups of Catholics. He went in disguise, sometimes escaping on horseback just in the nick of time.

4. Secretly, Campion set up a printing-press. He wrote the book called "Campion's Brag," and six men worked for nine weeks printing it, watching all the time for spies. In his "Brag" he gave Ten Reasons why the Catholic Faith was true and the Protestants wrong. Copies were spread round St. Mary's Church in Oxford, at dead of night.

5. Now the hunt was up! The whole country was searching for Campion who stopped at a house in Lyford. Forty Catholics gathered for Mass and to hear him preach. But there was a traitor in their midst! The Queen's men ringed the house round, searched it, broke the panel of a hiding-place and the Jesuit was caught.

6. Campion was tortured on the rack, his arms and legs almost torn from their sockets. He was tried in Westminster Hall, accused of plotting a rebellion against the Queen, and sentenced to death. He was tied to a hurdle and dragged through the London streets to Tyburn Tree. There he was hanged and cut to pieces.

OUR LADY OF GUADALUPE

1. More than four hundred years ago, in far-off Mexico, Juan Diego was hurrying down Tepeyac Hill. It was a Saturday in December, and he was going to Mass in Mexico City. Juan Diego was a poor Indian, fifty-five years old, and he had not long been a Christian. His country had been conquered by haughty Spaniards.

2. Suddenly he stopped. What was this? He could hardly believe his eyes. Before him stood a beautiful young woman. She was dressed like one of his own people. "Juan Diego," she said, "I am the Blessed Virgin Mary. I want you to go to Bishop Zumarraga. Tell him I want a church built, here on this spot."

3. Juan Diego was very frightened. He hardly dared to go to the palace of the great Spanish Bishop and tell him what he had seen and what the lady had said. But he went. The proud Spaniards laughed at him, but the Bishop was kind, and told him to go back and ask the Lady to give a sign to show that what he said was true.

4. Juan Diego had an uncle, and this uncle fell ill. So on the Monday Juan Diego was busy all day looking after him. Very early on the Tuesday morning he ran to fetch a priest, for he thought his uncle was dying. He went by a different way, because he did not want to meet the Lady. But she knew which way he was going, and there she stood.

5. "My son," she said, "what road are you taking? I will cure your uncle, but you must take my message again to the Bishop." Juan Diego said: "The Bishop asks you for a sign." "Go up that hill," replied the Lady. "You will find roses. Gather them." Juan Diego climbed the rocks, found the roses, and filled his cloak with them.

6. Juan Diego kept the roses hidden in his cloak. And came to the Bishop. Flinging back his cloak he let them fall. At once the Bishop and his court fell to their knees. Juan Diego looked at his cloak and on its lining saw a wonderful picture of our Lady of Guadalupe, gazing radiantly at them. The cloak is there in Mexico still.

OUR LADY OF FATIMA

1. "Do not be afraid. I am the Angel of Peace." Lucy, Francis and Jacinta see the angel messenger for the first time as they guard their parents' sheep in the Cova da Iria. The year is 1916. Francis and Jacinta are brother and sister. Lucy is their cousin. All three are devout children.

2. The children do not tell their parents of the angel's visits but the next year on May 13 the children see a beautiful Lady, brighter than the sun. The Lady asks them to come to the Cova six times in succession. Lucy's parents are furiously angry.

3. The villagers do not believe that the children have seen the Queen of Heaven. "Lies, all lies," they cry when Lucy and her cousins walk down the street. But the little Portuguese shepherd-children know that they must suffer and make sacrifices if the world is to be saved from war.

4. Lucy is brought before the officials. They question her about the appearance of this Lady. Lucy says over and over again. "She told us to pray, to say the rosary every day and to go to the Cova on the 13th of every month."

5. Now the children suffer persecution. They are put in prison and questioned hour after hour. They are very unhappy but they know this is something they have to suffer and they are determined to do what the Lady asked them.

6. In October Our Lady appeared and in the presence of thousands of people there happened the miracle of the sun when it "danced" before their eyes. "I am Our Lady of the Rosary," Lucy heard the Lady say, "and I desire a chapel in my honour. . . ." Today Fatima is one of the great places of pilgrimage.

THE SHOOTING OF FATHER PRO

1. Eagerly Miguel Pro listens to the training that will make him a priest. He has been driven out of his country, Mexico, by the men who have seized power, and are attacking the Catholic Church. Miguel has become a Jesuit and is studying in Europe. He is a gay young man, a mimic and a comic, and a great hand with a guitar.

2. It is the year 1925. In Mexico, under Calles, the persecution of the Church is growing very fierce. The Bishop's reply is to close all churches and order priests to withdraw. Meanwhile in Belgium, Miguel has been made a priest. But he is a sick man, and spends much time in hospitals having operations.

3. God's ways are strange. Miguel, the sick man, is summoned back to Mexico. At once he hurls himself into action; he preaches, gives retreats, hears confessions, attends the sick, the poor; always in disguise, under the very noses of the police who are hunting for him. All has to be done in secret. There are spies everywhere.

4. November 18, 1927. The police have got wind where Father Pro is. Before dawn they surround the house, force a way in and find where Miguel is sleeping, with Humberto his brother. "Stay where you are!" cries Basail the police-officer, covering them with his revolver. Miguel and his brother are taken to prison.

5. Of what are they accused? Three days before this, bombs had been thrown at General Obregon. The Pros had nothing to do with this. Father Miguel denies it solemnly. Humberto was playing tennis at the time. Although no trial takes place, the police assert that Father Pro and three others have confessed their guilt.

6. November 23. Troops mass at the Prefecture of Police. Generals in flashy cars arrive. A crowd collects. Pressmen with cameras are there. At ten o'clock Father Pro is led into the garden. He stands before the generals and the camera-men and the firing squad. "Long live Christ the King!" he cries, and the rifles reply.

YOUTH SAINTS

In the sixteenth century, it seemed God wanted to show that not only old people but also the young could do great things for his Kingdom. He showed this especially by raising up three Youth Saints.

All three lived in an age when the Church was torn by conflict, inside and out. Two, Stanislaus Kostka and Aloysius Gonzaga, were of aristocratic stock; the third, John Berchmans, was the son of a shoemaker, born over his father's shop in Diest. All three joined the Society of Jesus, that is, they became Jesuits.

Stanislaus Kostka

The father of Stanislaus was a senator of Poland, and Stanislaus was born in 1550 in the castle of Rostkovo. In the eighteen years he was destined to live he achieved sanctity. He died in 1568, the year Aloysius was born. Stanislaus set his heart on becoming a priest from an early age.

The dream looked like bearing fruit when his father sent him to the Jesuit College at Vienna. He was only fourteen when he insisted that he wanted to enter the Order. But his father and his elder brother, Paul, had other ideas, and the Father Provincial of the Society dared not oppose the Senator who threatened to banish the Jesuits from Poland should they accept his son.

Paul made Stanislaus's life miserable with his taunts and ill-treatment, but never once did he shake his young brother's firm resolve to become a priest. But the strain told on Stanislaus, and he fell seriously ill. The two brothers were lodging in the house of a Lutheran, and this man would not let a Catholic priest come into the house, though the sick boy was longing for Holy Communion.

One night Bilinski, the tutor of the boys, was watching by the bedside of Stanislaus. Suddenly Stanislaus sat up, shook the tutor by the shoulder and cried out: "On your knees! See Saint

"On your knees! See Saint Barbara! She's coming into the room"

Barbara! She is coming into the room with two angels, and they are bringing me the Blessed Sacrament!" He knelt up in bed and though Bilinski saw nothing, Stanislau felt himself receive the Food of Angels, and then he lay down again.

Some days later he was suddenly cured of his illness. Our Lady appeared to him, bringing her baby Son. The kiss of Jesus healed him, and she told him to join the Society of Jesus.

Finally the boy decided to take a long walk—a very long walk—all the way to Rome, to persuade Father Francis Borgia to accept him. But first he resolved to make for Upper Germany where the Provincial, Father Peter Canisius, might help him. He was singularly ill-equipped for such an adventure. The distance was three hundred and fifty miles!

One morning in August 1567, after going to Mass and receiving Holy Communion, he slipped out of the town. Coming to a wood near the roadside he turned into it, and there pulling off his

coat he put on a peasant's rough canvas blouse. He fastened it round his waist with a piece of rope and on that he hung his rosary. A large, broad-brimmed peasant's hat completed his disguise.

Paul and Bilinski, frightened out of their wits at his disappearance, took carriage and horses and galloped after him next day. They drove for forty-five miles. They caught him up. They passed him. And they never saw him. Either his disguise was good, or God held their eyes!

At Dillingen he made contact with Father Peter Canisius, and that great man accepted him. He knew very well what he was doing, and how dangerous might be the storm against the Jesuits that the angry Polish nobleman might raise over his son. But he had seen Stanislaus, and he knew that here was no ordinary boy. It was Stanislaus himself who urged that he should be sent on to Rome, and the Father Provincial agreed. But first he kept him in the College, working as a common servant in the house, unknown, for about a month, treated as any scullion might be treated. Stanislaus stood up to this test too.

At last he was sent to Rome. There he was favourably received by the General of the Order, and at the age of seventeen, in 1567, he entered the novitiate. He had just one more year to live, one perfect year with his soul on fire with God's love. Then came sickness, a sickness which his frail strength could not overcome in the treacherous climate of Rome. He died just one month before his brother arrived on the scene. The shock of finding that Stanislaus was dead completely reformed Paul, and many years later he entered the Society of Jesus himself, at the age of sixty.

Aloysius Gonzaga

A few years after the death of Stanislaus Kostka, a little boy of about five years old was playing at soldiers. It was something more than play, for even at that early age his father had taken him in hand to begin his training as a soldier. He had all manner of toy weapons made for his small son, and dressed him in light armour, with cuirass and halberd, such as officers carried, and made him march beside him and stand while he reviewed his troops.

The boy was Aloysius Gonzaga, and his father was Marquis of Castiglione, a fortress town in Northern Italy, from whose citadel the rich Lombard plain and the Alps beyond could be seen. Ferrante Gonzaga, the Marquis, was at the time in the service of the King of Spain, and in charge of all the Italian infantry Spain could then control.

Aloysius was thrilled by his life among the soldiers, and especially by the gunpowder, which was then coming into use, and which went off with such a splendid bang when the men let him fire their muskets. One hot noon, while everyone was dozing, he stole some gunpowder from a soldier's flask, loaded a small cannon and fired it. His father, imagining a mutiny, leapt from his tent and ordered the instant arrest of the mutineers. His men sprang to obey and a few moments later the guard returned

Aloysius, the small prisoner, under arrest

Canons stacking their swords before entering St. Peter's

with one small prisoner under arrest! It was Aloysius.

Ferrante Gonzaga, while in Spain, had fallen in love with a maid of honour of Queen Isabel of Valois, wife of King Philip II of Spain. She was Donna Marta, the saintly woman who became the mother of Aloysius, and one of the strongest influences in his life.

Aloysius was born into a perilous world. An enormous menace brooded over Europe, the Turk, who threatened the very existence of Christendom. But Christendom was threatened even more by the appalling corruption within it. It was, indeed, such as we can scarcely imagine. Picture the Canons going into the great new basilica of St. Peter's to chant the divine office: see them pausing in the entrance to slip off their worldly costume and stack up their swords, watch them take them up again as they come out, and you will have a glimpse of how bad things were. In church men sang worldly songs to music that was far from sacred, while some few sang the proper words, but sang them to the worldly tunes. The Counter-Reformation had begun, but as yet it had made little difference.

Life in the splendid courts and palaces was like a nightmare. Side by side with refinement and culture and the brilliant art of the time, violence and murder, debauchery and licentiousness were rampant. It is necessary to bear all this in mind if we are to have a true idea of St. Aloysius.

That little boy who fired the cannon, and upset the ladies in the castle by shouting out rude swear-words he had picked up from the soldiers, without knowing what they meant, was a tough little boy. He might have grown up into a violent man, like his father. He might have become like any of the hundreds of vicious profligates who thronged the courts of Italy. Instead God called him to be one of the most sinless of saints, a lily growing on a slag-heap. We have to remember what he might have been, if we wish to understand this youth of steel, whom God called to be a patron of purity for youth.

Nor is that all. We have to remember Aloysius' father, Ferrante Gonzaga, Marquis of Castiglione, a Prince of the Roman Empire, a man who would brook resistance to his will less easily than a lion will be robbed of its prey. His heart was set on making of his eldest son, not only a soldier, but one of the greatest men of his day. The story of Aloysius' life is soon told: it was a titanic struggle between two mighty wills, that of the father and that of the son. But God was on the side of the son, calling him to sacrifice, and the will of God prevailed.

Aloysius was about ten years old when he discovered that saying prayers is not the only way to pray. He began to find deep satisfaction in thinking, that is in meditation. It would be wrong to imagine that he was just a timid little boy with a liking for quiet corners. Some of his letters to his father about this time, describing the fun they had, show how lively and boyish he was. He was with Don John, and the Princesses arrived with a number of dogs, "because they said they wanted to run the race of the cloak of the dogs." Everyone ran, he told his father; Lord John, the Princesses, and Aloysius and his brother, "and the fun lasted till evening." But Aloysius was discovering that God is sweeter than any fun, and in a few years he had reached heights of prayer seldom reached.

It was soon after this that he met St. Charles Borromeo, to whom he was related. Aloysius was twelve, but had not yet made his First Communion. St. Charles, the Cardinal, himself instructed him and gave him Holy Communion. From this time the boy began to feel strongly that life in a world that was so mined with dangers to the soul could not satisfy him, and he began to practise austerities that were heroic, and indeed extravagant. People protested, but Aloysius was a bit of a rhinoceros where criticism was concerned.

12—III

In the year 1581 the Empress Mary of Austria decided to go to Spain, where her brother Philip was king. She took with her all the Italian princes who owed allegiance to Spain, and among these were the Gonzagas of Castiglione. An interesting detail of this very interesting journey was that the Empress had as chaplain the very same Polish priest who had advised Stanislaus Kostka to run away from Vienna; and this priest had also known Blessed Edmund Campion in Vienna, so that Aloysius may well have heard all about what was going on in England at the time, under good Queen Bess, in the days of Tyburn Tree.

In Spain, Aloysius was in the very midst of the greatest grandeur of pomp and ceremony that even the sixteenth century knew. He was made a page of the first class, which meant that he attended the Heir Apparent and shared his studies with him. In that age of violence, bull-fights and wild-beast shows were common, and we hear of Aloysius watching once from the balcony of a house when a pain-crazed tiger leapt the barriers round the square and dashed into the house. The court-life of Spain was ruled by very stringent laws of etiquette, and it was from about this time that Aloysius formed the habit of keeping his eyes cast down. This caused people to misunderstand him and think that he was a prude, the very last thing that he was! He was studying hard in Spain, in spite of all the excitements, learning Spanish, doing mathematics and astronomy (which he liked) and using "the globes"—which meant, in fact, finding out about the amazing new worlds of the Indies, East and West, where the King, his patron, had such vast empires, but best of all, learning about God from philosophy. He was a very grown-up boy, even then, and his father trusted him with confidential business and everyone was impressed by his maturity and poise. But it was in his

Aloysius looking on as the mad tiger leaps the barrier

heart that the real growth was going on.

He had practically made up his mind that he would turn his back on the brilliant prospects before him. He did not want to be a priest, not simply that, because that would have meant that family influence would have got him high position, a cardinal's hat, rich revenues, and all the entanglements from which he wanted to cut loose. He wanted to be a religious, some kind of monk or friar or hermit. He was getting to know the Jesuits. He had a Jesuit confessor. He liked especially the fact that they made a vow not to accept any Church honours or dignities. Also they taught boys, and he liked boys and got on well with them.

Then on the feast of the Assumption, 1583, he went to Communion at the Jesuit church, and knelt to make his thanksgiving in front of a picture of Our Lady. As he knelt he suddenly knew for certain what he was to do: he was to be a Jesuit.

Even Aloysius, who was brave enough to pull the teeth out of a crocodile, shrank from giving the news to his father. He got his mother to give it. Ferrante Gonzaga, when he heard it, gave a one-man impersonation of an atom-bomb going off.

But he might as well have puffed his cheeks and tried to blow a Spanish galleon through the Straits of Gibraltar. Aloysius was his father's son, a chip of the old block, and tantrums did not move him. The Heir Apparent died suddenly of smallpox. Aloysius decided that that meant his job was ended, so going out for a walk with his young brother, and a taggle of attendants, he walked into a Jesuit house, sat down, and said he had come to stay, and the others could go home and tell his father.

The pressure brought to bear on Aloysius to make him change his mind was terrific. Even the King of Spain talked to him about it, though it does not appear that he tried to influence the young lad. But the Father General of the Franciscans, who was a Gonzaga, a

Bishop sent by the Duke of Mantua, an archpriest, a famous Franciscan preacher, and an array of uncles and important people in the family, were all marshalled to batter at his resolution. His father, who could not bear the thought of being—as he felt—disgraced in Spain by having his son walk out and leave him, ordered the whole family back to Italy, and Aloysius went with them. There he was sent on a grand tour of good-byes, his father hoping that all the flattery he would receive and the luxury he would enjoy might bend his will.

Ferrante Gonzaga was not a bad man. He did not want to keep his son from God. He was simply convinced, and with very good reason, that this brilliant young man could raise the family to heights of achievement, and would without a doubt become one of the leading figures in Europe. Why should he be allowed to throw all this away and become one of a set of dingy and insignificant clerics . . . even if he was going to be the General of the Jesuits one day, as everybody expected?

So the battle went on. It was necessary for Aloysius to abdicate, and the Emperor had to agree to the abdication. There were moves and counter-moves, delays and indecisions. Everyone in Castiglione knew what was afoot, and wherever Aloysius went he was surrounded by throngs of his people; they ran to doors and windows as he passed; they felt they would be abandoned if he left them, and when at length he did leave Castiglione, his carriage was followed by weeping crowds.

Ferrante had yielded to the irresistible conviction of his amazing son. "Aloysius," he said to him, "you have wounded me to the heart, because I love you and have always loved you, as you deserve. On you are fixed all my hopes, and my family's. But since God, as you tell me, calls you, I will not stop you. Go where you wish, and I give you my blessing."

To the Father-General of the Jesuits Ferrante wrote: "I am giving into your Reverence's hands the most precious thing that I possess in all the world."

On November 25, 1585, accompanied by the Patriarch of Jerusalem, at whose house he had stayed on arriving in Rome, and by the General of the Jesuits, Aloysius went to the house where

Of his simple room he says "this is my rest for ever and ever"

he was to begin his life as a Jesuit. There he said good-bye to his suite of servants, and amid many tears sent last messages home. Then the Rector took him to his room. Seeing it Aloysius exclaimed: "This is my rest for ever and ever—here will I dwell for I have chosen it." At last he was alone.

In 1587 he took his vows as a Jesuit. Of the years of training before and after this we need say little. In 1591 famine and plague struck Italy. Starving peasants poured into Rome. The hospitals, wretched places as they were, swarmed with victims. In the low and stifling wards, amid the frightful overcrowding, such organisation as there had been collapsed. It was terrifying to be in the midst of dying men going about naked through the hospitals and falling down dead on some corner of the stairs. Into this purgatory of stench and misery Aloysius persuaded his Superiors to let him go, continuing the works of charity he had devoted himself to. But he was weakened himself in health, and after lifting an infectious patient out of bed and attending to him, Aloysius himself was stricken down by the plague. That was in March. On June 20 he died. He was twenty-three years old. The glories of the great house of Gonzaga have faded, but this young man who thrust the world aside to follow Christ has made the name immortal. As Patron Saint of Students he is revered by the youth of every country and every century.

John Berchmans

Eight years passed, years during which the Church continued her desperate struggle with heresy, years which saw great masses of men drift away from her altogether. From the ranks of the high-born God had given to the world two great saints of youth; now he chose that a third should come from the common people.

At Diest, a village in Belgium, on March 15, 1599, John Berchmans was born. His father was no aristocrat, but a humble shoemaker who looked to his son for help as he grew older.

Unlike St. Stanislaus and St. Aloysius, who spent their boyhood days in castles and palaces, John grew up in a humble cottage, and there was nothing to mark him out as one of God's specially chosen, nothing, except his determination to become a priest.

He went to school at Diest for a time, but if it had not been for the kindly intervention of two of his aunts, he would have been forced to leave, for his father's circumstances worsened as he grew older. They were, in fact, badly off, and John counted himself fortunate when at thirteen, he found himself working for Canon John Froymont, who, in return for domestic service, helped him with his studies. The Canon ran a kind of boarding-house for young seminarians, and one of John's duties was to wait at table.

John spent four happy years in this way. No matter what duty he had to perform, whether it was sweeping, or washing up, or serving at the banquets which the Canon frequently held, he undertook them all with the same quiet efficiency and cheerfulness which impressed everybody in the Canon's household.

Meanwhile in Diest, his father was labouring to support his wife and four children. Times were hard and business was not good. As the time grew near for John's ordination, his father, Charles Berchmans, began to look forward to the time John would become a priest and be able to help them financially. There was good reason to hope that some of his son's influential friends would see to it that he obtained a good living.

But alas for his hopes! They were

John Berchmans and Bartel Penneman starting on their eight hundred miles journey

dashed to the ground when John announced that he wished to become a Jesuit. His father protested violently, but John, though desperately unhappy at his father's displeasure, persisted with a kind of stolid courage in his course, and when the Jesuits in 1615 opened a college at Mechlin, he seized his chance and entered.

Charles Berchmans came to Mechlin angry, and resolved to take his son home by force if necessary, but John stood firm, and finally he convinced his father that his true vocation lay in the Jesuit Order. On September 24, 1616, John entered the novitiate. He was seventeen, and from the first, he became the saint of little things. His work was his prayer. Everything he did, he did perfectly, for he was always conscious of being in God's presence.

To his great joy, he had only been a novice a few months, when his father, now a widower, decided he too wished to become a priest. He was too old to enter the Jesuit Order, but he was accepted by the sympathetic Archbishop of the Mechlin diocese and ordained in 1618. John was present at the ordination and served his father's first mass. Sorrow followed swiftly on joy when only six months later, his father died.

"Blessed be God. Now I can confidently say, 'Our Father who art in heaven.'"

St. Aloysius, whom John loved and revered, had used these words at his own father's death—John, consciously or unconsciously spoke them again, as he gazed with tear-filled eyes on his father. In the same month, September, his novitiate ended, and John pronounced his first vows.

He began his philosophical studies at Antwerp, but all unknown to him, the General of the Society had written to the Flemish provincial for "two men, outstanding in religious spirit and intelligence, one to study theology and the other philosophy," at the College in Rome.

John was chosen and with him another scholastic named Bartel Penneman. Together they set out, and in the true spirit of the Order took neither money nor provisions. It was an eight hundred miles journey and the young pair made the journey all the way on foot.

On his arrival at the Roman College, John was almost overwhelmed to find that he had been given the very room which, thirty-one years before, Aloysius Gonzaga had used. God, it is true, often treats his saints "rough," but every so often grants them a wonderfully unexpected and thrilling favour. John would not have exchanged his bare, shabby room for any other in the world.

Gay, interesting and interested, John fascinated the Italians, and soon made many friends among them. He learned the language quickly, and was able to act as a guide to visitors.

But he continued still to be the saint of little things, and of "the little way." Without seeming to, he put himself at the disposal of anybody who needed a service done. How he found time to become the brilliant student and lecturer, the skilled linguist and historian, re-mains something of a mystery. Had he lived . . . if only he had lived ! But God has a way of taking to himself souls so perfectly surrendered to his will.

No one knew the reason for his sudden fatal illness in the year 1621. Certainly he had strained himself to the uttermost for his brilliant results, and then had come the request that he should take part in a public disputation. He was tired out, he needed a rest, but it was not his habit to put himself first. In August the fever took hold of him and apparently he had no strength to resist. In one short week, on the 13th, he was dead.

Scarcely known outside his Order, after his death, his reputation for holiness swept through Germany and Italy . . . so great can the "little way" become if God himself is at the beginning and end of it.

THE CHURCH AND SCIENCE

Space-ships are the galleons of today. Boys of the modern age do not sit by the sea listening to old sailors telling them of adventures on the Spanish Main; they dream of stream-lined rockets, powered by atomic energy, coasting among the planets and exploring the distant stars.

This, and a great deal more, we owe to science. In every walk of life, scientists have changed our way of living. In commerce and industry, by mechanisation and automation, in transport and communication, in medicine, food, clothing, amenities, even in our amusements, they have altered the pace of the world. They have also, alas, let loose on us the horrors of scientific warfare. And what is worst of all, science has been made to fog men's understanding of God's purpose in creation.

The "Modern Age" began in the sixteenth century, and the New Learning helped to begin it. In that new learning, science as we know it now lay germinating, as an acorn lies in the mould, beginning to grow into an oak. True

Christians and devout Catholics had their share in that early growth, as we have seen. Although a fierce revolt against the Catholic Church was going on, men did not think of science as an enemy to religion. In the eighteenth century things changed.

The Age of Reason

The eighteenth century has been called the Age of Reason. It was the age of the French Revolution. That revolution was not political only. The men who laid the train of gunpowder which exploded in the violence and bloodshed of the Revolution were also in revolt against God. It was from that time that the false idea was spread about, suggesting that science and religion were in conflict with each other. This false idea has hung about, like a pea-soup fog, down to our own lifetime.

One way to dispel it is to make known the teaching of the Church. Another way is to show how large is the number of good Catholics who have played their part in the development of science. This is mainly what we wish to do in this chapter on the Church and Science.

The Catholic View of the Universe

The universe, as Catholics see it, is a wonderful well-ordered system, created by God, the all-seeing, the ever-present, the all-powerful. Science is the discovery by human minds of the laws that govern the universe. It is concerned with material things, and with such spiritual things as the soul of man which form part of the universe. By innumerable experiments and calculations, the scientist formulates theories to explain the universe, and marshals facts to prove or disprove his theories. But the universe is God's creation; things behave in the way they behave, because he makes them behave so, and our discovery of this, which we call Science, is simply a discovery of the wisdom of God. There can be no conflict between this and religion, for religion is concerned with what God has revealed to us about himself.

The Church values and appreciates the work of scientists. Whatever will better men's living-conditions will help them in their attitude towards religion; fear, poverty, squalor and misery are fertile grounds for the spread of such evil theories as atheistic communism. The Popes, especially in recent times, have constantly expressed their encouragement of true science, and Pius XII in particular has repeatedly surprised us all by the accuracy and range of his up-to-date knowledge of scientific discovery.

Scientists who were Catholics

A good reference-book, dealing with the history of science, will list the names of about eight thousand men prominent for their work in science. About eight hundred of these, or ten per cent, have been Catholics. It should be remem-

MARIN MERSENNE
Religieux de l'Ordre des Minimes Thologi
Philosophe et Mathematicien celebre né a
Oyse au Maine Mort a Paris 1648 âgé de 60 ans

Photo Mansell

Friar Mersenne who worked on sound

bered that the advance of science went hand-in-hand with what is called the Industrial Revolution. Discovery and invention greatly improved industry; industry increased wealth; wealth made more possible and powerfully stimulated further research and discovery. It was chiefly in countries that were estranged from the Catholic Church that this was going on. Hence it is not inexplicable that the greater proportion of scientists were not Catholics. Of those who were not, many of the greatest were Christians, and believers in God. We have not space to write of all the great Catholic scientists, but even the story of the more famous will help to nail the lie that the Church is, or ever has been, the enemy of science.

Early History

When telling of the beginnings of the modern age, we mentioned Friar Roger

Bacon (not to be confused with Sir Francis Bacon), Copernicus and Galileo, and the great artist-scientists Michael-angelo and Leonardo da Vinci. It was to the Pope, Paul III, that the great book of Nicolas Copernicus was dedicated. The interest that sculptors and painters took in the shape of the human body was linked, as we said, to progress in the science of medicine, and especially anatomy, or the study of the body. Those of you who become doctors will come upon the names of Vesalius, Eustachius and Fallopius, for certain parts of the body have been named after them. These were Catholic scientists, and they led the way in overcoming prejudice against dissection of the body, thus heralding the precious knowledge and the skilful operations of today. With them we may mention the botanist Andrea Cesalpine, whose work on classifying plants led up to the achievements of Linnaeus, the Swedish botanist.

Mathematicians

The study of mathematics made great progress in the sixteenth century. Among Catholics who were distinguished mathematicians were Tartaglea (who solved the cubic equation) and his pupil Farrari (who solved equations of the fourth degree); Clavius, a Jesuit priest, whose calculations enabled Pope Gregory XIII to reform the Calendar; Mersenne, a Franciscan Friar, who collated the work of his contemporaries, keeping up correspondence with them; he did good work on sound, following Pierre Gassendi, the maker of the first attempt to work out how fast sound travels.

One of the best-known names in science in the seventeenth century was that of Réne Descartes. Although his line of thought had dangers in it, Descartes was a deeply religious man, and a sincere Catholic. He delved into many fields of science, developed rota-

tion for indices in algebra, invented analytical geometry and wrote on the theory of equations.

Among astronomers in the seventeenth century were the Abbé Jean Picard, who accurately measured a degree of latitude, and Giovanni Cassini, discoverer of the four moons and white polar caps of Saturn; he worked out that the sun was 87,000,000 miles away, which is very close to the modern estimate of 93,000,000.

Late Seventeenth Century

With the coming of the microscope biologists were able for the first time to study minute anatomy. One of the pioneers was Marcello Malpighi who was famous for his discoveries in connection with capillary circulation and in the anatomy of the skin, kidney and spleen. He made a special study of the organic structure of silk-worms and found that they and similar creatures breathed through a system of tubes in

Photo Mansell
Volta, the inventor of the electric pile which builds its own charge

Photo Mansell

Lavoisier analysing atmospheric air

the skin. He discovered how we taste with the papillae or taste-buds on our tongues, and made a minute study of how a chicken is developed in the egg, what we now call embryology. In 1691 he was appointed private physician to Pope Innocent XII and spent his last years in Rome. We must complete our list by including Nicolaus Steno, who was not only a great scientist but a great Church man. He was trained in medicine and won great fame as an expert on the anatomy of the glands, heart and brain. Later he became a geologist and stated definite principles under which the earth's crust was formed, and the strata then deformed by the action of fire and water. He became a convert from Lutheranism in 1667 and was later made a Bishop and Vicar Apostolic for Northern Europe.

Early Eighteenth Century

The eighteenth century opens with the Abbé Nollet, who discovered that plants subjected to electricity grow more quickly, and the Abbé Spallanzani, who demonstrated the work of the gastric juices in dissolving what we eat, and showed in a series of experiments that the theory that life could start from non-living matter, was unfounded. We have the work of Galvani and of Volta in electricity. Volta invented the electric pile which builds up its own charge. Charles Coulomb did a great deal of work in electro-statics, and his name is commemorated in the unit of current quantity.

One of the tragedies of the French Revolution was the execution of André Lavoisier. Chemistry owes to him its ranking as the equal of physics. His insistence on exact quantitative methods and his refusal to accept any proposition unless positive proof was forthcoming brought splendid results. He identified many of the elements and propounded the theory of the conservation of matter. He was the founder of modern chemistry and taught that combustion was the union of the combustible substance and the oxygen in the atmosphere. No wonder it was said of him that such a brain might not occur again in a hundred years.

Nineteenth Century

Astronomy came once more into prominence in the nineteenth century. Pierre Simon Laplace, in a monumental work of five volumes, dealt with laws of mechanics and gravitation, and their application to all the movements of the planets, and put forward an improved method for working out the orbits of planets. Early in the century the monk Piazzi discovered the minor planet Ceres, Joseph Laverrier predicted the existence and position of the planet

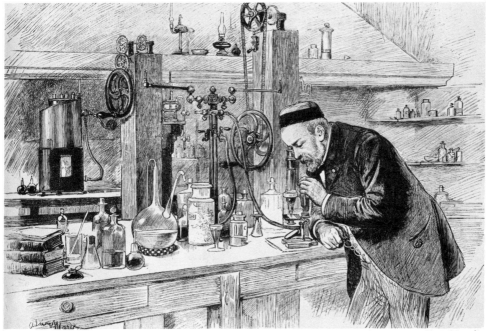

Photo Mansell

Pasteur working in his laboratory

Neptune later discovered by Dr. Gaile, and the Jesuit, Angelo Secchi, was able to classify several thousands of stars, and by photographing the sun during an eclipse, showed what the "corona" of the sun really was. André Ampère stated the rule concerning the magnetic field round a conductor carrying a circuit. He also discovered that an electrified wire coil behaves as a magnet and will magnetise a steel rod placed inside it. Any schoolboy interested in electricity can duplicate his experiment and get the same result. All our knowledge of electro-magnetism is based upon his work and his services to electricity were judged so highly that the unit of current has been named after him.

The nineteenth century did more for medicine than any until then. René Laennec invented the stethoscope, the instrument which the doctor uses to listen to your internal workings as you cough and keep saying "ninety-nine." One disease which had carried off generations of women in child-birth was puerperal fever. Then a Hungarian doctor working in Vienna, Ignatius Semmelweiss, had the courage to declare that most of these deaths could be avoided if only his doctor-colleagues and the midwives would observe greater cleanliness. After a long period of ridicule and discouragement he succeeded in reducing the percentage of deaths so much that the scoffers were forced to accept his theory.

Louis Pasteur

Semmelweiss' work was the forerunner of that of Louis Pasteur, who proved that disease and decay are caused by bacteria. Pasteur was one of the benefactors of humanity, and the greatest Frenchman of the century. His investigations into the work of microbes gave

Photo Mansell

Marconi and his assistant receiving the first transatlantic message by wireless telegraphy

the French wine-growers a cure for a disease that attacked their vines and saved the silk industry from ruin by another such microbe. Using Jenner's method of vaccination he found a remedy for anthrax in cattle and another for the horrible disease of rabies, which is caused by the bite of a mad dog. Milk is something that we drink every day and it is through the research done by Pasteur that we are today able to drink *safe* milk. Milk is made safe for us by pasteurization (from Pasteur)—a process which kills all the harmful bacteria.

Marconi

At the end of the century there had been several attempts to transmit signals through space and Lord Kelvin had suggested a probable use of what were called "Hertzian" waves. With this idea in mind Guglielmo Marconi had been experimenting with some success and on May 10, 1897, he succeeded in sending the Morse "V"—three dots and a dash—from Lavernock Point near Cardiff to the island of Flat Holme three miles out. Just think what that first experiment has led to in the sixty years that have followed.

In this short article we have mentioned but a few of the hundreds of Catholic scientists, but they should be sufficient to show that it is possible to be a Catholic and a scientist, and that no scientist need be agnostic or atheist.

THE MODERN PAPACY

To the blare of trumpets and the beating of drums the soldiers of King Victor Emmanuel II of Piedmont and Sardinia marched through the streets of Rome on September 20, 1870, and took possession of the Eternal City in the name of their king. Pius IX watched them in silence as they poured into his capital, flushed with victory against his own troops. It was a sad and bitter day for him, for he knew that it was the end of so much that he had fought to defend and preserve ever since he had become Pope in 1846. It was made all the sadder by the thought of what had happened in Rome only two months before.

On July 18, in fact, Pius IX had listened, with gratitude to God in his heart, to the tremendous explosion of joy that had greeted his own solemn definition of the infallibility of the Pope. His mind went back to that wild and stormy morning of July 18 when, with thunder and lightning rolling and flashing through the basilica of St. Peter's, he had declared that the Pope cannot make a mistake whenever he speaks as the

Teacher of all Christians and declares what they must believe or do to save their souls, for he speaks then under the direct guidance and protection of the Holy Ghost.

The very next day war had broken out between France and Prussia. The French, hard pressed by the Prussians, had recalled their troops stationed in the Papal States with the consent of the Pope. The Italian patriots had seized their chance. And now they were in Rome itself! Their presence there meant the beginning of the end for the Vatican Council which had been responsible for settling, after many months of patient examination and discussion, the question of the Pope's infallibility. It meant also, as many hoped and imagined, the beginning of the end for the Catholic Church.

Humanly speaking, then, it was a sad and bitter day for Pius IX when he saw the troops of a foreign king marching in triumph through the streets of his fallen capital. But there was no fear in his eyes, no despair in his voice, as he turned

179

King Emmanuel marching into Rome

to a little group of foreign diplomats standing in silence behind him, and said:

"I have written to the King. I do not know whether my letter has reached him. But whether it has or not, I no longer have any hope of touching his heart, or putting a stop to his ungracious proceedings. . . . Bixio, the notorious Bixio, is here at our gates, supported by the Italian army. He is now a General of the King. Years ago, when he was just a Republican, he promised that if he ever got inside the walls of Rome he would throw me into the Tiber!

"It was only yesterday that I had a communication from the young gentlemen at the American College, begging me, nay, demanding of me, to allow them to arm themselves, and to make themselves the defenders of my person. Although there are few in Rome in whose hands I should feel more secure than in the hands of these young Americans, I turned down their generous offer with thanks.

"I should like, gentlemen, to be able to say that I rely on you and on the countries that you have the honour to represent. . . . but times are changed. The poor, old Pope has now no one on earth on whom he can rely. Relief must come from Heaven!

"But," he added after a moment of deep silence, "remember, gentlemen, the Catholic Church is immortal!"

"The Catholic Church is immortal! ' said the seventy-eight-year-old Pope, that fateful day of September 1870 as he saw his own City fall into the hands of the enemy. He was only echoing the words of Our Lord eighteen hundred years before him. "The gates of Hell shall not prevail against it!" But to many non-Catholics the events of September 20, 1870 in Rome were the writing on the wall for the Catholic Church. The Papacy was finished, they said, and soon the Church would sink into the grave, never again to rise. The years ahead, however, were to prove that instead of the Papacy being dead and fit only for the scrap-heap, or a museum of antiquities, it was in fact very much alive and very much up-to-date. So that today it has more power and more say in the affairs of the world than it has ever had before.

As Pius IX said to the foreign diplomats that day: "Relief must come from Heaven!" And relief did come from Heaven. It came above all in the form of five wonderful and magnificent men whom Heaven sent, one after the other, to take over from Pius IX the command of the storm-tossed and battered Ship of the Catholic Church, and to steer her safely through fresh storms that were to burst upon Her to the comparative calm and tranquillity of our own age.

Leo XIII, Pius, X Benedict XV, Pius XI, and Pius XII were the names of these Captains of the Ship of the Church of Christ. To say even just a few words about the works and the achievements of these wonderful Popes we

should have to write at least five large volumes. All we can do, then, is to mention very briefly indeed, one or two of the more striking features of the pontificates of these five Popes who have stood at the helm of the Catholic Church during the past eighty-six years.

The first of these five Popes was Leo XIII who succeeded Pius IX in 1878. He is famous above all for his courageous and relentless fight to win better conditions for the working man, as well as for his efforts to get the nations of Europe and America to put a stop to the slave trade. His fight on behalf of the workers reached its climax in an Encyclical Letter that he wrote in 1891. This was the great *Rerum Novarum*, on the conditions of the working class. In this Letter Leo XIII protested with all his might against the inhuman hardships and the injustices imposed on the ordinary working man by so many employers. He condemned the system that made tyrants of the

Cardinal Lavigerie denouncing the slave trade

The paralytic child is cured

employers and slaves of the workers. And he warned the world that the lot of the working classes had to be improved or there would be an explosion.

The Pope's Letter caused a sensation at the time. But it was only very slowly that his plan to make sure that justice was done to the workers came to win practical support from employers.

No less unrelenting was Leo XIII's fight against the horrors of the slave-trade. He had been Pope only a few days when he set up two new missions for the White Fathers of Cardinal Lavigerie, and restored the See of Carthage in North Africa as a base from which to carry on his fight against the Arab slave-traders.

"Since Africa," he said, "is the centre of this trade we recommend to all missionaries to consecrate their strength and even their lives to this sublime work of redemption. We recommend also that they should ransom as many slaves as they can."

Between 1879 and 1890 Leo XIII poured more and more missionaries into Central Africa. At the same time he encouraged Cardinal Lavigerie to preach a crusade against the slave-trade in Paris, London, Brussels, Rome and Milan. But his first great victory in this fight came in 1888 when 2,000,000 slaves were set free in Brazil, and slavery in that country was abolished. Then finally, in 1890, Leo XIII published his Encyclical on the Abolition of Slavery.

In this letter the Pope told the world that he was filled with horror whenever he remembered how he had been told that "every year nearly 40,000 Africans of every age and sex were torn by force from their humble homes, and then, chained and whipped, they were dragged for long distances to markets where they were shown like cattle, and sold."

As a result of his efforts to help and defend the weak and the down-trodden Leo XIII grew to be so immensely popular that when he came to die in

1903, at the age of ninety-three, the whole world, non-Catholic as well as Catholic, mourned for him as for a father.

The old Pope had been the son of a nobleman and had been reared in the midst of luxury and ease. The new Pope, who took his place, was the son of a peasant, and had been brought up in poverty and real want. But the peasant boy proved to be as great a Pope as the nobleman had been before him. Pius X, or St. Pius X as we now know him, left an extraordinary impression on the Church and the world by the sheer holiness of his life. He was not content to tell people that they must be good. He showed them how to be good and holy by his own example. The fame of his holiness soon spread, and people began to come to him from every part of the world both to see and hear him and also to be cured by him of their diseases.

There was, for instance, the little boy, paralysed from birth, who was taken by his father to see the Pope. Pius X stretched out his arms when he saw the child and said to the father: "Give him to me, please." So saying, the Pope took the little boy, held him on his knees, and went on talking to the pilgrims who had gone to see him. Suddenly the boy wriggled out of the Pope's hands, slid to the floor, and raced round the room!

Not everybody, however, shared in the Pope's dreams of leading the world back to Our Lord by getting people to be better Christians. The rulers of France, Portugal and Mexico had ideas of their own about what their countries needed most to make them happier and more prosperous. So they declared war on the Catholic Church. Pius X did not hesitate to condemn their attempts to destroy the Church and Christianity, even though he was the meekest and gentlest of men.

He was at grips with these anti-Catholic governments when in August

13—III

1914 the First World War burst upon Europe and the world. It broke his heart, and sixteen days later he was dead.

His successor was Benedict XV. He was such a tiny man physically that when the Vatican tailor tried in vain to find a white cassock to fit him after his election, he said to him:

"My dear man, you had quite forgotten me!"

From every other angle, however, the new Pope proved to be a giant. When he became Pope it was thought by many that he would keep silent about the war. Benedict XV however had no intention of holding his tongue while the nations of Europe poured out their life-blood on the battlefield. Time and time again he appealed to them to put a stop to the slaughter that was turning Europe into a vast graveyard. Time and time again they refused to listen to him, and even accused him of favouring the other side. The fighting became more and more inhuman and murderous, and Benedict protested against it all, especially when the Germans stepped up their submarine warfare in their efforts to starve Britain into surrender by sinking neutral ships on the high seas. And when the war at last came to an end, Benedict XV continued to appeal on behalf of what he called "the inconceivable number of enfeebled people, particularly children and young people, who bear in their bodies the ravages of this atrocious war."

His courage in speaking out as he had done during the war, and his tireless charity towards all who were in need both during and after the war, made such an impression on the world that when he died in 1922 the number of countries represented at the Vatican had risen from fourteen in 1910, to twenty-five, among them France and Portugal!

The one and only aim of the pontificate of Pius XI, who succeeded Benedict

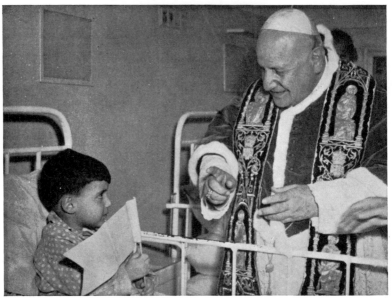

Courtesy Associated Press Ltd.

Pope John XXIII visiting children in hospital at Christmas time

XV, was to give peace back to the world. Men had lost peace, the new Pope told them in his first Encyclical Letter, because they had banished God from their lives, and had thrown overboard the teaching and the example of Jesus Christ. To find it again they had to bring God back into their lives, and allow Jesus Christ to reign over them once again.

Pius XI was determined to help them to do so with every means in his power. That is why, as he told a group of boys from a college near Rome who had gone to see him, he was ready to deal with the devil himself if the good of souls required it! One of the most important steps that he took in his efforts to win peace for the world in general and for the Catholic Church in particular were the treaties or concordats that he signed with countries such as Latvia, Poland, Russia, Germany, Yugoslavia and others. By means of such concordats he guaranteed the right of Catholics in these countries freely to practise their own religion.

Perhaps the most spectacular of all these treaties and concordats was the one with Italy in 1929. This was the Treaty of the Lateran which put an end to the state of tension that had existed between the Church and the Italian Government ever since 1870. It put an end also to a problem that was at least 1200 years old! The problem was this: how to give the Pope the powers of a completely independent ruler and yet spare him all the worries that usually go with such powers. "All I want," said Pius IX in 1871 after he had been robbed of the Papal States, "is a little corner of the earth where I shall be master. Not that I would refuse my States if they were offered to me! But so long as I have not that little corner of the earth I cannot exercise my spiritual mission in its fullness." That is precisely what the Treaty of the Lateran did: it recognised the Pope's supreme authority as King over a "little corner of the earth," the 108 acres of the City of the Vatican created by that Treaty.

Equally important for the cause of

Courtesy Associated Press Ltd.

Pope Paul VI

eace was the work of Pius XI on behalf f the Foreign Missions. In the course f the 1914–18 War the Foreign Missions ad suffered disastrous losses, and it was ear that if something was not done for em they would collapse altogether.

Apart from this consideration, however, Pius XI was convinced that the best way to win peace for the whole world was to make more and more men know and love Jesus Christ, and that the best way to do this was to develop the Foreign Missions.

In 1923, then, he organised a wonderful missionary exhibition in the Vatican. This created a deep impression, and made Catholics everywhere realise that the Pope had not been exaggerating when he had told them that to help the Foreign Missions "was the greatest and the holiest of all Catholic undertakings." After a great deal of spade-work he was able in 1926 to give the Foreign Missions their Magna Carta in the form of an Encyclical Letter called *Rerum Ecclesiae*. Ten years later he had the joy of consecrating with his own hands the first six Chinese Bishops in the history of the Church.

Yet in spite of all this unsparing work for peace, the pontificate of Pius XI was anything but a peaceful one. On the one hand the rulers of Russia, Mexico and Spain (his "terrible triangle" as he called them) refused to listen to his appeals to put an end to the religious persecutions in their countries. And on the other hand Pius XI had to contend with Nazi Germany despite the concordat of 1933. Against the evil rulers of that unhappy country the Pope waged a relentless struggle in defence of Christianity and of humanity long before World War II broke out.

Even less peaceful was the pontificate of the successor of Pius XI, the saintly, gentle and wise Pius XII who became Pope in 1939. Pope Pius XII set himself the mighty task of working for peace like his predecessor, and like him also of fighting tooth and nail against falsehood and injustice, oppression and tyranny in the name of humanity.

Like Benedict XV he laboured with all his power to put an end to a world war. Like Pius XI he waged war against the horrors and excesses of Nazi Germany, and, more and more, of Communism. Like Leo XIII he made the most skilful use of the weapons of diplomacy and statesmanship in his fight against the enemies of the Church and of mankind. But like Pius X he relied above all on the weapons of prayer and of the striking holiness of his own life.

Pope John XXIII who succeeded him in 1958 was a man of the people, born of peasant stock and his winning personality made him popular throughout the world. Two of his Encyclical Letters were acclaimed by all men; the first, *Mater et Magistra*, set out the social teaching of the Church in the changed conditions of modern times, while the second, *Pacem in terris*, was an impassioned plea for peace and justice among all peoples. Perhaps his greatest work, however, was the summoning of the Second Vatican Council, which began in 1962. Pope John did not live to see the completion of the Council, but when he died, in June, 1963, the whole world, Catholic and non-Catholic, Christian and non-Christian, mourned his loss.

In the same month of June, 1963, the Cardinals met in conclave, and soon their choice was known to the world Cardinal John Baptist Montini, Archbishop of Milan, who took the name of Paul VI. His first act as Pope was to declare his firm resolve to work without ceasing for the Reunion of Christendom and to continue the Vatican Council which his predecessor had begun.

The outstanding holiness of the Head of the Catholic Church, perhaps more than anything else, has won for her the admiration and the respect of vast numbers of non-Catholics. It is this holiness also that is convincing more and more of those outside the Church that a Church which can produce such holiness must be the true Church of Christ, the infallible Guide of all men to Heaven.

HOW A POPE IS ELECTED

In the bedroom of his apartment in the Vatican Palace in Rome, the Pope has just died. Standing by his bedside is the Cardinal Camerlengo, the Cardinal appointed by the Pope to direct the affairs of the Church until a new Pope is elected. In the presence of the Camerlengo and other officials of the Papal Court, the white veil which covers the face of the dead Pope is removed, and prayers are said for the repose of his soul. Then an official reads the *rogito*, or solemn announcement of his death. The "Ring of the Fisherman." which the Pope had received upon his election, is entrusted to the Camerlengo, who will take it to the first meeting of Cardinals when it is broken into pieces.

When a Pope has died, the Church has lost its supreme head. The Congregations which deal with the affairs of the Church no longer have any authority. There is no longer any office of Papal Secretary of State, and until the election of a new Pope there can be no move in diplomatic relations involving the Holy See, no matter how important or how advanced they may be. Even if a General Council of the Church is in session, it is automatically suspended and can only meet once more if the new Pope gives his approval.

The Church throughout the world goes into mourning, and many of its buildings are draped in black, like a widow mourning a husband, or children mourning a father; and the sorrow is shared by all men of goodwill throughout the world.

Now, no structure as great or as important as the Catholic Church can remain for long without a Supreme Authority, and it becomes the duty of the College of Cardinals, who have already assumed the responsibilities of the government of the Church, to elect a new Pope. They begin to arrive in Rome as soon as they have heard of the Pope's death. For some days the body of the dead Pope, clothed in red vestments and with a golden mitre upon the

187

The Sistine Chapel arranged for the election of the Pope.   Along the sides are the Cardinals' thrones with a small square table in front of each.   On the large table is the chalice, a silver paten, a silver box, and ballot forms

head, is exposed for the veneration and prayers of the faithful, in St. Peter's basilica. After the lying-in-state, the body is placed in a triple coffin, a purse containing the coins and medals of his pontificate is put at his feet, the absolutions are pronounced, and the coffin is taken for burial in the crypt of the basilica. Then there follows the *Novemdialis*—the nine-day period of official mourning, with a solemn Mass each day in St. Peter's.

Sorrow over the death of the Pope is universal and sincere, but the Church must continue its God-given task, and a new Pope must be elected without delay. Therefore, as soon as the *Novemdialis* is over, the Cardinals must turn to the task of the election. The machinery of administering the Church, usually very slow and deliberate, is now seen to be moving very fast indeed.

At one time, the papal election had to be commenced within ten days after the death of the Pope, but the time has now been extended so that the election must begin not less than fifteen days, and not later than eighteen days, after the Pope's death. In this way every Cardinal no matter how far away he may be, may take part in the election. In fact, under his vow of obedience, he must do so unless he is prevented by grave illness. From all over the world, then, by land, by sea, by air, the Cardinals hasten to Rome. On their journey they are bound to secrecy. They must not discuss the election with anyone, they must give no interviews, they must not offer any opinion upon any candidate. The Pope must be elected upon merit alone.

There are three ways of electing a Pope: (1) by inspiration or acclamation, when the Cardinals are unanimous in the choice and cry his name aloud; (2) by compromise, when all agree to accept the decision of a group of three, five or seven cardinals, who have been unanimously chosen to represent the others; and (3) by ballot, which is the normal procedure.

Election by acclamation last took place in 1621, at the election of Gregory XV. Compromise was resorted to at the election of Gregory X in 1271, when differences among the Cardinals held up the election of the new Pope for nearly three years.

Nowadays a Pope is usually elected by ballot and, to be elected, a candidate must obtain two-thirds of all possible votes, unless the number of Cardinals cannot be divided into three equal parts, in which case the successful candidate must receive two-thirds plus one of all the votes.

All those Cardinals who have arrived within the time-limit of eighteen days will take part in what is called a "conclave" for the election. Conclave means "under lock and key", from the Latin words *cum clavi*, with a key. This means that until they have reached a decision, the Cardinals are locked away from the outside world. Once upon a time, when a decision was slow in coming, the Cardinals' food was reduced in quantity and quality as a means of inducing them to come to an agreement. Once inside the conclave, the Cardinals stay there, unless there is a very grave reason, such as an urgent need for a surgical operation.

During the time which has elapsed between the death of the Pope and the

The Sistine Chapel after the Pope has been elected showing only the Pope's canopy standing

Photo Mansell

Pope John XXIII being robed before his coronation with the triple Crown

opening day of the conclave, an army of workmen has been busy inside a wing of the Vatican Palace itself. Every Cardinal must have a cell in which he will live for the time before a decision is reached. He will be allowed to take one attendant with him to the conclave.

The conclave itself must be absolutely secret. To ensure this, all entrances to the area of the Vatican where the Cardinals will stay are sealed off, and any windows facing the outside world are covered with whitewash. The only entrance from outside is at a wicket-gate, watched by five officials, whose duty it is to check everything that passes through, even the food which the Cardinals and their attendants will eat. Only with the

permission of the senior official, who is called the Marshal of the Conclave, is a message allowed to pass, and anything debatable will even then be refused.

The actual balloting takes place in the Sistine Chapel. There, as many thrones as there are Cardinals have been set up. Each throne is covered in violet cloth and has a violet canopy. In front of each throne there stands a small square table covered also in violet; upon this table the Cardinal will mark his record of the voting, as the names are called out. On the altar will have been placed the paraphernalia for voting which is kept for the election of a Pope: a supply of ballot forms; a large chalice, used as an urn for the votes; a paten on to which the votes are poured out for counting; a silver box, in which the votes are deposited; and a box which will be carried to the cell of any Cardinal who is too ill or infirm to leave his cell. In this box he will place his vote.

At the other end of the chapel a small stove is set up, with a pipe leading from it directly to the roof. In this stove the ballot papers are burned and the assembled crowds, thronging St. Peter's Square in their thousands, watch tensely as the smoke rises into the air. If no candidate receives the necessary two-thirds of the votes, then the ballot is unsuccessful. The ballot papers are put on one side, and a second ballot takes place immediately. If this too is unsuccessful, both sets of ballot papers are gathered together, wet straw is mixed with them, and they are burned in the stove, so that the smoke shows black against the sky, When, however, the necessary two-thirds of the votes have been obtained, the voting-papers alone are burned, and the smoke is now white.

The ballot papers bear the words: Eligo in summum Pontificem Rev. mum D. meum D. Card ... (I elect as Supreme Pontiff my Lord Cardinal . . .). Each Cardinal writes his nomination in the space provided and then folds the ballot paper. The Cardinals go one by one, in order of seniority, to the altar. Each in turn kneels for a moment in prayer. He rises and, holding up the paper for all to see, cries aloud: "I call to witness the Lord Christ, who will be my judge, that I am electing the one whom under God I think ought to be elected." As he says these words, he has before his eyes the tremendous fresco by Michelangelo, showing Christ coming in judgement. The Cardinal then places the ballot paper on the paten and tips it into the chalice, before returning to his place.

When all the votes have been cast,

and any sick Cardinals have put theirs into the ebony box which is carried to them by three of their number, the papers are poured out on to the paten, while three other Cardinals, chosen by lot, act as scrutineers. One opens the paper, reads it, and passes it to the second, who also reads it before passing it to the third, who reads the name aloud. If no candidate receives the two-thirds of the votes that are needed, then all immediately vote again, and each Cardinal may now, if he so chooses, vote for a different candidate. If this second ballot is also unsuccessful, then the papers are mixed with wet straw and burned. There are four ballotings each day, two in the morning and two in the afternoon, and the process of burning the ballots is therefore repeated twice each day, to give the "black" smoke, until finally a Pope is elected.

While the outcome of each ballot is being announced, each Cardinal will take note of the results. These notes, and any other notes relating to the balloting, are not burned but are gathered together and placed in sealed envelopes; the envelopes may not be opened without the express permission of the reigning Pope, who may allow historians in the centuries to come to study them.

Once locked away inside the conclave, the Cardinals of course are able to discuss freely among themselves the various "papabiles" or likely candidates, to advance the abilities and suitability of their choice, and to attempt to sway individuals or groups to vote with them.

By tradition the Pope is elected from among the Cardinals, but by tradition only. It lies within the power of the College of Cardinals to elect anybody: an unknown, humble priest, a layman, even a married man if they so wish, to become the Supreme Pontiff. It was in 1059 that a Council, called by Nicholas 11, declared: "If there is to be found in

Pope Paul VI is carried across St Peter's Square to his coronation

the Roman Church a subject fitted to govern it, let him be of the clergy; otherwise application should be made to another church." A Pope, then, may be chosen from outside the Diocese of Rome, and a layman may be elected, as long as he caused to be conferred upon himself all the necessary ordinations after his election. In point of fact, since the decree of 1059, no layman has been elected Pope, and since the time of Urban VI, 1378, who, when elected, was Archbishop of Bari, and not a Cardinal, all the Popes have been chosen from the College of Cardinals.

During the conclave the Cardinals wear a woollen robe, still in the violet or purple of mourning, sleeveless and with a long train. Over this they may wear a coat, also violet, for warmth. Their mantellettas, the distinguishing mark of their rank, they will have removed as soon as the news of the Pope's death reached them. What happens during the conclave can but be guessed, for everyone inside, Cardinals, attendants, servants, are sworn to secrecy.

When at last the balloting has proved successful, the violet canopies over the thrones are lowered, leaving only that of the Cardinal who has been elected. Then the Dean of the College of Cardinals, who is the senior of the Cardinal Bishops, presents himself before the throne of the Cardinal who has been elected, and asks him whether he will

Pope Paul VI being crowned by Cardinal Ottaviani

accept election. If he does accept, in that moment he becomes Pope, with the full authority of the Vicar of Christ. The Cardinal Dean then asks him the name by which he would wish to be called.

Escorted by two Cardinals, the new Pope enters the sacristy where three sets of robes, one large, one medium and one small, are waiting. He dresses in the white cassock, white stockings, and puts on the red slippers, each embroidered with a golden cross. Returning to the throne he is adorned in the vestments of his office and in turn all the Cardinals, in order of seniority, advance to kiss his hand and to kneel before him. After this the Cardinal Dean places upon his finger the Ring of the Fisherman, which the Pope then removes so that his name may be engraved upon it. This ring is not again worn by the Pope; it is a seal-ring, used at one time to seal important documents, and is now purely symbolical.

Outside the Vatican, in the great square of St. Peter's, the faithful gathered in their thousands are waiting. They know that a Pope has been elected. Nowadays the Vatican Radio will broadcast the news in many languages, and while lifting their voices in a *Te Deum* they watch the balcony expectantly. At last the windows open and the senior Cardinal Deacon appears. It is he who will announce to the City and the world the name of the new Pope.

The announcement is in this form:
Annuntio vobis gaudium magnum. Habemus Papam.
I announce to you a great joy. We have a Pope.
Eminentissimus et Reverendissimus Dominus, Dominus ——

The most eminent and reverend Lord, the Lord ——
Sanctae Romanae Ecclesiae Cardinalis
——
Cardinal of the Holy Roman Church qui sibi accipit nomen ——
who takes to himself the name ——
There is a roar of cheering, and the waiting crowd grows more expectant, more intense. Suddenly there is a hush, the crowds sink to their knees, and the white-robed figure comes out on to the balcony and raises his hand in blessing "Urbi et Orbi"—to the City and the world.

A few days later, the basilica of St. Peter's is thronged when the new Pope enters it to sing his first papal Mass at the altar over the tomb of St. Peter. As the procession moves towards the altar, it is halted three times. At each halt, a piece of tow is set on fire; it flares brightly for a moment and then dies away; meanwhile the Pope hears the words, "Pater sancte, sic transit gloria mundi"—Holy Father this is how the glory of the world passes away; for in the midst of the pomp and splendour of his crowning, the Pope is reminded that he is but a mortal man.

At the end of the papal Mass, the crowds gather once more in St. Peter's Square, and watch, while in full view of all of them, the great triple tiara, the crown of the Supreme Pontiff, the Holy Father of the Church, is slowly and solemnly placed upon the head of the Pope. Once more, there is the blessing and the square resounds with a roar of "Viva il Papa!" "Long live the Pope" and the Pope, on the Sedia Gestatoria, the portable throne, is borne away to the Vatican.

The labels in the diagram, clockwise from top:
Congregation of the Holy Office
Congregation of the Council
Extraordinary Ecclesiastical Affairs
Congregation of the Rites
Congregation of the Ceremonial
Seminaries and Universities
Fabric of the Basilica of Loreto
Congregation de Propaganda Fide
Fabric of St. Peter's and the Vatican
The Eastern Church
Congregation of the Index
Affairs of the Religious
Discipline of the Sacraments
Congregation of the Consistory

THE SACRED CONGREGATIONS

Try to imagine for a moment or two the vast extent to which the Catholic Church has grown in just under two thousand years. It seems a long way from the small congregations of believers left behind by St. Paul on his missionary journeys, or the little groups who met furtively in the catacombs beneath Imperial Rome, to the immense structure which is the Church of today.

Today the Church has spread wherever man has found it possible to go: farthest north, among the Esquimaux; among the jungles of Africa and South America; to the islands of the East Indies; among the teeming millions of India; to Australia; Japan; there is no country where the Catholic Church does not have its priests, its missionaries, its religious. Think of all the things it possesses; not as a miser who gathers his selfish wealth, but as a mother who looks forward with loving care to the future. There are its glorious churches, a heritage from the Middle Ages; its new modern churches which have been built to house the growing numbers of those who come to worship; its schools, abbeys, hospitals, convents, missions, and lands. The Church grows continuously: there is a perpetual need for priests to carry the word, and the Church must have colleges, seminaries and universities where the priests can be trained. All these various places and things must be built, repaired, supplied, governed, controlled, financed. We know that any country, however small it may be, maintains a body of people whose work it is to deal with the business of the country from every aspect. Some of them deal with its relations with other countries, some with affairs at home, some deal with education, some with finance. Put together these people form what we know as the "Civil service," and individually each of them is a "civil servant."

The Congregations

How much more, then, must it be necessary for the Church to maintain a

195

"civil service," to deal with her affairs, both religious and civil, in all those countries of the world where the Catholic Faith can be found. Therefore the Church has set up a great organisation in which its best brains are placed at the service of His Holiness the Pope.

For the most part, this organisation consists of "Congregations," formed by the Holy Father from the members of the College of Cardinals, aided by large numbers of highly qualified officials.

In the days when the Popes governed not only the Church, but also large areas of land, known as the Papal States, in Italy, the Congregations were as many as nineteen or more in number. With the loss of the Papal States, as the Church in modern times deals only with matters of religion, the number of Congregations has dropped to thirteen, or if we count that of the Propagation of the Faith as two separate entities, then fourteen. Congregations were established in their present form by Pope Pius X in June 1908, and between them, they cover the whole of the government of the Church in all its aspects. At the head of each Congregation we find the Cardinals, varying in number according to the importance and amount of the work to be done. The major officials are selected by the Pope and are appointed by a letter of the Cardinal Secretary of State. The minor officials are chosen by examination and appointed by a letter of the Cardinal Prefect.

As in everything else, all decisions taken by any of the Congregations are subject to the approval of the Pope.

The fourteen Congregations are those of: (a) The Holy Office, (b) the Consistory, (c) Discipline of the Sacraments, (d) the Council, (e) Affairs of the Religious, (f) the Propagation of the Faith, (g) the Eastern Church, (h) the Index, (i) Rites, (j) Ceremonial, (k) Extra-ordinary Ecclesiastical Affairs, (l) Seminaries and Universities, (m) Fabric of St. Peter's and the Vatican, (n) Loreto.

If the Pope wishes he can form a special Congregation from among the Cardinals. This is done when any special points of argument or discussion arise. In 1881, for instance, Pope Leo XIII formed such a Congregation to consider certain grounds of disagreement which had arisen between the bishops and the Religious Orders of England and Scotland.

Suppose we take each of the Congregations in turn and examine the work that its members are asked to do. The Congregation of the Holy Office is the supreme court for dealing with matters or threats of heresy. It was set up by Pope Paul III in 1542 when the danger to the Church was at its height and the struggle among the German princes, due to the heretical teaching of Martin Luther, threatened the very existence of the Faith. In those days it was called the Congregation of the Holy Office of the Inquisition, but then it could rely on the help of the civil power in putting down heresy. That is not so today and the Inquisition, as understood in the Middle Ages, has no place in the modern world. Nowadays, the Congregation, with its twelve cardinals, supported by learned theologians and doctors of canon law, watches, judges, and condemns any deviation from the established teaching of the Church, especially in books, in sermons and in pamphlets.

The Congregation of the Consistory has the duty of deciding and then preparing the business which shall be brought before the Consistory. The Consistory is the "Senate" of the Church where the Pope presides over the whole body of the Cardinals. At its meetings which are held about once a fortnight the serious ecclesiastical affairs of the Church are debated.

A sitting of the First Ecumenical Council in St. Peter's

The Congregation is responsible for the setting up of new dioceses, for the appointment of bishops and for the supervision of bishops in their dioceses. It reviews the reports which bishops must send to the Holy See, it announces the times and places of apostolic visitations and is responsible for the government, discipline, administration and studies in seminaries, and so for the training of future priests.

The Congregation of the Sacraments is the authority which regulates all sacramental discipline. It has taken over some of the work previously done by the two tribunals, the Dataria and Peniteniaria. If you want to marry a relative within the forbidden decrees then you must apply to this Congregation for a dispensation. It controls the discipline of the six sacraments other than matrimony and before it come requests for permission to say Mass in various places or at certain times: Masses in private chapels; Masses in the open air; Masses on board ship; Masses before dawn; and sometimes for priests suffering from blindness.

Next on our list comes the Congregation of the Council. The Council referred to is the Council of Trent (1545–1563) and the full title was originally "the Congregation for interpreting the Council of Trent." The great Council was held at a time when strife and dissension had placed the Church in such a position that her unity must be restored, maintained and strengthened or the whole fabric would crumble. To ensure that the decrees of the Council should be interpreted as correctly as possible the Holy Father gave the Congregation the power to deal with all questions of the discipline of the secular clergy and people. It deals with fasting, abstinence and feast days. Under it come parish priests, canons of the Church, the various sodalities and societies. It handles such things as stipends for Masses, the tributes from the dioceses, and ecclesiastical benefices. To himself alone the Holy Father reserved the power to deal with such decrees of the Council as concerned the Faith. In the latter half of the nineteenth century one of the Congregations bore the title "of Bishops and Regulars." By the decree of Pius X in 1908 this Congregation was abolished and replaced by that of "Affairs of the Religious." Before it come disputes between bishops and the communities of religious within their dioceses, which used to come before the earlier Congregation. Broadly speaking, we may say that in relation to property, to the rules of their Orders and their ordinary life, the regular communities are exempt from the jurisdiction of the bishop: they have their own strict rules and discipline, for which they are answerable directly to the Holy See. Everything relating to that discipline and to the conduct of the regular communities comes under the congregation for "Affairs of the Religious." It deals also with oblates and the third orders of the regular communities. It handles and decides on disputes which sometimes arise between Orders, a state of affairs which was a frequent occurrence in early mission days, although happily a rare event in these times. The Congregation of Propaganda is too important to be treated here at any length. It will have a chapter of its own. Sometimes named as a separate Congregation, but in actual fact forming part of the "Congregatio de Propaganda Fide" is the Congregation of Eastern Rites, which has jurisdiction over the spiritual affairs of all Catholics belonging to the Eastern Rites. These include such Churches as the Coptic Church of Egypt, the Coptic Abyssinian Church, the Maronite Church, and several branches of the Greek Rite.

We have seen already, in the work of the Congregation of the Holy Office, how strict a watch is kept so that the morals, the doctrine and the liturgy of the Church can be kept unchanged and unpolluted by any taint of heresy. This work is carried to a conclusion by the Congregation of the Index, in Latin "Indicis librorum prohibitorum," the list of books, the reading of which is prohibited to the faithful of the Catholic Church. Early in the history of the Church, the danger of the influence and subversive teaching of bad books was realised by successive Popes, and several times during the Middle Ages, lists of books were compiled which were forbidden to be read. With the invention of printing, the danger became far more acute and finally Pope Pius V set up the Congregation of the Index, constituted of a number of Cardinals and a great number of professors and experts. Their instructions in the matter of the examination of books were laid down most minutely by Pope Benedict XIV in 1753. The list contains books of heresy, all books that are obscene, certain controversial works and works of magic and astrology.

One of the great Congregations is that of Rites (see "The Canonisation of a Saint"). Its duties are twofold. Ordinarily it has the duty of seeing that there is a general uniformity in the form of worship, in the services of the Church, that is to say, the Liturgy, throughout the world. It gives permission for various differences of detail, according to custom or tradition. Secondly, it has the duty, and a very important though long-drawn-out one, of examining, discussing and judging any claims which may be brought before it for the beatification and, later, the canonisation of saints.

Whenever any of the great feasts of the Catholic year call for ceremonies in St. Peter's, or whenever there are the ceremonies of the beatification or canonisation of a saint, then the magnificence and splendour are beyond imagination. At such times His Holiness the Pope is attended by a great

A procession of Bishops entering the Council chamber for the First Ecumenical Council

retinue of the Hierarchy of the Church, Cardinals, Archbishops, Bishops and many other great and important dignitaries. It would be impossible to hold any ceremony if all these important Churchmen had to scramble for their places or had no idea of where to go or when, and so the Congregation of Ceremonies takes charge of all ceremonies in which the Pope or the Cardinals will take part. At the head of the Congregation is a Grand Master of Ceremonies, and he, with the help of the Congregation, deals with all questions of etiquette and precedence.

A Congregation which does not meet except when needed is that of Extraordinary Ecclesiastical Affairs. As its name conveys, it deals with situations which arise beyond the scope of the other Congregations. That is why this Congregation is sometimes referred to as a Congregation of State.

Right at the beginning of this article we mentioned, among other institutions which the Church maintains, the Universities, colleges and seminaries. Some of the great Orders such as the Jesuits, the Franciscans, the Dominicans, and the Benedictines have colleges and seminaries of their own. The studies of all these, whether the university training for a degree, or the seven years training for a priest, come under the Congregation of Studies. When the number of students justifies the setting up of a new Catholic University it is this Congregation which initiates it and carries it to its opening, and watches over it from then on. Finally we come to two Congregations which deal with the most important buildings that the Church possesses, the basilicas of Loreto and, of course, Saint Peter's with the Vatican. In both cases, the duty of the Congregations is to keep watch over the

14—III

sacred buildings, to see that they are kept in good repair, that any damage is quickly made good. To the great body of the Catholic Church there can be few places so worthy of veneration as St. Peter's and the Vatican, the home of His Holiness. We know that St. Peter's was built over the site of several famous buildings of Roman pagan times. Below it there lie layer upon layer of history, both pagan and Christian: the burial place of St. Peter is there, and excavations are continually taking place. At the canonisation ceremonies of a saint, at the election of a Pope, the Vatican is illuminated and decorated. All these activities must be carefully studied and controlled lest the fabric suffer any damage.

These are the great Congregations and between them they deal with the greater part of the business of the Church. There are also three tribunals: the Rota, the Signatura, and the Penitentiaria.

The Roman Rota is a court of the first instance, or of appeal, or of final appeal, according to the origin and history of the case to be tried, for *all* contentious cases which require judicial action and examination of evidence and, unlike the Sacred Congregations, it must give reasons for its decision. It tries cases, *including criminal cases*, which the Pope may send before it, and is best known as a court of appeal from the courts in matrimonial cases. Cases may also be brought before it, not for judgment, but for a considered opinion.

The Penitentiaria, headed by the Cardinal Penitentiary, is a tribunal dealing with matters of the internal forum. It grants absolutions and dispensations, decides cases of conscience and deals with indulgences. It is a court of mercy held in secrecy and charging no fees. Any Catholic may write to the Cardinal Penitentiary. Cases are set out in letter, the characters bear fictitious names, and in order to keep the anonymity of the writers, such cases are usually made out on their behalf by their father confessors.

The Apostolic Signatura is the Supreme Court of appeal, ranking above the Rota, and deals with appeals and other matter arising from that court. It is also the court of appeal for *civil* and *criminal* cases of the Vatican City.

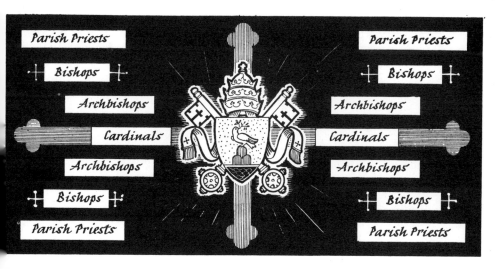

THE ORGANISATION OF THE CHURCH

In this article we are going to see how the Church here on earth is organised. From the tiny body of men to whom Our Lord gave his instructions to go forth and teach has emerged the mighty society which has nothing to equal it in the world. As Catholics we make far too little use of its powers. If we were to use the Church efficiently and as Christ willed that it should be used, the world would be a far different place. How lucky we are that the enemies of the Church can never have such an organisation! They do and will do their best to imitate it, for they know that if ever such an organisation fell into their hands they could conquer the world. Think of all the great empires of history, beginning with Alexander of Macedon, and going on to the Persians under Xerxes, to the great Roman Empire which extended over all the then known world to the Indian Empire of the Moguls, to the empires of Spain and Germany. Where are they now? Gone, like the dust of the statue in Nabuchadonosor's dream. Not all their riches nor their mighty armies

were able to hold them together and keep their conquered peoples in subjection.

Now think for another moment of the great square of St. Peter's in Rome. There is an expectant hush; suddenly a white-robed figure appears on a balcony and there is a roar of welcome from half-a-million throats, "Viva il Papa! Long live our Pope! Vive le Saint Père!" and a hundred other tongues echo the cry. Who are these half-million people who have gathered in tumultuous welcome for this man? Are they Italians because St. Peter's is in Rome? Of course not! They are of every colour, race and tongue and from every country in the world; and they are there of their own free will to pay homage to His Holiness the Pope as Christ's representative here on earth. Nowhere else could you look upon such a scene nor ever will. The Visible Church: The Pope. The Church itself has been described as the "union of all the faithful under one head." Our Lord founded His Church and he is its invisible and supreme Head, but when he returned to His Father he left behind his chosen successor, the man who was to be the Head of the Church here on earth. Christ said to Peter: "*and I say unto thee: thou art Peter and upon this rock I will build my church, and the gates of hell shall not prevail against it. And I will give to thee the keys of the kingdom of heaven. And whatsoever thou shalt bind upon earth, it shall be bound also in heaven; and whatsoever thou shalt loose on earth, it shall be loosed also in heaven.*" (Matt. xvi, 18–19.) By these words he promised to set him at the head of the Apostles, making sure in this way of the unity of the Church and of the Faith. Later in his Apostleship Peter became the Bishop of Rome, and the right of succession as Head of the Church has passed down through nearly twenty centuries to those who have followed him in that Office. In the few kingdoms that are left in this world today as well as in the great republics, the power of the ruler is limited by the will of the people in the shape of parliaments, but the Pope has no limits set to his powers of office. At the Council of Trent in 1565 all the traditional powers of the Pope were confirmed to him and those who would have curtailed his authority were discomfited. He is the direct and supreme authority over all Catholics the whole world over, and he is responsible for his actions and his decisions only to himself and to God. In all matters of administration, of beatification and canonisation, of absolution, of censure, of appeal to the courts, the last word is his. He is the supreme judge and law maker. As a man the Pope is as capable of human error as any of the rest of us, but when he speaks as the Head of the Church on matters of faith and of morals then he is infallible, unable to make any mistake. You see, he is then speaking as the Vicar of Christ, sustained and strengthened by the power of the Holy Ghost, and what he says under such circumstances may be taken as the "Word of God" put into man's mouth.

The Pope is the Bishop of Rome, the Vicar of Christ, the Supreme Pontiff and many other titles besides, but to himself he is always "Servus Servorum Dei," the servant of the servants of God, to remind himself of his Master's humility here on earth, and of the time when he washed his disciples' feet. The ordinary dress of the Pope is white, the insignia of his office are the pallium, which he wears as an Archbishop, since he is Primate of Italy and Archbishop of the Roman Province, the keys, which signify the Keys of Heaven handed down by St. Peter, and the triple tiara, or crown, showing him as teacher, lawgiver and judge.

We do not know for certain how many Popes there have been since St. Peter; the usual list gives 262 names. What we do know is that Pope has followed Pope in unbroken succession through the centuries, through strife and struggle, rise and fall, and that Pope will follow Pope as long as the world shall last.

Nobody could give very much thought to the position which the Pope holds without realising that he must be one of the busiest of men. No one man could possibly cover all the work which being the Head of the Church involves. Do you know that there are over two thousand ecclesiastical jurisdictions, that means two thousand different areas ruled by bishops? Think of the vast amount of lands, of buildings, schools, churches, orphanages, hospitals, and convents that belong to the Church, and add to all that the care of the souls of millions of the faithful and try to total it. The result would be beyond imagination. So much of the government of the Church must be delegated to others. To do this the Pope appoints the cleverest and most learned men to the dignity of Cardinal. Altogether there are seventy offices of Cardinal: six of them are Cardinal Bishops, fifty are Cardinal Priests and fourteen are Cardinal Deacons, and together they form the College of Cardinals. To be a Cardinal is a dignity and not an Order; the Cardinal is a Prince of the Church; he ranks next to the Pope himself and is responsible to the Pope alone.

The Cardinal's dress is scarlet, and he wears a biretta of the same colour. The most important part of his insignia is the "red hat." If you ever happen to visit the great cathedral of Notre Dame in Paris look up at the ceiling above the Choir. There you will see several "red hats" belonging to former Cardinals.

The chief duty of the Cardinals is to assist and advise the Pope in the government of the Church. Some of them are in charge of the various Sacred Congregations which deal with the affairs of the Church, and of the tribunals or courts which deal with disputes, appeals, law cases and benefices. When all the Cardinals meet together in the presence of the Pope to deal with claims for beatification or canonisation or other all-important matters such as the creation of Cardinals, that is known as a Sacred Consistory. When the Pope dies, all the Cardinals meet in a Sacred Conclave to elect a new Pope. There are also Cardinals in charge of the Apostolic Chancery and of the Secretariat of State, those are the offices which deal with other governments and with letters issued by the Pope to be sent to Bishops all over the world. There must be a Cardinal-Secretary of State to deal with foreign affairs, because the Pope sends

Photo Mansell

Pope St. Pius X wearing the triple tiara. Over his cassock and rochet he wears a cope and stole

his representative to the government of most other countries, and in return these countries are represented in Rome.

The representative of the Pope in a foreign country may be a Legate, the highest rank, usually a Cardinal or Archbishop; a Nuncio; or an Internuncio, who is sent to small countries.

A Nuncio is an official with diplomatic standing : he deals both with the Catholic Bishops and with the civil government of the country to which the Pope has sent him. Sometimes the Pope wishes to have a representative to deal with the Catholic Bishops only, and not with the government of the country; such a representative is an Apostolic Delegate.

Photo Mansell

An audience day at the Vatican. The Pope's bodyguard crossing the Sala Clementina on the way to the audience chamber

The Archbishops

Next in dignity after the Cardinals come the Archbishops. Some of them have the title Patriarch, as they rule over the dioceses of very ancient cities such as Jerusalem or Constantinople. Others have the title of Primate; at one time a Primate had authority over the dioceses of a whole country, or several provinces. Others are called Metropolitan Archbishops; this means that they have certain rights and jurisdiction over a province, as for example the Archbishop of Westminster has over the Province of Westminster. Some are Titular Archbishops. This means either that they rule over one diocese, or that they have no diocese, but take their title from an archdiocese that no longer exists. The Pope usually sends to an Archbishop the pallium, a badge of white wool, worn round the shoulders, with pendants on breast and back. It is the symbol of his sharing in the full authority of the Pope.

The Bishop

Remember, then, that the highest Order in the Church is that of Bishop. The Pope himself is Bishop of Rome, the Patriarchs are Bishops and so are the Archbishops. To be a Bishop is to have reached the highest rank of all in Holy Order, for the Bishop holds his rank in direct succession from the Apostles: St. Peter himself was the first Bishop of Rome; St. James was the first Bishop of Jerusalem. In the early days of the Church the Bishop was chosen from a list of suitable candidates by lot or by vote, just as Matthias was chosen to fill the place of Judas Iscariot by the other Apostles. Nowadays the Holy See is usually provided with a list of names of those considered worthy of the honour and the Pope chooses from this list. If he wishes, he can, of course, go outside this list altogether to make his choice. The Bishop wears a mitre, the double-pointed cap which has been in use for about nine hundred years: he carries a crozier, the shepherd's crook, to remind him of Our Lord's words to Peter: "*Feed my sheep.*" On his right hand he wears a large ring as a symbol of faith: and around his neck is suspended a "pectoral cross" of precious metal, usually gold.

In addition to the reports which are sent back to the Pope at frequent intervals by the Apostolic Delegate about the state of the Church in the various countries, every Bishop must go to Rome and tell the Pope all about the diocese over which he rules. If he is a European Bishop, he has to go every five years, but Bishops from other continents have further to come, and they visit Rome once every ten years. In this way the Pope is able to keep in contact with the Church all over the world and is able to advise or suggest or even direct as the case may be. Many of the dioceses over which the Bishops rule cover large areas or large populations, and then the Bishop has the help of a Vicar-General, who ranks above all other clergy in the diocese, and next to the Bishop himself. The organisation of the diocese is very much like that of the Universal Church itself. There is a tremendous amount of business to be dealt with in any diocese, apart from matters of faith, and so the Bishop has a staff attached to his office, who deal with the various problems, subject to the final approval of the Bishop himself. So, if we visit "Bishop's House" in any diocese, we shall find the office of the Chancellor, where most of the business is dealt with, and we shall meet the Bishop's secretary who deals with all the personal business concerning his superior. Just as the Pope has the help of his College of Cardinals, the Bishop has a Board of Consultors to give him their advice on important matters, and, since he is the chief authority in his diocese, he must have certain people who will act for him as lawyers; as examiners where requests for the Bishop's help arise: and as judges in the matrimonial court: there must be a Superintendent to see to all the Catholic schools in the diocese and that the Faith is carefully taught, and the Censor, whose approval must be obtained before any book dealing in any way with matters of faith can be printed. You will be able to see the "Nihil Obstat" as it is called, and the Censor's signature at the beginning of this very book. Before the script was sent to the printers the publishers were careful to send it to the Censor for his certificate.

Abbots

The Pope, the Cardinals, Archbishops and Bishops are known as Prelates. Also ranking as Prelates are the Abbots. The Abbot is the "father" of his community of monks and the word "abbot" is taken from the Chaldean "abba" meaning father, because the Greek word for father was used in talking of bishops. In the Middle Ages many Abbots were extremely important, and were allowed to use the mitre, crozier and ring as if they were Bishops.

The Parish Priest

On our visit to the Bishop at Bishop's House we should probably come across a map of the diocese and find it marked out into hundreds of small areas, each fitting into place among the others as the parts of a jig-saw puzzle make up the whole. Each of these areas is a parish and the Church places each parish in the charge of a Parish Priest, and he is responsible for the spiritual care of all the souls in his parish and for the finances of the church also. The Parish Priest is one of the busiest of men. His home is always open house for the members of his congregation to seek his help, ask his advice, to pour out their troubles at all hours of the day (and night). He says his Masses, reads his Office, hears confessions as his Order as Priest demands. He must visit the sick and infirm in their homes, carrying the Holy Eucharist to the bedridden and ill; the hospitals see him daily, the schools very frequently: he visits the waverer, seeking to strengthen him in his Faith and to draw him back to the Church: he instructs the would-be convert in what he must know of the Catholic Faith. In the larger parishes he has the help of Assistant Priests whose lives are as busy as his own.

In its general structure the Church can be compared to a triangle, with the Pope at the highest point, and descending in rank in the order we have described: Cardinal, Archbishop, Bishop, and with the Parish Priest forming the base. To these may be added those dignitaries as we call them, whose duties are necessary for the smooth running of this vast and complex society. The Pope has for his assistance in the government of the Church, twelve Congregations, working under the College of Cardinals, and which deal with the affairs of the Church in all its branches. You should read the article on "Sacred Congregations" to see how carefully the Church watches over its affairs and those of the faithful, and then you will be able to see how lucky we are to be members of a society never equalled on earth.

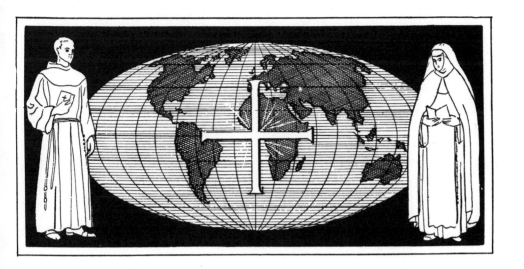

MISSIONS TODAY

"Daddy! What are foreign missions? This morning Miss Burney, my teacher, said that our money was to be sent off to the Foreign Missions in Africa to buy medicines and things for the natives. Aren't there any doctors in Africa?"

Mr. Morton considered his last piece of ham for a moment. He swallowed it hastily and pushed away his plate. "Well, Johnnie, there's quite a lot of explaining to do about that. First of all, let's see what a mission land is. Some countries are mission lands because the peoples of those countries are heathen who have never heard of Jesus and the Apostles and the True Faith, and who still worship idols. Before there can be a Church with an hierarchy —that means rulers of the Church, such as Archbishops and Bishops—and Priests—these heathen must be taught all about God, about his Divine Son, and about the Holy Eucharist. Remember, people like this don't know anything

about what we worship: they find it difficult to even imagine other lands and other people differing from themselves in the colour of their skins and in their way of life. In most cases their life is bound up with whether they will have enough to eat until the next harvest and whether they will have sun and rain to give them good crops. This means that the missionaries must educate these people in a very simple way to know about God.

"Still, we will come to that later. Let's go back to Europe, to our own continent. About four hundred years ago, as we know, a large part of Europe turned away from the Mother Church and became what we call Protestant. Some of the countries which broke away were regained for the Faith, but there are some where the Catholics are very small in number compared with the whole population, and in these countries there is no hierarchy. These countries too are mission lands. This country,

207

England, in which we live, was a mission land until 1850, but hard work and prayer are beginning to lead her back into the Church.

"Usually, though, when we speak of the missions we think of the countries among the heathen, where people have never heard of Jesus Christ and his Blessed Mother, or of that Christmas at Bethlehem or of the glory of Easter Sunday."

"But Daddy!" Johnnie interrupted his father, "if there are no rulers of the Church in these places, who sends out the missionaries? I mean—well, a little while ago we had a Father in church to talk about the missions. He was a Holy Ghost Father, wasn't he, and he said there are hundreds more like him. Do they all go out among the heathen just as they wish and hope they will be sent enough money to keep the mission going, and if not, who tells them where to go and sees that they get the money and things like that?"

Johnnie's father looked at him in mild amazement. "My goodness, that's a lot of thinking for such a small fellow as you are, but it's a good question all the same. There are many Orders, just like the Holy Ghost Fathers, who send out missionaries, and all these missionaries must be trained specially for the work in the mission lands. You see, Johnnie, a missionary doesn't go to foreign lands just to preach, and so he must go to a college to be trained in all kinds of things.

"First, he must learn to speak the language of the people among whom he will work, and he must learn all about their lives, their pagan gods whom they worship, and their laws and customs. He will need to be a teacher, and build schools; he must know something about medicine, to care for the sick and injured; and in between times he must build his church, where he can say his Mass. All

this takes several years of training before the missionary-priest is ready to be sent on his mission."

"When he is ready then," demanded Johnnie, "can he choose where he would like to go, or must he go to some special place?"

"I think most of the colleges train their students for certain special regions," replied Mr. Morton. "Just think how awkward it would be if every priest in the college needed to learn a different language from all the others. That is why the White Fathers became missionaries in Africa; the Scheut Fathers went to China or Africa, and the French missionaries of the Society of Lyons went to Africa. Here in England missionaries are trained at Mill Hill and there is a famous missionary college at Maryknoll in the United States. Of course the great Orders, the Jesuits, the Franciscans and the Dominicans have always been foremost in the mission field; the Franciscans in California and the Jesuits in South America and China, for instance. Then too, there are the Redemptorists, the Passionists and the Lazarists, together with the Colleges of Milan and Paris, the Consolata of Turin, the Divine Saviour and of the Holy Ghost. They were founded especially for the training of missionaries. You asked me just now who directed the missionaries and the work in mission lands. Well, you know that the Pope has a College of Cardinals who help him with all the work of the Church, and the work of the Church is divided up among the Sacred Congregations. Well, one of these Congregations is called 'De Propaganda Fide.' That's Latin, and perhaps its hard for you to remember but it means 'for spreading the Faith.'

"You see, Johnnie, missionary work isn't new, and as far back as 1622, over three hundred years ago, a very

A mission nurse with a Chinese mother

famous Pope, Gregory XV, first founded this Congregation to look after the Church in the mission lands. Pope Gregory died only a year later, and it was the Pope who followed him, Urban VIII who completed Pope Gregory's work and set the Congregation working. He set up a college in Rome for the training of missionary priests. It is still there, and it is called after him, the Urban College. You mustn't think that missionary work began only in 1622. There had been missionaries in America for over a hundred years, and in India, too. By then St. Francis Xavier, you know all about him, had been dead for seventy years, and the famous China missionary, Ricci, had been dead for twelve years. Pope Gregory's idea in setting up this special Congregation, 'Propaganda,' was to take control of the missions all over the world directly into the hands of the Holy See. The idea now was that the Pope should appoint bishops who would be known as Vicars Apostolic, and they in turn would be responsible directly to the Pope for all the missionary clergy in their territory.

"As time went on, Johnnie, there would be more and more of the heathen converted to our Faith, and it was hoped that one day there would be so many native Catholics that it would be possible to have native priests, and even native bishops.

"It took a long, long time, but in the end, over two hundred years after the Congregation was founded, there were regions where the Faith was so strong that native bishops were consecrated, and today we can find men of many different races who have Bishoprics.

"And that, Johnnie, is where your sixpences and half-crowns come in. You can't build schools, colleges, hospitals and mission buildings without money; and when you have built them there must be more money for books, medicines and a thousand and one other things. Do you know how many territories there are which depend for their work on the pennies, shillings and pounds of the rest of the Catholic world? There are almost seven hundred now. Some of them are small places, tucked away in an odd corner of the world; others are great regions where the people can be counted in millions, but where the Catholics are still all too few. That is not because the people don't want to believe. It's because the money just doesn't run to enough missionaries and missions. Think of all the countries of South-East Asia. In Indonesia as it is called nowadays, in 1951 there were only 780,000 Catholics out of a population of 77,000,000; in India where there are 5,700,000 Catholics out of 412,000,000. We can travel all over the world and find them. Ethiopia, Nigeria, Burma, Siam, Japan.

"Let me give you a few figures to show you how much your money is needed."

Johnnie's mother, who had been washing up tea-things, and listening too, stopped in the doorway. "This is why Mummy and I never say no when you ask us for money for the missions. They are big figures for a small boy to grasp, but if every little boy's mummy and daddy could read them I think your collection would be much, much bigger than it is now. I know all these figures. I copied them down when the Father gave us a talk about the missions at our meeting of the Knights of St. Columba. In 1961, which is the latest date for which world figures were given, in the territories which come under the congregation 'Propaganda' (apart from Australia and New Zealand) there were 24,700 priests, 8,300 brothers, and 56,700 nuns, together with 92,000 native catechists. There were 47,000 schools, with 4,000,000 children; 3,100 dispensaries, 1,100 hospitals, 1,720 orphanages, and 174 leper hospitals. Altogether the Catholics numbered 32,600,000 and

there were 3,000,000 under instruction. Enough to make your head whirl, isn't it? And collecting enough money to keep all this going, and getting enough to meet all the extra demands that come in every year, would mean another terrible headache. Yet it all started from pennies like your own.

"If you could visit the Palace of the Congregation de Propaganda Fide in Rome and go into the room where the Pontifical Mission Aid Societies hold their meetings you would see on the wall the picture of a young Frenchwoman called Pauline Jaricot. She lived about one hundred and fifty years ago in Lyons, in France. She had always been interested in missions, and when her brother joined the Paris Foreign missions she used to collect money from all her friends to send to him. One day she thought of getting many other people to join, and soon there was a wide system, built up in circles of ten people, which collected money and sent it off to Headquarters in Rome for the use of the missions. Today that movement is world-wide. Here in England we have the Association for the Propagation of the Faith, and the Society of the Holy Childhood, who send the money they collect to Rome; and so do people in France, the United States, Holland, Germany, Belgium and other countries far and wide.

"The first collections in England in the year 1837 came to just over £95. In 1956 they reached £60,000. Even that seems a small sum when we look at the United States. The Catholics there are nine times as many as in England, but they gave nearly sixty times as much, £2,945,000. France gave £275,000. Germany £200,000, and even India, which is still a mission country, gave £15,000. It seems a lot of money, but it still isn't enough. There is always a demand for more schools, more

Bringing the Love of God to the Nigerians

hospitals, more orphanages, more colleges, and they all cost money. So the work of collecting money goes on. There are many societies, all grouped under the name of Pontifical Mission Aid Societies, and if we can't all be missionaries, we can at least help with our sixpences. And what do we see for our money? Look at Formosa, where the Catholic population has gone up from 20,000 to 180,000 in ten years, and there are still 60,000 under instruction. In 1945 there were 100,000 Catholics in Japan; today there are 277,000. In Africa in 1900 the Catholics numbered 1,250,000; today there are almost 25,000,000. In India the Church has fifty-five colleges. In Togoland, in West Africa, there were no Catholics in 1892; today, only seventy years later, there are 216,000. Yet there is a tremendous amount of work still to do. Hundreds of devoted priests and nuns go out every year into the far places of the world to preach the Faith, but hundreds more are needed. There are one hundred and fifty million Catholics in Central and South America, but only fifty million of them have priests. No wonder, Johnnie, that the Church is always glad of your sixpences. And now, I think, you had better run off and play or bedtime will be here. Away with you!"

The following day Johnny finished his tea so quickly that his mother looked at him in mild reproof, but he sat so quietly that she forgave him, and Johnny remained in anxious silence until his father had settled himself comfortably in his armchair, and had lit his usual after-tea cigarette.

"Now then, young fellow, what's this all about? Why are you so anxious to have me on the carpet? What have I done?"

"Of course you haven't done anything, Daddy. You do tease! It's just something that came up in school today.

We were talking about the Far East, about China and Japan."

"Well, what about them? China and Japan are two of the oldest civilisations in the world, even if they do lag behind a little by modern standards."

"That's just it. That's what teacher said. He says that the Chinese were civilised when the Ancient Britons were still using flint implements, and that the Japanese were too, and that they knew all about all kinds of things long before we ever heard of them."

"Very true, too. They knew all about gunpowder, and the mariner's compass, and paper and printing, and how to make silk hundreds of years before we did. But what about it? Why are you so bothered?"

Johnny considered for a few moments. "Well, Daddy, what I want to know is this. If the Chinese have a religion called Buddhism and the Japanese have Buddhism and Shintoism how do the missionaries manage? It's easy to go to some African tribe and show them what it means to be a Christian, because you can help by having schools, and hospitals, and looking after the people, but in countries like Japan and China, where people have hospitals and schools and colleges, and towns and cities just like our own, how do the missionaries manage?"

"Heigh-ho! Here we go again! Another long lecture to be given by your poor long-suffering father. What makes you think that I always know all the answers to all your questions?"

"Of course you do, my dear." Mrs. Morton chuckled as she cleared the table. "Boys' daddies always know all the answers. That's the main use daddies have. And don't tell me you don't enjoy it."

"Well, there's no arguing about that, I suppose. I hope, Johnnie boy, that I can make you understand a little of what I have to say. It's going to take all the evening, so you'd better make yourself comfortable. Now, let's look at this problem of yours about China and Japan first of all. You will remember that I told you how missionaries were usually trained for different regions, and your question will help you to see why it must be so. The Chinese and the Japanese are nations whose civilisations are among the oldest in the world. You have learned at school that people in the Far East were civilised when the Ancient Britons were still using stone axes. We know that the Chinese people settled in the fertile valley of the Hwang-Ho or Yellow River two thousand years before the birth of Christ. The first of their great teachers, Lao-Tse, was born in the year 604 B.C. He was a very wise man, and wrote a book called Tao, or True Way of Life, and which is still one of the most famous books in the whole world. After him came Kung-Fu-Tse, born 551 B.C. He is known as Confucius and his teaching spread all over China. Later on, Buddhism spread into China and it was a Buddhist monk who discovered the tea-plant. The Japanese started out with a Nature worship called Shintoism and then became followers of Buddha.

"Supposing, then, you became a missionary and you were sent off to China or to Japan to try and teach the people about Our Lord and his death on a Cross in a tiny country thousands of miles away. You see what a difficult thing it would be. You would be trying to persuade people who had been worshipping in a certain way for hundreds of years to change to your God, of whom they would know nothing. Because of this, the progress of the Faith in such countries is slow, very slow, and patience and example are the best means of putting forward the Catholic Faith."

Father Damien among the lepers

"Yes, Daddy. I see that," said Johnny solemnly, "but I thought you said missionaries had to be doctors and teachers, and build hospitals and schools."

"So they do, so they do! Look Johnny, you know lots of stories out of the Bible and particularly those told by Our Lord; these we know as parables. Have you ever noticed how he went about his teaching? Our Lord always altered his stories to suit his listeners. When he was talking to the poor people he spoke about food and crops; do you remember the story of the Sower, and of the Shepherd and the lost lamb; but when he talked to the rich he spoke about the Owner of the Vineyard, or of the rich man who gave a feast, or the man who lent out his money. That's what missionaries have learned to do. They have learned that when a man and his family are poor, hungry and suffering, they need help. So they build the hospitals and orphanages and schools,

and try to show that the love of Our Lord means love of man by his fellow-men. The poor, the sick and the needy who flock to the schools and the hospitals learn to lose their distrust and their fear, and are ready to listen when they hear the priest talk of his God, and of how his Son came down to earth to lay down his Life for the sins of mankind. And that is something which is quite against most pagan ideas. You can read in your history books how most pagan religions were built upon fear. There is no love for the gods in them, but horrible stories of human sacrifices; and of terrible punishments by offended gods. To try and tell them that the Son of the All-powerful God took on the nature of man, and died like a criminal on a Cross is very, very difficult, and the missionary can succeed only if he tries to live his life as near to the pattern of Jesus Christ as possible. In that way he can show that he means what he is teaching, and persuade his people to follow his example. It must be heart-breaking to give up a whole lifetime, as missionaries do, and to die feeling that so little has been done."

"That's what I'm beginning to think," said Johnny, solemnly once more, "I've always thought that I'd like to be a missionary and go off and make thousands of converts, and become famous like Father Damien."

"Father Damien didn't become famous because he made thousands of converts, Johnny . . ."

"Of course not, Daddy. He lived among the lepers, didn't he?"

"Yes, he did, and you mustn't think that because the work he did among the lepers made him famous, that Father Damien was in any way different from thousands of others who have gone out to preach the Faith. There is nothing easy about the life of a missionary. Supposing he is sent to Central Africa, or to the islands of the East Indies, or to Brazil. He will have a mission away in the tropic heat of the jungle, probably a hundred or even hundreds of miles from the nearest civilisation; he must himself struggle against jungle fever, malaria and leeches, and at the same time look after the sick who will come to him for help. There will be poisonous snakes and insects, savage animals and people, and always the heat and the loneliness. The missionary may not see another white man for months at a time, and there will be no one to whom he can turn for help when difficulties come, as they are certain to do. I have just been reading about the work of missionaries in South America. Listen to this! Although there are one hundred and fifty millions of Catholics in the countries of South America, there are still great areas where the natives have hardly seen a white man. Take, for instance, the region known as Matto Grosso in Brazil. Away out in the jungle there is a mission which has to

Fighting their way through jungle on their mission in the Matto Grosso

On a long missionary journey in the Sahara

cover an area of 187,500 square miles, more than three times the area of England and Wales. And how many missionaries would you think there are to cover this tremendous region? Just twenty! Eight Jesuit priests, four Scholastics, and eight brothers; and to help them twenty Little Sisters of the Immaculate Conception. Their journeys into the jungle to the settlements take months at a time; they must live on the game and fish they can catch, and travel on horseback or on foot. Their people are very poor, ignorant and often suffering from disease. So these wonderful missionaries run three dispensaries, a hospital, two homes for old people, two schools for children and two for adults, as well as a kindergarten.

"In the Sahara desert in Africa there is a diocese called Laghouart with an area of a million and a quarter square miles, the largest diocese in the world. The people are scattered all over the area, moving with their flocks from one oasis to another. Think of the travelling to be done. In the Sahara the missionary lives on camel-back as he tries to visit as many of these scattered tribes as he can. There are just seventy lay missionaries at work in the schools and dispensaries, while the White Fathers carry the Faith as far and wide as they can. Then, from places like Africa and Brazil you can go to the Far North——"

"Ah yes! I know something about that, Daddy. Our teacher has told us about the Eskimos and their kayaks and of how they hunt seals and knock holes in the ice to fish and . . ."

"Steady, my boy, steady. Take a deep breath."

"Do missionaries go right up there though, Daddy? There are not very many people, are there?"

"If you are a missionary, Johnny, you don't mind where you go. Just because there are vast areas and very few people is no reason why they should be denied any knowledge of the Faith. What did Our Lord say?—'Go ye forth and teach all nations!' And so you can go to Labrador, or Hudson Bay Territory, or Kuwatie, or any of those places right away in the far north of Canada, where the land is measured in thousands of square miles and the people counted in hundreds. In 1941 for an area of 1,300,000 square miles the North-West Territories had a population of twelve thousand, yet those few thousands must not be neglected. Far beyond the Arctic Circle in the frozen wastes where daylight in summer lasts for months and where the night is just as long in winter, live the Eskimos, and to them the story of the True Faith must be carried. The loneliness is still there for the missionary, but instead of the heat there is the cold, cold so great that the temperature cannot be measured with a mercury thermometer such as we use but only with an alcohol thermometer. There the missionary travels on foot with a sledge and a dog-team, so wrapped in furs that nobody can tell him for a priest, living on dried meat and frozen fish, and fighting against snow-blindness and frostbite. The only other white people who venture into these regions are a few traders and Canadian Mounted Police. There cannot be any schools and hospitals because buildings are something unknown, and the Eskimos live in igloos in winter and skin-huts in summer, but there are always sick and injured to be tended and while he is doing this the missionary can tell the story of Our Saviour and his Love.

"Perhaps now you won't have any more ideas of glamour about the life of a missionary. Be a missionary by all means when you grow up, Johnny, but now you won't have any doubts about the kind of life it will be. Being a missionary means a lifetime of hard work and patience; a lifetime of struggle against poverty, disease and intolerance; a lifetime spent among strangers,

A missionary struggling through a blizzard in the frozen north

A welcome chat with a mounted policeman

perhaps never to come back home again, and finally, to be forgotten except in the prayers of Mother Church."

"There's one place you haven't said much about though, Daddy. What about China? We had a story at school about Father Ricci and the early missionaries, and there are still millions of people in China who still worship false gods, aren't there?"

"I'm afraid, Johnny," his father replied, "that China is one of the great tragedies of the Catholic world of today. Since the Communists came to power in China, the Church has been gradually deprived of its missionaries. In 1948 there were almost six thousand missionaries in China and about eight thousand five hundred Chinese religious. In a few years they have all been driven out, so that by the beginning of 1957 there remained only twenty-three; one bishop; eleven priests, of whom seven were in prison, and eleven sisters. We must just hope that China's three and a quarter million Catholics will remain constant to their Faith and we can all help with our own prayers. Good gracious! Look at the time! Your mother will want to know why you are not in bed. Off you go, and remember the missions in your prayers."

ARTISTS OF DISTANT LANDS
TELL THE CHRISTMAS STORY

Courtesy United States Information Service

A highly decorative painting from Nigeria illustrating the "Adoration of the Magi"

In this section are reproductions of paintings and bas-reliefs by artists from far and wide. These modern artists give us their own interpretation of the Christmas Story which has stirred the imagination of countless artists through the ages. The illustrations are interesting because the artists have used their own local surroundings and the Holy Family are given the features and colour of the artists' own people. This may be strange to us but the sincerity and imagination of the artists make us realise there are other conceptions than ours of the wonderful story.

"*The Nativity,*" *by Castera Bazile, well-known Haitian artist*

"The Adoration of the Magi."   *A Vietnamese artist places the scene against a tropical background*

"Christ in the Manger" is the work of one of Japan's leading religious artists, Teresa Kimiko Koseki

"Madonna and Child"—a bas-relief of coloured plaster, by the Cuban painter José Quintero

"Madonna and Child" in the true Chinese fashion by a Chinese artist

e Flight into Egypt" by the Indian artist Jaimini Roy. This shows a bold Indian pattern and the wide-open eyes which are peculiar to Indian art

"*The Flight into Egypt.*"   *This is a simple and charming interpretation by an artist from French West Africa*

ECCLESIASTICAL DRESS

Hierarchical Insignia

Cardinal   Pope   Archbishop

...ishop wearing cappa magna over rochet and violet ...ssock. In winter the cape is of white ermine

Archbishop in full pontificals. Under the chasuble he wears the dalmatic and tunic, and over it the white woollen pallium, the symbol of his Apostolic authority

219

Bishop in violet mozzetta worn over rochet and violet cassock, on his head is the zuchetto

Bishop in mantelletta, rochet and violet cassock. The mantelletta is also violet faced with red. On his head a violet biretta

Bishop wearing black cassock edged with crimson, crimson sash and feriola

Canon with black cassock edged with red, and short violet cape (mozzetta) edged with fur, worn over the rochet

220

Priest in cassock and biretta

Priest in cape-cassock

Franciscan friar's habit showing hood and cord

Benedictine monk's habit showing scapular and hood

221

A contemplative nun of the Carmelite Order   *A French Sister of Charity*

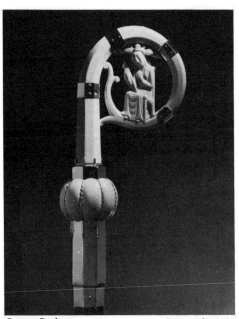

Dunstan Pruden   Courtesy the Artist

Crozier in ivory and silver made for St. Mary's
Abbey, Buckfast

HOW A SAINT IS CANONISED

We are all familiar with the names of saints, aren't we? St. Peter, St. John, St. Paul. "Why, of course," we say, "they are the names of apostles; those men whom Jesus chose to carry his message to the world."

But sometimes we read of other saints, perhaps in a history book, perhaps in a story book. There is St. Augustine, who came to this island to bring the faith to the people whom St. Gregory had called "Angels—not Angles"; St. Alban, who was killed by the Romans because he believed in Jesus Christ; St. Francis of Assisi; St. Teresa of Avila; St. Teresa of Lisieux, and the peasant girl who became St. Bernadette.

We always think of them as saints, but do we ever ask ourselves why? Who says that they shall be known as saints? Do we just call them that because they have lived holy, devoted lives? It can't be that, because thousands of people try to live good lives—ordinary people like ourselves; and not one of us would claim to be a saint, would he?

Let us think a long way back, right back to the times of the Old Testament. We find that even in those days some men were famous for their good deeds, for their efforts to lead good lives.

"Let us now praise famous men," says the scripture, and goes on, "Let the Church declare their praise." These were men like Abraham, Isaac, Jacob and Moses; the great leaders of that little race who were to become known as God's chosen people.

So you see, from earliest times people wanted to pay honour to the memory of those who deserved it. From this the whole system of the making of saints has been built up. It has gone on through the years of the persecution of the Church and the martyr's death that so many died, down through the centuries to our own times, to Saint Bernadette of Lourdes, and Saint Marie Goretti, whose relatives are still alive as I write.

The earliest saints known to us

Edward the Confessor's Shrine

are the early martyrs. Their bodies, whenever possible, were buried. This was not always possible, because many of those who died at the Roman Games, at the hands of the gladiators or the jaws of wild beasts could not be buried. Many more were thrown into the river Tiber to be washed away to the sea. Those whose bodies could be recovered were buried, and above the remains an altar was erected, to serve as a table upon which the Mass could be offered. It was also a protection, for the superstitious Romans would not disturb the place of the dead. Many of the oldest churches in existence were built as monuments to all the saints who lie buried beneath their altars. Of course, we have no detailed knowledge of the early martyrs. They must have numbered thousands. It is only in very special cases, where martyrs were especially famous or heroic so that the news spread to other churches, that their names have been handed down to us.

Careful Enquiry by the Church

Whenever it was possible, the authorities of the Church did make careful enquiries. Only when these proved satisfactory, was the name of the martyr placed on record.

Sometimes, after a period of years, or even of centuries, the relics of the martyr would be "translated," that is to say, taken up and reburied under an altar in a church. And so, for several centuries the majority of martyrs were revered only in the district where they lay buried. Often this reverence was paid by permission of the local bishop, without any reference or appeal to Holy Mother Church. Nearly a thousand years passed before the Church actually decreed that the word "Saint" should be added to a name. In the year 99?

this honour was given to St. Uhlrich. About two hundred years later, in our own country St. Edward the Confessor and St. Thomas of Canterbury were declared saints.

These famous men received this honour by a decree issued at a council of the Church and this practice persisted for several more centuries. Then, about the year 1634, Pope Urban VIII, in a series of decrees, decided that, except for those holy martyrs whose names had been handed down through the centuries, no honour must be paid to anyone who had not been "beatified" by the Holy See.

In this last sentence I have used a new word, "Beatified" which means "made blessed." Nowadays "beatification" or the state of being made blessed is the first step towards "canonisation," that is, being made a "saint." Now, since no-one can be made a saint while he is still alive, somebody must put some kind of machinery in motion to obtain this "canonisation." Let us see how this is done. To begin with, you must try to understand that the Church is as careful in this as she is about everything else. Only after the most careful enquiry, and years after the proceedings have begun, will "canonisation" take place.

The Early Proceedings

Anybody can set the machinery in motion by petitioning his bishop to begin enquiries. If he agrees, then a priest, called a "postulator," is appointed to take charge of the cause, to collect the names of witnesses, and to gather all possible documents that can be put forward as evidence. From the very beginning there will be expenses and as the case is built up, these expenses will increase until they may reach a final sum of anything up to £10,000. For these tremendous sums the "postulator" is responsible. Of course, when the cause

is well-known, there will certainly be offerings from far and wide to help forward the work.

The early enquiries will be made locally, in the bishop's court, where if he finds it possible, the bishop himself will preside, and if he cannot, then three judges appointed by him.

Don't think that everything is made favourable because an enquiry has been started; far from it. The Church puts forward every possible objection, for to be numbered among the saints is something which is not given lightly. The duty of objecting falls to an official, also appointed by the bishop, who is known as the Promoter of the Faith, and to most people as the "Devil's Advocate."

Every word of the proceedings must be taken down, and since shorthand is not permitted, the notary or clerk has an enormous amount of work to do.

Finally, everybody is bound by oath to secrecy, to be faithful, to be honest, and to be truthful. As the case goes forward, enquiries will be made in all likely places for evidence, particularly any that could be unfavourable, and all kinds of witnesses will be called, even though they may belong to other denominations, or are infidels.

Suppose now that the case is well under way. What is there to find out? First, all writings by the deceased must be collected and examined. There will be books, notes, sermons, letters and diaries, and there must be nothing in any of these to prejudice the cause. Next, evidence must be offered to show either martyrdom or extraordinary virtue, and that miracles have been worked through his intercession. The martyr, of course, has made the supreme gift of charity, that of laying down his life for his friends and for his God. Lastly, it must be proved that in obedience to the decrees of Pope Urban VIII there has been no public honour to the dead, without permission from the Church and the Holy See.

Proceedings in Rome

When all these enquiries have been completed satisfactorily, then the results are forwarded to Rome together with a letter from the Bishop guaranteeing that they are true.

Now the case moves forward another step. The Congregation of Rites, which deals with all these things, appoints a Cardinal to study the case, and to report on it. Once more the writings of the dead man or woman are examined in detail, and so too is the evidence of holiness and virtue, and the accounts of the miracles. Once again the Promoter of the Faith sets out his objections, and these must be answered in writing.

Then the case, with its arguments for and against, goes to the Congregation of Rites. If their report is favourable, then the Cardinals of the Congregation send a recommendation to the Pope that he give permission for the cause to go forward. From now on the case is taken out of the hands of the bishop, and put under the authority of the Congregation of Rites.

Apostolic Processes

Now again, we return to the court of the local bishop for more and more detailed enquiries. This time, however, the judges are nominated by the Holy See. They are five in number, and with them are two important priests who have been appointed by the Promoter-General of the Faith in Rome. The main discussion is now concerned with the extraordinary or heroic virtue shown by the dead person, although as before, if it is a question of a martyr, the fact of martyrdom and the cause of it will be sufficient. The body will be taken from its grave and examined carefully, and the report of the medical specialists carefully studied. If, however, there is no martyrdom, then the process is much longer and may run into a hundred or more sessions, because it must be shown that all the virtues have been exercised to an outstanding degree.

What are these virtues? They are Faith, Hope and Charity, the three theological, that is, those relating immediately to God—and the four moral—prudence, justice, fortitude and temperance. Finally, at least two miracles must be proved in detail, and here again the court calls in the help of doctors and specialists.

More Proceedings in Rome

Remember, every word of these proceedings must be copied in ordinary writing, and when you are told that this may amount to two or three thousand pages you can realise what an enormous amount of care and attention is involved. Then all this must be copied, and the copy sent to Rome, where the Congregation of Rites once more takes over. Again, the degree of heroic virtue and the miracles have to be examined, and again the Promoter of the faith will put forward every objection he can find.

There will be three sessions to discuss each of these points. The first is held by the Cardinal in charge of the cause, the second in the presence of all the Cardinals of the Congregation, and the last in the presence of the Pope himself. If the Cardinals vote favourably, then the Pope, if he decides that way also, will issue a decree announcing that the virtue or martyrdom has been proved, and the name of the dead subject of the decree may now have the title "Venerable" placed before it. Next follow three more sessions for the enquiry into the miracles.

The Miracles

For this the help is sought of specialists in the diseases said to have been cured

Pinturicchio

Photo Mansell

Canonisation of St. Catherine of Siena

The cure must not only have really taken place, but the specialists must be sure that it can be explained only outside the law of nature. Among the wonderful miracles which have been brought forward at these enquiries we find instantaneous cures of fracture of the skull, of the last stages of tuberculosis, of bad cases of rupture, of incurable skin diseases, and of internal diseases which gave the sufferers no hope of living. In all these cases the cure was instant and perfect, and no trace whatsoever of injury or disease remained. How could such things be other than miraculous! After these sessions, and when the miracles have been proved, the Pope, if he so wills, will order the decree of "beatification." You will notice that twice I have said "if the Pope so wills." This is because, no matter what the votes of the Cardinals in the Congregation of Rites might be, the Pope is the Supreme Authority, and he only can issue the decree.

Beatification and Canonisation Ceremonies

The ceremony of "beatification" must seem splendidly solemn to anyone seeing it for the first time. Anyone who visits St. Peter's on that day gains a plenary indulgence: the decree is read aloud in the presence of the Cardinals of the Congregation of Rites: The Te Deum is sung: the picture of the new "Beatus" or "Blessed"—is unveiled, the relics are incensed and High Mass is sung. Later in the day the Holy Father himself will arrive to pay his homage to the "Beatus."

From beatification the next step forward is to canonisation. At least ten years have passed since we saw the proceedings first set in motion by the petition to the bishop. Now there must be a further wait, for although "beatification" can be shown, more miracles must be proved, and these must have taken place since the ceremony of beatification. When these have been proved in detail, as before, then the Pope after great consideration and thought, and with the help and guidance of the Holy Spirit, will arrange the day for the solemn ceremony of canonisation.

Nowadays both beatification and canonisation take place in St. Peter's. Splendid as the ceremony of beatification may seem, the ceremonies for the solemn canonisation of a saint are the most magnificent that the Church can offer. And this is as it should be, for as you and I have seen, the new Saint put the service of God and His Church first throughout his life, even to laying down that life itself.

So the ceremonies build up to a fitting climax to all the long waiting; to the endless detailed enquiries; to the thousands of pages of evidence sifted and re-sifted; and the long years that have passed.

The immense building of the Vatican is decorated and illuminated. Pictures of the new Saint, and scenes illustrating the outstanding events of his life hang from the walls, and the Pope, with the support of a magnificent company of Cardinals, Archbishops, and Bishops, presides.

The ceremonies are quite formal in character, and because of that they are all the more impressive.

A request is made to His Holiness the Pope that "canonisation" be granted. Three times the request is repeated, the first time that it be granted "instanter," that is immediately; the second time "instanter, instantius," as quickly as possible; and lastly "instanter, instantius, instantissime," now, at this very moment.

The first request is held up while God's help and guidance are sought and

Murillo   Photo Mansell

St. Francis' Vision

the Litanies of the Saints recited. The same reply is made to the second request and the "Veni Creator" is sung.

Finally the prelate or bishop who is replying on behalf of the Pope announces that His Holiness will grant the request.

Listen to the words with which the Pope makes the announcement:

"To the honour of the holy and undivided Trinity, for the exaltation of the Catholic Faith and the increase of the Christian religion, by the authority of Our Lord Jesus Christ, of the Holy apostles Peter and Paul, and of Ourselves, after mature deliberation and many petitions for the Divine Assistance, with the advice of Our venerable brethren, the cardinals, patriarchs, archbishops and bishops at present in Rome, We decree and define that —— is a saint, and we insert his name upon the catalogue of the saints, commanding that his memory be annually venerated by the Universal Church upon the —th day of —th month. In the name of the Father and of the Son and of the Holy Ghost."

On behalf of the postulator for the petition thanks are offered, a solemn Te Deum is sung and the bells in all the churches in the city are rung.

Then the Pope recites the collect of the Saint, and sings High Mass in his honour.

Perhaps all this will help you to realise what the Saints were like: men and women of every station in life; poor and rich; religious and laity, who have offered up themselves to God's service, and who by their intercession have worked miracles for some of us here on earth, and who now stand numbered with the glorious company of the Apostles and Martyrs.

"Blessed be God in His Angels and in His Saints! Amen!"

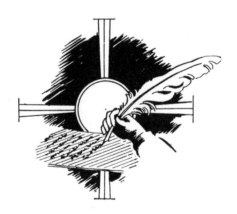

THE SACRAMENTS

"Good-morning, boys!"

"Good-morning, sir!"

Mr. Laverty looked down at the small boy hopping from one foot to the other in excitement in front of his desk.

"Well, Terence! Has the good news come at last, then! Which is it, a baby brother or a baby sister?"

"Please, sir! It's a sister, born last evening."

"Ah! that's just what you wanted, isn't it? And how about your mother and the baby, are they both well?"

"Oh yes, thank you, sir!"

Terence still looked full of news and in the end he could hold it no longer.

"Please, sir, the Bishop himself is coming to baptise the baby."

"Is he now?" Mr. Laverty smiled down at the excited little face, "and with you being confirmed this year and your sister Veronica being married you seem to be having a special interest in the Sacraments. And when Lawrence finishes his training at the Seminary and is ordained that will make four out of the seven. For your sake and perhaps for that of all the others in the class I think we could have another talk about them during the next few days. We all know what the Sacraments are called, how many there are, and so on, but I wonder how many of us ever give much thought to the meaning behind all the ceremonial. It will do all of us good to spend a little time studying just that."

Later that morning Mr. Laverty stopped as he walked between the desks and looked down at Terence. "It's still an exciting day, Terence, isn't it? Much too exciting for arithmetic, or history, or geography. Supposing we put all our books away now and begin our talk about the Sacraments, well, the first of the Sacraments, anyway. I don't have to ask you how many there are, do I?"

"Seven, sir," the reply came in a chorus. "That's right!' and now give them to me in the right order," and he wrote them on the board.

"Baptism, Penance, Confirmation, Holy Eucharist, Holy Order, Matrimony and Extreme Unction."

He underlined the first word.

231

Baptism

"Supposing we think for a little while this morning about Terence's new baby sister. Some time very soon the Bishop will baptise this very small baby in a ceremony which is one of the most ancient in origin in the Church. Tell me, where do we find the model for the ceremony of Baptism?" Hands shot up everywhere. "Yes, Michael!"

"Please, sir, Jesus was baptised in the river Jordan by John the Baptist."

"That's true! and how was Jesus baptised? Not by having water poured over him but by being dipped entirely under the water; and in the early days of the Church when people were publicly baptised on Holy Saturday, that was how it was done. Many people, you know, have the idea that the water means cleansing, to show that the stain of original sin has been washed away. Well, so it does, but it means much more also. I spoke just now about early baptism for grown-ups taking place only on 'Holy Saturday.' Nowadays we have a reminder of that because the baptismal water is blessed on that day, and during the blessing we hear several Bible stories where water played a very important part. We hear how in the beginning the Spirit of God moved over the waste of waters and out of them rose the dry land. Think for yourselves, can you tell me about another story?"

"The Flood, sir!"

"Well done! The Flood; when the earth was purified from wickedness and a new and better earth was born. And again, when the Egyptians were destroyed in the Red Sea, while the poor, downtrodden Hebrews passed over to a new life. And that is really what baptism means. It means new life in the Kingdom of God, a destroying of sin and evil and a new living with Christ. Without it we cannot hope for Heaven. Jesus himself said to Nicodemus, 'I say unto thee, unless a man be born again of water and the Holy Ghost, he cannot enter into the Kingdom of Heaven.'

"The Holy Ghost moved over the waters at the Creation; the dove that Noah loosed was his symbol, and he appeared as a dove at the baptism of Our Lord in Jordan. Baptism brings us into the living Church of Christ. Before baptism we are outside with the guilt of original sin on us, but afterwards we are members of the Body of Christ, and we can look forward to being one with him in the living Church to come. Now most of you have brothers and sisters, and you have seen some of them baptised. Let's see how much you remember about it. Since most of the baptisms in church nowadays are of infants, how can they be expected to know anything of what is happening and how can they be expected to make a profession of faith, to renounce Satan, and to make the necessary promises?" Up went the hands once more.

"You, Dominic!"

"All babies have god-parents, sir, and they make the promises for the baby."

"That's true, Dominic, and you must remember that, boys, if ever you are asked to be god-parents. It isn't enough just to hold the baby through the ceremony and then to go away and forget all about it. When you become a god-parent you have a special duty towards the baby; to see that he or she is brought up in the True Faith, that in time she, supposing we are talking of Terence's sister, goes regularly to Mass and to Confession, and that she lives as good a

The god-parents present the child at the church door

on the baby to drive away the Evil Spirit and to impart the Holy Ghost. This is followed by marking her forehead and breast with the sign of the Cross, the sign of victory over the powers of evil, and the sign that the baby has given herself to be part of the household of God. Then the priest lays his hands on the baby's head, and prays for her to have the power to resist the snares of the devil, and the desire to serve God and lead a good life.

"Immediately after comes a very interesting part of the ceremony, when a few grains of salt are put into the baby's mouth. Could you think of any meaning for the salt? What use has it in your homes and in your food?"

"It makes it taste better, sir!—The food hasn't any taste without it!—It keeps meat and fish from going bad!" The answers came tumbling out in a torrent of eager words.

"Yes! Yes!" Mr. Laverty held up his hand. "Most of what you say is

life as possible. That is what will be expected of your baby's god-parents, Terence. So many people forget that they owe this duty to their god-children and after the baptism is over neglect to do anything more, and that something is very often needed. So, suppose now that we are there to see Terence and his father and mother, his brothers and sisters bringing the baby to church.

"The god-parents bring the child to church, where the priest is waiting. Do you remember what he says? He asks what the baby expects and the reply is 'Faith,' which is to bring it to 'Life everlasting' and the priest reminds the child of the great commandment, 'Thou shalt love the Lord thy God with thy whole heart and thy whole soul and thy whole mind, and thy neighbour as thyself.' That is one of the commandments which the god-parents must see that the baby obeys as soon as she can realise what it means.

"Then the priest breathes three times

The priest breathes on the child to drive away the Evil Spirit

The forehead is marked with the sign of the Cross

The priest lays his hand on the child's head and prays for her

A few grains of salt are put in the child's mouth

The priest lays his stole over the child, and leads her to the font

right. The salt is the wisdom that makes what she learns about God pleasant to her. It is a sign that having been admitted to God's family we must not be corrupted by sin. Three times during the ceremony we have what are known as exorcisms, that is, the driving out of evil. The first time is at the beginning of the ceremony when the priest breathes on the baby: the second is after the giving of the salt. The soul of anyone unbaptised is at the mercy of the powers of darkness and so the Father, the Son and the Holy Ghost are asked to drive away the devil and become the Almighty Protectors of the new member of the great Family. Then, while the priest lays his stole over the baby and leads her to the font, the godparents, in her name, say the Creed and the Lord's Prayer, 'Our Father'—showing that the baby is now a real 'child of God.'

"This is followed by another exorcism. Can you remember, any one of you, when Jesus used his own spittle in one of

The child is anointed on the breast with holy oil

his miracles?—No!—Give me my Bible, somebody, and now listen to this from the seventh chapter of St. Mark." And he read to them the story of the deaf and dumb man whom Jesus cured by putting his fingers in the man's ears and by touching his tongue with his own saliva, saying, "Eph pheta—Be opened." "And with this very word," he continued, "in the same language that Jesus spoke the priest touches the baby's ears and nostrils, opening the child's ears to the word of God, and her taste to the sweetness of God's grace, for without smell there is no taste.

"Then, on behalf of the baby the godparents renounce Satan and everything connected with him, and the baby is anointed with the holy oil, the oil of chrism, on her breast and back, the shield of the Christian on her breast and the burden of Christ on her back.

"Then comes the actual baptism when the water is poured over the baby's head and the priest says the words of the Sacrament, 'I baptise thee in the name

The priest touches the child's ears to open them to the word of God

Water is poured over the child's head and the priest says the words of the Sacrament

The god-parents hold a lighted candle for the child

of the Father and of the Son and of the Holy Ghost.'

"Finally, the baby is anointed on top of the head to show that she is now a Christian, and she is draped in a white cloth to show that the stain of original sin is washed away. The last ceremony of all is the command to the baby through her god-parents, who, during this short period hold a lighted candle, to keep the Baptism without blame and to obey the Commandments.

"The candle can be compared to the candle of the Easter Vigil in the dark, empty church—'The light of Christ'—which has brought the baby out of darkness into her 'Father's triumphant light.' And there, boys, we had better leave the Sacrament of Baptism. I expect Terence will have much more to tell us after the Bishop's visit. Another time we will talk about Confirmation, and you yourselves will have a good deal of interest in that."

Penance

"Penance is a sacrament, whereby the sins, whether mortal or venial, which we have committed after baptism, are forgiven.

"Those are the words of the catechism—our sins are forgiven. And who is going to forgive them?" The class was having another of its talks about the sacraments.

Mr. Laverty had just recited the definition of "Penance" and was now waiting to see the hands go up in answer to the question. "Come along now. You must know the answer. You have all of you made your first confession and received your first Holy Communion. Now, who forgave you your sins?"

"Father O'Malley, sir!" The class sat back triumphantly.

"Well, shall we say the priest in the Confessional. It can't be Father O'Malley in every Confessional, you know; but Father O'Malley would be the first to say that he forgives you your sins, not by his own power, but by the power of God. You have heard him say, 'I absolve thee from thy sins, in the name of the Father, and of the Son, and of the Holy Ghost.' The Church teaches us that a baby who dies directly after Baptism, even without receiving the sacrament of Confirmation, goes directly to Heaven. But as we grow older we begin to think and act for ourselves: we know the difference between right and wrong, but because we have the gift of free will, we are allowed to choose, and unhappily enough, we don't always make the right choice. That means that we have sinned, just as Adam sinned when he had the choice in the Garden of Eden, and let himself be led astray. What do we do then? Do we go on living, letting our sins grow into a bigger and bigger burden? Of course we don't. We confess our sins, and the priest, by the power given to him by God, absolves us, as long as we show that we are completely sorry, and promise to do our best to see that the offence will not occur again. Remember this! You must be truly sorry or the absolution that you receive will be worth nothing.

"And you must remember, too, that as Catholics you will have to put up with a lot of misunderstanding about this very thing. Outside the Church itself, most people look upon 'confession' as something peculiar, a means by which we are supposed to think that we may get rid of all our sins and their punishment, and start again with a clean slate. We are supposed to believe that we can do this as often as we wish and that we consider ourselves after confession as entirely ready for Heaven.

"Now let's see what we do believe, and why! We believe that sins can be forgiven, and to help us in this belief we can repeat Our Lord's own words to his Apostles: 'Receive the Holy Spirit, whose sins you shall forgive, they are forgiven them, and whose sins you shall retain, they are retained!' Those words definitely place the power to forgive sins in the hands of the Apostles and consequently of their successors, but you must remember what I said just now, that there can be no forgiveness unless we truly repent. The first words that Our Lord said when he began teaching were: 'Repent, for the Kingdom of God is at hand.' St. Matthew, instead of 'Repent' said 'Do penance.' Both these words come from the word 'poenitentia,' a word which showed a state of real sorrow for wrong things done. Now if I do something really wrong, against the law, and have to appear before a judge and am found guilty, I shall be punished. Well, then, if I appeal to the priest to use the power which Our Lord has given him to absolve me from my sins I must tell him what those sins are, or how can he judge me and say whether they can be forgiven? God will know what sins I have committed against him, but no one else but myself. And how does God feel about me? How many of you can tell me the story of the Good Shepherd? Tell me then, Brendan."

"The Good Shepherd went out one day to look for one of his lambs that had strayed, and he hunted everywhere until he found it, and he climbed up out of the pit with it where it had fallen, and carried it home." Brendan rushed it all off in one long breath, and sat down again gasping, but thoroughly pleased with himself.

"Well done, Brendan!" Mr. Laverty was always quick to give praise where it was deserved. "There we have in a simple story from the lips of Our Lord

Kehren   Photo Mansell

The Good Shepherd

himself just how God feels towards us sinners. He doesn't want us to remain with our sins, but he is ready to lift the burden from us. Even the Hebrews of the Old Testament felt like that about God. Isaias says, 'If your sins be as scarlet, they shall be white as snow,' so you see he realised that God could and would forgive sins, and that the mercy and compassion of God had no bounds.

"Coming back to the beginning of our talks on the Sacraments we said as an answer in our Catechism: 'A character is given to the soul by the Sacraments of——?'"

"Baptism, Confirmation, and Holy Orders," the class finished for him.

"Yes, those three leave a mark or seal which cannot be effaced and so those Sacraments may be received only once. But since we are free to choose between right and wrong, and wrong often wins, then Penance must be repeated frequently. All the same, every time we go to confession God works a change in our soul. If we truly repent and really intend not to fall again into sin, then the guilt of sin is washed away from our soul and we return to the innocence we had after our baptism.

"In the early days of the Church 'Penance,' like Baptism and Confirmation, was a public affair, although, of course, confession has always been secret as between the penitent and his confessor. Nowadays we make our confession in church, in an enclosed kind of cell called a Confessional. You boys are all familiar with it, and if you want to live good Catholic lives you will go to confession regularly. Inside the Confessional, as you know, the Father Confessor is seated and there are side alcoves in which the penitents kneel and where a screened opening allows them to speak their confession.

"It is interesting to note that although the priest may, although it is not usual,

17—III

leave off his surplice, yet he must wear the purple stole which shows he is a priest. And although every priest is given the power to hear confessions and to forgive sins when he is ordained, not every priest can make use of this power. A priest can administer the sacrament of Penance only in the diocese where the Bishop has given him the right. The only exception to this is when the penitent is in danger of death, as perhaps in a street accident or a railway smash.

"Suppose now, you were going to confession this evening. What would you do? Would you go straight into the Confessional? You wouldn't! Very well then, what?"

"We ought to kneel and pray while we are waiting and make sure that we are in a true state of repentance."

"Good boy, Terence! And when we are ready and in the Confessional how would you begin?"

"Please, sir, with the Confiteor."

"And then we make our confession. Have you ever listened to the priest when he gives the absolution? Listen carefully next time and you will find that there are really two absolutions. The first absolves you from excommunication and interdict, as far as the priest is able so to do, and the second absolves you from your sins. Can you give me a reason for that? No! Well, I'm afraid plenty of Catholics don't know, but, you see, a priest cannot absolve a sinner if he is cut off from the Church and so he must first be brought back into the Church, and then his sins can be forgiven. Remember the words which Our Lord used to Peter when he made him the Head of the Church on earth and gave the keys of the Kingdom of Heaven into his keeping. 'Whatsoever thou shalt loose upon earth, it shall be loosed also in Heaven.' That is what makes Penance a sacrament, that although it is something which is administered here on earth, yet it has the supernatural power of taking effect in Heaven, and so gives grace to our souls which no longer bear the stain of sin.

"Too many Catholics often treat the sacrament of Penance far too lightly, as though it were a habit, like cleaning your teeth, or having a bath. Try never to look upon it as though it were something familiar, to be got over as quickly as possible. That kind of confession is useless. I've explained to you about your conscience, which tells you what is right and what is wrong, and about free will, which allows you to choose between them. When the time comes for you to make your confession, then you must examine your conscience thoroughly. All the times when you have put your conscience on one side you have committed a sin, and all those sins must be confessed if the matter is serious. It isn't enough to say 'I was late for Mass' or 'I told a lie' or 'I was uncharitable.' 'All right,' you say, 'what else is there? I haven't murdered anyone, or robbed a bank.' Perhaps you haven't, but if you think carefully you will find that there are plenty of sins to admit; sins of omission, through lack of will, or not caring, or from pure selfishness. And if you are still doubtful, try reading the lives of the saints. They thought themselves eaten up by sin, and spent their lives trying to atone. Next time you go to confession remember some of the things you have done—been lazy and neglected your work—been a glutton for something you liked and made yourself sick—helped yourself when nobody was about—boasted about things you have done or would do when you know very well you couldn't do them—used bad language because somebody used it to you. Then you will be making a real confession. It doesn't matter that the same sins keep occurring. That's because you are built that way, and all your life you will find those sins cropping up. Never mind! Keep confessing them and you will find that they will become easier to struggle against, and you yourself will become more humble, more peaceful at heart, and less critical of others. Then you will be living up to the Christian faith, that is, trying to grow in virtue by copying Our Lord.

"That is why the sacrament of Penance comes before the sacrament of the Holy Eucharist, because with the sin lifted from our souls, we can receive him, knowing that we have made ourselves as worthy of his sacrifice as we possibly can.

"When you have received absolution listen to the prayer which the priest says: 'May the passion of Our Lord Jesus Christ, the merits of the Blessed Virgin Mary and all the saints, all the good that you do and all the evil that you bear procure for you the remission of your sins, an increase of grace, and the reward of eternal life. Amen.'

"Beautiful words indeed, and a wonderful thought to keep in our minds as we go to receive Him at the Holy Eucharist."

Confirmation

"Boys! Father O'Malley has been in this morning to tell me that the Bishop will be visiting the parish next month to confirm all those who are ready. That means nearly all of you, doesn't it?"

Mr. Laverty looked round the class. All the faces had taken on the excited, expectant look that he knew so well.

"I expect the Bishop will remember you, Terence. You had quite a long

The Bishop, with hands extended, prays for those who will be confirmed

talk with him when he came to baptise Cecilia Anne, didn't you?"

He picked up the chalk and turned to the blackboard. "What does the catechism tell us about Confirmation? Say it for me all together."

"Confirmation is a sacrament by which we receive the Holy Ghost in order to make us strong and perfect Christians and soldiers of Jesus Christ." The words died away.

"There we are, boys. Baptism makes Christians out of us; Confirmation makes soldiers out of us, to wage war on Satan and all his works. Once we have been given the Sacrament of Confirmation we must live up more than ever to the vows and promises made for us by our god-parents at our Baptism, and show by our actions that we do mean to live up to them. Let me tell you a little about Confirmation as it was in the early days of the Church. You remember how I told you that many,

many people were baptised together. It was always on one particular day." He paused, waiting for the class, and was not disappointed.

"Holy Saturday, sir!"

"Yes, Holy Saturday: when these people were baptised they were dipped right under the water and when they came out they were rubbed all over with oil. Then they put on their new white clothes again and came before the Bishop. This time, since they had been anointed all over with oil before he 'signed' them with the sign of the Cross on their foreheads and they went straight in to church to hear the whole of the Mass for the first time and to make their first Holy Communion. So, you see, in those days Confirmation was the completing of the Baptism; it was the sacrament that completed and perfected the receiving into the 'living Church.' Perhaps now you will be able to understand why the modern sacrament of Confirmation has only a short ritual, because it was part of a very long ceremony of the Easter Vigil.

"Later on, when ordinary simple priests were allowed to administer the sacrament of Baptism, the Bishop could not be expected to confirm every baby who had been baptised immediately after the ceremony, and so, when he was able to visit, as he did, each of the parishioners of his diocese in turn, which might happen only once in several years, he would find quite a number of people to be confirmed.

"Now, what did I say a few moments ago about early Confirmation? What did the Bishop do?"

"Please, sir, he marked them on the forehead with Holy Oil."

"That's right, and that is why Confirmation is still the Bishop's Sacrament, because the chrism, the mixture of pure

The Bishop anoints the forehead of the boy

oil and balm, can be consecrated only by the Bishop. And after all this that I have said, what would you say Confirmation is going to do for you? Think of what the water meant at Baptism!"

"We hope it will give us the Holy Spirit, sir!—Please, sir, it brings us the Holy Ghost!—It makes us stronger to believe, sir!"

"Good, good! In the same way that the Holy Ghost came to the Apostles in the Upper Room on that first Pentecost, and in the same way that Peter and John went down to Samaria, where many people had been baptised by Philip the deacon, and laid hands on them so that they received the Holy Ghost, so Confirmation brings the Holy Spirit into our hearts.

"When you kneel before the Bishop your sponsor, who is like the god-parent at baptism, puts his hand on your

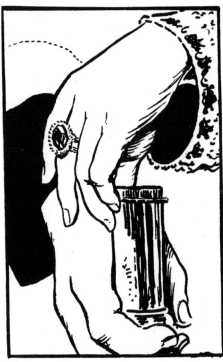

The Bishop dips his thumb in the chrism

shoulder. Then the Bishop will 'sign' you on the forehead with the thumb of his right hand, which he has dipped in the Holy Oil, and he will say, 'I sign thee with the sign of the Cross and I confirm thee with the chrism of salvation in the name of the Father, and of the Son, and of the Holy Ghost,' and he will lay his hands upon your head. From then on you will be soldiers of Christ, you will have been marked with the cross to show all the world that you are a Christian, and ready to lift up your head and do battle for him; and ready to live up to the example which Our Lord set in his life here on earth. Listen carefully to the Bishop's blessing at the end and you will hear what you may hope to gain. 'May the Lord bless you from Sion, that you may see the good things of Jerusalem all the days of your life, and may have life everlasting, Amen.' "

The Eucharist

"Hurry! There's somebody at the door. Shall I go?"

"If you will, Johnny! Tell whoever is it that I won't be a minute."

Away goes Johnny to the door and—bump—in the hallway his head makes violent contact with a very solidly filled waistcoat.

"Ouf! Johnny, are you trying to play at billy-goats? I'm sure you've ruined all appetite for my supper." Father O'Malley chuckled a trifle ruefully.

"Oh! Father! I am sorry." Johnny protested, just as ruefully rubbing his head where Father O'Malley's watch-chain had proved a trifle hard. "Mummy! Daddy! Here's Father. Do come in, Father, please!"

Father put his head round the door. "No! No! Don't get up for me. I just popped in to see how you all are, particularly this bundle of energy. All ready for Corpus Christi procession, eh?" He sank gratefully into the chair which Johnny's father brought forward and sighed.

"I wish all my visits could be as easy and as pleasant as this one always is. But no—that is being too selfish."

Johnny's mother looked up inquiringly, and Father O'Malley smiled.

"I've just been talking with a young fellow who has been asking for instruction in our Faith." He paused.

"What's his difficulty, Father?" asked Johnny's father. "Dislike of confession, or what?"

"No, not this time," Father replied. "More serious than that. It's the doctrine of transubstantiation." His face lit up, and his voice became warm and eager. "Never forget, Johnnie, how wonderfully fortunate we are in having the faith we have in the miracle of the Eucharist. So many people have faith enough in the ordinary things of life but lack the faith to believe in the things that matter most. They want miracles and signs, or as they so often say, proof positive. So many Thomases! I wonder why they can't see that that is just why God ordained it that way. There is the Body and Blood of Our Lord upon the altar and they won't believe unless they see him in his glory and surrounded by angels." He sighed again, "If I had but greater faith——"

Johnny broke in: "But, Father, Our Lord's Body in the Blessed Sacrament is not a mortal body, as it was when he was on earth, is it?"

"No, Johnny; when he rose from the dead he made his Body glorified. That means that though it was truly the same Body, it was not in the same way subject

"For this is the Chalice of My blood of the new and eternal covenant"

to the laws of nature. When the Bread and Wine are changed at the Consecration, it is the glorified Body and Blood of Christ which become present, with his Soul and Divinity.

"We believe that although the Host looks and tastes like bread, and although the wine in the chalice looks and tastes like wine to the priest, yet there is no bread nor is there any wine, but the real Body and Blood of Our Blessed Lord, and that from the moment of Consecration he has come down again upon the altar, to offer again the sacrifice of himself to his Eternal Father. That's where faith is so much needed, to be able to believe with all our hearts that it is Jesus himself who is present there. And we believe that in the words of Our Blessed Lord himself, 'He that eateth my flesh and drinketh my blood, hath eternal life.'

"Those words were not spoken at the Last Supper but in the synagogue in Capharnaum the day after the miracle of the feeding of the five thousand."

"But isn't it true, Father," Johnny's father interrupted, "that the Last Supper, at which Our Lord spoke the words which the priest now uses at the Consecration was an ordinary Jewish feast?"

"Why, of course it was," Father O'Malley replied. "Jesus was a Jew, and was brought up in the Jewish faith. He lived according to Jewish law, and kept all their religious feasts. What Our Lord wanted to do, and what with the help of his Eternal Father, he did, was to substitute the Sacrifice of himself for all those sacrifices which had been offered to God up to that time. From that time forward the old sacrifices were no longer needed, the one Triumphant Perfect Sacrifice was to be sufficient for all time. And as sacrifice had always been a part of heathen and pagan religion, Our Lord intended by the

Sacrifice of himself to separate his Church from all false religions. St. Paul was thinking of this when he said, 'Ye cannot partake of the Table of the Lord and the table of devils.' The great St. Augustine says, 'His Body is offered up instead of all these sacrifices and oblations, and it is given to the communicants.' As a Sacrifice, the Eucharist is perfection. There is the offering of the Body and Blood; the offering is made by a priest, who at the moment of offering is as Christ himself, and there is the acknowledgement that God is all Supreme, for the Mass can be offered to no one but God himself. It pays homage to the One Eternal God; it offers a perfect victim, and in offering it, we ask for and receive God's grace, through the entry of the Holy Ghost into our hearts. Tell me, Johnny, what grace would you expect to gain from Holy Communion?"

"Sanctifying grace, Father," replied Johnny promptly.

"And sanctifying grace is . . .?"

"A supernatural gift of God, freely bestowed upon us for our sanctification and salvation, Father," came the reply.

"Good boy! I see that you don't forget your Catechism. And one last question. Can you tell me the difference between the Sacrament of the Eucharist and all other Sacraments?"

Johnny thought hard. He looked at his father and mother but he found no help there. At last he shook his head, "No, Father, I can't think of anything."

"Well, Johnny, it's this. The Eucharist is 'permanent,' but all the others pass. With the others, of course, the effects remain. We say, don't we, 'Once a priest, always a priest,' but the Sacrament of Baptism or Confirmation, or of Holy Order, lasts only for the moment

"May the Body of our Lord Jesus Christ keep your soul unto life everlasting"

or two in which it is given. The Blessed Sacrament is different. From the moment when the priest says the words of Consecration, although the outward appearance is still that of bread and wine, it is Our Lord's Body which is there. We can reserve It in the tabernacle for the communion of the faithful; we can adore It in the Exposition at the service of Benediction.

"And now I must go. Pray for me, everybody, that with the help of his Sacrifice and of his Love I shall be able to strive and overcome. May he fill all our souls with his warmth and comfort. Good-night, good-night, everybody."

Ordination

"We shan't see anything of Terence today," remarked Mr. Laverty to the rest of the class as he closed the register. "I saw him with all the rest of his family on the way to the station. Today is another great day for Terence: his brother is to be ordained priest."

He glanced round the class. "Terence, I know, has a vocation, and so too, I believe has Brendan. Is that right, Brendan? In a year or two, then, you'll both be leaving us for the Seminary. It means long years of hard study but you will consider it worthwhile at the end. And when both Terence and Brendan have been ordained priests, how many degrees of Order will they have received?"

"Please, sir, seven!"

"And how are the seven made up?"

"Four minor, and three major Orders, sir." Before he could go on, a hand went up at the back: "Why are the first four called minor Orders, sir?"

"Well, boys, these first four Orders go right back to the time when the duties were performed by men who were chosen from among the faithful. Sometimes they went on to become priests, sometimes they were content to carry on with these minor posts all their lives. But every priest nowadays receives the tonsure and the minor orders, never more than one at a time though. Before Terence and Brendan receive any one of these orders they will kneel before the Bishop to be tonsured, that is to have the six little clippings of hair in the form of a cross to show that they have put away all worldliness and from then on are the servants, even the slaves, of the Church. They will next become doorkeepers, the guardian of God's house; lectors, the readers of the Scriptures; exorcists with the power to cast out devils; and acolytes, to serve at the altar at Mass. Those are the Minor Orders of the Priesthood. They do not bind a man in any way and he is free to return to the world at any time. Indeed, so careful is Holy Mother Church in her choice that if any student in the seminary shows that he may be unfitted for the priesthood he will be advised by his superiors to leave. You will have seen, at Solemn High Mass, the priest with his two assistants, because there must be a Deacon and Sub-Deacon. Can you tell me what particular duty each has?"

"The Sub-Deacon sings the Epistle, and the Deacon sings the Gospel, sir."

"That's right, and you will notice that all the priests in the parish do at times act as Sub-Deacon or as Deacon. Supposing, then, that Terence and Brendan have been chosen to be raised to the Order of Sub-Deacon. They will be advised by the Bishop at the Ordination Mass to think carefully, for from now on they will live their lives in chastity,

Offering themselves

while the congregation sings the Litany of the Saints. Then they will be told what the Church expects of them and as Sub-Deacons they will receive the amice and the maniple, the tunic and the Book of the Epistles. Later on, they will be raised to the rank of Deacons. You heard me tell about the Deacon Philip, who had baptised many converts, and of how Peter and John went to confirm them with the Holy Ghost. St. Stephen, the first martyr, was another Deacon. So you see, the office of Deacon, the assistant to the priest, goes back to the very beginnings of the Church. As Deacons, they will receive the Deacon's stole, the dalmatic in place of the tunic, and the Book of the Gospels. Finally comes the great day when they will be ordained priests, as Terence's brother is being ordained this very day. There is nothing higher than Priest in Holy Orders. The Holy Father himself, his Cardinals, Bishops and Prelates are all priests, as Jesus Christ is himself, The Priest.

The Bishop addresses the ordinands

giving up most earthly things, and spending the rest of their lives in God's service. There is no more moving sight in all the ceremonies of ordination than to see all these eager young men, anxious to enter God's service, prostrate themselves and lie full length before his altar,

"It was to Timothy St. Paul said, 'Neglect not that grace that is in thee, which was given by prophecy with the imposition of the hands of the priesthood,' and after the Bishop has pressed hands upon their heads, all the priests present, in slow and solemn procession,

The sacred vessels delivered

"Receive ye the Holy Spirit"

will do the same, passing on their priest-hood to their younger brethren. It is during this ceremony that the hands of the priest are anointed on the palms. That is why, when a priest receives the sacrament of Extreme Unction, his hands are anointed on their backs.

"From the offering of the bread onwards the newly ordained priests say the words of the Mass, their first Mass, with the Bishop, and the Bishop, laying hands upon them again says, as Our Lord Jesus Christ did to his Apostles on the first Easter Sunday, 'Receive ye the Holy Ghost, whose sins ye forgive, they are forgiven them. Whose sins ye retain, they are retained.'

"From this time onward the priest, in the highest rank of Holy Order, must try to live up to the example of his Lord and Saviour, who was truly God and truly man. At the sacrifice of the Mass he will be as one with Christ himself offering once again his Body and Blood for our redemption; in the Confessional he will be as one with God, taking from God the power to forgive sins, and in his ordinary life he will be as the Son of Man, calling himself as does the Holy Father, 'Servus Servorum Dei—the servant of the servants of God.' "

Marriage

". . . in the Church Hall . . . six different sorts of sandwiches, and ice-cream, and jellies, and fruit, and the biggest whacking cake . . . three layers, I mean tiers . . . and lemonade and orange-squash. Oh! and about the confetti . . . listen, all of you!"

Mr. Laverty stood in the doorway of his class-room and listened with amusement to Terence holding forth. Terence was surrounded by six or eight of his more particular friends in the class and they had now gone into a huddle in the corner.

"And when they come out we pelt them all down the steps . . . and all the way round to the Hall!" There was a burst of laughter; somebody looked up; the laughter became a sudden hush. Then there was a concerted rush towards their teacher. Surrounded by a milling crowd of excited, laughing boys, Mr. Laverty edged himself into safety behind his tall desk.

"Sir . . . sir! . . . sir!"

"Sssh! Now then, one at a time. What's all this about? Have the Town drawn Arsenal at home in the Cup? I'm not taking anybody's grandmother's funeral as an excuse for not doing your homework, you know."

The class roared with laughter.

"Ah well! I don't have to guess, and you don't have to tell me. Terence's sister is being married on Saturday week, and you've all been invited. How do I know? Because Terence's mother and father very kindly sent me an invitation by this morning's post. I expect they think that if all you boys are going, then I may come in useful to keep you in order. Now! be off and sit down or the rest of the class will be raising the roof."

The register was closed, the odds and ends of business, dinner money, school funds, notes for absence were dealt with, and the class settled down for its morning period of religion. Mr. Laverty surveyed his class with a somewhat sardonic grin.

"From what I heard of your conversation, Terence, my young man, I fancy that your mind and the minds of these fellow-conspirators of yours are dwelling rather much upon material things. Did I hear a mention of ice-cream, and jellies, and lemon-squash?"

The rest of the class broke out into open laughter and the wedding-guests wriggled in their seats and blushed furiously.

"Well, don't let me spoil your enjoyment of the great occasion, but for this morning we could spend a little time in thinking of the more serious side of the ceremony. You know, Terence's sister and her husband-to-be don't believe that

The priest pronounces the couple husband and wife

marriage is all jellies and ice-cream and lots of fun. They know that 'Matrimony is the sacrament which...?'" The class joined in; 'Sanctifies the contract of a Christian marriage, and gives a special grace to those who receive it worthily.'

"I would like to talk this morning first of all about the actual ceremony of marriage, then about the sacrament which gives it a special grace, and lastly about the care with which the Church lends her sanction to the ceremony.

"To begin with, the marriage ceremony is a very simple one. It is really an agreement between the two people concerned to take each other as man and wife, usually in these words: 'I, N.N take thee, M.N., for my lawful wife (or husband) to have and to hold, from this day forth, for better, for worse, for richer, for poorer, in sickness and in health, till death do us part.' A very, very solemn and impressive promise to make, isn't it?

"Then the priest blesses the marriage in the name of the Holy Trinity: the ring is blessed and sprinkled with holy water before being placed on the bride's hand and prayers are said asking for God's protection for the bridegroom and the bride. There in a very short summary, is all that there need be to the marriage service, but since Terence's sister and her husband-to-be are both good Catholics they will be married during the celebration of a special Mass, called...?"

"A Nuptial Mass, sir!"

"Yes, a Nuptial Mass. The Church asks that whenever possible a marriage shall take place with a Mass, and ever since the second century this has been a common practice. So on Saturday week we shall have this beautiful Mass which is filled with passages from the Scriptures to show exactly what marriage means. Just after the Pater Noster the priest will give the Nuptial Blessing, and again just before the usual blessing at the end of the Mass he will pray that the happy couple may enjoy fruitfulness, peace and happiness.

"The Nuptial Mass is not only a lovely ceremony, but an added means of grace, so no matter how simple the celebrations for the marriage may be, the Mass is something which should never be left out.

"Marriage existed from the beginning of mankind. God the Creator instituted it, by making man what he is. Marriage is according to the nature of man. It is a contract made between a man and a woman, to live together as husband and wife. What Jesus Christ did was to make this contract a sacrament, an outward sign of inward grace, for Christians. It is the bridegroom and the bride who are the ministers of this sacrament and they administer it to each other by the very act of making the marriage-contract.

"The Epistle read at the Nuptial Mass, taken from St. Paul's letter to the Church at Ephesus, tells us: 'Husbands, love your wives as Christ also loved the Church and delivered himself up for it.' In the same way that Christ became the bridegroom of the living, eternal Church —'a glorious Church, holy and without blemish'—so man and woman 'shall cleave to each other and they shall be one flesh.' St. Paul ends in these words: 'This is a great sacrament, but I speak in Christ and in the Church.'

"From the very beginning, then, Matrimony has had God's blessing, but since Our Lord's coming on earth it has had the added grace of a sacrament. When Terence's sister and her husband leave the church after the Nuptial Mass they will go with God's blessing 'to increase and multiply' and have children born into the Faith.

The ring is placed on the bride's finger

Bride and bridegroom receive Communion at the Nuptial Mass

"Marriages among those who do not believe as we do are none the less marriages, but if, by the grace of God, a husband and wife are converted and baptised, then their marriage gains the added grace of the Sacrament of Matrimony.

"Remember this, boys, that in all the other sacraments, Baptism, Penance, Confirmation, Holy Eucharist, Holy Order, Extreme Unction, the sacrament is administered by one person to another, whether by a bishop, or by a priest, or, it may be, in baptism, by a layman, but in Matrimony the sacrament is administered by the man and woman themselves. The priest is there to bless the marriage in the name of the Church, but by the very fact that they exchange marriage vows they themselves are the ministers.

"The sacrament of Baptism makes us members of the living Church for all eternity: Holy Order makes a man into a priest for ever: and Matrimony is a lasting state which nothing can break until one or the other partner dies. That is why I said the happy couple will soon forget the confetti, the feasting and the fun and will settle down with each other to share all the joys and the sorrows that will come during what I hope will be a long married life.

"Having done my best, perhaps a very poor best, to explain why Matrimony is a sacrament, it should be clear to you all that marriage is not something that the Church regards lightly.

"Perhaps now you will be able to see the reasons why the Church is so very strict about marriage. Apart from the fact that the Church insists that a marriage is for life, which means that there is no such thing as divorce, she takes very great care before the marriage is allowed to take place to see that there is no impediment which should prevent the ceremony. There are many of these impediments, or causes which could prevent a marriage from being lawful in the eyes of the Church and the priest must be satisfied that none of them exist before he will consent to marry anyone.

"In the matter of divorce the Church says that although the State has the power to lay down rules before it allows a marriage, it has no power at all to dissolve a marriage, and therefore the Church refuses to recognise the right of the State to grant divorces in a civil court.

"People not of our Faith will argue with you and say that what I have told you isn't true and that the Church does grant divorces: they will even go as far as to say that 'Catholics who are rich can get a divorce.' Don't believe it. Nothing could be more untrue. What occasionally happens is that after a marriage has taken place it is found that one of these 'impediments' existed and that therefore the 'marriage' is no marriage in the eyes of God and of the Church. Then the case is sent to Rome, to a special court called the 'Rota'; and after a long enquiry and lots of argument, if the court decides that the reason did exist, it gives a decree of 'nullity,'

which says that there never was a marriage. And, an important thing to remember, there are no fees, either for rich or for poor. A secret marriage cannot take place because the Church requires that the banns, that is, the notice of the marriage, must be called out in church on three different Sundays, and if the man and woman live in different parishes, then they must be called in each parish. The parish priest must be present at the marriage ceremony, or the bishop, or a priest who has been delegated specially. Even when the State insists on a civil ceremony, this is not recognised as a valid marriage for Catholics; only the contract made before the representatives of the Church is valid for Catholics. The priest himself is bound by certain rules. He can marry people only in his own parish, unless he is authorised by another parish priest or his bishop. He must, as soon as the marriage has taken place, enter the details in the parish register, and also in the register of baptisms if the couple were baptised there.

"We may be sure that in the case of Terence's sister and her fiancé everything we have mentioned has been carefully considered, and all that confetti that some of you young mischiefs are reckoning to throw, will be thrown over a couple who are safely married in the Church."

Extreme Unction

Mr. Laverty's class had a surprise one morning when they entered the classroom after assembly to find their class teacher missing. A moment or two later the Headmaster came in looking grave.

"I'm sorry, boys," he said, "but Mr.

Laverty's father was taken very ill during the night and he died just before I came to school. Suppose we all stand and say a prayer for his soul.

"'May his soul and the souls of all the faithful departed through the mercy of God rest in peace. Eternal rest grant

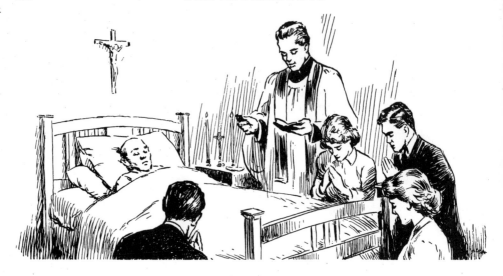

The sick person and all in the room are sprinkled with holy water

unto him, O Lord, and let perpetual light shine upon him. May he rest in peace. Amen.'

"Thank you, boys. Sit down." He paused for a moment. "You won't expect to see Mr. Laverty today, I know, but I will send him a message from us all to say how sorry we are. We must be as thankful as he is that his father lived long enough for Father O'Malley to administer the Sacrament of Extreme Unction, so that he died fortified by the rites of Holy Church. I was at Mr. Laverty's when Father arrived, and I

"May the Lord pardon thee whatever thou hast sinned by sight"

was able to help by waiting for him at the door with the lighted candle.

"This morning I have seen and heard one of the most magnificent and moving ceremonials of the Church and I should like to say just a few words to you about it. I know that Mr. Laverty has been talking to you about the Sacraments and I am sure he won't mind if I have a little more to tell you.

"It was St. James the Apostle who said in his Epistle, 'Is any man sick among you. Let him bring in the Unction, and it should not be left so late that the dying soul is beyond sight, sound and hearing. Wherever possible, and it was so in the case of Mr. Laverty's father, the priest will bring with him the Holy Viaticum, 'the provision for the journey' which the departing soul is about to take. The Holy Viaticum is of course the Holy Eucharist, and can be given to anyone in danger of death, or, as is commonly said, 'at death's door.' There is no obligation to be fasting when receiving Holy Viaticum. For the dying

The Last Blessing

priests of the Church and let them pray over him, anointing him with oil in the name of the Lord. And the prayer of faith shall save the sick man, and the Lord shall raise him up, and if he be in sins, they shall be forgiven him.'

"Notice this, boys. There is in that no prayer for the dying. It brings hope to the sick person and asks that he shall be cured and return to his ordinary life. But when someone is obviously near to death, it is then that the Church prepares him for his journey into the next world by the sacrament of Extreme

18—III

the Holy Viaticum is the bread which Our Blessed Lord described in these words: 'This is the bread which cometh down from Heaven. If any man eat of it he shall not die. . . . He that eateth this bread shall live for ever.' Even if a dying person has received the Holy Eucharist already during that day, the Holy Viaticum can be given. So, as I stood by the bedside, I saw the Blessed Sacrament brought by the priest for a man who knew that it would be the last time on earth that he would receive it, and who was ready for the great crossing

The crucifix is kissed as a symbol of the resignation to the will of God

from Death into Life Eternal. It may sound queer to you boys, but I saw no fear of death, only a man at peace with himself. I watched Father O'Malley dip his thumb into the Holy Oil and make the sign of the cross with it upon the dying man's eyes, saying these words: 'By this holy unction and his most loving mercy may the Lord pardon thee whatever thou hast sinned by sight.' And so he did with his ears, his nose, his lips, the palms of his hands and his feet, using the same words, naming each sense in turn. Then followed the prayers and the Apostolic Blessing with the final exhortation.

"Baptism brought him out of the stain of Adam's sin and the sacrament of Extreme Unction restored him to the innocence of Baptism, so that he could face his God strengthened by all the help and hope that Holy Mother Church could give him.

"'May our Lord Jesus Christ, son of the Living God, who gave to Peter the power to bind and to loose, receive thy confession and restore to thee that first robe of innocence which thou didst receive in Baptism, and I, by the power given to me by the Apostolic See, grant thee a plenary indulgence and remission of all thy sins, in the name of the Father, and of the Son, and of the Holy Ghost.

"'Through the most sacred mysteries of man's redemption may God remit unto thee the pains of the present and of the future life, open to thee the gates of Heaven and bring thee to everlasting life.'

"And may God in his mercy, boys, deal as kindly with us as he will with the soul of Michael Laverty."

SACRAMENTALS

Ash Wednesday

As usual the school had gone to church on that day for the ceremony of the "ashes" and to Mass. The dry palms of the Palm Sunday of the year before had been burned, and the ashes sprinkled with holy water and blessed.

The boys once more were back in school and looking curiously at each other's foreheads, where the dark cross of the ash stood out against the light skin. There was a subdued mutter in various parts of the room, but in one corner something was being discussed rather noisily. Suddenly a hand went up from the middle of the group and a voice asked hopefully, "Please, sir, why do the choir stalls and the priest's stall too have fish carved on their ends?" "Ah!" Mr. Laverty shut the book in front of him quickly, and moved out in front of the class. "So you've seen some fish carved on the ends of the stalls. What else have you seen in church? What other unexpected things? You should take a look round your parish church occasionally, and notice some of the interesting things. It's not always the large and obvious things that are most interesting. Think of these fish, for instance. Well, has anybody anything to say?"

"Please, sir, on some of the walls there are memorials and above them are small tablets with a cross carved on them and let into the stone."

"Sir, the candle-holders, the large ones, have IHS on them!"

"Sir, there are holy-water stoups inside the door!"

"Sir—Sir—Sir!" Hands were going up everywhere and the hubbub was terrific.

"Wait! Wait a moment!" Mr. Laverty held up his hand and the noise died away. "Before we start to deal with the first question about the fish, can you tell me what we call all these things you've mentioned. Let me see, there's the fish, the carved cross, the holy

Photo Mansell

Easter Candlestick

water, the sign IHS, the candles, and, yes, when I come to look at you, there's also the mark of the ashes that you have on your foreheads this morning. There are many others that you could have told me and which we shall be able to talk about in a few moments, but first I want to know what the Church calls them. They are not Sacraments—we have talked about each of those in turn —but these are linked up with them in various ways. Now! What is . . . ?"

"I know, sir, they are sacramentals!"

"Right! They are called sacramentals by the Church because of their close association with the sacraments. Many of them are referred to as 'Holy' or 'Blessed'; for instance, the Holy Oils, Holy water, Blessed candles, which means that the Church has blessed their use, their prayer use, of course, and has

prayed that they may help us to gain additional grace. They will help you in your inmost thoughts and your every-day life, by recalling the wonderful and supernatural graces you have received through the Sacraments, in particular the Blessed Sacrifice of the Mass. Mind you, there is nothing to say you must use them. That is entirely up to yourself. I myself use them. You have all of you seen my St. Christopher medal when I've gone down to the swimming pool with you. I never take it off and I never tire of the story of the giant who spent his life ferrying people across a deep, dangerous river. I turn to it sometimes in my missal, where it has been put in to fill a small space at the bottom of a page, and I picture to myself this huge fellow with the Child on his shoulder: 'Child, why art thou so heavy? It seems to me I am carrying the whole world.'—'Not only art thou carrying the world but him who made it. I am the Christ, thy God, and thy Master, he whom thou must serve. Henceforth thou shalt be called Christopher, the carrier of Christ.'

"I find it a very fine thought that I am a little like St. Christopher, carrying some of Our Lord's burden through life, and I know that the prayers of St. Christopher will protect and shield me through his intercession with the Holy Child whom he bore on his broad shoulders. There, then, is my own instance of the use of a sacramental. I expect many of you wear medals too— the Miraculous medal, the St. Benedict medal, Our Lady of Lourdes—yes Jamie, what's that you're showing? Of course, the brown scapular. That's not a medal, but none the less it's a sacramental and one particularly dear to the Mother of God. But before I go on to talk about scapulars and any other sacramentals, we had better have them in some sort of order, instead of all in a muddle. Today is Ash Wednesday, and we can be forgiven if we take a little extra time for our talk. So many among the sacramentals have stories attached to them that we could spend much more time than we can spare, but we will do our best with the time that we have.

The Sign of the Cross

"Let us begin then, with the most important sacramental of all, one that I heard mentioned at the beginning of this talk. What did we have—the fish, the ashes, the candles, the holy water? Which, then? Of course, the cross, or rather, the sign of the cross. We all of us use it more frequently than any other. Have you any idea how often the priest makes the sign of the cross during Mass? Fifty-two times, each time remembering the sacrifice of himself which Our Lord offered for the redemption of our sins. When we use it we say *in the name of the Father, and of the Son, and of the Holy Ghost*, and so show that we believe in the One and Indivisible Trinity, the three Persons in one God. There is no ceremony in the whole liturgy of the Church without it. In our talks on the Sacraments you have heard it mentioned time after time. The baby at Baptism is signed several times: it is used many times in the blessing of the holy water; you saw it several times in this morning's ceremony of the burning of the ashes, and if you think hard you will remember my telling you that the priest who receives Extreme Unction is anointed with the cross on the backs of his hands because his palms were anointed with the sign when he was ordained. Make the sign for me, now, slowly and reverently, right hand to the forehead—*In the Name of the Father*—now to the breast, *and of the Son*—to the left shoulder, *and of the Holy Ghost*—to the right shoulder—*Amen.*

The Crucifix

"This morning in church as I knelt at the altar rail I looked up at the figures above the altar itself. There I saw the image of Our Lord hanging on the cross while Mary, his Blessed Mother, and the beloved disciple John gazed upon him. I looked at the side altars, and saw the same image, above each of them, and I remember seeing it on a chain round the neck of Terence's sister when she was married. There we have another sacramental, the crucifix, with the image of Christ crucified. Sometimes the cross alone is used, as on the altar-stone, where we see it five times, but we of the Catholic faith use mainly the crucifix. I expect many of you have a crucifix at home—over your bed!—beside your bed!—in the hallway!—I thought so.

"One difference between the Sacrament and such sacramentals as I have just mentioned is that the Church does not say we must use them, but the crucifix should be in all our homes, to remind us of the Infinite Sacrifice. That is why we find it hanging from the rosary, so that every time we use it in our prayers we have before us the memory of the Crucifixion and Our Lord's agony on Calvary.

Relics of the True Cross

"Some time ago I knew someone who was very, very ill. She was a friend of the Mother Superior of the Convent nearby, and as well as praying for her, the community sent her one of their greatest treasures, a splinter of wood from the True Cross, in a beautiful crystal container. Sometime you must ask me to tell you the story of the finding of the Cross by St. Helena. There are many similar relics of the Crucifixion. In the Sainte Chapelle, Paris, is kept the Crown of Thorns; the veil of St. Veronica, with which she wiped Our Lord's face as he passed on his way to Calvary, is in Rome, and I expect many of you read the story of how Group Captain Cheshire, V.C., recently went to Turin with a little crippled girl so that

Sainte Chapelle where the Crown of Thorns is kept

she might see the Holy Shroud which many think is the winding sheet in which his body was wrapped when taken down from the Cross.

Holy Water

"This morning, as you went into church, what was the first thing you did after entering the doorway? You used the holy water, and you used it again when you left. Some of you may have a holy-water stoup at home. If you go to High Mass, the first ceremony is the *Asperges*, when the priest goes round the church and sprinkles the congregation; in fact you may be sure that anything blessed has been sprinkled with holy water. What is this holy water, then? It is water with a little added salt, and which has been blessed by a priest. Don't forget that there is also the baptismal water, which is mixed with Holy Oils: water for consecration of an altar, used by the bishop, to which is added wine, salt and ashes; and the Easter water, which is distributed to the faithful on Holy Saturday. We know what a great part water has played in the story of the Church, from the very beginning when the Spirit moved over the face of the waters, to the cleansing of the world from evil by the Flood, down to the Baptism of Our Lord in Jordan. The beginning of the *Asperges* puts into words all that the Church thinks of its use: *Asperges me*—'Thou shalt sprinkle me with hyssop and I shall be cleansed. Thou shalt wash me and I shall be whiter than snow.'

Stations of the Cross

"One thing you did not give me just now and which I would have expected you to mention is the series of scenes which are placed round the walls of the church. Yes, I mean the Way of the Cross. Just one point before I say anything about the pictures themselves. They are not, as most people seem to think, the Stations of the Cross. The stations are the crosses placed above the pictures, and the pictures are there only to help us remember the outstanding moments of Christ's journey to Calvary. How many stations are there, do you know? Yes, there are fourteen, each representing some event on that terrible journey. We shall not find all of them in Holy Scripture; some of them have been handed down by tradition, like the story of St. Veronica, who wiped Our Lord's face with her veil. Not many of us will ever be able to make the journey through the narrow streets of Jerusalem to the mount of Calvary, as pilgrims often did in the Middle Ages, but we can all of us follow Our Lord as he carried his Cross, and share with him the anguish and suffering that he endured; and at every station we can meditate for a little while on all that the Crucifixion has meant for us.

Holy Oils

"A few moment ago I said that the ashes on your foreheads was a sacramental. Can you think of any other time when you have been marked on the forehead with the sign of the cross? Quite recently it was."

"Please, sir, we were all marked at our confirmation by the bishop!"

"Yes, you were, but not with ashes. What did he use?"

"Sir, he dipped his thumb in the holy oil."

"And when else have you heard of the use of holy oil during the Sacraments? During Baptism — Extreme Unction — when the priest is ordained. It is little wonder then, isn't it, that the Church looks on the Holy Oils with very great reverence, and that the ceremony on Holy Thursday when the oils are consecrated is full of great pomp and solemnity. You notice that I use the word 'oils.' That is because there are three different Holy Oils used in church : the oil of catechumens, the chrism, and the oil of the sick.

"The catechumen was the convert who was preparing to be baptised, and

Photo Vasari

Font in the Cathedral of São Paulo, Brazil

at his baptism he was to be anointed. That gave the oil used in Baptism its name. It is used for making the sign of the cross on the breast and back of the person who is to be baptised. The chrism is used to anoint the crown of the head after the water has been poured on at baptism and to anoint the foreheads of the candidates at confirmation. It is into the chrism that the bishop dips his thumb. When a bishop is consecrated the chrism is used, and the bishop himself uses it to consecrate some things which are set apart for God's service, such as chalices and patens. There is a very interesting story in the book of Exodus which tells how God commanded Moses to make a special oil with which Aaron and his sons were to be anointed priests. The words used by God to speak to Moses of the holy oil are used of the chrism: '*This Oil of Unction shall be holy to me through all your generation. The flesh of man shall not be anointed therewith and you shall make none other of the same composition, because it is sanctified, and shall be holy unto you.*'

"Because the Holy Oils are a sacramental which commands such reverence they are guarded in our churches with very great care, and at the end of the year, if any of them remain, they must be poured into the sanctuary lamp and consumed, and the new oils used. The reverence and homage with which the oils are consecrated and guarded show how much value the Church places upon their use, and how much grace we must gain from their use in the Sacraments.

Candles

"There is one thing that has formed a part of all religions ever since the world began; I mean light. Among pagans, who knew nothing about God, it was natural to worship something that gave warmth and drove away darkness, of which they were afraid. Down among the catacombs beneath the city of Rome the early Christians needed light, and so they used candles, and the candles soon came to be recognised as the symbol of Our Lord. They must be of wax—bleached wax—Our Lord's most spotless body—not of tallow or fats—and the wick represents his Soul, while the flame shows the union of the nature of God with the nature of man. Every year on the second of February the Church holds the feast of Candlemas: the blessing of the candles which are to be used in the services of the coming year. We shall see them at Mass, at Benediction, and at Vespers, lighting the altar with their warm glow.

"And there, perhaps, we had better leave our talk on Sacramentals for today. We will go on with it again tomorrow and perhaps by then you will have a whole long list of sacramentals for me, and if they are small enough you may bring them along. I don't expect you to bring the bell from the church tower, although it is a sacramental, but there are many others small enough to slip into a pocket or into your satchel, and,

who knows, among them we may find something quite unusual."

Next morning, as Mr. Laverty could feel when he walked into his classroom, was to be one of those exciting lessons to which his boys looked forward with great delight. There were eager faces everywhere, hands were continually wandering into pockets, and occasionally a desk lid was furtively lifted for a quick peep inside. The registration minutes passed more quickly than usual, for the class was quieter than might have been expected, but the suppressed excitement grew noticeably as the master began to clear his table of exercise-books and odds and ends.

"From the look of your bulging pockets, and the various packages I have spotted in the last few minutes," he said, "I think this promises to be a very interesting lesson. Suppose you all file past the table and put on it what you have brought. I hope you will remember what belongs to you. We don't want any disputes over ownership when you go home."

By the time every boy had deposited what he had brought on the table, it was covered with an assortment of medals, crucifixes, statues, scapulars, and rosaries.

"My goodness! You certainly took me at my word!" exclaimed Mr. Laverty, "I couldn't possibly mention every single one of these, so I'd better choose here and there for examples."

The Agnus Dei

He turned over the different objects. "Rosaries, medals of all kinds, scapulars, —ah!" He picked up a small leather case and took out a white oval. "I thought we might find something unusual. Here is an Agnus Dei. Who brought this? You, Michael? And how did you get it? Your aunt got it a long time ago on a visit to Rome? She

Pinturicchio

Photo Chauffourier

Christ on the Cross with St. Jerome and St. Christopher carrying the Holy Child

Antique carved group at Aylesford Priory showing St. Simon Stock receiving the Scapular

The Rosary

"Here is a sacramental which goes back a very long way in the history of the Church, back to the days when few people could read and write. They learned what prayers they could by heart and repeated them over and over again. In order to keep count they made strings of beads, and that's how the Rosary came into being. St. Dominic, the founder of the Order of Preachers, made its use famous and the prayers of the Holy Rosary spread throughout the world. It is not the mere repetition of the prayers that makes the Rosary so valuable a sacramental. It is that it gives us the opportunity of meditating on the important events in the life of Our Blessed Saviour, and on his sacrifice of himself for our redemption. Each of these rosaries has five decades, that is, five sets of ten beads each, separated by a larger bead. There are fifteen mysteries, divided into three groups of five: the joyful, the sorrowful, the glorious. Therefore anyone reciting the Rosary says five times 'Our Father,' fifty times 'Hail Mary,' and five times the 'Gloria.'"

The Scapular

Mr. Laverty put down the rosaries and picked up two small pieces of cloth, joined by two fairly long pieces of tape. He slipped his head between the tapes so that the oblongs of cloth hung down on his breast and back.

"If I had been a monk in the early Middle Ages," he said, "these small pieces of cloth would have been long and wide enough to cover my other clothes, and I could have gone to work in the fields without spoiling the habit I wore underneath. Nowadays these small pieces of cloth represent the 'scapular' of the monk's habit, and they are worn by people who are known as 'oblates,' people who still live in the world but

must have been lucky with her pilgrimage, then, because these are blessed by the Pope and only once every seven years. Look, boys!" He held up the plain leather cover and the white oval. "This is a symbol, just the same as the fish, about which you asked me yesterday. Agnus Dei means, of course, Lamb of God, so it is another symbol of Our Saviour, and since it has been blessed by His Holiness, who asked for protection from evil and accident for whoever wears it, that makes it an especially valuable means of grace. Now, let's see. What shall we take next?" He picked up several rosaries and looped them over his fingers.

who share in the prayers of the monks and their devotions and good works. There are sixteen different kinds of scapular, worn as I am wearing this one, except that they are worn under the clothing, as you saw Jamie wearing his.

"Look again! You will see that on each piece of cloth there is a picture. Don't make the mistake, as some people do, as with the Stations of the Cross, of thinking that the picture is the sacramental. It is the woollen cloth which is the real scapular, and the picture doesn't make any difference to it. The oldest of all the scapulars is that of Mount Carmel, which tradition says was presented by Our Lady to St. Simon Stock, as long ago as the year 1251. Anyone wearing this scapular is sure of enjoying her blessing and protection, and of her intercession for his eternal welfare. Sometimes people wear a scapular medal, especially if they have been invested with several different scapulars. Of the others, the most important are those of the Seven Dolours or Sorrows of Our Lady; the Blessed Trinity; the Immaculate Conception; and the Passion. The scapular medal can be worn to represent all five, but whether we wear scapular or medal we can be sure we are sharing in the devoted life of the great religious orders and we can gain indulgences and added grace by wearing them to the glory of God and his wonderful Mother.

Courtesy Intercontinental Photo Service, Australia

Symbol of a fish carved on the font in the Church of St. Francis Xavier, Ashbury, N.S.W., Australia

Medals

"I've already spoken about my St. Christopher medal, and I see several here, among the many that you have brought. What others have we? Medals for your first communion, of Our Lady of Lourdes, of the Sacred Heart, of St. Benedict; the Miraculous Medal: just a few out of the hundreds that there are. Next time we have a history lesson, have a look at the picture of Louis XI of France. He was a great wearer of medals, and you will see them all round the crown of his hat. That's how they were worn in the Middle Ages, quite large, and made of lead. Later on, they became smaller and were made of silver, more like those that I have here. Of all those I have mentioned perhaps I could choose the story of the Miraculous Medal. It shows on one side Our Lady standing on a globe, and on the other the 'M' of Mary, with twelve stars, and the hearts of Jesus and Mary, one wearing the crown of thorns, and the other pierced with a sword. The medal itself was the result of a vision granted to St. Catherine Labouré, a French nun. Our Lady herself appeared to St. Catherine and commanded that the medal should be struck in the form we have here. Listen to the words around the image of Mary: 'O Mary, conceived without sin. Pray for us who have recourse to Thee.'

Symbols

"And now, before our time runs out, I must come back to where we started, to the symbol of the fish. If we look around any Catholic church, yes, as you have seen, even round our own church, we shall find symbols everywhere. There have always been symbols in our religion, from the earliest Christian paintings in the catacombs to the wealth of carving on the glorious cathedrals of the Middle Ages.

"We have already spoken about the cross and the lamb which you saw on the Agnus Dei. Then there is the fish. The fish was a favourite symbol with the early Christians. In Greek the word for fish is 'ichthus.' Now look at the beginnings of these words as I write them on the board.

"'Iesous Christos, Theou Uios, Soter' —Jesus Christ, Son of God, Saviour.'

"You see the first letters make up the word ichthus and so the fish became a symbol of Our Blessed Lord. Another of his symbols is the Lion, for he was the 'Lion of Judah.'

"There isn't time enough to speak of them all. Look for yourselves and you will find many others; the rose for Our Lady—The Mystical Rose; the dove for the Holy Ghost; the ship of salvation for Holy Mother Church; the crossed keys for His Holiness the Pope, and the letters IHS on the great candlesticks: they are the first three letters of Iesous, because the Greek capital E is like our H.

"All of them are beautiful because of the thoughts behind them. They help us to think all through our daily lives of the things that the hurry and bustle may make us forget, and they remind us of that supernatural, eternal world to which this life is only a preface."

THE MASS IN MODERN TIMES

Have you ever sat behind a small, wriggling boy in church and remembered that once you too were small and "not very well behaved" when Daddy took you to Mass? One day that small naughty boy will come to realise that the Mass is the most wonderful gift God has given his children. Perhaps like Michael he will become a server and stand close to the altar where the Sacrifice of the Mass takes place.

For the Mass is a sacrifice, the Sacrifice of Calvary, but Michael did not properly understand this until he was older. As far back as he could remember he had been going to church every Sunday morning, and on weekdays too —on Holidays of Obligation, and on other days like his birthday, and the day Mass was said for his grandmother who had died.

Something of the wonder of the Mass had come to Michael before he was asked to serve on the altar. But the morning when he found himself in the sacristry was the proudest of his whole life. The cassock reaching down to his ankles, black and dignified, and the white cotta, gave him a sense of being dressed for a very special purpose.

Ready long before he need be, he had watched Father Roberts vesting, and he had remembered that centuries before, the priestly vestments which seemed so splendid now, would have seemed just ordinary everyday clothes of the Roman citizen.

"Not quite the same," Michael told himself as he watched, "not quite the same shape, for the chasuble had been the Roman's cloak and was shaped more like a cycling cape, and not cut away at the sides to leave room for the priest's arms to move easily."

He was suddenly grateful that he knew something of the history of the vestments. That made him feel even more properly belonging. He saw Father Roberts put the maniple on his arm, and he didn't have to wonder what that

A tabernacle. A monstrance, used for Benediction of the Blessed Sacrament or for processions. A lunette, in which the Host is set for insertion in the monstrance; and a pyx in which it is kept in the tabernacle. A ciborium, filled with hosts, for the Communion at Mass. A bell for use on the altar. Cruets for the wine and water used in the Holy Sacrifice, with a finger-towel for the *'Lavabo'*.

was for, because he knew already that it was just a symbol, like the blue and white armlet of a policeman on duty. Once it had been a cloth like a napkin or a handkerchief which the priest actually used.

It was good to think that there was a special dress for saying Mass, and that it was very, very old in shape and style —like the coronation robes of a king.

And he was thinking that, and about the King of Kings, when Father Roberts picked up the chalice, bowed to the crucifix over the vesting table and put on his biretta. Now they were almost ready to start. Michael picked up the heavy Missal, proud that he could carry it easily. Father Roberts nodded, and they set off for the altar.

HIGH MASS

The entry procession

The full ceremony of the Eucharistic Sacrifice is the *Missa Solemnis* or High Mass. It is sung, and the Celebrant is assisted by Deacon and Subdeacon. (Usually two priests perform these functions.) Following p. 270 there is an artist's impression of the Entry Procession. If the Blessing called the *Asperges* is to be given before the Mass, the Celebrant will be vested in a cope, not a chasuble, for the entry

Looked at from the outside the Mass is a ceremony that takes place in church. Understood from the inside it is a profound Mystery. It is the sacrifice of the Body and Blood of Jesus Christ, really present on the altar under the appearance of bread and wine, and offered to God for the living and the dead. "What is the Mass?" the Catechism asks, and you give the answer in these words, so they are already familiar to you and to every Catholic. The Mass is your link-up with God. Without God you would not be you, you couldn't move or even exist without him because he gave you life. God is like the engine and we are like the carriages of a train. The carriages are coupled to each other and to the engine. The Mass is like the coupling links. It joins us to him.

The Mass today, according to the Roman Rite, is the same as it was four centuries ago. There were then, as there are now, different words for different days of the year, but only in certain parts of the ceremony. During the last four centuries some new "Masses" have been introduced, meaning that some new words for new feasts—like the Feast of St. Maria Goretti—have been added, but only in the changeable parts. The fixed parts of the ceremony have not been changed at all.

One of the proudest days in Michael's life was when he was allowed to serve Mass. Another was when he was given his first "grown-up" Missal, and shown how to use it.

"Missale Romanum, ex decreto Sacrosancti Concilii Tridentini restitutum, Summorum Pontificum cura recognitum" he read on the front page, and his father translated it: "The Roman Missal, restored according to the decree of the Sacred Council of Trent, and revised by the authority of the Popes."

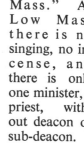

And then his father went on to tell him how in 1570 Pope Pius V reformed the Missal or Mass Book at the request of the Council which said it needed "tidying up." Since that year the whole of the Western Church has used the same Missal. It was the development of printing which made it easy for the same Mass book to be used everywhere. And, of course, Michael at once understood, that explained why in the early centuries the ceremonies of the Mass were different in different places.

In Volume II of this Book you have read about the ceremony in the Middle Ages. Now we are going to look at the Mass as it is today, remembering that when we get to church we are not there to look at the ceremony, but to take part in it, for all the Mass belongs to us and we to it. It is our Sacrifice united to Christ's Sacrifice and the one perfect gift which we can offer to God; the one most perfect way of adoring and worshipping Him.

The first thing to know is that "High Mass" and not "Low Mass" is the standard form. In this book the pictures show what happens at "High Mass." At Low Mass there is no singing, no incense, and there is only one minister, a priest, without deacon or sub-deacon.

It would take a big book to write down the full story of the Mass, its ceremonies and history. The tiniest spark is enough to set a whole forest ablaze. Michael's interest in the history of the Mass began when he was told that the vestments had once been the ordinary clothes of the Roman citizens; after that, he just went on asking questions.

Every time he mounted the steps and placed the heavy Missal on the altar, he liked to remember what Father Roberts had told him once, that the altar represented Christ. And since then, he had especially loved the moment when the priest kissed the altar.

Father Roberts had said to him then: "It was made a rule for the altar to be over a martyr's grave, and now every altar-stone has to have some relics of martyrs in it, and the kiss is a greeting to the martyrs and through them to the whole triumphant Church."

If Michael had lived in the time of Henry VIII and you had been one of the congregation you might not have seen the beginning part of the Mass at all, for in those days priests said the "preparation" prayer and the Confiteor in the sacristy. It was Pope Pius V, the

HIGH MASS

The Incensation of the altar

At High Mass, after the Prayers at the Foot of the Altar, the Celebrant incenses the altar. He then reads the Introit, which the Choir have been singing, and says the *Kyrie eleison*. When the Choir have finished singing the *Kyrie eleison*, he goes to the centre of the altar and intones the *Gloria in Excelsis*. He completes it in a low voice, and while the Choir sing it, he goes with his ministers to the *sedilia* and sits down. Returning to the altar he sings the Collect

same Pope who "tidied up" the Missal, and who lived in the reign of Queen Elizabeth, who said that these prayers should be said at the foot of the altar and they must be part of the Mass.

These and the Confiteor are the prayers which help you to get ready. It is a great pity when you are even a little bit late for Mass and miss these prayers, for you and everybody else need them.

After these prayers a new part of the Mass begins. Father Roberts goes up the steps to the altar and he asks you to pray with him: "Dominus Vobiscum" he says aloud. "Et cum Spiritu tuo" answers the server.

"The Lord be with you." Michael learned the Latin for that and for the answer he had to make "And with thy

spirit" more easily than the other responses, perhaps because it often occurs and perhaps too because it was such a beautiful kind of way of saying: "This really is your Sacrifice and Jesus is here on the altar."

Now the Teaching and Praising part of the Mass has begun. The priest kisses the altar. Until Michael became a server he was never quite certain which part of the altar Father Roberts kissed. Afterwards he knew the priest's lips touched the corporal, the white cloth which was kept in a square envelope—like a case and called a burse—until the priest spread it on the altar.

The Introit long, long ago began as a psalm which was sung while the Pope, or the celebrant, was going in procession from the vesting-room near the door of the church to the altar. Now it is just a short sentence followed by only the first verse of a psalm, but it sets the note for the Mass of that day.

Michael couldn't remember the reasons for the Introit until he heard Wilfred Pickles say in his "Have-a-go" programme: "Give him the right note"; this was sounded on the piano and then the boy sang—in tune. The Introit begins the real Mass, and the ancient cry the Kyrie eleison carries it on. A deacon used to read out petitions at this time and the servers answered: "Lord have mercy on us" to each, now only the Kyrie is used. This prayer in Greek is so ancient that it goes back to pagan times, long before Jesus came to earth. It is very beautiful and useful too.

The more often Michael served the more he was thankful for the prayer. It is both terrible and wonderful to be taking part in a sacrifice to God. That is why some of the saints took hours to say Mass and others could not utter the words without tears of joy and humility streaming over their cheeks.

The "Gloria in excelsis Deo . . ."

Salvador Dali   *Glasgow Art Gallery and Museum, Glasgow*

Christ of St. John of the Cross

Facing p. 270

F. M. Lea

High Mass, Entry Procession

CVMEO
ERAM
CVNCTA
COMPONENS

LVDENS
CORAMEO
OMNITEMPORE

Modern tapestry over the altar in the Church of Notre-Dame de France, Leicester Place, London

The Elevation of the Chalice

F. M. Lea

used to be sung on Christmas Day only, but now it is always said except during Lent and on special "sad" days. The Angels' Hymn it is sometimes called and it is very beautiful.

"Dominus vobiscum," said Father Roberts, turning round, and opening out his arms. It was as if he were gathering them all together, Michael thought, and the next part of the Mass is just this: it is the "Collect." The priest "collects" all the petitions that have been made (at the "Kyrie," though the Gloria has now crept in between), and he prays one of the short, simple but impressive prayers which are so clearly the voice of the Church.

HIGH MASS

The Epistle

At High Mass the Epistle is sung by the Subdeacon.standing on the floor of the sanctuary while the celebrant and deacon sit and listen

After the Collect, Michael turned the pages of his own Missal quickly to find the Epistle for the day. He knew Epistle meant "letter"; it was usually but not always taken from the New Testament.

After the Epistle the priest leaves the right-hand side of the altar, and Michael prepares to carry the Missal to the Gospel side, while the priest, in the middle of the altar, prays for grace to preach the Gospel well.

During the first centuries the Catechumens—the name given to those who were preparing to become Christians,

19—III

always left after the reading of the Gospel or Creed.

The Gospel was then and is now a very important part of the Mass. In High Mass the incense and carrying of candles leaves no doubt in our minds, but in Low Mass there is no ceremony and as we stand, making the sign of the Cross on our forehead, lips and heart, we should be emptying our minds of everything except the words we are preparing to read in our Missals. Jesus is talking to us, and frequently the sermon which follows is connected with the Gospel for the day. If there is no sermon and it is a Feast Day on which the Creed is said, we keep standing.

Michael could both say and sing the Creed in Latin, but it was some time before he knew when the Creed was not said. He knew it was said on Our Lady's Feast Days; what he did not discover for a long time was that no other female saint had the Creed included in her Feast Day—which seemed rather hard. And yet not so hard—they were after all in good company—that of the martyrs and confessors.

It was right and proper that not only the Apostles but also the Evangelists

HIGH MASS

The Gospel Procession

Before the Gospel, the Celebrant puts incense in censer and blesses it. The Deacon receives the Gospel Book, kneels before the Celebrant to ask his blessing, and then with Subdeacon and attendants forms the Gospel procession. They go to the Gospel side of the sanctuary, the Deacon facing the side of the church, and after incensation of the Book, the Gospel is sung by the Deacon

HIGH MASS

Singing the Gospel

This photograph was taken at Westminster Cathedral in London during Midnight Mass at Christmas.   The Deacon is singing the Gospel, the Subdeacon holding the Book.   The Celebrant faces them from the Epistle corner of the altar.   On this occasion the Celebrant was a Bishop.   Behind him is seen the Attendant Priest, vested in cope

should have the Creed because they spread and defended the faith so wonderfully, but surprising to learn that for a very long time indeed—in fact for the whole of the first ten centuries—the saints had to do without the Creed on their feast days.   It wasn't part of Holy Mass at all.   But it was said during baptism.   To begin with there were several Creeds, but these were "tidied up" at the Council of Nicea in 325, and what we all say now is the Nicene Creed. Babies when they are being baptised have the very ancient Apostles' Creed all to themselves.

The Gospel or Creed ends the Instructing Praising part of the Sacrifice.

Michael often held his breath at the Offertory; he couldn't quite explain why. Nor could he say why he was glad that he didn't serve Mass in the old days. Somehow the idea of a procession of people, of the whole congregation getting up from the benches and coming up to the tables set out before the sanctuary was a bit disturbing.

It wasn't only bread and wine they brought, but fruits and the first lambs and all sorts of things.   If Michael had a distraction as the collecting plates were taken round, it was often a sudden clear picture of a little lamb skipping along the table!

As soon as Father Roberts took the

veil from the chalice Michael felt a strong sense of union with the people behind him. There they were and here he was, and in a moment—just as soon as Father Roberts took up the paten on which the Host lay—they would be all one, united in a tremendous offering of their whole selves to God the Father.

HIGH MASS

Preparing for the Offertory

When the Celebrant has intoned and said the Creed, he sits with his ministers while Choir and People sing the Creed. During this the Deacon rises and going to the altar receives from servers the Chalice and the Paten with a Host upon it. He spreads the Corporal upon the altar and sets the Host and Chalice in readiness

A vivid picture of the Last Supper swept away distractions. The altar-breads made by the nuns were the same kind of unleavened bread that Jesus broke and gave to his disciples at the Supper. The wine was fermented as it had been then, and as the priest poured the water into the chalice, Michael always whispered to himself the prayer which he had long ago learned by heart.

As this water is made one with the wine to be
  made by a greater wonder still
Your Precious Blood,
So may we be companions close with you,
Who shared on earth our human life

The Mass is divided into three parts though it would be wrong to try to separate the parts. The Offertory ends the Second Part. When the priest moves to the Epistle side of the altar and washes his fingers, the third and last part of the Mass begins; the preparations are over;

the way is prepared for the Sacrifice itself, and though nowadays the washing of the fingers is merely symbolic, long ago there was real need for it.

Then, the people did not only bring themselves, but as we said earlier, they brought their gifts too, and the priest selected from them the bread and wine which he required for the Sacrifice. In the beautiful prayer to the Holy Trinity which the priest makes at the centre of the altar he asks that our Sacrifice should be acceptable and he calls upon all the angels to surround the altar.

Everything is now prepared for the supreme act of the Sacrifice itself, and the priest turns to the people, arms outstretched as if he would draw them to him.

"Orate, Fratres" he says aloud. "Pray, brethren . . . that my sacrifice and yours may be acceptable to God the Father Almighty," and the server replies: "Suscipiat Dominus . . . May the Lord receive the sacrifice at thy hands in the praise and glory of His name, to our own benefit and to that of all his Holy Church."

The priest then turns to read The Secret Prayers from the Missal. These change every day and they are very, very old, and very beautiful. Why secret?

A Chalice. A Paten, with a Host upon it. A Purificator, or cloth for wiping the Chalice. A Pall, linen card for covering the Chalice. A Corporal, linen cloth laid upon the altar when the Blessed Sacrament is to rest on it. A Veil, or outer covering for the Chalice. A Burse, or case to contain the Corporal

HIGH MASS

The Offertory of the Chalice

Having offered the Bread, the Celebrant receives the Chalice, into which Deacon and Subdeacon have put wine and a drop of water, and offers it to God.   The Deacon assists, with his right hand beneath the Chalice, and holding the Celebrant's chasuble. The Subdeacon, with Humeral Veil about his shoulders, stands ready to receive the Paten, which he will hold during the Canon, until the Paternoster has been said.   In this photograph, the Bishop's Priest Assistant, in cope, stands at his left

Nobody knows for certain, but in Latin the word *secreta* means chosen, something chosen, and Father Hubert McEvoy suggests that one explanation might be that when the people brought their gifts, the priest made his choice and then said a prayer over the offerings which were to be consecrated for the Sacrifice. The remainder of the gifts were blessed and afterwards distributed among the poor.

The Secret Prayers and the Offertory part of the Mass and the Preface which follows begin with a conversation between priest and server. One of the first things Michael did was to learn by heart his part in the dialogue.

"Per omnia saecula saeculorum" (For ever and ever), says the priest.

"Amen," says the server.

"Dominus vobiscum" (The Lord be with you), says the priest.

"Et cum spiritu tuo" (And with your spirit), says the server.

"Sursum corda" (Lift up your hearts), says the priest.

"Habemus ad Dominum" (We lift them up unto the Lord), says the server.

"Gratias agamus Domino Deo nostro" (Let us give thanks to the Lord our God), says the priest.

"Dignum et justum est" (It is meet and right), says the server.

Michael knew there were special Prefaces for Christmas and Lent and Easter, but he did not know until he looked them all up in his Missal that there were fifteen special Prefaces, and after that he was very particular about reading the correct Preface for the day. His favourite one became the Preface for The Holy Trinity.

"There were actually more than a hundred different Prefaces" Father Roberts told him one morning after Mass, "in the very old Missals and they were very long, but the word Preface which just means 'Introduction' did not appear in Missals until the Middle Ages."

"What about the Sanctus?" Michael had asked, thinking how much he liked ringing his little brass bell.

"That's one of the oldest and most beautiful prayers," Father Roberts answered. "It became part of the Mass in the very first century . . . so you see when you ring your bell three times, you are calling attention to words which have echoed down nineteen centuries; words which come from the Book of Isaias. And don't forget," Father Roberts had added, "that the Preface and Sanctus are part of the Canon—just as the Preface to a book is part of the book, and an important part too, when you think about it."

And after that Michael hadn't forgotten even though on the very next page of his Missal were the words in black type: The Canon or Rule of Consecration. The word "Canon" he knew was a Greek word which meant "rule" and he understood much better what the Canon was when he thought of his own ruler which was a fixed length; it never varied and just as there was only one way to measure with a ruler so there was only one way to say the Canon.

In Missals there is a picture of the Crucifix which helps us to prepare for the Canon and as if that wasn't enough, the priest bows low and kisses the altar. Then silently he asks God through Jesus Christ to accept our offerings and he makes three signs of the cross over the Host and Chalice.

The rustle and sighs and coughs as we get down on our knees at the Sanctus have all died away. Michael was always vividly conscious of the silence as the priest asked God to receive through his

HIGH MASS

The Preface

The Celebrant sings the
Preface, the Choir respon-
ding. Behind him stands the
Deacon, and on this occasion
the Assistant Priest also.
Below them is the Subdeacon

Son, "these gifts, these offerings, these holy and unblemished sacrifices."

And then as he went on reading the prayers slowly to himself he understood, and always with the same sense of astonishment, what they were really saying. Jesus took the whole burden of the world and the Church on his shoulders. And he could do this because he was God and because he had died for the world on a wooden cross in the beginning. And because the priest and everybody in church were saying these prayers and sharing them, Our Lady, St. Joseph and the Apostles, Popes and Martyrs were brought in—to help them along, as it were.

And immediately after—the two beautiful prayers in preparation for the Consecration; the first asks God to graciously accept our sacrifice of self, to save us from eternal damnation, and to bring us safely to him. And as the priest prays he stretches his hands over the bread and wine and the server rings the bell.

During the Second Prayer the priest makes the sign of the Cross five times over the bread and wine, asking that God will bless them, that he will approve them and make them worthy and acceptable and pleasing; that they may be consecrated to become the Human Body and Blood of Our Lord.

Now comes the most solemn moment of the Mass, the priest speaks the words of Consecration. The Consecration is the Mass in the sense that without it there is no Mass.

Sometimes theologians talked about the great drama of the Mass. The Consecration is the climax of the drama; Jesus Christ consecrates the bread and wine and they become his Body and Blood. And at the same moment he enters into the priest so that the priest is no longer just Father Roberts or Father Brown or Father Smith, but the instrument by which Jesus is consecrating the Sacrament.

Jesus Christ is now both the High Priest of the Sacrifice and the Victim. He has taken our worship and united it with his own to make it worthy of God. God has always wished to be worshipped by sacrifice. Before his Son became Man and gave the world a New Law, the Jews worshipped God by sacrifice. Do you remember how Noah built an altar and sacrificed the birds and beasts which God told him to sacrifice after the flood?

"After the Order of Melchisedech"—you read in your Missal: "Melchisedech, a priest, who worshipped the one true God, offered bread and wine in sacrifice." Jesus wished us to have his own Sacrifice of Calvary to offer to God in worship. But we could not all be present at Calvary, so he gave us the Mass. The Mass is the Sacramental Sign which makes present for us the action of Jesus on Calvary. And the sign which Jesus chose was the Sign of Melchisedech, the offering of bread and wine. The Mass is our offering of bread and wine which Jesus (through his priest) takes and changes into his Body and Blood.

And so at the supreme moment, Christ's own words at the Last Supper are used: Take ye all and eat of this:

For This is My Body.

The priest genuflects in adoration, the server takes hold of a corner of the chasuble, and rings his bell. Then the Sacred Host is raised so that all the people may see It, and once again the server's bell rings out. Then the priest genuflects again and the server rings his bell again too.

The ceremony of The Elevation was not introduced until the twelfth century and not until the revised Missal of 1570 were the genuflections permitted, though it is impossible to think that the priest did not "kneel down" in his heart before the Mystery of the Transubstantiation.

Then follows the Consecration of the Wine:

For this is the Chalice of My Blood of the New and Eternal Covenant:

The Mystery of Faith, which shall be shed for you and for many unto The Forgiveness of Sins.

And once again the bell rings out as the chalice containing the Precious Blood is raised.

Even the small, wriggling little boy is still, head bowed. He could not answer the easiest questions in the Catechism, but he knows that Jesus is present on the altar, truly present, and something of the wonder of the mystery of the Real Presence stays his busy little hands and kicking feet. He is even too small to be consciously saying: "Dear Father, I too am in this Sacrifice . . ." But that doesn't matter. He is in it. He is part of the gift of adoration and worship and love which God has been accepting from the moment of Calvary.

Following the Consecration the priest raises his hands and now until the ablutions his thumb and first finger are pressed tightly together. There is a reason for this. There might be just a tiny fraction of the Host sticking to his fingers and this action prevents the danger of It falling.

The prayer which he now says is divided into three parts; it is called A Prayer of Offering. In it he (extending his hands) makes our offering to God; he asks him to accept; and he begs his blessing, and to show how profoundly he realises the Presence of Jesus Christ there on the altar, the priest bows low and kisses the altar. He ends this first prayer with the words: "Through the same Christ Our Lord. Amen."

And now because nobody may be left out, he begins prayers for the souls in purgatory, praying silently as he joins his hands, for those of the dead he wishes particularly to remember. He prays for sinners, for all sinners, for us . . . "To us also, to us sinners . . .", and he asks that we might have a share in the companionship of the apostles and martyrs, mentioning some of them by name. And then the Canon ends with that wonderful spirit-lifting prayer to The Holy Trinity, and the priest during it makes the sign of the Cross eight times, just as if he could not emphasise strongly enough that it is only through Christ that we can offer honour to God.

The very last act of the Canon is when the priest raises the Host and Chalice together, but not very high, so that perhaps the congregation do not see.

The server says "Amen" quite loudly, and the congregation echo it, in their hearts. It is sometimes called The Grand Amen and once it really was Grand because it was taken up and spoken aloud by all the worshippers.

The last part of the Mass is sometimes called "The Sacrifice Banquet." We have given our gift to God; now God invites us to his Banquet. There he will return to us the gift of himself in Holy Communion.

"Christ has given himself to us in the Holy Eucharist to be the life and the food of our souls. . . ." Before Michael made his first Communion and long before he learned to serve, he had to learn the answers to the Catechism questions on the Holy Eucharist.

"Christ is received whole and entire under either kind alone." Michael found that puzzling until Father Roberts explained that in the first four centuries Christians were free to receive Communion under both kinds (that is drinking from the Chalice as well as receiving the Host) or under one kind only. But there was a heresy which led to confusion and wrong-thinking and two popes of the fifth century said that the faithful must communicate under both kinds.

"Then," Father Roberts had continued, "the heresy was finally squashed, and once again the people were permitted to choose. In the fifteenth century it became a strict law of the Church that the lay people should receive Holy Communion under the form of bread only."

The Communion part of the Mass begins with the Pater Noster.

Michael always said it silently with the priest so that he could be quite ready to come in with his line: "Sed libera nos a malo." He was always glad that in the prayer, the phrase which asked for us to be saved from evil, should go through, (besides Our Lady) Saints Peter and Paul and Andrew, especially Andrew. He liked the way Father Roberts blessed himself with the paten and kissed it, making it ready for its Sacred burden.

For his tenth birthday Father Roberts had given him a book which showed pictures of what the priest was doing at the altar. Michael liked particularly the one, in colour, showing the action of the priest breaking the sacred Host in two equal parts. When this was happening Michael usually shut his eyes but sometimes he watched. He knew exactly what happened.

After the Breaking of the Host, one part lay on the paten, and a tiny particle

HIGH MASS

The Kiss of Peace

The Canon of the Mass is the same in High Mass as in Low Mass, save that the Paternoster is sung by the Celebrant. After the *Agnus Dei*, and the first of the prayers which follow it, there occurs in High Mass the ceremony of the *Pax*, or the Kiss of Peace. The Deacon approaches the Celebrant and they embrace in the sign of Christian brotherhood. The Deacon then descends and gives the *Pax* to the Subdeacon

The prayers at the foot of the altar. The Celebrant being a Bis

This photograph was take

of the other part (after he had opened his eyes and said Et cum spiritu tuo) was allowed to fall into the Chalice.

At the Last Supper Jesus took bread and broke it. He was following a custom which the Jews knew and understood, for the father of a Jewish family did just that on special occasions with the small, round flat cake made from unleavened flour, and gave it to his children. At Mass the breaking of the bread formerly took a very long time because the priest was using the offerings of the people, and the bread was brought by them in the form of loaves, not the little wafers we now use.

The fragment of the Host dropped into the Chalice was at one time taken from the Host of the Mass said the day before so that there was a kind of continuous thread from one day's Mass to the next binding together every Mass with Calvary.

Father Roberts explained to Michael that the Agnus Dei used to be sung (as it is now during High Mass) while the Bread was being broken. "It is a prayer for forgiveness and peace addressed to the Lamb of God," he explained. "That is how St. John the Baptist greeted Our Lord, and that is how we salute him now on the altar."

The beautiful ceremony of the Kiss of Peace which in the early centuries took place at the beginning of the Canon is omitted altogether from Low Mass but the prayer properly belonging to it is said: "Lord Jesus Christ, you told your Apostles: Peace I leave with you. My Peace I give unto you . . ."

Before Michael got ready to ring the bell he prayed with the priest that he might make a worthy Communion.

The priest genuflects and takes the Host.

I will take the Bread of Heaven, and call upon the name of the Lord.

Striking his breast, he says, "Domine, non sum dignus . . . Lord, I am not worthy that Thou shouldst come under my roof; but only say the word and my soul will be healed . . .", using the words of the humble centurion, taken from the Gospel of St. Matthew.

After the priest's Communion, the

HIGH MASS
The Priest's Communion

As at Low Mass, the Celebrant at High Mass takes and eats the Bread of Life and drinks the Chalice of the Precious Blood

HIGH MASS
The Communion of the People

Communion of the people follows. The priest has not faced the people for a long time; now he turns to them, holding the Host over the ciborium.

Ecce Agnus Dei . . . (Behold the Lamb of God.
Behold Him who taketh away the sins of the world).

Then he says again three times, Domine, non sum dignus, and for the last time the bell rings out.

The communicants come to the altar rail and the priest steps down from the altar. Over each communicant he makes the sign of the Cross with the Sacred Host: Corpus Domini nostri Jesu Christi custodiat animam tuam in vitam aeternam. Amen. (May the Body of Our

Lord Jesus Christ keep thy soul unto life everlasting. Amen.)

The Banquet Sacrifice is over. The priest pours first wine and then wine and water into the Chalice. Satisfied that it is purified, he drinks the "ablution," praying at the same time that what we have taken with our lips may we keep in a heart that is pure; that the Sacrament may stay with us for ever wiping away all traces of sin.

Then he turns to the Missal and reads a verse of one of the Psalms that used to be sung while Holy Communion was being given. Then a prayer called the Post-Communion completes the Sacrifice.

Once again the priest faces the people.

"Dominus vobiscum," he says.

HIGH MASS

The Blessing

When the Communion is finished, and Deacon and Subdeacon have put away the Chalice and Paten, the Celebrant says the Communion versicle, which the Choir have been singing; then the Postcommunion Prayer, and after the Deacon has sung *Ite Missa Est* the Celebrant gives the Blessing. In this photograph the Celebrant being a Bishop wears the mitre, but he was not the ruling prelate of the diocese and therefore is not holding the crozier

"Et cum spiritu tuo," says the server.

"Ite Missa est." (Go, you are dismissed.)

"Deo gratias" says the server, meaning thank you, God, for the wonderful Gift of Yourself which we have given and been given. The Blessing was added in the eleventh century like the beautiful Last Gospel of St. John which sums up for us so perfectly the Mystery and Wonder and Glory of the Holy Sacrifice of the Mass.

Dunstan Pruden   Courtesy the Artist

Bronze crucifix in the church at de Chamblac prés Brogue, France

VESTMENTS

All through the ages it has been the custom for those holding public offices to wear a distinctive dress. Man has always been impressed by the robes of kings and pontiffs. They have added to the importance of their calling. They have distinguished the wearers from ordinary people, giving respect due to them. Even the soldier and the policeman is distinguished by his uniform and the uniform makes him more conscious of his duty.

With religious garb this is even truer. The priest's dress helps us to distinguish him from ordinary laymen and helps him by the reminder that he forms the link between us and God.

As the king in his rich robes with his crown and his sceptre impresses us with the importance and dignity of his position in the temporal life of a nation, so the Pope and his cardinals' vestments impress us with the dignity of their calling as spiritual leaders.

Since the world began, every religion, pagan or Christian, has had vestments in some form or other and we know that in the Old Testament by the command of God the Jewish priests wore distinctive dress for the Tabernacle and Temple services. When God spoke to Moses he ordered vestments to be made for Aaron "in which he being consecrated may minister to me." These vestments, richly gilded and with many accessories, are described in Exodus xxviii, where God says, "And Aaron and his sons shall use them when they go to the tabernacle of testimony, or when they approach to the altar to minister in the sanctuary, lest being guilty of iniquity they die. It shall be the law for ever to Aaron and to his seed after him." It was then by divine command that every single vestment in the Jewish religion was provided for and there were severe penalties if the minutest details were not observed.

When Christianity came no divine command was given about the dress to be used by the priests, so it was left to the heads of the Church to decide. There is no record of any special vestments during the first four centuries of Christianity, due no doubt in part to the persecutions under the Roman Empire. No special dress was set aside for the priesthood. Men of those days wore long flowing garments which were a modification of the Roman toga. Gradually the garments used for divine service became distinguishable from ordinary dress by the richness of the material used and by the costliness of the decorations, and priests were forbidden to wear them except during liturgical services.

After the fall of the Roman Empire the luxurious dress of the Romans was replaced by the fashions brought by the "barbarians." The Church however kept the long dignified dress for the service of the altar though she did allow her priests to modify their ordinary dress. The Church still continues to use these vestments. They are precious heirlooms and links with the past. They —the Mass vestments—are a symbol and reminder of Christian duty.

Colours of the Vestments

The Church permits the use of five colours in the sacred vestments—white, red, green, purple and black. Rose-coloured vestments are used at the Solemn Mass on the third Sunday in Advent and the fourth in Lent. Gold too may be used as a substitute for white, red or green.

Each of these colours has its own meaning. The Sacrifice of the Mass is offered for many purposes and in honour of many kinds of saints. All these purposes are symbolised by the colour of the vestments which the Church prescribed for each Mass.

When the Church wishes to symbolise joy, purity, innocence or glory she uses white, so white is used on the feasts of Our Lord, the Blessed Virgin, Angels, Saints who are not martyrs, and the Sundays after Easter.

Red, which is the colour of fire and of blood, symbolises love. It is used in the Masses of the Holy Ghost such as Pentecost when it reminds us of the tongues of fire, and on the feasts of the Martyrs who shed their blood for their faith.

Green is the colour used to show the growth of the Church and it symbolises hope. It is worn on the Sundays after Epiphany and Pentecost.

The Amice

Purple which is the symbol of penance is worn during Advent, Lent (except on Saints' days), on the vigils outside the Easter season, on the festival of the Holy Innocents and on Rogation days.

Black is the colour of mourning for the dead. It is used for all Requiem Masses and also on Good Friday.

The vestments which the priest wears at Mass are the amice, the alb, the cincture, the maniple, the stole and the chasuble, and at certain other services he uses the cope, the humeral veil and the surplice.

The Amice

This is a square or oblong piece of linen to which two long tapes are attached at the upper corners. It has been worn in the Mass since about the year 800 and the word amice comes from the Latin *amictus*, a wrapper. The priest touches it to his head, places it over his shoulders, and ties it around his waist as he prays: "Put on my head, O Lord, the helmet of salvation, to repel the assaults of the devil." In this way the amice is the symbol of a helmet used for protection, against idle or sinful thoughts during Mass.

The Alb

This is the long white linen dress which the priest wears over the cassock. It is gathered round the waist by the cincture. The word alb means *white* and originally this was the ordinary undergarment worn by the Romans. Today the lower part is frequently made of lace. The vesting prayer is "Make me white, O Lord, and cleanse my heart; that being made white in the Blood of the Lamb, I may deserve an eternal reward." So the white colour symbolises purity of soul and body in the priest who offers the Immaculate Lamb of God to the Eternal Father.

The Cincture

The Cincture

We mentioned the cincture before as the girdle worn around the waist to keep the alb in place. It is made of braided linen or wool and can be white or of the same colour as the vestments worn. It is symbolic of continence and the prayer the priest says while putting it on is "Gird me, O Lord, with the cincture of purity, and quench in my heart the fire of concupiscence, that the virtue of continence and chastity may abide in me."

The Maniple

This is a long silk band worn looped over the left forearm of the priest. As he puts it on the priest says, "May I deserve, O Lord, to bear the maniple of weeping and sorrow in order that I may joyfully reap the reward of my labours." Originally the maniple was a strip of linen used as a handkerchief because of the dust and heat in hot countries. It is symbolic of hard work and its reward, and is the special badge of the Order of Sub-deaconship. It is not used by those in minor orders.

The Alb

The Maniple

The Stole

At Mass, and also in nearly every other religious function, the priest wears around the neck a long narrow vestment with ends hanging down in front. When worn at Mass the ends are crossed over the breast. As he vests with the stole the priest says, "Restore to me, O Lord, the garment of immortality which I lost through the sin of my first parents and, although unworthy to approach Thy Sacred Mysteries, may I deserve, nevertheless, eternal joy."

We do not know the real origin of the stole, but it was originally a sort of robe or cloak which was gradually modified until it became a narrow strip of cloth. According to the prayer it symbolises immortality and worn on the neck it also symbolises the yoke of obedience to the Lord.

The deacon at a Solemn Mass wears a similar vestment to the stole but it is worn in a different way—diagonally from his left shoulder to his right side. The diagonal stole is therefore the badge of the order of deacons.

The Chasuble

The chasuble is the large and most conspicuous garment worn by the priest at the Mass. It is worn on the shoulders and hangs down in front and behind. The back part is often, though not always, ornamented with a large cross or rich embroidery. While putting the vestment on the priest says, "O Lord, who hast said my yoke is easy, and my burden light; make me so able to bear it, that I may obtain thy favour, Amen."

The word chasuble comes from the Latin *casula* meaning "little house," because during the first centuries of the Christian era it was the heavy outer garment worn for travelling, and was in the form of a large piece of material with a central opening for the head and completely covered the wearer. As a vestment it has gradually become greatly altered over the centuries. Originally it was so large that it had to be raised to allow the hands to be extended outside it. Assistants at the Mass used to help the priest by holding up the sides of the chasuble. What is left of this practice is still to be seen in Solemn Masses, when the deacon and sub-deacon ceremoniously hold the edges of the priest's

The Stole

The Chasuble

chasuble although now there is no necessity for actual assistance.

The chasuble symbolises perfection and charity because of its size and fullness.

The Cope and Veil

The cope is used at the Asperges before a High Mass, and at many of the Church's solemn functions. It was originally worn only at outdoor processions and was used as a protection against rain. Its Latin name *pluviale* shows us this derivation. The cape which is attached to it no longer has any use, but is just a reminder of the hood which used to be worn over the head in bad weather. The English "cope" is from the Latin *coppa*—a cloak with a hood.

The humeral veil is a vestment which looks like a wide scarf. It is worn on the priest's shoulders at the Benediction of the Blessed Sacrament when he holds the Sacred Host for the blessing of the people. It is also used when the Blessed Sacrament is carried in procession. The sub-deacon also uses the veil in Solemn Masses except Requiem Mass.

20—III

Its use then is to hold the paten from the offertory to the Pater Noster.

The Surplice

The surplice is a shortened tunic with very wide sleeves. Usually it is of white linen, sometimes decorated with lace. At the administration of the Blessed Sacrament and various other services of the Church it is worn over the priest's cassock. The cotta, which is like it, is worn by servers at the altar who are not priests.

The word surplice comes from the Latin *superpellicium* which means a dress worn over furs. In the Middle Ages the clergy and the monks were allowed in cold countries to have clothes lined with fur. Over the fur-lined clothes was worn a linen gown in choir. It was a large version of the alb and at one time reached down to the wearer's feet. Gradually as the years passed it was much more convenient to have it shortened.

The Tunic and the Dalmatic

The Sub-deacon wears the tunic and the deacon wears the dalmatic. They

The Surplice

are exactly alike though the tunic should be smaller than the dalmatic. They are about the same length as the chasuble of the priest. The tunic and dalmatic hang from the shoulders which sometimes have projecting flaps covering them. The flaps are substitutes for real sleeves which are often used. On the back there are usually two ornamental vertical stripes, but no cross. The name tunic simply means an outer garment and dalmatic is the name given in ancient times to a Roman dress made from Dalmatian wool. This garment was worn under the outer clothes.

The tunic symbolises joy and the dalmatic is the symbol of righteousness and charity.

The Dalmatic

THE MISSAL

"Saltere and pistol-boc, god-spell-boc and mæsse-boc . . . thas bec sceal mæsse-preost nede habban."

These strange words are English words. They were written about a thousand years ago, by Ælfric. The meaning of them is this: "Psalter and Epistle-book, Gospel-book and Mass-book . . . these books a Mass-priest needs to have."

It is only the quaint old spelling that might make you think the priest in those days packed a gun when he went to the altar! "Pistol" just means "epistle."

The interesting thing about the rule that Ælfric laid down is that it tells us how many books a priest had to have in Ælfric's time, in order to say Mass. Nowadays it is quite different. Only one book is needed, and that book is the missal.

The missal of today contains all the prayers that are used in the Mass. It has been so since the days of Pope Pius V, in the sixteenth century, after the Council of Trent.

Nowadays nearly everyone—in this country—has a missal, and many follow the Mass by reading (usually in English) the prayers which the priest is saying (in Latin). Centuries ago, not very many people could read, and books were costly and rare; they were not small, neatly printed things like ours.

But the reason why there were several different books needed for the Mass was not at first that books were large and scarce; it was rather that different persons read, or sang, the different parts of the Mass. Something of this remains today at High Mass. The sub-deacon sings the Epistle (from the "pistol-boc"); the deacon sings the Gospel and the choir sing the Introit, Offertory and Communion antiphons, and the responses, in which sometimes all the congregation join.

As Father Jungmann says: "These

older liturgical books are thus laid out like the actors' parts in a sacred play, as the share of each individual in a community performance." As time went on, it became customary for the priest who was celebrating Mass to read all the parts, even those that were sung by the choir. So the missal of today developed, and now it is common for the faithful to have the book in their hands, as well as for the priest at the altar.

There are parts of the Mass that are the same every day, no matter what the feast may be. These form the "Ordinary of the Mass." Because they are always used, they are printed for convenience in the middle of the book, where it opens most easily. The chief part of the Ordinary is called the Canon, and consists of the prayers said at the consecration of the Bread and Wine.

There are also parts of the Mass which change from day to day. They consist of the Epistles and Gospels, of the Collects and of those parts that were originally sung by the choir. They are called the Proper of the Mass. The Propers are placed in the missal apart from the Ordinary. The first Mass-prayers printed in the missal are those of the Proper for the First Sunday in Advent. That is the beginning of the Church's year. Then come the Propers for the Sundays and Feasts, and certain weekdays like those in Lent, up to Holy Saturday. After Holy Saturday's Proper, the Ordinary is placed in the book. After the Ordinary, the Propers begin again, with that for Easter Sunday.

But, as everyone knows, a great many feasts are Saints' feasts. The Propers for Saints' feasts are not printed in the missal in the same series as those for Sundays. They are set out in a separate series, which you find after the Last Sunday after Pentecost. So when you go to Mass and want to find the place in the missal, you must first find from the calendar what feast is being celebrated in that church on that day. You may have to look for the Proper in the series that begins at the beginning of the book, or in the Saints' series.

The other important thing to know about the arrangement of the Propers in the missal is this: although there is a Proper for each Saint's feast, many of them are alike. For instance most of the Saints who were martyrs have one Proper common to them all; most of those who were Confessors have the same. To save reprinting these parts every time they come, they have been arranged in another part of the book. This is called the Common of Saints. Therefore when you are following the Mass in the missal, you will probably have to open the book at several different places, and you will understand why the missal on the altar has ribbons for markers.

There are other things printed in a complete missal. Chief among these are the rubrics, or rules for the correct carrying out of the ceremonies. These are given at the front of the book. But for the use of the Faithful missals are published which do not contain all these things, nor even all the Masses for the year. The Pope says: "We therefore highly commend the zeal which, to enable the Faithful to take part more easily and profitably in the Mass, seeks to adapt the Roman Missal to their use so that they may join in prayer with the priest, using his very words, and uttering the sentiments of the Church herself." That is the idea of the missal; it is the chief prayer-book of the Church.

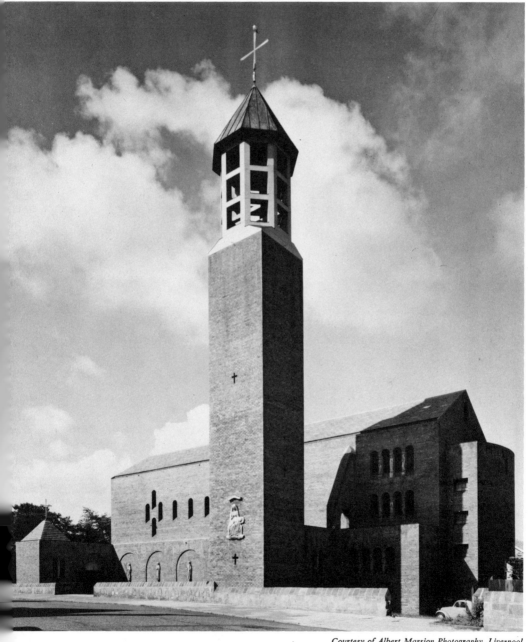

Courtesy of Albert Marrion Photography, Liverpool
Church of the English Martyrs, Wallasey, Cheshire

Church of Our Lady of Lourdes, Blackpool

*Exterior and interior view of the Church of Our Lady of Visitation, Greenford, designed by David Stokes, F.R.I.B.
seating 675. It has an entrance porch larger than usual, for the use of mothers and babies. The beautifully shaped p
bolic pre-stressed concrete trusses are left exposed and the brickwork walls have reconstructed stone dressings. The Ch
is designed with its upper roof covered in aluminium. The campanile on the left is to be added later and an interesting
is that it has to be built on stilts as it is a restricted site and cars will have to pass underneath the tower.*

St. Mary's Church, London Colney, England. Designed by David Stokes, F.R.I.B.A., with a reinforced concrete barrel vault supported on four corner columns with brick external walls and an aluminium roof. The photograph shows the main front with the big west window formed of reconstructed Portland stone, with tinted glass in the openings. The concrete framed side windows of stained glass give a picture-frame effect internally.

Courtesy Unity Studios, London

Courtesy Elsam, Mann & Cooper Ltd., Liverpool

Church of St. William of York, Liverpool

Courtesy Lofthouse, Crosbie & Co., Hampton

St. Monica's Church, Bootle

Courtesy Stewart Bale Ltd., London

St. Mary and St. Joseph's Church, Poplar.
Completed 1954

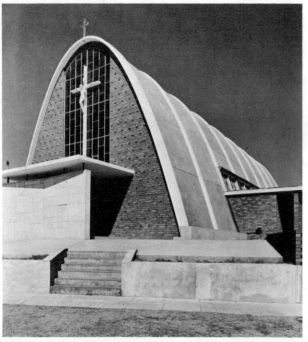

St. Bernard's Church, Botany, Sydney, Australia, made mainly of concrete in a "parabolic" shape. The building was prefabricated and assembled later in its position. The exterior is finished white marble chips, embedded in concrete with patterned brick on front wall

Courtesy Fox Photos Ltd.

Courtesy Fox Photos Ltd.

Interior of St. Bernard's Church, Botany, Sydney, Australia

Interior of St. Dominic's Church, Flemington, Sydney, Australia. Showing the radial grouping of seats converging on the altar

St. Dominic's Church, Flemington, Sydney, Australia, in red texture brick with concrete canopy and silver cross; designed by Architect Kevin J. Curtin

Courtesy Fox Photos Ltd.

Courtesy Fox Photos Ltd.

St. Francis Xavier's Church, Kansas City, U.S.A., built in 1950 and planned by the architect Barry Burne in the outline of a fish, the symbol which was familiar to Christians from the earliest times. It was derived from the Greek word for fish of which the letters form the initials of the title "Jesus Christ, Son of God, Saviour," and was a brief profession of faith in the divinity of Christ, the Redeemer of mankind. It appeared in the catacombs, in early frescoes, on carved gems and has been used in sculpture over the centuries. In many new churches today it is also seen in ironwork such as Sanctuary rails etc.

Courtesy Warren Reynold , Minneapolis, U.S.A.

Interior of St. Francis Xavier's Church, Kansas City, U.S.A., showing the High Altar

Courtesy Warren Reynolds, Minneapolis, U.S

Recess over the main doorway of St. Augustine's Church, Yass, New South Wales, Australia, completed 1956. In the centre is a stone cross with the figure of Christ in bronze. On stone panels above are the peacock and the phoenix, symbols of the Resurrection. On the other panels are the chalice, the sponge, the wine and the lance, the palm leaves, the seamless robe and the scourges and flagellation pillar.

On the left below is the High Altar of St. Augustine's Church, Yass, New South Wales, Australia. The altar rail is inscribed with the words "He gave His flesh, their food to be" and below are two pelicans which are supposed to bring their young to life with their own blood and so are used as symbols of the Resurrection.

On the right below is the Sanctuary of St. Ethelreda Church, Chicago, U.S.A. On the left of the Crucifix above the altar is St. Ethelreda and on the right some of the instruments of the Passion.

Courtesy Axel Poignant, Sydney, Australia

Courtesy Douglas Baglin, N.S.W., Australia

Courtesy Daprato Studios, U.S.A.

On the left the altar in the chapel of Carmelite Priory of St. Cyril, Chicago, U.S.A., and on the right the altar in the chapel of St. Thomas More Convent, Chicago, U.S.A. The front of this altar is decorated with the Cross and under the arms of the Cross are the first and last letters of the Greek alphabet, Alpha on the left and Omega on the right. The symbol indicates that in Christ the beginning and the end are joined into one.

Sanctuary and altars in Alexian Brothers Novitiate Chapel, Gresham, Wisconsin, U.S.A.

Courtesy Fr. Odilo Schwarz

Sacred Heart Church, Inkamana, Zululand, consecrated in 1953, designed by a Mission Brother and built by fellow Mission Brothers and unskilled native labourers

Interior of St. Mary's Church, East Finchley, London

Courtesy Morris Allen, Dunfermline

Altar in St. Patrick's Church, Lochgelly, Scotland

Interior of the Church of the Most Precious Blood, Cabra, Dublin, Eire

*St. Peter in Chains Church,
Ardrossan, Scotland*

*Interior of St. Bartholomew's
Church, Coatbridge, showing
the diffusion of bright sunlight
through the cruciform window
above the altar*

Courtesy J. W. Boyd, Saltcoats

Courtesy W. Ralston Ltd., Glasgow

Sanctuary of Christ The King Cathedral, Queenstown, S. Africa

Instead of a pulpit there are two ambones, one of which can be seen in the foreground on the right. These raised des go back to early Christian practice. From one is read the Epistle and from the other the Gospel. The altar and t bishop's Chair are carved from local sandstone and under the altar-table is the Lamb of God worked in silver. Behi the altar stands the altar-cross decorated with precious stones. The bishop's Chair stands centrally behind the altar in the earliest Christian basilicas in Italy. Behind the altar are three panels—the central one, as the Cathedral dedicated to Christ the King, represents Him as the King and Judge, with His right hand raised in blessing and His le holding the "Lily Sceptre". The left panel depicts Mary, the Mother of God and the right one St. John the Baptist. (either side of the bishop's Chair are the symbols of the Four Evangelists.

Courtesy Hardie's Studio, Witbank, South Africa

Interior of Witbank Cathedral, Transvaal, South Africa

Courtesy Hardie's Studio, Witbank, South A

Exterior of Witbank Cathedral, Transvaal, South Af

Exterior of Woodlands Church,
Durban, South Africa

Interior of Woodlands Church,
Durban, South Africa

Courtesy John Lucey, Durban, South Africa

Courtesy John Lucey, Durban, South Africa

Photo Van Berkel, N.V.F., South Africa

Front view of the Church of St. Pius X, Southfield, Cape Province, South Africa, built in 1956

Photo Van Berkel, N.V.F., South Africa

Side view of the Church of St. Pius X, Southfield, Cape Province, South Africa

Courtesy Northern Aluminium Company

Exterior view of the Church of Our Lady Queen of all Creation, Hemel Hempstead, England, designed by Colin A. B. Gowers, A.R.I.B.A.   It is built of pre-cast concrete and reinforced lead bearing brickwork.

Church of the English Martyrs, Horley, Surrey

d by Justin H. Alleyn, B. Arch., F.R.I.B.A., to seat 450 people.   This church is octagonal with the Sanctuary one wall of the octagon.   The construction, of pre-cast concrete trusses and beams, has a folded slap concrete ered with copper.   In-filling panels of brickwork complete the nave, while load-bearing brickwork is used for the es, side chapels, etc.   Triangular windows under the roof and recessed splayed windows around the aisles will give excellent lighting.

Perigueux Chapel, Dordogne, France, showing a wall relief of Christ in concrete over the simple altar. The chapel is one of the world's most modern architectural conceptions

Church of Our Lady of the Alps, Waiho, Franz Joseph Glacier, New Zealand, opened 1952

St. Mary's Church, Rotorua, New Zealand, built of steel framing and cement sheathing, plate glass and aluminium, opened in 1954

THE EDUCATION OF A PRIEST

Somebody's mother is going to be very proud one day. It will be the day when her son is ordained a priest. Please God, his father will be there with her, proud too, and grateful, and they will kneel together at their son's feet, and receive his blessing, and kiss the palms of his anointed hands.

That day will be the crown of a long uphill road. The education of a priest is a long and careful one. It begins with a vocation. A vocation is a call to the priesthood, and it comes from God. "You have not chosen me, but I have chosen you," said Jesus to his Apostles. "Nobody can take on himself such a privilege as this," St. Paul wrote to the Hebrews. But Almighty God gives this call by means of his Church on earth; that is to say, a young man can only know that he has a vocation to the priesthood through being accepted by the Bishop of the diocese.

That, however, is not the first step. To be accepted by the Bishop, you must ask to be accepted. This means that the seed or root of a vocation is a desire to serve God as a priest. It is the Holy Spirit who inspires this desire in one whom he wishes to lead to the priesthood, but the young man himself will usually only be conscious that he thinks it would be a good thing to become a priest, and that he wants to be one, not that he is inspired by the Holy Spirit.

A boy who has this desire asks his parish priest to apply to the Bishop. It is for the Bishop to decide whether the candidate is suitable, but naturally the parish priest will only apply to the Bishop if he thinks there are good hopes of the boy being a worthy student for the priesthood. Coming from a good Catholic home, being a frequent communicant, and being an altar-server, are encouraging signs of this.

Not all those who hear the call of Christ are boys. Older men are called to the priesthood, sometimes after years of life as doctors, lawyers, soldiers, and indeed from any walk in life. There is in Rome a College called the Beda which

Oscott College

is especially for such "late vocations." The Holy Father, Pius XII, says of those who come to the priesthood from schools and colleges other than seminaries: "Such students, even though they enter the priesthood late, often excel in solid virtue, precisely because they have already faced grave difficulties, had their souls hardened in the battle of life, and have engaged in work closely connected with the priestly office."

But the Pope also says, in the same Apostolic Exhortation (Menti Nostrae, 1950): ". . . Seminary students at the beginning of their course are very young boys taken from their natural environment." That is the normal thing in the Church: the education of a priest begins in boyhood.

It begins at the seminary. The red-letter day comes, and young John—let us say—says good-bye to his father and mother, travels to the seminary and joins a crowd of other boys, some of them new boys like himself, a bit nervous perhaps, but excited and eager to find their way round their new home. Probably John knows a boy who went to the seminary before him, maybe from his own parish, who will show him the ropes.

John has had a talk with his Bishop, who has made sure that he has the right ideas about being a priest . . . "they aspire to the priesthood for no other reason than the sublime nature of the priestly office and the spiritual good of themselves and others," as the Holy Father expresses it. John has passed a medical, too. The Pope has urged all Bishops "to enquire carefully . . . into the physical fitness of the aspirants." And the Bishop is satisfied that he has enough brains to do the studies that lie before him.

He finds his new companions are of all sorts. The Catholic priesthood is as near a "classless society" as anything in the world. Rich and poor are all one here. Pope Pius XII belongs to the Roman nobility; Pope Pius X, now canonised, walked barefoot to school to save shoe-leather, so poor were his people.

A Seminary is very like any other boarding-school. In fact in England there are boarding-schools—Ushaw College is one—where the boys are not all going to be priests, though most of them are. The studies are those of any grammar school, with perhaps more lessons in Christian Doctrine and in Scripture. There are plays and concerts in plenty; often an orchestra, with the chance of learning a musical instrument. There are jobs and hobbies of all kinds, even printing in some seminaries, and there are games. "Their life," says the Holy Father, "should correspond, as far as possible, with the normal life of boys," and no one who has seen Seminarians play, or heard them discussing results and star-players, has any doubt of this.

While at the seminary, a boy is not cut off from his home. He goes home for holidays, and if these are a little shorter than at some boarding schools, they still amount to some eight weeks in the summer, and two or three at Christmas.

The education of a priest includes ordinary studies, but the Holy Father says: "It is self-evident that nothing can have greater importance in our eyes than their spiritual and moral training." Every day the young seminarian hears Mass, on Sundays and feast-days High Mass. He is given ample instruction concerning it, and has constant opportunities of serving it, and taking part in other ceremonies. Once a week he will hear a sermon, and all the masters who teach him are priests.

His training, according to the mind of the Pope, will induce "self-discipline and a sense of responsibility," and his Superiors will see to it that he has knowledge of current affairs and is enabled to form a mature judgement on events. From the beginning he learns obedience, for in this the Catholic priesthood should excel even the Brigade of Guards. He learns chastity, since, in the words of the Holy Father, "it is on this virtue that their determination to be priests and their perseverance in the life largely depend."

At length, when the grammar school part of his education is complete, when in the ordinary way he would be leaving school, and perhaps going to the University, young John leaves the minor Seminary and passes to the major. This is an important step. He changes his dress. He puts on a Roman collar, and

Upholland College

his suit is black. He begins the studies that are special to the priesthood. "The greatest stress," the Pope declares, "must be laid on philosophy and theology 'according to the system of the Angelic Doctor.'" These last words come from the Canon Law, which is the law of the Church. The "Angelic Doctor" is St. Thomas Aquinas, and if you will now turn to the second volume of this book you will be able to read there who St. Thomas was, and why the Church insists that he should be the guide and inspiration of her priests in their sacred studies.

St. John's Seminary, Wonersh

The first part of these studies is called philosophy. One of the duties for which John is being trained at the seminary is to preach and teach what Jesus taught; John is to be a priest of the Church, spreading the message of which she is the bearer. To do this well, he must have a trained mind. He must be taught how to think clearly and reasonably. This he learns in Logic. He must understand all that can be understood of the marvel which is knowledge.

He must grasp clearly the great truths that lie behind all science, such as the meaning of truth and of goodness. Though he is not called upon to be an expert in such special sciences as physics and biology, he must know the principles on which they rest. He will be taught enough of the special sciences to help him to explain such doctrines of the Church as the Real Presence of Jesus in the Blessed Sacrament. He must know also enough of the science of psychology, or the workings of the human mind, to help him in the care of souls. He must be able to prove by reason that God exists, and to show that religion is a truly reasonable thing, and he must learn the laws of human conduct, and what is right and wrong, as the conscience of man can know them. All these things John will study in philosophy.

But philosophy is only the preparation for theology. John's proper study will be theology. First he will learn afresh what the Church is, the Mystical Body

Ushaw College

Aero-Pictorial Ltd.

The late Cardinal Godfrey celebrating Mass in the presence of the Hierarc

d and Wales on the occasion of his enthronement as Archbishop of Westminster

Courtesy Independent Newspapers Ltd., Dublin

Maynouth College

of Christ. He will learn how she teaches, and how to recognise her infallible voice. He will be instructed in the Law by which she is governed, and told the main outline of her history. He will be taught how to read correctly the Sacred Scriptures which she guards, and how to follow the living stream of her tradition.

Above all he will be taught the mystery of Jesus Christ, and of the divine life of grace which is given by him to Christian souls. For John will come to realise more and more, as he studies, what the Pope says: that he is to be, "as it were, a living image of Jesus Christ; and all those he teaches will feel an inner conviction that it is God's word he speaks, and that it is by God's power that he operates."

When he is ordained, John will have to minister to the spiritual needs of the faithful. For this he must be prepared by careful training in the use of the sacraments. In particular he will be trained for two full years in moral theology, in order that he may be a sure guide and a helpful physician to those who come to him in confession. For moral theology is the science of human

Cotton College

conduct, and of the laws of right and wrong, as these things are made clear by the light of the revelation of Jesus Christ, and the living voice of the teaching Church.

All that John learnt as a boy concerning the ceremonies of the Mass will stand him in good stead, for now, as a theologian, he makes himself ready for the great day when he himself will go unto the altar of the Lord, and offer sacrifice for himself and for the people.

At every great moment of a Christian's life a priest is at hand. He baptises the new-born infant; he gives the first Holy Communion, and all that come after; he absolves the sinner, and blesses bride and bridegroom; he is there when the hour of death comes, to prepare the Christian soul for its flight into eternity. He is teacher, counsellor, consoler, guide and minister of grace, and for all these heavy responsibilities he is prepared by the long and toilsome education of a priest.

St. Edmund's, Ware

CATHOLIC EDUCATION IN ENGLAND

Just before Christ ascended into heaven, he told his apostles, "Go out into all the world, and preach the Gospel to all creation." And this is how Catholic education began.

Since then, without interruption, men and women have been teaching people about God and how to lead good Catholic lives. But this was not always done in the kind of schools we have today. The very first Catholic schools were for boys who wanted to become monks or priests and for girls who wanted to be nuns. At every monastery and convent there was a school for those boys or girls who wanted to join the Order. There was also, at every cathedral, a choir school, as there is today. Little by little, these schools admitted pupils who did not want to be priests or religious. In the later Middle Ages, many towns and guilds founded grammar schools, and every parish had a school for poor children. Before the Reformation England had a very large number of schools, and there were many

English laymen who were famous for their learning. The most outstanding of them was St. Thomas More.

At the Reformation, all Catholic schools were either taken over by the Protestants, as in the case of the cathedral schools, or they ceased to exist because all the monasteries and convents were abolished, and anyone who was discovered teaching the Catholic religion was put to death. At least ten Catholic lay teachers and many more priests who had been schoolmasters were condemned and died as martyrs. Many of the monks and nuns who had been driven out of their monasteries, went to France and Belgium. There they joined communities of their own Order, and in some cases it was possible to open an entirely English house. Well known among these were St. Monica's, Louvain, a convent of English Canonesses of the Lateran, Beaulieu convent in Douai, of the Canonesses of St. Augustine, and the English Benedictine Abbey of Douai. Catholic parents who were sufficiently

Douai Abbey

well off, sent their children abroad to ensure their receiving a Catholic education, although this was against the law, and if it was found out that children had been sent abroad, the parents were very heavily fined. In this way, English Catholic education continued uninterruptedly in spite of the Reformation and Elizabethan penal laws, but it was possible for only a small number. By far the greater part had no Catholic education.

But the Reformation did not only happen in England. Holland, Germany, Switzerland, Scandinavia, and large parts of Central Europe became Protestant. Wars broke out between Protestant and Catholic countries, and there was very much misery and poverty and ignorance everywhere. People did not know what to believe any more. Then began the great movement which we know as the Counter-Reformation. And in the forefront of this movement were the members of the Society of Jesus, or "Jesuits," as they were soon called. The Counter-Reformation was to reconquer many countries that had been made Protestant. It was a fight of the truth against false doctrine—a new crusade, only this time in Europe.

St. Ignatius of Loyola, who founded the Jesuits, did not at first think of starting schools for boys. Indeed his first idea was not even to found a religious order; he began by simply gathering a group of men who wished to do priestly work in the true spirit of the Gospel. But it was not long before the Jesuits saw how important education was, for the real reform of the Church, and they took up with energy the work they found to hand, opening everywhere colleges for boys.

St. Ignatius himself, after his "conversion," when he set out to be a distinguished soldier not of the King of Spain, but of the King of Heaven, found it necessary to go to school. From school among boys, he went to the university among young men. To find his food, he had to beg, and one of the

Stonyhurst College

Courtesy Aero Pictorial Ltd

places he begged in was London, where he was given most generous alms.

St. Ignatius never forgot England. In his lifetime, it was impossible to send anyone to England, though he did send two Fathers to Ireland. But they could not stay there. The only thing that could be done was to found an English Jesuit College on the Continent, and this was done at St. Omer in Flanders, conveniently near the Channel. All through the reign of Queen Elizabeth, English Jesuits, trained at St. Omer, went secretly into England, although there was a price on every Jesuit's head. Fifty-seven Jesuits were martyred because they had come to bring the Faith back to England. The stories of their lives make thrilling reading, especially that of Bd. Edmund Campion. It was not till 1794 that the first Jesuit College could be opened in England—Stonyhurst in Lancashire, a foundation from St. Omer.

While St. Ignatius was forming his "Company of Jesus," one of whose aims is the education of boys, St. Angela Merici was forming the "Company of St. Ursula" for the education of girls. There is a parallel in their way of looking at things, a gallant, soldierly spirit. The Spanish officer and the Italian peasant girl both had the glory of God passionately at heart; they both lived with their eyes wide open, so that they understood the needs of the times they lived in.

St. Angela's Ursuline Convent, Forest Gate

And the main need was for sound and thorough education. So far, there had been no organised education for girls, either in England or elsewhere. Teaching Orders such as we know them to-day, did not exist. St. Angela did not intend to found a religious order. She wanted to found something very much like what we know as "Secular Institutes." Her "Company of St. Ursula"—called after the leader of a group of virgin martyrs—was to be an association of lay teachers living in their own homes, wearing ordinary clothes, distinguishing themselves from other girls and women only by their intensely Catholic lives and their teaching activity. Later on, the Ursulines, as they were called, became a religious order, the first teaching order in the Church. The Ursuline Order is also the first missionary order, for it was a French Ursuline, the Ven. Mother Mary of the Incarnation, who went to Canada and founded the first convent of nuns in the Missions.

From the Jesuits and the Ursulines, all the "active" religious orders and congregations, that is those who teach, nurse, and do social work, have taken their inspiration. These two Orders were breaking entirely new ground, and it is through them, even because of them, that the hundreds of active religious congregations have come into being. And the story of many of these congregations is the story of Catholic education in England.

So many there are, indeed, that it is quite impossible to mention them all. They have come to England from almost every country in Europe: from France, Spain, Italy, Germany, Belgium, Holland, Poland and Ireland—all working to make England Catholic again.

But the first convent of teaching nuns in England was, as is only fitting, an English foundation. Many English girls, who had a religious vocation, went secretly to the Continent to enter a con-vent there. One of them was Mary Ward, daughter of a well-to-do Catholic family from the north of England. She wanted to lead a strictly enclosed religious life, and entered therefore a convent of Poor Clares in St. Omer. But through some misunderstanding she was admitted, not as an enclosed nun, but as an Extern Sister, who has to go out begging for the nuns' food. This was not Mary Ward's vocation, and she left the convent to found a Poor Clare Convent for English nuns only. For a time she was very happy, but she became more and more convinced that this was not her vocation either. She wanted to work for the conversion of England, yet there was no possibility of returning to England as a nun. The Jesuits were religious, yet they went over—but not looking like priests. They wore ordinary clothes; there was nothing to distinguish them from other gentlemen. Something like that, thought Mary Ward, ought to be possible for nuns— nuns without enclosure, nuns who looked like other ladies. At last it became clear to her that her place was not in the Poor Clare Convent of St. Omer. For the second time, Mary Ward left a convent. The people of St. Omer shook their heads. And then they were really shocked; Mary Ward put her plan of having nuns without enclosure into practice. This was something unheard of—nuns who went about the streets collecting little girls for their lessons! Even though the "English Ladies," as they were soon called, proved to be excellent teachers, they had to go. In Bavaria and Austria, Mary Ward and her companions were received quite cordially at first. Their schools were very good and filled a real need. But the idea was too new, and, so soon after the Reformation, new ideas were immediately suspected of being heretical. For a time, Mary Ward was imprisoned

Courtesy Aerofilms Ltd

Convent of the Holy Child Jesus, Mayfield

Beaumont College

Convent F.C.J., Poles, Ware

for suspected heresy and disobedience to the Church. The Pope dissolved her Institute. In 1645, Mary Ward died at the age of sixty, having apparently achieved nothing. But after her death, the Institute of the Blessed Virgin Mary came to life again, and in 1686 the first English Convent since the Reformation was founded. The Bar Convent, York, was to remain the only convent in England for over a hundred years. Mary Ward was after all the pioneer of Catholic education for girls in England.

In 1822, an Irish girl, Frances Ball, made her novitiate at the Bar Convent, York, and then went back to Ireland to found the first house of the Institute at Rathfarnham Abbey in Dublin. The Irish branch of the Institute is known as Loreto. From England and Ireland the Institute spread all over the world.

It was not till the outbreak of the French Revolution at the end of the eighteenth century that convents were founded again in England. There was, up to that time only one monastery in England, namely Ampleforth Abbey.

This was a foundation from the English Benedictine Abbey of Douai. Today Ampleforth, Ealing, Downside, Douai, Belmont and Ramsgate, have large boys' colleges.

In 1790, Benedictine nuns who had been driven out of their convent by the French Revolution, came to London, and went from there to Princethorpe. This is the only Benedictine convent in England to which there is a school attached.

Meanwhile in Ireland, where the only way of giving Catholic teaching was by means of the "Hedge Schools"—classes being literally held behind hedges and hidden from government spies in clumps of trees and bushes—Mother Catherine McAulay in 1787 founded the Sisters of Mercy. They were not expressly a teaching order, but were to meet any need—sick nursing, social work, teaching. Now they have many large schools and colleges in Ireland and England and in other parts of the world.

Almost at the same time, Edmund Ignatius Rice of Dublin founded the

Irish Christian Brothers for the education of boys. The inspiration for this congregation came from the De La Salle Brothers, the first teaching congregation for men, which St. John Baptist de la Salle founded in 1680 for the education of poor boys. Schools for the poor hardly existed at that time, and where they did exist, the children were more often beaten than taught. St. John Baptist de la Salle changed all this and insisted that the boys in his schools should be treated kindly, even with respect. This was quite a revolutionary idea then, but it worked. The success of the De La Salle Brothers' teaching methods led Edmund Ignatius Rice to found the Irish Christian Brothers on the same lines. This congregation received the first confirmation by the Church of a congregation of religious men in Ireland. It spread to England, America, Canada and Australia.

The Presentation Brothers are a branch of the Irish Christian Brothers.

They, too, work in England and Canada.

In France, the seventeenth and eighteenth century brought many new religious foundations, both of teaching congregations and for the relief of the poor. Many of those came to England, either at the time of the French Revolution, or after the passing of the Catholic Emancipation Act in 1829, or at the beginning of the twentieth century, when French anti-clerical laws forbade religious to teach.

The most famous congregation founded in France in the seventeenth century is that of the Sisters of Charity, St. Vincent de Paul. Originally, they were founded for visiting the poor, nursing them in their homes, looking after children, and doing anything and everything that needed doing. This included teaching children the catechism and preparing them for their first communion. From there it was only a short step to teaching them to read and write, and when the Sisters of Charity came to

Ampleforth College

England, the greatest need was for teachers, and now they have large schools and colleges here.

Another congregation founded in France in the seventeenth century are the Sisters of Charity and Christian Instruction of Nevers, also primarily for the service of the poor. Their most famous pupil is St. Bernadette of Lourdes who later became a nun in that congregation.

had entered the convent of the Canonesses of The Holy Sepulchre in Tougres, Belgium, on condition that she should be allowed to found an English convent later on. This she did in Liège a few years later, and this convent became famous for its boarding-school. New Hall, near Chelmsford, is its home in England now.

Another, even older, teaching community which was an English founda-

St. Mary's Convent, South Ascot   *Courtesy Aero Pictorial Ltd.*

St. Peter Fourvier and St. Alix Leclerc founded the Canonesses of Our Lady, who conducted a famous boarding-school in Paris which was called "Les Oiseaux" (the Birds). They had to leave France at the time of the French Revolution, and made a foundation in England in 1794, which they also called "Les Oiseaux" to show the unbroken tradition which links the Westgate convent with the Paris foundation.

Also in 1794, there came a famous English community from Belgium to England. In 1641, Miss Susan Hawley

tion on the Continent, came back to England. When Henry VIII suppressed the convent of Augustinian Canonesses Regular in Burnham, Bucks, one of the nuns, Elizabeth Woodford, fled to Louvain and entered a convent of the same order, St. Ursula's. Soon there were so many English nuns at St. Ursula's that they made a separate foundation, St. Monica's, Louvain. Twenty years later, St. Monica's founded the "English Convent" in Bruges. Most English Catholic noble families sent their daughters to school there.

New Hall Convent, Chelmsford

From Bruges a convent was founded in Hayward's Heath.

It was, however, after the French Revolution, that the greatest number of teaching congregations were founded. It is quite impossible to mention them all, because they would fill a whole book. The very first teaching order founded after the Revolution was the Society of the Sacred Heart. Its foundress, St. Madeleine Sophie Barat, had had a quite unusual education for a girl of her time. Her brother Louis, eleven years older than she, and her godfather, became a priest. He noticed that his sister was very intelligent, and so he drew up a course of study for her which was identical with that used in the Jesuit colleges. St. Madeleine Sophie studied Latin and Greek, Mathematics, Literature, History, just like the boys in the colleges. Her brother was a very good, but extremely strict teacher, and would not allow his sister to make any mistakes or to spend time on anything except study and prayer. After the revolution, Father Varin, S.J., wanted to found a congregation of teaching nuns, but could not find anyone who was suitable to take charge of such a congregation, until he met St. Madeleine Sophie who was then twenty years old. At first she hesitated chiefly because she wanted to be a Carmelite, but also because she was too young to be Superior. Father Varin pointed out to her that her unusually wide and thorough education could be best used in teaching, and she consented at last. From small beginnings, the Society grew very quickly and now has convents in almost every part of the world. Already during the foundress's lifetime, the boarding-school of the Society was famous and Catholic noble families sent their daughters there. But there was an elementary school attached to every Sacred Heart convent, so that the Society was and is educating girls from every walk of life. The Society came to England in 1842. Roehampton Park, now at Woldingham, is the best known of their schools.

A few years after St. Madeleine Sophie had founded the Society of the Sacred

G. P. King Ltd

The Convent of the Sacred Heart, Woldingham

Heart, Bd. Julie Billiart founded the Sisters of Notre Dame. The aim of the two congregations is identical, namely the Catholic education of girls. But no two women could have been more different than the foundresses. When St. Madeleine Sophie Barat became the first superior of the Society of the Sacred Heart, she was a lively, highly educated girl of twenty. Bd. Julie Billiart, born in 1751, was an invalid for most of her life. For some time she had even been completely paralysed. During the Revolution, she did much to help priests who were in hiding, and she prayed and suffered much for France. This seemed all she would ever be able to do, until she was cured miraculously. Then, with a few companions she began to teach the catechism to poor children. The first Notre Dame Convent was opened in Namur nine years before the death of the foundress. Then the congregation developed fast, sending nuns to America in 1840. The first English convent was opened in 1851, the year of the restoration of the Catholic hierarchy.

Throughout the nineteenth century, very many teaching orders came into England. The Faithful Companions of Jesus, founded in France after the Revolution, were indeed the first of the new congregations to come here. The Ursulines of Jesus, founded in 1802, went to Scotland, and opened there the first convent since the Reformation: St. Margaret's, Edinburgh. From Scotland, they made foundations in England and Wales.

The Sisters of Providence came to England in 1843, opening girls' schools just as the Rosminian Fathers were opening colleges for boys. The Sisters of La Sainte Union des Sacrés Cœurs, who had been founded after the Revolution for the teaching of poor children; the nuns of La Retraite who, having been founded for the work of giving retreats, changed their activity after the Revolution for the teaching of poor children; the Bernardines founded by three Cistercian nuns who had been driven out of their convent by the Revolution, the Religious of Christian Instruction, the Ladies of Mary, the Marist Fathers and Sisters, the Ursulines from Paris and Thildonck, the

Servite Sisters, founded as early as 1284 in Florence—these and many other congregations came and helped to restore and develop Catholic education in England.

Special mention must be made of the Salesian Fathers and Sisters founded by St. John Bosco in Turin. St. John Bosco had a very special love for poor boys. He collected them from the streets, taught them their prayers, heard their confessions, let them serve his Mass, played games with them and became their guide. He opened schools, colleges, and workshops for them, and there were always more boys wanting to get into his schools than there was room. One of his first pupils, St. Dominic Savio, urged St. John Bosco to go to England which he had seen in a vision. Shortly afterward, St. Dominic Savio died at the age of fifteen, but St. John

Bosco never forgot England. In 1887 Battersea College was opened. What St. John Bosco was doing for boys, St. Maria Mazzarello was doing for girls in the convents of the Sisters of Our Lady Help of Christians, who came to England with the Salesian Fathers.

But not only teaching communities from Continental countries came to England in the nineteenth century. Three large teaching congregations were founded in England itself: The Society of the Holy Child Jesus by Mother Cornelia Connelly, an American convert who, having made herself familiar with the religious life at the Convent of the Sacred Heart, came to England at the request of Cardinal Wiseman to open English boarding-schools. The Society has houses in many countries overseas and on the Continent.

Downside Abbey

The Italian Passionist Fathers, working in the North of England, soon realised the need for all types of girls' schools, and Fr. Rossi under the patronage of Bishop Turner, founded the Congregation of the Sisters of the Cross and Passion.

Mother Margaret Hallahan and a few companions, all of them Dominican Tertiaries, began to teach poor children. Bishop Ullathorne formed them into a religious community, and the Dominican congregation founded by Mother Margaret Hallahan in great poverty now has many large schools and colleges.

But there could never be enough religious to meet the need for Catholic teachers in England, especially after 1870 when education became compulsory for all children. A number of the teaching orders therefore opened training colleges for Catholic teachers. The Society of the Sacred Heart, the Sisters of Notre Dame, the Sisters of La Sainte Union, the Society of the Holy Child Jesus, the Assumption Nuns, the Vincentian Fathers, and others, all have training colleges for Catholic teachers in primary and secondary schools. These Catholic secular teachers play a very large and important part in the work of Catholic education in England. They are to be found on the staff of every convent school, and very many primary and secondary schools attached to parishes have secular teachers only. In addition, there are some Catholic boarding-schools for both boys and girls, conducted by secular teachers.

Matins · Lauds · Terce · Prime · Sext · None · Vespers · Compline

THE BREVIARY

Have you ever travelled on a long train journey sharing the compartment with a Catholic priest and seen him reading a book that looks like a prayer-book? It might have gilt edges, and coloured ribbons for markers. Or have you ever had a priest staying in the house and heard him say, "Well, now I really must say some Office"?

The book is called a Breviary, and the Office is the Divine Office, the official prayer of the Church. The word "office" means duty (though we mostly think of it as meaning a room where people work!).

What the Pope says

To learn what the Divine Office is, we could not do better than read what the Holy Father, Pius XII, says in his Encyclical Letter on Christian worship. He writes:

"The public prayer of the community, offered to God by all, was in the earliest times made only on certain days and at certain hours. But prayer was offered not only at the public assemblies, but also in private houses, and often in common with neighbours and friends. It soon became the custom, however, in various parts of the Christian world to set apart special times for prayer: for example the last hour of the day, as evening approaches and the lamps are lighted; or the first hour of the day, as night comes to an end, that is, after cock-crow and just before sunrise. . . . These various prayers took definite form as time went on, especially under the influence of monks and ascetics, and gradually came to be introduced, by the Church's authority, into the sacred liturgy.

"The Divine Office, therefore, is the prayer of the Mystical Body of Jesus Christ, offered to God in the name of all Christians and for their benefit, since it is recited by priests, by other ministers of the Church, and by religious, who are officially appointed by the Church to that function."

309

Private and Public

The priest whom you may have seen reading his Breviary in a railway carriage was saying it privately, or to himself. If you were to go to Westminster Cathedral in London, at the right time, or to a great abbey like Downside Abbey, you would hear the Office carried out publicly. It would not be just read, but sung or chanted. The priest who says it privately says it when he conveniently can; but when it is public the times for it are fixed. The Holy Father in the Encyclical reminds us that the Apostles and early Christians followed the tradition of the Jews, in this matter of choosing certain times for prayer. It was when they were praying "at the third hour" that they were all filled with the Holy Ghost. It was at noon that Peter went up on to the house-top to pray there. Peter and John went up to the Temple "at the ninth hour which is an hour of prayer." And at midnight Paul and Silas were at their prayers, praising God. These things we read of in the Acts of the Apostles.

The "first hour" was six o'clock, or the beginning of the day. The "third hour" was what we should call 9.0 a.m. The sixth was mid-day, and the ninth was three o'clock in the afternoon. You will remember that in the Gospel account of the Passion, St. Matthew says "Now from the sixth hour there was darkness over the whole earth, until the ninth hour." This was while Jesus hung on the Cross. If you saw a notice giving the times for Divine Office in a cathedral, you would meet these same "hours"; only they would be called Prime, Terce, Sext and None. If you looked into the breviary that the priest was reading you would find the same; and you would also find other parts of the book, or other "hours" of the Divine Office, which were called Matins, and Lauds, and Vespers and Compline.

On the notice board of a church belonging to the Church of England, you are likely to see times for Mattins (with two T's) and for Evensong, which is Vespers.

Beginnings

Now what are the prayers that are said in the Divine Office? The Holy Father has told us that they took definite form as time went on; what were they like at the beginning?

You know that this Divine Office is part of the liturgy; you know that the chief part of the liturgy is the Mass; and you know that the Mass ceremony is made up of two parts, the first of which is called the Foremass, or the Mass of the Catechumens. This part contains traces of psalms that used to be sung, and readings from the Gospel and other parts of Holy Scripture. If you remember this, you will be able to understand what the public prayers of Christians were like in the very early days; at least you will know what a learned Benedictine monk, Dom Fernand Cabrol, thought they were very probably like. And if you think of a sturdy plant growing strongly and straight for a time and then gradually producing offshoots, you will come closer to understanding how the Divine Office came into being.

On Easter Sunday we now have a midnight Mass. Before it there is a very interesting service; it is a Vigil. The early Christians did not celebrate the Eucharistic Sacrifice as often as we do; but when they did celebrate it they did so with great fervour. They might spend the whole night preparing for it. This preparing was the Vigil. Sometimes, also, when they could not have the Holy Sacrifice, they just had the Vigil by itself. You could imagine a group of Catholics in our own days, living together on an island, with no priest, and saying to one another: "Since we cannot have Mass on Sunday, let us all meet together and

Fox Photo

Benedictine monks chanting office in their new monastic church at Glenstal Priory, Limerick

read the first part of the Mass, the Mass of the Catechumens, and have that for our prayer-meeting."

Perhaps the Vigil was divided into a Beginning, a Middle, and End, or in other words an Evening part, the Vigil itself, and a part for the Morning; or else the service for the previous Evening and the service for the following Morning were gradually separated from the Vigil itself. In one way or another, there came into use the Evening Service, called Vespers, and the early morning one, called Lauds. But why was the Morning service not called Matins? Does not "Matin" mean Morning? The answer seems to be that it was called Matins at first, and the part that belonged to the middle of the night was then still called the Vigil. But later on the name Matins was given to the night part, and the name Lauds came in for the morning part. Behind this changing of names there may have been one very

human fact: the fact that it is not very easy to stay up all night praying, or to get up in the middle of the night to pray.

Even now monks and nuns who lead a very austere, penitential life do get up in the middle of the night to pray, and the part of the Office that they celebrate then is Matins and Lauds. It is much less exacting to wait till one gets up in the morning before saying Matins and Lauds, so it is not surprising that the name Matins came to be used for what is still the longest and most important part of the Divine Office for the day. Priests who say the Office privately are allowed to say this part the day before; this is called "anticipating."

Prime, Terce, Sext and None are the parts of the Office that belong to the hours of daytime. Compline comes after Vespers (or Evensong). It is "Night prayers," in the sense in which we think of night prayers as rounding off the day, giving thanks to God, examining our conscience and renewing our sorrow for sin, and asking God's protection during the night. The name "Compline"—in Latin "Completorium"—means a completing or filling-up.

Once we know that the Church's prayer grew out of the traditional prayer of the Jews, we can guess at once the composition of the Divine Office. The Holy Father says in the Encyclical: "The psalms, as everybody knows, form the main part of the Divine Office." Each of the eight "hours" is a pattern of psalms, with the addition of some readings from Holy Scripture or the Fathers of the Church or other writings.

Jesus himself used the ancient psalms and canticles. On the Cross he appears to have been saying one, for he cried out in the words of the psalm "My God, my God, why hast thou forsaken me?"

To the psalms and lessons (or readings) are added hymns and other parts which are especially suitable for the musical adornment of the Divine Office by a choir. In the days when books were scarce, and had to be copied out by hand on parchment and bound in leather covers, it was hardly possible to put into one book all that was needed for the full celebration of the Office. There were separate books for the psalms and for the readings and other parts. Nowadays a priest can have in one book, with small print and fine paper, all that he needs. That is how the name Breviary came in. It is a kind of abbreviation or shortening. Moreover a certain amount of shortening had been done, besides getting all that was needed into one binding.

The Breviary used by the priest of today is usually in two volumes, one volume for winter and spring, and a second volume for summer and autumn. Sometimes there are four volumes, one for each season. This corresponds nearly enough to four parts or seasons of the Church's Liturgical Year, beginning with Advent, the winter volume of the book.

If you have watched a priest saying his Office, you will probably have noticed how he keeps turning from one part of the book to another. When you are using your own Missal for Sunday Mass, you have to do the same. The reason is similar: like the Missal, the Breviary is arranged in a special way. First come the psalms; these are set out according to the day of the week, some for Sunday, some for Monday, and so on. Then the portions of Scripture that are to be read; these are arranged according to the Church's calendar. Further on in the book there are the short Saints' lives and other passages that go with the feasts of the saints. Then, just as in the Missal, there are the "commons" of Saints; this means that just as there are special Masses for Doctors, Martyrs, Confessors, Virgins and other classes of Saints, so there are special "Offices" for them. This gives you an idea why on any one day the priest saying his Office will have to turn to several different parts of the book; that is why they usually have markers, just as the Missal does.

Thus through the centuries the Church's prayer-book has grown. We could not end better than by giving once more the words of the Pope. "In ancient times the faithful used to attend the recitation of the Office in greater numbers; but this custom has gradually died out and now, as we have said, its recitation is the duty only of the clergy and religious. The law, therefore, lays no obligation upon the laity in this matter; but it is greatly to be desired that they should take part in the recitation of Vespers or Compline on Sundays and feast-days in their own parish churches."

DEVOTIONS

Janet's grandmother was a rather special person. She was very old, and very kind, and very good, but the nicest thing about her was that she knew what you meant even though you got things mixed up trying to explain.

"You see, Grandma," Janet explained one day, "it's because of devotion to the Sacred Heart, and we're having a procession, and I'm to wear my First Communion dress and carry a basket of flowers, and throw them . . . we had a practice yesterday. . . ."

Janet's grandmother settled herself in her rocking-chair and Janet pulled up the stool—she called it her "listening" stool—and sat down.

Grandma nodded once or twice, then she said: "And you'll be able to use your beautiful white rosary, won't you?"

"Yes," said Janet, "isn't it lovely? I like its smooth white beads—and the cross. Grandma, I do like the cross, but please tell me about devotions. Tell me about Devotion to the Sacred Heart especially, but I want to know about the others too. . . ."

And so, to the accompaniment of Grandma's gentle rocking, Janet listened, and learned.

"It's a very big subject," Grandma began, "this subject of devotions. Lots of people who aren't Catholics don't understand about it all. They even say we are so busy with these devotions that we haven't time to be loving God."

"Grandma, how could they?" Janet looked up into her grandmother's wise face. "Everybody knows why there are devotions. Devotions are just a way of showing a very special love of Jesus. What I'm asking is how did they begin? Who thought about them first?"

"Let's begin," said Grandma after a pause, "let's begin by making a list of the chief devotions, and then perhaps we'll be able to say how they began. But first of all, Janet, you must understand that there's never any new truth or teaching when a new devotion starts. It's only that people get specially interested in some doctrines, and start thinking and talking about it. . . ."

"And then perhaps they make up

Legend of the Rosary of Our Lady

special prayers and hymns," Janet broke in, "and maybe they make statues and pictures, and think of things they can do . . . is that it, Grandma? Like—like processions."

"Yes," replied Grandma. "That's just about it. All the things they do, the devotional acts they make, help them to understand better about the truth they have realised."

"What shall we put first on the list, please?" Janet liked making lists, especially tidy ones.

"I think," said Grandma, "that we'll start the list with the Devotion to the Blessed Sacrament. Do you remember the story of the saintly nun to whom Our Lord showed a vision of the moon with a portion missing from it? Christians had always known that Jesus was in the Blessed Sacrament, but they hadn't properly realised all it meant. When they did, they found all sorts of ways of making the wonderful truth shine out, and rousing people to a special love of Jesus because of it. The vision which Our Lord showed to Blessed Juliana of

Cornillon indicated that a feast was missing in the liturgical year . . . a feast in honour of the Blessed Sacrament, and that was as long ago as the thirteenth century. But it helped most wonderfully to encourage people to love Jesus in the Eucharist. . . ."

"Is a devotion just a special love, Grandma, do you think? That's what I said it was. . . ."

"Well, that is what matters most about it," Janet's grandmother rocked herself gently to and fro, and Janet curled herself up on her "listening" stool, her eyes bright. "But usually when we speak about a devotion we mean a special love and a special way of showing it, or making it grow inside ourselves. Sometimes, you know, and it's sad, people think more about the outward showing than about the inward loving. It doesn't really matter an awful lot if you don't manage to kneel very straight and still, but it does matter that your thoughts should be loving, prayerful ones."

Janet nodded; her grandmother was

very wise and she was very proud of her: "What comes next?" she asked at length. "For my list."

"I remember," her Grandma replied, "that you were reading once about devotion to the Sacred Passion of Jesus, and perhaps that would be the next for your list, although I am not quite sure of my history to be able to give you things in their right order. . . ."

"That was when I was reading about Crucifixes and St. Francis of Assisi," Janet exclaimed. "He had the Wounds of Jesus in his hands and feet and . . . Grandma, I know—the Stations of the Cross."

"We know very well where we are with this devotion," Grandma said, smiling a little. "There are prayers to say, and things to do, and it is all meant to make us love Jesus more and remember his love for us. Did you know that the Stations of the Cross started with pilgrimages? Long ago, the Christians loved to go to the Holy Land and see the places where Jesus suffered. Once there, they followed the Way of the Cross. But when the Moslems took possession of the Holy Places in the Middle Ages, they began to put pictures up in their own churches and follow the Way of the Cross there. . . ."

"They just made miniature 'Stations of the Cross' for themselves, didn't they?" Janet cried, who was thinking most especially of the wonderfully carved Stations at Lourdes. "And there are fourteen special thoughts to think about Jesus before each of the fourteen Crosses. Was it the same when they had the devotion to the Five Wounds of Jesus?"

"Yes, it was all part of trying to understand the great love Jesus showed by suffering for us, and to love him back. Now tell me, Janet, what do you think is one big Catholic devotion—one we haven't yet talked about?"

Janet screwed up her face in an effort

to think hard—all the while letting the smooth white beads of her rosary slip through her fingers. Grandma's eyes fixed themselves on the rosary, and all in a flash, Janet knew:

"Our Lady! Devotion to Our Lady! The Rosary, of course."

"Yes, the Rosary," said Grandma. "One of the greatest and most important of Catholic devotions is to Our Lady. And the best known practice of this devotion is the Rosary."

Janet fingered the beads: "Why Rosary, Grandma? Why do we call it the Rosary—is it to do with roses? I saw a garden once with fifteen flower-beds—one for each Mystery—and it was lovely!"

"A very old legend tells how Our Lady was seen gathering rosebuds from the lips of a young monk as he recited Hail Marys, and that she wove them into a garland and placed it on his head—but that is a legend. The word 'rosary' meant a 'garland,' even before the Rosary of Our Lady began. . . ."

"Who began it, Grandma?" Janet sat still on her "listening" stool trying to memorise the legend so that she could tell her friends in the morning: "Who began it?"

"Nobody can say when the custom of counting prayers on beads began," her Grandma answered thoughtfully. "It's very, very old. Do you remember the great explorer, Marco Polo? I've seen you reading about him in your *Great Discoveries Book*. Well, he found that the King of Malabar used a string of precious stones, not ordinary beads, to count his prayers. St. Francis Xavier, too, when he went to Japan, found Buddhist monks using beads, and—I don't think you will know this—Lady Godiva of Coventry left in her will a circlet of precious stones on which she had recorded her prayers exactly.

"It's a very old custom," Grandma

In the centre is a 17th century South German Rosary. The beads are Venetian glass, the emblems of the Passion are in silver-gilt, and the pendants are filigree.
Rosary with the crucifix is in pink coral and gold filigree-work and is Spanish of the 19th century.
The third Rosary is late 17th century, South German, and is of amber and silver filigree with two pendants enclosing gilt medals of the Virgin of Altötting.

went on quickly to stop Janet from interrupting just then, "and very widespread. In fact the word 'bead' meant 'prayer' in Old English, and a pair of beads is the old name for rosary in England . . ."

"I love my Rosary," said Janet, "but I didn't know all that about it. Anyway Grandma, I do know our Rosary is fifteen decades, with an Our Father and ten Hail Marys in each; but I do want to know why we have the Mysteries, I mean just those things out of the life of Jesus."

"Well, Janet, they are the chief things, aren't they? What matters more is to see that the way to say the Rosary is to think about the life of Jesus while you are saying the Hail Marys. It's meditating, really. That means keeping your thoughts firmly fixed on some scene in the life of Jesus, and you know it does help to keep on repeating the same prayers over and over again. Do you know how I like to think of the Hail Marys?" Grandma went on with one of her sweetest smiles, "I think they are like a sort of music accompanying my thoughts---like the murmur of a stream . . . you know how you can sit by a stream and think—sometimes much better than if you were just sitting in a field. . . ."

"Yes, I do know that," Janet said eagerly. "I really do."

"The greatest of saints have loved the Rosary and Our Lady herself has urged us to say it," Grandma continued. "It's a real Catholic practice, and part of the great devotion to Our Lady."

Janet looked down at her rosary in silence for a little while before she asked:

"What's next?"

"There's a special Rosary called the Dolours Rosary," her grandmother said, "and that is to make us remember the Sorrows of Mary—seven chief sorrows we call to mind—and we try to love her more because of them. . . ."

"And that's a devotion too, isn't it?" Janet felt they were making quite a good list.

"And then there's the 'Quarant Ore' —the Forty Hours.' Did you see the notice about it in the church porch? There's a list of churches and dates."

"Yes, I did," said Janet, "and I wondered about it."

"Well, each church has a date which the bishop of the diocese fixes. You can easily see," Grandma went on, "that it is a special practice of devotion to Jesus in the Blessed Sacrament."

Janet nodded: "Yes, it's lovely. The altar is beautiful—all candles and flowers . . . somehow the flowers look even prettier once they get on to the altar, and there are so many candles. . . ."

"Twenty . . ." said her grandmother quite briskly. "Twenty candles there must be and all kept alight. Did you know that, Janet? And did you know there had to be twelve for Benediction?"

"I think so," Janet looked doubtful. "I think I knew about the candles for Benediction anyway." She made a secret resolve to count the candles next time. "And I think that Forty Hours is a lovely idea because it means that somewhere every day of the year people are loving Jesus in the Blessed Sacrament and he is never left alone. I'm glad it's our turn soon. I shall watch too. Daddy watches at night, but, Grandma, who began it?"

"We can only say for certain that in the city of Milan in Italy, in the year 1537, the practice was introduced," Grandma answered. "Then two years later the Pope gave a special approval, and said that it was to appease the anger of God for the offences of Christians. It was to be used as a spiritual weapon against the Turks who were threatening to destroy Christendom. . . ."

"I see—but why is it Forty Hours? It is because the Body of Jesus was in the tomb for about forty hours after he was crucified? I do know that."

"Perhaps. In fact most likely," Grandma replied. "In the Middle Ages, the Blessed Sacrament was left for forty hours in the Easter Sepulchre. You remember, don't you, that the Forty Hours ceremony begins with a solemn High Mass and ends with one, and at both there is a procession of the Blessed Sacrament, and the Litanies of the Saints are sung. . . ."

"Yes," said Janet. "I think I remember, only I do forget sometimes. Are there any other devotions for my list, please?"

"I doubt if we could make a complete list, even if we tried," said Grandma, "there are so many, but the one I most want to tell you about and the one in a way which made you come and sit on the 'listening' stool is the one we began with—Devotion to the Sacred Heart of Jesus."

Janet put her rosary away in its neat little green case. "Go on, Grandma. That's the one I particularly want to hear about most specially."

"When you are older," her grandmother told her, "you will read for yourself the Encyclical Letter on Devotion to the Sacred Heart. That letter was written by Pope Pius XII on the 19th of May 1956. The chief thing to understand is that by this devotion we try to realise that Jesus loves us with divine love and human love; he loves us as God, for he created us, and he loves us as Man, with the Human Heart he made his own when he became the Son of Mary. And he wants us to love him back, and to know that he feels hurt —just as we do—when, instead of loving him we treat him with forgetfulness and ingratitude and even worse."

Janet rested her head on her grand-mother's knee. There was something in her Grandma's voice which made her long to understand all she was saying.

"There was a French priest," her grandmother continued, "who understood this truth so well that he longed to bring about the public worship of the Sacred Heart of Jesus. He lived during the first half of the seventeenth century during the reign of Louis XIII. This burning love which he had for the human heart of Jesus inspired him to compose an Office and Mass for the Feast of the Sacred Heart, and the bishops of the dioceses where he founded his seminaries permitted the celebration of the new feast. His name was John Eudes, St. John Eudes now, for he was canonised at the beginning of this century. . . ."

Janet repeated the name slowly, looking puzzled.

"There was another name, Grandma," she said at last, "but it wasn't that name at all. I remember seeing it on a holy picture I had once; it was a picture of The Sacred Heart. . . ."

"Yes, I know," her grandmother replied; "it was on the picture I gave you myself. On the back was printed a little life of Margaret Mary Alacoque . . ."

"That's it!" Janet's eyes lit up; it was wonderful not to have to go on explaining and explaining. "Who was she, Grandma?"

"She was a very holy nun—a Visitation nun—who strove to love Jesus with all her strength. She was born in a farmhouse surrounded by mountains and forests of giant pines—which is the kind of scenery you get in Burgundy, and though at first she was happy, after her father died, she was often lonely and unhappy, but for all her sufferings she clung fast to Jesus. . . ."

"Did she live about the same time as the other saint?" Janet asked.

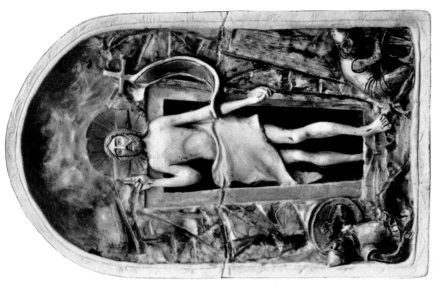

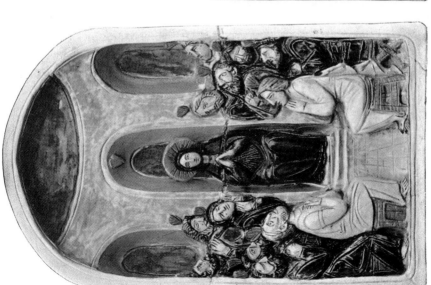

Three of the fifteen jewel-like ceramic plaques depicting the Mysteries of the Rosary on the ancient wall and on the trees along the Rosary Way at The Friars, Aylesford. On the left "The Visitation", in the centre "The Virgin Enthroned", and on the right "The Resurrection". The beautiful ceramic work has been designed and executed by Adam Kossowski.

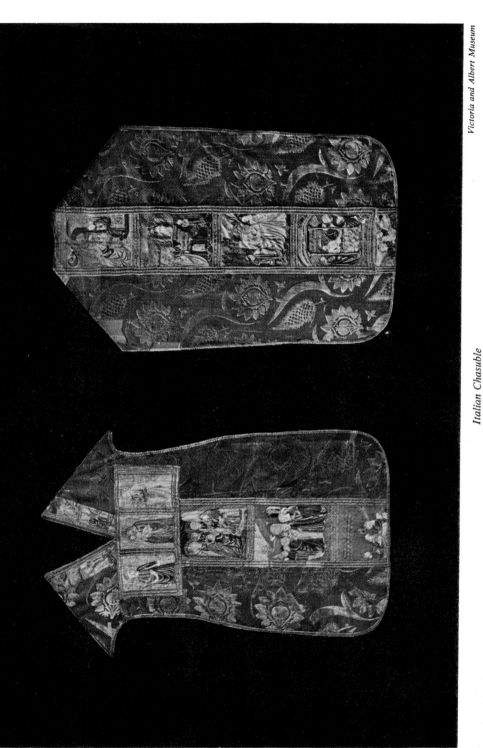

Italian Chasuble

Front and back views of an Italian (Florentine) Chasuble of the early fifteenth century. On the orphrey (the embroidered panels) are scenes from the life of the Virgin and Child, St. Catherine of Alexandria and St. John the Evangelist

Vincent Van Gogh   Rijksmuseum Kroller Muller Otterlo(G), Holland

The Good Samaritan

*The man who fell among thieves, who stripped him of some of his clothes and stole his money, is being helped by
the Good Samaritan.   In the distance is the priest who ignored the man's sufferings and went his way, as also did
the Levite who has just passed by*

elvet Italian (Florentine) cope of the late fifteenth century. The hood and orphrey are early sixteenth century. On the hood are the Martyrdom of St. Margaret and Christ with the Woman of Samaria

St. Margaret Mary's Vision

"John Eudes was born in 1601," her grandmother replied, "Margaret Mary in 1647, but she did not join the Visitation nuns until she was twenty-four, mostly because she could not bear to leave her mother. The convent at Paray-le-Monial was a charming house surrounded by gardens and Margaret Mary was radiantly happy, with a happiness which the world finds hard to understand. She was happy just to suffer because through suffering, Jesus told her, she could draw close to him. . . ."

Janet watched her grandmother's face intently. It seemed almost as if she had forgotten Janet was there. Perhaps she was thinking of the time she had suffered too.

"Did Jesus show her His Sacred Heart?" Janet asked. "I think that's what the holy picture said."

"Yes, St. Margaret Mary had four great visions, the first in 1674 just a few years before Saint John Eudes died.

23—III

One of them showed her his heart enthroned and surrounded by fire and flame, and Jesus told her that he wished men to see this picture of his human heart so that they might realise how much he had suffered for them and how much he loved them. . . .".

"June is the month of Sacred Heart Devotions," Janet said eagerly. "Did Margaret Mary see all this in June?"

"She had the greatest of her visions in June in 1676 when Jesus asked her to make His Heart honoured by all men, and he made her wonderful promises which you will better understand when you are older, Janet. And he gave her someone to help her, a holy Jesuit, Père la Colombière. . . ."

"What happened next?"

"It is a long story," Grandma said, her eyes no longer misty. "Margaret Mary suffered a great deal; she was misunderstood and persecuted and she only lived until she was forty-three . . . but the Devotion spread like a forest flame sweeping right across France, and then spreading across the world. . . ."

Grandma stopped speaking and for a while there was a deep kind of prayerful silence in the room broken only by the gentle creak of the rocking-chair. Then Janet spoke again.

"Grandma," Janet asked, "was Father Eudes . . ."

"St. John Eudes," put in her grandmother gently.

". . . 'St. John'" Janet corrected herself, with a smile of apology. "Was he the first person to have devotion to the Sacred Heart?"

"Oh, no!" replied her grandmother, "not at all. The Holy Father in his Encyclical mentions other saints who lived long, long before St. John, who had understood about the Sacred Heart; St. Gertrude, for example."

"What made them think of the Heart of Jesus?"

"As you know," Grandma answered, "Jesus died upon the Cross for us, and by that he showed his love for us, more than he could have shown it any other way. And when he rose again he kept the wounds of the nails and spear even in his glorified body."

"I saw a picture once," Janet cried, her eyes bright with remembrance, "and it was Jesus showing the wound in his side to Thomas!"

"That's right. Now the saints who spent their days praying used to think with joy of those wounds and of the great love of which they were the proof. They began to think, in a kind of sacred fancy, of the wound in the side as a shelter into which they could creep, to be safe from the storms of temptation. Then they began to think of the Heart which pierced by the lance, had poured out the last drop of blood for them."

"Jesus was dead, wasn't he," Janet asked quietly, "when the soldier pierced his side?"

"Yes. But it was still his Body. It was the dead Body of the Son of God. '. . . He loved them to the end,' St. John says. Do you see now how the saints found their way to the Sacred Heart?"

"Like you said: it's the love of Jesus!"

"That's right. The Heart stands for the love. A devotion, like devotion to the Sacred Heart, always has something you can think of quickly and easily, and be reminded by it of all the rest. A sign or a symbol. The Sacred Heart is a wonderful sign meaning all the love of Jesus, his divine love and his human love. Pope Leo XIII said that it was 'a symbol, nay an express image, of the infinite charity of Jesus Christ, which moves us to love him in return.'"

"You know, Grandma, we have the Sacred Heart on our badges, in the Apostleship of Prayer."

"I know," replied her grandmother, "Jesus himself chose the symbol, and said to St. Margaret Mary that he should be honoured under the figure of this Heart of flesh, and its image should be exposed."

"I shall think of this, Grandma," she said softly, very softly because her grandmother's head was nodding. "I shall think of it all when I throw the petals from my basket and wear my First Communion dress, but best of all I shall truly be taking part in the Devotion to the Sacred Heart, because I understand about it so much better now."

And with a last look at her grandmother, Janet tiptoed quietly from the room.

THIRD ORDERS, CONFRATERNITIES, PIOUS ASSOCIATIONS

The first Christians lived a family life, having all things in common, and looking after one another in illness, or poverty, or any other emergency. As Christianity spread more and more widely, this kind of common life became obviously impossible. Only groups of people specially dedicated to God lived this common life. In the fifth century St. Benedict established the Western form of religious life. Communities of men or women following a rule of life under an abbot or abbess, lived as one family with the same duties and privileges for all. Soon, benefactors of the various monasteries were given some of the privileges of the monks and nuns. They were allowed to wear the habit and be buried in the monastery cemetery, participating in the prayers and good works of the community, although they did not take vows. These "Oblates," as they were, and still are called in the Benedictine Order, were the beginning of the "Third Orders." They are seculars who, living in the world and following their own occupation, yet live in close union with and under the guidance of, a religious order. They wear a part of that Order's habit (usually a small scapular), have the right to be buried in the Order's habit, follow a rule of life, saying a part of the Order's office or, if unable to do that, a stated number of Our Fathers and Hail Marys. They share in all the merits of the First and Second Order (the first being that of the monks, the second of the nuns).

Apart from the Benedictine Oblates, there are four Third Orders: the Carmelite, the Franciscan, the Dominican, and the Servite Tertiaries, as members of Third Orders are called. The object of the Third Orders is the same as that of the First and Second Orders, to sanctify their members by prayer and penance, to help one another and all those around them by mutual charity, and to share in all the indulgences and good works of the parent order. Membership of a Third Order can be a very powerful means of sanctification: we only need to remember that such great saints as St. Catherine of Siena and St. Rose of Lima were Dominican Tertiaries, and St. Pius X one of the many canonised Franciscan Tertiaries. In each case, the three orders form one family. The members support one another by their prayers and good works, share in each other's merits, and follow the same ideal of perfection, encouraging one another and being guided by the Superior of the Order.

But Third Orders are only one form of close association of groups of people with a common spiritual and charitable bond. As early as the seventh century there were the "Guilds" established in England. These, too, developed out of the idea of the family, and there were different kinds of these voluntary associations. Some were purely religious; these were the forerunners of the confraternities, sodalities, and pious associations of today. Others were for social and commercial purposes, like the various guilds of merchants and craftsmen. There were, in the Middle Ages, special "Peace Guilds," associations with a corporate responsibility for the good conduct of their members. Very often, the rules of the guilds became the law of the town, ensuring peace and concord among the inhabitants.

The guilds took care of the spiritual and temporal welfare of their members, and looked after their business interests. The religious guilds took care of the sick, especially at time of epidemics, and saw to the burial of the dead. Guilds founded schools—some of them still exist, such as the famous Merchant Taylors. They also founded hospitals, and they had a carefully worked out system of social welfare: insurance, pension schemes, care of members' widows and orphans. Deceased members were not forgotten; Masses were said for the repose of their souls. In short, members of the guilds, in a spirit of brotherly love, supported one another, and those around them, in their spiritual and temporal needs.

From these medieval guilds the many confraternities and pious associations of our own days are derived. Their primary object is the sanctification of their members and the promotion of special works of Christian charity and piety. Some are purely religious, such as the Apostleship of Prayer, others are chiefly for charitable purposes, others again for people engaged in special professions. Some are for men, or women, or children only, others for everybody. There is a confraternity or pious association for every purpose, and, as the life of the Church grows and develops, and new needs arise, their number is being constantly added to. It would be quite impossible to mention them all, because there are so many.

The difference between a confraternity and a pious association is a matter of Church law. A confraternity must be canonically erected and guided by competent ecclesiastical authority. A pious association, on the other hand, does not need to be canonically erected. This is the only real difference between them, and very often the name "confraternity" or "sodality" is applied to what is in reality a pious association.

Some of the oldest confraternities are the Scapular Confraternities, the best known among them that of the Brown, or Carmelite, Scapular. Others are: the Servite, or Black, Scapular, in honour of Our Lady of Dolours, the Red Scapular in honour of the Sacred Passion, and many others. The members must have been invested with the scapular by a priest authorised to do so, and the scapular must be worn, if the indulgences attached to it are to be gained.

The Scapular Confraternities can be joined by all the faithful, as can also the Holy Rosary Confraternity, and the Bona Mors ("Good Death") Confraternity. Membership of these two depends on being formally received into them—a certificate of membership is issued to every member—and saying the fifteen decades of the rosary every week in the case of the former, and of three Our Fathers and Hail Marys in the case of the latter, is necessary to gain the many indulgences granted to these confraternities.

The Eucharistic Crusade of the Blessed Sacrament, divided into three sections— Knights (men), Handmaids (women and girls) and Pages (boys) has for its special object the devotion to the Blessed Sacrament and frequent communion.

The Archconfraternity of St. Stephen is for altar servers, men and boys, to promote devout serving at Mass, and ensure that ceremonies are carried out with dignity.

The best known and most widespread sodality is that of Our Lady. It began in a very small way in the sixteenth century. Fr. John Leunis, S.J., who was teaching in the Roman College, assembled the most devout senior boys for special meetings of prayer and meditation in honour of Our Blessed Lady. Very soon, other boys, having learnt from their privileged companions of these meetings and how much they helped in acquiring true devotion to Our Lady, asked to be allowed to come, too. The sodalists were the élite of the college. In a short time, there had to be three groups of sodalists, for the senior, the middle, and the junior school. The effects of membership of the sodality on the conduct of the boys were so striking that other Jesuit colleges adopted the system, too. The Holy See granted many privileges to the sodality, and it was canonically erected as the "Sodality of the Blessed Virgin of the Annunciation," because the senior sodalists of the Roman College held their meetings at the Church of the Annunciation. Later on, other associations in honour of Our Lady were affiliated to the Roman sodality which is also called "Prima Primaria." — "First and Foremost." They were given all the privileges granted to the Prima Primaria.

Members of the Sodality of Our Lady must strive by means of prayer and meditation to acquire true devotion to Our Lady and to promote this devotion by every possible means, chiefly by the example of a life that is in every detail worthy of a Child of Mary.

What the Jesuits did for the Sodality of Our Lady among boys and men, the nuns of the Society of the Sacred Heart did later on among girls and women. They adopted the system of the three age groups in their boarding-schools. They extended the Sodality to their old pupils, and then to various groups of women and girls. In time, Sodalities were established in almost every parish, independent of the Jesuits. They have proved a very powerful means of sanctification and apostolic activity.

If it is quite impossible to even mention all the confraternities and arch-confraternities, the impossibility is even more evident in the case of the pious associations. It is only possible to touch upon the best-known and most widespread.

There are those for professional people, mostly called "guilds": the Guild of St. Luke, St. Cosmas and Damian, for Catholic doctors; the Catholic Nurses' Guild; the Catholic Pharmaceutical Guild (for chemists). The Guild of St. Francis de Sales for writers, journalists and publishers; the Printers' Guild of St. John; the Guild of Catholic Artists and Craftsmen; the Catholic

Teachers' Federation; these and other professional unions help their members to uphold Catholic principles in their work.

The Society of St. Vincent de Paul is formed by men who undertake active charitable work, visiting the poor and sick, and helping with money, food and clothes.

The League of Christ the King—known as L.O.C.K.—promotes the lay apostolate among men students.

The Knights of St. Columba are an association of Catholic men who assist the parish priest in various activities.

For women, there are among many others, the Catholic Women's League (C.W.L.) for the promotion of religious, educational and social welfare, and to represent Catholic women's interests on national and international affairs; the Union of Catholic Mothers, for the preservation of the family and sanctification of the home; the Catholic Needlework Guild providing clothing for the poor; the Association of Perpetual Adoration, providing vestments and altar linen for poor churches and the foreign missions.

Especially for children there is the Association of the Holy Childhood for the benefit of Foreign Missions, (1) through devotion to the Holy Child obtaining the sanctification of children, both at home and in the missions, and (2) by prayer and alms for the missions. Members say daily one Hail Mary with the invocation, "Holy Mary, pray for us and the poor pagan children," and pay an annual contribution.

The Association of the Holy Childhood is the children's branch of the Association of the Propagation of the Faith for the assistance by prayers and alms, of priests, brothers and nuns in pagan and non-Catholic countries.

The Legion of Mary is an association of men and women for the sanctification of its members by prayer and active apostolic work.

Perhaps the most universal of all pious associations is the Apostleship of Prayer, or, as it is also called, "The League of Prayer in Union with the Sacred Heart." In order to become a member it is only necessary to have one's name entered on the register of one of the Apostleship's centres. Members make the Morning Offering: "Oh, Jesus, through the Immaculate Heart of Mary, I offer Thee the prayers, works, sufferings, and joys of this day for all the intentions of Thy Sacred Heart in the Holy Mass." The children's section is called the Eucharistic Crusade. We said it was the most universal, because everybody can belong to it, and because it reaches out to embrace all the needs of the Mystical body of Christ. Members of the Apostleship of Prayer make the infinite desires of the Sacred Heart their own and pray for their realisation.

These are but a few of the unaccountable number of confraternities and associations, all richly indulgenced, powerfully effective for the sanctification of their members. But even this very much abbreviated enumeration shows that there is no one in the Catholic Church who cannot take a very real and vital part in her life and activity. For everybody, no matter how old or how young, ill or well, rich or poor, there is a place in one or the other association, where he or she can be actively engaged in apostolic work and help in the extension of the Kingdom of God. Every member of the Mystical Body has its part to play, and no one need feel lonely or isolated or unwanted. In the give-and-take of the family life of the Church there is a part for everybody.

THE SAINTS—OUR FRIENDS

Mary-Rose read a book once—about saints. In it were told the stories of a great number of saints, saints of many nationalities and from many different walks of life. Mary-Rose read the book straight through, from cover to cover. When she came to the end of it, she thought it would be hard to remember just exactly why so many men and women, and boys and girls, too, became saints. She could not even decide which—out of so many—she would like to meet.

Mary-Rose did not read the book again for a long time; she did not really think very much about the saints for a long time, until a grown-up suggested she should try to "make friends with the saints." "Do not try to learn all about all the saints at once," her grown-up said. "Choose one or two, and try to get to know their lives properly. You see to know the saints is to love them . . . but there are some whose lives are not easily understood all at once. It is hard

for instance to love Benedict Joseph Labre unless you see that his great, burning love for the suffering Jesus compelled him to accept every kind of physical hardship."

Mary-Rose started all over again with her Book of Saints. But this time she read each life slowly and tried to make a picture of the particular saint about which she was reading. Mary-Rose began to understand that the saints are our friends, and with that understanding came the wish to know them.

Now, no one volume would hold the stories of all the hundreds of men and women who have loved God with that kind of "divine folly" which has made them saints. But the following stories concern some of the "modern" saints— and they are the ones which Mary-Rose liked best to read at first. Some of the stories are about saints who had much to do with children; all of them concern saints who lived and died within the last two centuries.

John's thrilling tight-rope act

John Bosco

In the fields at the back of his mother's cottage a tousle-headed, dark-skinned little boy was practising—on a tight rope slung between two trees. Time and again he fell off, but he always got up and tried again.

At last the day came when he considered himself as expert as any of the acrobats and jugglers who came to the village on market days.

He ran down the cobbled streets shouting his news:

"Grand performance! No entrance fee . . . except a decade of the rosary . . ."

Some of the bullies came to the field with the idea of breaking up the show, but like the rest they found themselves listening and watching. And the show was good. It was grand fun. Young John gave them a performance as thrilling as a one-man circus. And afterwards when he began telling them stories from the Bible—he told them so well,

that they really couldn't stop themselves listening.

John was only ten, but already he had begun his great work for children. He was born in a little village called Becchi in Piedmont, a province of Italy. His father was a peasant farmer, his mother was hard-working, devout and wonderfully alive to the gifts which John soon began to show.

His father died when he was two, and John's young life was made miserable by a stepbrother, a great, surly youth who resented everything about his clever little half-brother.

You can see John, can't you, his dark eyes flashing, as he clenched his fists all ready to shout at his bully of a stepbrother and yet for his mother's sake holding back.

But there were certain things John stood firm for as he grew older. One was learning. Jeer and scoff as Antonio might John was determined to educate himself, and every morning he set out on a six-mile walk to school. When his boots wore out he trudged barefoot, and he went in all weather; all through the broiling hot days of an Italian summer, and through the bitter hard days of winter when the wind pierced his shabby suit and his fingers grew numb with cold. And he learned quickly and easily with the help of a prodigious memory and an indomitable will.

The long tramp to school toughened him physically, but it was a dream which forged his will to bring boys to Jesus. It was a strange dream—later he had two more—but the first came to him when he was only nine.

In it he saw a crowd of children quarrelling; then suddenly and terrifyingly the children turned into wild beasts, wolves and bears and tigers, and he was among them . . . then the beasts changed again—into little white lambs.

John had no doubt about the meaning of his dream. His own village was full of bullying, quarrelling children who knew nothing of the love of Jesus. How could they? Italy in the early part of the nineteenth century was overrun with beggars and rogues; there were few teachers and schools and scarcely anybody cared about the children of the ordinary working people most of whom were growing up without being able to read or write.

But how could he persuade the boys to listen? It was then he remembered the jugglers and acrobats who thronged the village square on market days. They could always draw a crowd with their tricks . . . and what they could do, he could do. But first he must learn their art. From that moment John haunted every fair, studied every juggler and acrobat that he came across, and then in the seclusion of his mother's field he practised, practised until his whole body was bruised black and blue with his falls.

John owed a great deal to his mother; it was she who gave him his first love of Bible stories. From her he learned his catechism and the value of saying his prayers night and morning. It was largely because of her that he was able to hold his audience after each performance, with his stories about Jesus.

One Sunday night on his way home from evening service he met and talked with a kindly old priest who was deeply moved when John repeated back to him the whole of his own sermon.

"If you come and see me tomorrow," Don Carlos told him, "I'll give you a lesson in Latin."

That night John could scarcely sleep for happiness. To learn Latin was one of the first steps on the way to becoming a priest. But his stepbrother, when he heard of the Latin lessons, made life at home intolerable, and soon it became clear that the lessons must stop. Worse was to follow.

"You must leave us, John," his mother said to him at last. "Antonio will make your life such a misery that you had better go . . ."

And John went; already he was brave and self-reliant, and though it seemed that his dream of becoming a priest was over, he made the best of his new life—as a cowhand.

He stayed on the farm for two years until an uncle took pity on him and arranged for him to return home promising that he would speak to Antonio. And so once again John was able to study, to visit his friend Don Carlos, and to go on with his Latin lessons. And just when all seemed to be going smoothly, the old priest died, and John lost both friend and tutor.

His mother made valiant efforts to send him to school again. She found

John studying with Don Carlos

him cheap lodging with a tailor and John helped to pay his way by learning the trade; he was older and bigger than any boy in his class and to begin with he was a long way behind, but soon even those who teased him most had to admit that he knew how to work, and that he was brilliantly clever.

And still he found time to collect the roughs of the town and bring them to Mass; and he found time to keep up his acrobatics and so expert was he by now that he was able to challenge a rival who tried to draw the boys away from church by giving performances on a Sunday. John beat him hollow, and his following increased by leaps and bounds.

Somehow the money was raised to send John to college and it was there that he had his second dream. Again he saw the children turned into wild beasts, but now Our Lady appeared and told him that she would put him in charge. And once more the beasts became little white lambs.

From college to seminary—and the third and last of the dreams; he saw himself with a priest sewing new patches of cloth on to an old coat.

"When you are ordained," the priest told him, "you will work among the under-dogs, the young hooligans who know nothing about Christ, and you will save them and give them new life. That is the meaning of your dream."

John's ordination took place on June 5, 1841, in the chapel of the Arch-bishop's Palace at Turin; he was twenty-six years old, and already he had been a juggler, ploughboy, preacher, tailor.

His first real conquest for the school which he visualised starting was a boy who had been chased out of church. John brought him back, talked with him, persuaded him to promise to come again for instruction.

In a short time he had no less than 400 boys—the young toughs of Turin—clamouring for help. Time and again he found suitable clubrooms, only to be ejected. The boys were noisy; many of the good citizens were terrified at the idea of attempting to educate such hooligans.

But John persevered—until he found a ramshackle old building which his boys helped him to rebuild . . . and out of it rose his Oratory, a school where boys, even the roughest and toughest of them, could learn a trade and at the same time come to know Jesus.

His influence for good over his pupils made him many bitter enemies, and some went to desperate lengths, even as far as attempted murder, to put an end to him and his work. His mother who had left home to come and act as his housekeeper worried for the safety of her son. But there was one great consolation: that was Grigio—Grigio "the grey one"—a huge grey mongrel which suddenly and mysteriously appeared one day at the Oratory in Turin and from that moment was John's official body-guard. More than once Grigio with some mysterious sixth sense prevented his master from walking into almost certain death.

John fed and housed his boys—now numbering close on a thousand—with boundless optimism and faith, but soon he began to realise that he must have helpers, and the idea of forming a Society came to him. Four years after his helpers arrived, he journeyed to Rome, in 1858, to consult Pope Pius IX regarding its foundation. Already he had resolved that it should be under the patronage of St. Francis de Sales.

Not only in Italy but all over the world there was need for schools and teachers. After the Holy See's official approval of the Order, the first band of Salesian missionaries left for South America in 1875.

The small peasant boy who had bruised himself all over in order to become an acrobat was now one of the best known and most loved priests in

John's dream

Italy. And his care was not only for destitute boys. In May 1872 he founded the First House of the Daughters of Mary, Help of Christians, whose primary work was to help and educate girls.

He died, worn out by his tremendous labours, in his Oratory at Turin on January 31, 1888, with the knowledge that his Religious had no less than sixty-two houses. Today there are Salesians in every corner of the world—and about him Pope Pius XI wrote: "God gave him largeness of heart as the sand on the seashore." Don Bosco was canonised in 1934.

Dominic Savio

They had much in common these two, Dominic Savio, the little peasant boy from Mondonio, a village not half an hour's walk from Becchi, and Don Bosco, founder of the Salesians.

When they met at last at Becchi, where John had taken some of his boys for the Feast of the Rosary, Dominic was a delicate, wide-eyed boy, gentle and quiet.

For Dominic it was the most important moment in his life; everything depended on what the great Don Bosco thought of him. Then he remembered the letter and shyly drew it from his pocket.

Don Bosco took the letter and read it. He looked down at the boy again and smiled, and the smile was warm and friendly. "Yes, Dominic Savio," he said, "you may join us at the Oratory. Your schoolmaster writes well of you. . . ."

So Dominic joined the boys at the Oratory in Turin which Don Bosco had founded eight years before. He was twelve—and the year was 1854.

He never saw his home again—until he returned there—to die—just two years later. As he studied and worked and prayed he must have wondered sometimes what his father was doing; was he out in the field or perhaps shoeing one of the village horses at the smithy? Was his mother baking or sewing or perhaps weeding the rich soil in the garden?

If he missed his parents and sometimes longed for the comfort of his mother's arms, he did not show it. Above all else he desired that his life should be modelled on the life of his Saviour, and he understood with astonishing clarity that its foundation must be perfect obedience.

Watching him, Don Bosco marvelled at his unobtrusive sanctity and the wonderful influence he had over the other boys. His merry smile and high spirits helped him to make friends with the most surly and rebellious of characters, and his skill at telling stories and teaching catechism reduced the noisiest to silence.

But they loved him best when he joined in their games; then he was one of them . . . and yet, strangely, not one of them.

Who but Dominic would think of sleeping through a cold winter night with only a sheet for covering, and who would think of giving as an explanation: "I shan't die of cold. Our Lord at Bethlehem had less to cover him than I have . . ."

Beside the other boys, Dominic looked frail and delicate, but he had such an energy and enthusiasm for all the tasks he was given that his companions forgot he wasn't strong, and Dominic would have been the last to remind them . . . until the morning came when he no longer had the strength to rise for prayers.

Don Bosco sent for the doctor: "I can find nothing definitely wrong with him," the doctor said after making an examination . . . "Nothing definite." It almost seemed as if his constant striving to do everything perfectly for the love of Jesus had exhausted his natural strength . . . and better than anyone, Don Bosco understood. Dominic, he said, must go home. The boy protested but Don Bosco realised that once away from the city the pure air of his own country village might bring his little friend back to health.

But it was not to be; four days after his homecoming Dominic died—less than three weeks before his fifteenth birthday.

His death was a great sorrow to the saint: "Dominic catches more fish with his games than many preachers do with their sermons . . ." over and over again he had said this as he watched the peasant boy at play; and the Oratory seemed strangely empty with no Dominic. But one thing he could do and that was to ask his boys to pray privately for his intercession, convinced as he was that one day the Church would raise Dominic to her altars.

The saint's prophecy came true in 1914 when Dominic's Cause was introduced to Rome, and his body was taken to Turin. His canonisation in 1950 was something very rare in the Church's long history . . . something rare and very splendid—a magnificent testimony to the courage and sanctity of a little boy.

Frances sailing her missionary boats

St. Frances Xavier Cabrini

Children all over the world have made paper boats and sailed them down streams and rivers. When Frances was a little girl she put violets in her boat: they were her "missionaries" and she was sending them to China. China was the centre of all her dreams. On her father's farm at Santangelo in Lombardy she prepared herself in countless ways for the day when she would journey eastwards as a missionary nun.

In New York, in Chicago, in London —she would remember her childhood dreams—but with no regret. God had given her another work to do which called upon all her courage and trust— and she had plenty of both.

At eighteen Frances had not even achieved the first of her ambitions, which was to be a nun; instead, to please her parents, she became a school teacher. Two years later, in 1870, both mother and father died, and Frances was heart-broken. She turned to one of her elder sisters for comfort. Rosa was strict but understanding, and she did not try to prevent her "little" sister from offering herself almost immediately to a religious congregation.

"They may not want you," she warned, "because you are not strong enough." Rosa was right, and Frances went on teaching, until the chance came to take over an orphanage and to serve a kind of novitiate with the idea of turning its present staff into a religious community.

Frances soon found she needed all her reserves of patience and strength to work under the eccentric foundress of the orphanage. Antonia Tondini resented her presence and heaped on her every kind of petty persecution in an effort to get rid of her. But Frances stayed on until eight of the staff including herself were permitted by the bishop to take their first vows. It was a strange roundabout way of becoming a nun, but not strange if you had known Mother Cabrini; whether it was founding schools, or defending law suits, or reconciling warring authorities—no matter what—she had a remarkable aptitude for achieving the desired end.

Antonia Tondini's strange ways developed into a kind of insanity and the bishop finally closed the orphanage.

To Frances he said: "If you want to be a missionary, you will have to found a congregation of missionary sisters yourself—for there isn't one you can join . . ."

And that was exactly what Mother Cabrini proceeded to do. She founded the Missionary Sisters of the Sacred Heart, and the first seven sisters were those original members of her orphanage staff.

In 1887 Mother Cabrini, with her community now safely housed, journeyed to Rome—not only to get Papal approval for her little congregation, but also to ask if she might open a house in the city.

After setbacks, both approval and permission were forthcoming, and Frances permitted herself to think again about the East and China.

But it was westwards and not eastwards the Holy Father directed her eyes. Across the Atlantic the vast continent of America was receiving almost daily thousands upon thousands of immigrants—many of them from Italy.

In New York City alone there were Poles, Czechs, Croats and, inevitably, Italians. Besides the almost insuperable barrier of language, many of the refugees were without hope and—perhaps worse —without energy; they had fled from their own countries because of economic and social conditions. America had promised a new life; but America was young and she had her own problems. For the most part, she was almost indifferent to the plight of her refugees, and besides there was no one strong enough to organise homes and schools and orphanages so that at least the children could be cared for.

The Archbishop of New York felt his responsibility keenly. Many of the immigrants had been of the Faith—once.

Mother Cabrini and her nuns embarking

The Holy Father—in distant Rome—was also concerned. Would Mother Cabrini accept the Archbishop's invitation to cross the Atlantic and start at least one orphanage in New York itself where some of the homeless children could be cared for.

Mother Cabrini could not hold out for long against such an appeal. She set out accompanied by six of her Sisters for the New World.

But it was no Promised Land that awaited the Sisters. For the blue sun-lit skies of Italy they had exchanged the dull, grey, rain-soaked clouds of a great city on a winter's day. They had been assured of a house of their own; instead they spent their first night in a filthy hotel room so dirty that the Sisters dared not sleep in the beds.

The Archbishop greeted them kindly but with embarrassment; the benefactor who had promised money for the scheme had now withdrawn her support. The best thing the Sisters could do was to return home.

But Mother Cabrini—who suffered all the time from chronic illness—was made of sterner stuff. Go home? Admit defeat . . . when the Pope himself had asked her to come to America? Not likely.

In the morning the rain clouds had cleared. Mother Cabrini set her Sisters on to cleaning the vermin-infested room, and herself went out to persuade, organise, cajole. Within weeks the scheme was re-organised, a suitable building had been found for the orphanage, and the first Italian children were taken from the streets and given a mother's love and care, and a good scrub-down.

So often God gives his saints the strength to overcome obstacles which humanly speaking seem insuperable. Frances, despite her frail appearance, was one of the ablest women in history. She never learned the language of the country properly, but her extraordinary ability to get the best out of people and circumstances whirled her along on a wind which swept before it every barrier. Her love for children spread like a bright flame across half the world, fanned by the wind of her faith and courage.

The New York settlement flourished. Requests for her help poured in—from Buenos Aires, from Panama, from Costa Rica, Los Angeles, Chicago. Mother Cabrini met them all, until her programme looked like a super tourist guide's itinerary.

In her own lifetime St. Frances made more than fifty foundations. Her Sisters —numbering seven to begin with—increased to a thousand. Orphanages, high schools, hospitals; homes for immigrants, for prisoners, for the destitute, were established, embracing men, women and children of every nationality.

For England she had a special affection, and she visited the country in 1902 and again in 1906 where the first school at Brockley was by then quietly progressing.

But in the years which followed she became increasingly frail although her work still continued. She died alone in her room in the new hospital at Chicago in 1917.

Fifty years before her canonisation in 1946 Pope Leo XIII said of her . . . "Mother Cabrini is a woman of fine understanding and great holiness . . . she is a saint."

St. Benedict Joseph Labre

"You look like the beggar Labre. . . ." Long after the saint's death, the country women who remembered him as he passed through their villages, would chide their children as they ran, dirty and ill-kept, through the streets.

"Would it then be so very terrible to look like the beggar Labre?"

"Not terrible, mon petit, not terrible, if the dirt and the mud were suffered for the love of Christ. . . ."

"And the lice, Mamma, and the heavy cross of wood he carried sometimes through the forests . . . he passed through this place, did he not? And he begged for scraps and gave them to those worse off than himself. And he walked many times between Loreto and Rome . . . and to Compostella to the shrine of St. James. . . ."

"Yes, mon petit, and to Montserrat and to Bari and many other places . . . and the mountain paths among the Alps and the Pyrenees knew his blessed feet . . . and the shepherds heard his voice raised sweetly in praise of God. . . ."

"And he was born, Mamma, in a village like ours—at Amettes in the Province of Artois. And he could see the mountains as he worked with his father in the fields—could he not, Mamma, as we can see them?"

"Yes, mon petit, if we lift up our eyes we too can look upon the mountains . . . but we cannot see them with his eyes for he was a saint, that one, a beggar saint. . . ."

Benedict Joseph Labre was born on March 28 in 1748. When he was still quite small he went to live with his uncle who was a priest in a neighbouring village, and Benedict took part in the life of the parish. He was a serious, thoughtful child, lovable and loving; he was clever too, and his parents were proud of him. With confidence they looked forward to the time when he would become a parish priest like his uncle.

In the presbytery library Benedict found books which he read and absorbed and which helped to form his resolve to give everything to Christ.

The beggar Labre

He began in a small way, denying himself the fruit from his uncle's orchard, his favourite sweets, observing perfect obedience to those in authority over him. Slowly he grew convinced that he could serve God best by withdrawing himself altogether from the world, and there was one Order which appealed to him above all the others because of the utter severity. This was La Trappe, the strictest religious Order for men in the whole world. But his parents when they heard of his decision opposed it with all their might. He was too sensitive, too delicate. Did he want to die before he was twenty?

Acting on the advice of his priest uncle, Benedict gave up all thought of La Trappe. Instead he asked their permission to become a Carthusian. The name "Carthusian" terrified them less—their eldest son need not go so far from home, and so at last they gave their consent.

To their secret astonishment, the prior of the monastery would not accept

their son, saying that he was not strong enough to endure the rigid discipline imposed on his monks; it was to be the first of many refusals.

Benedict returned home heart-broken. In the months which followed he helped his father in the fields in the daytime, but at night in the seclusion of his attic, he spent many hours in secret prayer, before lying down to rest on the bare wooden plank which served as his bed.

His mother watched over him anxiously. He was so strange, this son of hers, so different from the rest of her children; so obedient and good and gentle—and yet for that all so resolute. Then what she had been subconsciously dreading came to pass. Benedict told her that God did not mean him to be a Carthusian, that he must, after all, offer himself to La Trappe.

Reluctantly, his father gave him not only his consent but his blessing, and Benedict set out. He journeyed a long way, through forests, across moors and over mountains, until he came to the monastery of his dreams—and there too he was met by a refusal.

And so—once again, Benedict returned home in a pitiable state of poverty and exhaustion. Time passed. Benedict could not forget La Trappe; he resolved to try again, and this time the entire village united to prevent him . . . to no avail.

It must have been a moment of supreme joy to Benedict when the gates of the monastery closed—shutting him in—not out. But it was a joy which disappeared when his prior told him: "We want you to go. You have no vocation."

This time the saint did not make tracks for home. Convinced at last that God did not want him to be a monk, he asked himself: "What does He want?" There was no lightning-flash from heaven to tell him—only the growing conviction that he could serve his Master best by undertaking a series of pilgrimages to give honour to His friends.

The hardships of the road equalled anything Benedict could have found at La Trappe. And besides, he deliberately added to the hardships, for what could equal the sufferings of his beloved Christ? He who had once been neat and careful about his clothes and person was now content to tramp the roads as a beggar, an outcast of society, as his Master had been. He journeyed to the shrine of St. James at Compostella and from there to most of the shrines in Europe. He endured bitter cold and burning heat. He slept in barns, under hedges, in open fields. His clothes were in rags, his broken shoes no protection from the flints of the mountain paths. The children threw stones at him, the dogs snapped at his heels, the youths mocked him.

The only outward sign of his vocation was the wooden rosary which hung round his neck. He talked little but sometimes a passer-by would listen in astonishment to the Latin prayers which came to his lips.

Sometimes he would ring a small bell after the manner of the lepers of the sixteenth century to warn pilgrims to keep their distance . . . not because he wished to worship solitarily before the shrine, but because he knew he was verminous and in fairness desired other men to know it too.

Only as we grow older shall we be able to understand something of the love which the saint held for Christ Crucified. The lice and filth, and the shame they caused, which he embraced with such passionate sincerity, were for Benedict landmarks along the Way of the Cross. Our Lord chose to be the most despised and rejected of men. Benedict was surely while he lived the most despised and rejected of beggars.

Eighteenth-century Rome was teeming with beggars; there were no official government schemes either to house or feed them, but there were plenty of private charitable organisations—many of them in the hands of priests and nuns —which set out to relieve their wants.

The saint made six pilgrimages to the tombs of the apostles before in 1777 he made up his mind finally to settle in Rome, and except for one more pilgrimage to Loreto, his journeys round the shrines of Europe came to an end.

Beggars in their hundreds thronged the Colosseum, but even so, Benedict soon became noticed. Morning and evening he made the Stations of the Cross, his tall, gaunt figure moving quietly from one Station to the next. Sometimes he would remain for hours on his knees, arms outstretched before the Image of Christ.

At night, despite charitable efforts to persuade him to sleep in one of the hospices for the destitute, he chose a hole among the ruins. No longer now

Mocked and stoned by the urchins of Rome

permitting himself to beg for scraps, he accepted—when it was offered to him— a crust of bread or a bowl of soup, which as often as not he gave to one he considered more in need than himself.

The Roman urchins mocked him and stoned him as he walked through the streets—and yet these same ragamuffins were the first to set up the cry: "The saint is dead" when death at last claimed him.

Among the small shopkeepers who peddled their goods in the slums which then bounded the Colosseum on all sides was one, Zaccarelli, a butcher by trade. And it was to his house Benedict was carried after he had collapsed on the steps of the church of the Madonna dei Monti. It was the Wednesday of Holy Week in the year 1783. Those who had come to know him well believed that so close was he to Christ in his Passion that he would surely die during the Holy Week ceremonies, and so there was no surprise, only a tremendous sense of loss as the beggar of their Colosseum closed his eyes in his last long sleep.

St. Catherine Labouré

The story of St. Catherine Labouré is the story of The Miraculous Medal. It is, too, the story of a little French girl called Zoe, who did not take the name of "Catherine" until she became a nun.

Zoe was born in the French village of Fains-les-Moustiers, in the year 1806, one of a family of ten. It was a happy and united family, but all too soon the mother died, and Zoe, still young enough to be playing with her dolls, found herself taking her mother's place in the home. She swept and dusted and cared for her brothers and sisters, and when there was a moment to spare, she visited the beautiful little village church to say

Catherine's first vision

her rosary and ask Our Lady to help her to perform all her duties well.

And every night as her father came home from working his bit of land, Zoe was there to greet him, often in the yard near the pigeon house. The pigeons— her father kept seven hundred of them— knew her so well that sometimes as she fed them they seemed to form a crown as they circled over her head.

Everybody in the village loved the little girl, not only because she worked so hard to make things comfortable for her family, but because she was so good. Nobody was surprised when at last, at the age of eighteen, Zoe said that she would like to become a nun. But she had to wait six long years before her father would consent to let her go.

For a time, she was undecided about the choice of an Order, and then one night St. Vincent de Paul appeared to her in a dream and Zoe's mind was made up. She would enter the novitiate of the Sisters of Charity, which St. Vincent had founded. This she did, on April 21, 1830.

The mother house of the Order was in the Rue de Bac in Paris, and it was there that Zoe, now taking the name of Catherine, had her visions.

Just four months after entering, Catherine was suddenly awakened one night by the call of a young child. The child, shining with light, beckoned to her, and Catherine, startled and afraid, hesitated. "Come to the chapel," the child said. "Come quickly."

Catherine still hesitated: "They will hear me," she whispered nervously. "The other Sisters will waken."

But the child whose brightness filled the whole room, insisted, and Catherine dressed herself and followed him.

Her child-guide led her straight to the altar rails. Catherine knelt down, suddenly conscious that the whole chapel was brilliantly lit. She knelt there for a long time, not daring to speak. The child too was silent as he watched her from a place inside the sanctuary. Then, he spoke: "Here is the Blessed Virgin. Here she is."

The little Sister was scarcely able to believe that Mary, the Mother of God, should choose to appear to somebody as humble as herself, but the child spoke to her quite sternly, and, convinced, Catherine flung herself at the feet of the Virgin. Mary talked to her, telling her that a mission was about to be entrusted to her and that she would have much suffering before it was finally accomplished.

"I cannot tell," Sister Catherine said afterwards, "how long I remained with the Blessed Virgin. All I know is that after speaking with me for some time, she vanished like a shadow."

The child then, with sweet courtesy, conducted her back to the dormitory, before he left her.

Catherine did not see the Blessed Virgin again until November. She was making her evening meditation in the chapel when Our Lady appeared to her "white as the dawn." She stood upon a globe and she held in her hands another globe, and suddenly, "her fingers were covered with rings, set with rare precious stones, from which sprang rays of such brilliance that her feet and robe were no longer visible. The stones were of different sizes and the rays varied in their brilliance. I cannot tell all I felt or how much I learnt in that short space of time. . . ."

Our Lady then spoke to her: "This globe which you see," she said, "represents the whole world, and France in particular, and each person individually . . . behold the symbol of the graces I bestow on those who ask for them."

Catherine described afterwards all that she saw. It seemed to her that Our Lady was all at once framed by a kind of oval frame around which were written the words "*O Mary conceived*

Catherine's second vision

without sin, pray for us who have recourse to Thee" in letters of gold.

"Then it seemed," she went on, "as though the frame turned round, and I could see at the back of it the letter M, surmounted with a crown of thorns. And as I looked the voice spoke again: 'Have a medal struck according to this pattern. Those who wear it when blessed will receive great graces, especially if they wear it round their necks. There will be abundant grace for those who have confidence.'"

But although Catherine faithfully reported her visions to her director, no steps were taken to carry out Our Lady's wishes for a long time, and the gentle lay-Sister suffered a great deal. It was so hard to wait patiently for something which the Blessed Virgin had so very specially asked might be done. Then at last the medal was struck and Mary kept her promise. Miracles of grace followed which convinced even the most sceptical.

Sister Catherine, her mission accomplished, lived out her years in the convent —hidden, humble years with nothing showing either in her conversation or conduct that she had had to do with The Miraculous Medal. She died on December 31, 1876, and was canonised on July 27, 1947.

St. John Baptist Vianney, The Curé D'Ars

If John had lived in our own age he would have been labelled "backward." He didn't make much of the job his poor, harassed parents set him—that of ploughboy—and they were thankful indeed when the Abbé Balley, a good and understanding man, said that their son might come and live in his house and be trained for the priesthood.

But France, under Napoleon, was in a state of unrest. Every available young man was being conscripted into the mighty French army. John was called up, and he made as poor a soldier as he had a ploughman. He even lost his regiment, having fallen out on one of the long marches.

John must have sighed with relief when he found himself back in the Abbé's house, but there were battles ahead of him—intellectual battles— which all but defeated him. He simply could not get Latin into his head—and as for theology—most of it was so far above his understanding that his kindly tutor all but gave him up. And yet— John was learning how to pray, learning to love God with such purity and intensity that when at last he was ordained and became for a time the Abbé's curate, people clamoured to hear him preach. And John was terrified!

During the Revolution, France had been spiritually in a state of decay. Churches had been closed, bells silenced, and priests when caught, guillotined. When John was given the sleepy little village of Ars for his parish, he found in it every sign that the people had forgotten their faith. His new parishioners were quite polite, some of them even friendly, but they had been so long without a priest, that they saw no reason to take notice of one when he came.

They cared nothing about their duties, and after long days in the fields were content to spend the nights drinking heavily, or dancing wildly.

To begin with, they met the fiery blue eyes of their new Curé without shame. But later and without any fuss or advertisement, the whole character of the village changed. "Ars is no longer Ars!" the Curé exclaimed once, and it was true. And yet M. Vianney preached

St John Baptist Vianney preaching to his parishioners

no new, startling truths, it was just that when he talked to his congregation he made every one listening suddenly and vividly conscious of God and of God's love for every soul.

Something happened also to the Presbytery—all but the essential bits of furniture disappeared; the bed was given away, so were the armchairs and the cushions. The Curé made do very well with two planks, and as for his meals—he allowed himself so little time to eat that he found the most practical way of lunching was to boil enough potatoes to last a week . . . what he did for breakfast and supper nobody quite knew, but he was so little interested in his material comforts that it seemed most likely he went without.

M. Vianney was able to read men's hearts. You couldn't pretend with him. He knew and was able to direct the lives of perfect strangers. And the fame of this humble parish priest spread like a rainbow across the sky. It drew men from every part of France. And from countries across the seas. Thousands flocked to Ars to speak with him, to wait for days and weeks for the chance of going to his confessional.

And to keep pace with the demands laid upon him, the Curé rose at one in the morning. He made his way then to the church and was there alone with God until the first of his penitents arrived. After Mass, he was available to all who sought him. At eight, he drank half a glass of milk, at eight-thirty he heard confessions again—for three hours at a stretch.

Then came the children for catechism. At twelve he made his way through the crowds to the Presbytery where he ate his hasty meal, usually standing up. Half an hour later he was on his rounds, visiting the sick. His visits completed, back to church to hear confessions which lasted until eight. Evening service, prayers, confessions followed. At midnight he went to bed.

He tried to run away, not because he was afraid of the hard work, but because he was so humble he felt the village might gain from having another pastor. The village ran after him and brought him back.

He was attacked and criticised by some of his fellow clergy whose lives fell so far short of his own, and meekly and with most wonderful charity he accepted their rebukes. The devil tried to burn him out of house and home by setting fire to his bed and by plaguing him with attentions—but what can the devil do against a saint?

Born three years before the Revolution in 1786, he died just under one hundred years ago in 1859—so worn out that people felt they could almost literally see through him, and yet as he was dying he murmured: "I do not know if I have well carried out my ministry."

St. Teresa-of-the-Child-Jesus, The Little Flower

Have you ever taken your watch to be mended and waited while the watchmaker prised open the case and peered into its works? If you had lived in the French town of Alençon, towards the end of the last century, and your watch had gone wrong, you might have taken it along to Monsieur Louis Martin, the watchmaker.

But the world at large would have shown no interest in M. Martin if he had not had a daughter christened Marie-Françoise-Thérèse.

So many books have been written, so many sermons preached, so many miracles wrought, that the name of "The Little Flower" is known in every corner of the earth, and hundreds of thousands of pilgrims visit the Carmelite convent at Lisieux, where on April 9, 1888, Teresa, the watchmaker's daughter, became its youngest novice. She was fifteen.

Two of her sisters were there already; Marie, the eldest, had gone when Teresa was nine, and Pauline who had looked after the little family after their mother's death, entered when she was fourteen. Impatient to follow them, Teresa while on a pilgrimage to Rome with her father broke the rule of silence in the Pope's presence to beg him to permit her to enter Carmel at fifteen.

"You shall enter it if it be God's will," Pope Leo XIII said, with great kindliness, and Teresa completed the pilgrimage in a spirit of hope. At the end of that year, permission, previously refused, was given by the bishop, and Teresa entered Carmel.

Teresa had been her father's favourite child; she was so gay, so attractive and so lovable, and both suffered intensely when the hour of parting came, but there was never a doubt in her mind that this was her vocation, and from the start she determined to be a saint.

We shall all be saints when we see God in heaven, but Teresa resolved to make her heaven on earth. The life of a Carmelite nun is a hidden life and a hard one by our worldly standards.

Although Teresa's health was delicate, she desired no dispensation from the austere rule, and was given none. She suffered intensely from the cold and from exhaustion in carrying out some of the exterior physical penances customary to the rule.

"I am a very little soul, who can only offer very little things to Our Lord," she said once, "but I want to seek a way to Heaven, a new way, very short, very straight, a little path . . . I would like to find a lift to raise me to Jesus for I am

Photo Mansell

St. Teresa, the Little Flower, as a novice at the age of fifteen too little to go up the steep steps of perfection. . . ."

Teresa found her lift; it bore her swiftly through dark periods of spiritual suffering, through long nights of bodily pain, upwards and upwards, until she was safe at last in the arms of her Beloved Jesus.

Before she died, she completed her autobiography written at the request of her prioress. It was called *L'Histoire d'une Âme* (The Story of a Soul), and has since been translated into many different languages; it is full of beauty and wisdom and courage, and from it you can learn something of The Little Flower's sanctity, for she tells how she made of herself a plaything of Christ. He could pick her up like a ball, cherish her or throw her away. Whatever he did, she was secure in his love.

Sister Teresa of Lisieux died on September 30, 1897. In the June of that year she had been taken to the infirmary of the convent suffering from severe haemorrhages, and she never left it again.

Three of her utterances made about that time have since gone round the world, and no note on The Little Flower however short would be complete without them:

"I have never given the good God aught but love, and it is with love that he will repay. After my death I will let fall a shower of roses." "I will spend my Heaven in doing good upon earth." "My little way is the way of spiritual childhood, the way of trust and absolute self-surrender."

Almost immediately after her death, miracles through her intercession were so numerous that the Holy See dispensed the customary fifty years which should normally pass before a cause of canonisation is begun.

In 1922 she was solemnly beatified by Pope Pius XI and two years later, Teresa-of-the-Child-Jesus was canonised.

As one of the chief tasks of the Carmelites is to pray for the missions, it was not surprising that in 1927 St. Teresa was named the heavenly patroness of all foreign missions with St. Francis Xavier.

For Catholics and non-Catholics alike, The Little Flower continues to let fall her shower of roses, and those who are wise enough to grasp the precious petals find themselves drawn irresistibly to Jesus.

Pope St. Pius X

Two boys perched on a ramshackle old donkey-cart trundled along the road that led from Riese, their village, to Castelfranco, that lovely old Italian city, where they went to school. They were brothers, and the older of the two was Giuseppe or Bepi Sarto.

The donkey was slow and obstinate and the road was rough, but it was better than trudging the four miles barefoot, and there was so much to think about and so much to talk about. Soon now Bepi would be entering the seminary. And if things worked out well it would be to the seminary in Padua he would go.

If things worked out well . . . but his father was only the village postman and they were so poor.

"But you are so clever," Angelo his young brother would sometimes console him. "Even at the village school you were cleverer than all the rest. And everybody loves you. Surely things will turn out well for you . . ."

Every night Bepi enquired anxiously if there was a letter, a letter which would decide his fate. For a time the whole

Bepi and Angelo on the way to school

family could think and pray about nothing else, for Bepi's vocation was so obvious. And then it came. Bepi had been accepted at the famous seminary, and that night not only his family but the whole village rejoiced with him.

And so at fifteen, the merry, generous-hearted young peasant set out for Padua. Not even his best friends could have predicted the brilliant future that was to be his, but they would have said confidently: "Whatever his successes, our Bepi will stay as he is, modest and humble and great-hearted."

In 1858, at the age of twenty-three, Bepi's seminary life was over. And although normally his ordination would not take place until he was twenty-four, a dispensation was granted, and Bepi did not have to wait. He returned to Riese where as a newly ordained priest he sang his first Mass.

For ten years Don Bepi was the curate in the sleepy little village of Tombolo in the province of Padua, and became so greatly loved that his people were heart-broken when at last he was appointed Rector of Salzano.

"We could not hope to keep him," they told each other, "his sermons are so beautiful, and he is kind and good and understanding, and so hard-working."

Even when Giuseppe was made a Canon and then a Bishop, they still said of him that "he was everybody's servant."

As Bishop of Mantua, his first care was to teach Christian doctrine. Everywhere throughout his diocese he established schools and confraternities, and often on one of his pastoral visits, he would gather round him the children and himself instruct them. How he loved the children and how they loved him!

From Bishop to Cardinal! On June 12, 1893, Pope Leo XIII named Bishop Sarto Cardinal of the Holy Roman Church and Patriarch of Venice. He

Courtesy Hoxton & Walsh Ltd.

Pope Saint Pius X

returned to Riese, and in his scarlet cappa magna, stood by his mother's bed. She was very old and very frail and she did not live very long afterwards, but it must have been for her a moment of pure joy. Her son was a Prince of the Church; her little Bepi who had run so often barefoot along the dusty roads, who had helped her so willingly with all the work.

In 1903 Leo died, and Cardinals all over the world received notice to attend the conclave for the election of his successor.

Cardinal Sarto set out late from Venice. The people crowded round him at the station, begging for his blessing, half afraid that they were going to lose him for ever. But no thought of leaving them was in the Cardinal's mind: "Alive or dead, I shall come back," he assured them.

But he did not come back, for the Cardinals voted that he should become Pope. At first he pleaded "I am unworthy, I am not qualified, forget me." Later he accepted—in tears, and robed in the white cassock with the ring upon his finger, he sat upon St. Peter's throne to receive their obedience.

He chose the name of Pius, and he became a great and wonderful Pope who ruled over his spiritual children with understanding love and deep wisdom.

There is space here to mention only one of the many important Encyclicals which he wrote, and it was the first. In it he said that the frequent use of the Blessed Sacrament was one of the ways of restoring all things in Christ, and on December 20, 1906, he issued a Decree which said: "The primary purpose of the Holy Eucharist is not that the honour and reverence due to Our Lord may be safeguarded, not that the Sacrament may serve as a reward of virtue, but that the faithful, being united to God by holy communion, may thence derive strength to resist sinful desires, to cleanse themselves from daily faults, and to avoid those serious sins to which human frailty is liable. Frequent and daily communion, as a thing most earnestly desired by Christ our Lord and by the Catholic Church should be open to all the faithful of whatever rank and condition of life. . . ."

That is why sometimes Pope Pius X is known as the Saint of the Holy Eucharist, and his Decree, which put an end to all controversy about frequent or infrequent communions, affects all our lives. Pius was not just thinking about grown-ups; children too, he said, should be encouraged to receive Holy Communion as often as possible.

One of the things which gave the Pope so much delight was the number of letters which came to him from children who had made their First Communion.

And whenever the opportunity arose he gathered children about him. The children were never shy or afraid; they loved him and he loved them. It was all as simple as that.

The outbreak of the First World War in 1914 all but broke the Holy Father's great and tender heart; he had striven so hard to restore peace to the world that he could not contemplate without the deepest sense of grief all the suffering that lay ahead for his children.

He did not live to see it, for in the August of the same year he became suddenly ill. He died, as he had lived, very simply and very quietly, and on the 23rd he was buried in the crypt of St. Peter's.

The Inscription on his tomb translated reads thus:

Pope Pius X
Poor yet rich
Meek and humble of heart
Undaunted champion of the Catholic
Faith
Having done so much
To restore all things in Christ
Died holily August 20, A.D. 1914.

Having done so much . . . and in recognition, Bepi, the peasant boy, the village postman's son, was canonised in St. Peter's at Rome on May 29, 1954.

Epstein
Virgin and Child, statue on the outside wall of the Convent of the Holy Child of Jesus, London

SHRINES AND PILGRIMAGES

Besides the Holy Land, where Jesus himself had lived, there have been many other places to which pilgrims travelled.

Rome, the See of Peter and the centre of Christendom, was—and is—a goal for pilgrim hearts. For centuries, the town of Compostella, in the West of Spain, has drawn throngs of devout visitors, for there, in a magnificent tomb in the Cathedral, rested the body of the Apostle St. James.

It would take a whole book even to give the names of famous shrines and places of pilgrimage. England alone had so many that a whole shelf of books could be written about them because behind the story of the shrine itself lay the history of the saint, and all the miracles which took place after his death. Waterton's *Pietas Mariana Britannica* is one famous book telling about shrines of Our Lady in Britain. Ely, Evesham, Fountains, Ipswich, Islington, Muswell, Westminster, Willesden—these are only a sprinkling of great names, echoing the stories of centuries of loving prayer and courageous pilgrimage. Of all the many we will tell of two: of Walsingham and of Canterbury.

The story of Walsingham, a village in Norfolk, begins with a lady, a grand lady, called Richeldis de Faverches, who in the year 1061 had a vision.

Having prayed for a long time that she might in some way do honour to Our Lady, Richeldis was shown in her vision the little House in Nazareth where Jesus had lived as a boy with Mary and Joseph; she was told to build it exactly to measurement, and to build it at Walsingham.

The house, which was in fact a replica of the famous Little House of the Holy Family preserved at that time beneath the Basilica of the Annunciation, was fashioned by skilled craftsmen under her direction.

On its completion the problem of where it should rest was solved in a miraculous way. A heavy dew soaked the entire meadow close to where the carpenters were working—all but for

Our Lady of Walsingham

two small patches of ground, one of which was close to two holy wells.

The widow chose the spot nearest to the wells and the builders laid down the foundation stone. To their dismay, the construction would not fit, and they gave up in despair. Not so the practical Richeldis! Convinced that Our Lady would do something about it, she spent the night in prayer, and lo, in the early morning, angels removed the House to the second spot marked out by the dew and some little distance from the wells, where it rested perfectly securely for the next five hundred years.

In time the Little Holy House was enshrined in a magnificent Lady Chapel; it passed into the hands of the Augustinians who built a priory there in the reign of Edward III.

Pilgrims in their thousands made their way to the Shrine of Our Lady at Walsingham, and England became known as the "Holy Land, Our Lady's Dowry." The statue of Our Lady, it is generally accepted, was made of wood, and

wonderfully bejewelled; in her hand she carried a lily-sceptre; on her knee sat the Holy Child; under her feet was a toadstone, a symbol of evil.

A medieval pilgrim on his way to Walsingham wore the pilgrim's badge, and carried the pilgrims' staff. The miles he trod, usually barefoot, were marked off by the crosses set by the wayside. The monasteries opened their doors to him and gave him food and shelter.

The great as well as the lowly trod the Pilgrim's Way. Practically all the kings of England from Henry III until Henry VIII gave honour to Our Lady at Walsingham, and made rich gifts to the priory and chapel.

At the Chapel of St. Catherine, better known as the "Slipper Chapel," pilgrims finally rested, and if they were wearing sandals they left them there so that they might walk the last mile or so barefoot; even royalty halted there, and Henry VIII as a young and devout pilgrim left his royal slippers in the chapel. Later, he was responsible for the total destruction of the shrine, and the death of eleven men of Walsingham who tried in vain to save it.

In 1538 the shrine at Walsingham perished in flames, the statue of Our Lady being publicly burned at Chelsea, and no more was heard of it for three hundred years. During the last century excavations were started among the ruins of the priory, and the thoughts of the faithful turned once again towards Walsingham.

In his fascinating book *Famous Shrines of Our Lady*, H. M. Gillet tells the story of how it was decided to build a replica of the Holy House of Loreto at the parish church of the Annunciation at King's Lynn; of how, at the very end of the nineteenth century, a lady named Miss Charlotte Boyd purchased "the dilapidated but still intact chapel of St. Catherine's desiring nothing better than to see this chapel restored as a shrine of Our Blessed Lady. . . ."

In 1934 there took place along the Walsingham Way, a great national pilgrimage led by the late Cardinal Bourne, then Archbishop of Westminster—Our Lady was once more enshrined at Walsingham. Fourteen years later, in 1948, groups of men carrying heavy crosses of oak, converged on Walsingham, and on July 16 a procession as mighty and impressive as any in the Middle Ages, and led by the late Cardinal Griffin, Archbishop of Westminster, made its way slowly along the Pilgrim's Way to the Shrine of Our Lady.

Canterbury

Sacrilegious hands stripped the shrines of England as they laid waste her abbeys and monasteries in the days of Henry VIII. They robbed Canterbury, but though the wealth and splendour of the Martyr's tomb has gone, the memory of this great place of pilgrimage will never fade; it is set for ever in men's minds because of Geoffrey Chaucer.

This great genius, among the foremost poets of England, wrote the story of a pilgrimage to Canterbury. He wished

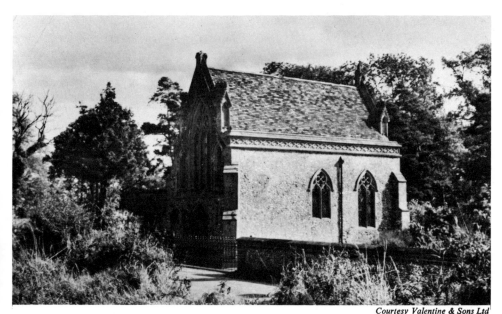

Courtesy Valentine & Sons Ltd

The Slipper Chapel at Walsingham

to paint a picture of English life, so he took a scene that was at the very heart of English life, the pilgrimage to Canterbury.

Who is there who does not know that Canterbury was the shrine of the "holy blissful martyr" (as Chaucer calls him) St. Thomas Becket? The story of his resistance against King Henry II, in defence of the rights of the Church, is part of English history.

"Who will rid me of this troublesome priest?" the angry king had cried. The murder in the cathedral which followed these words horrified all Christendom, and it was to atone for the sacrilege that the shrine of the martyr was made so magnificent that it defied description. For three hundred years it was a place of pilgrimage for all the Christian world.

But it was not only because of St. Thomas Becket that Canterbury was a pilgrim's goal. Long, long before it had been a shrine for prayer. It was the cradle of Christianity for the Angles and Saxons whom Augustine had converted. It was the resting place of a long line of Archbishops, many of whom were hailed as saints. Here lay Dunstan. Here lay St. Alphege, whose courage had saved the country from the savagery of the Norsemen in A.D. 994.

The story of this hermit-saint is not nearly so well known as it might be; here it is. After the death of the wise Dunstan, our island, always a tempting proposition to the barbaric Norsemen, was once again invaded. At the time, Alphege was a holy hermit shut off from the world in his hermitage at Bath, though his sanctity was widely acclaimed.

The Norsemen swept through Kent, death and destruction in their train; nothing could stop them. Nothing: certainly not an army. In the humility of their defeat, the people turned to Alphege. The hermit faced the invader at Southampton. He routed him—by

the power of the Faith. What actually happened was that so bravely and convincingly did he put Christ's cause that he converted the Norse Prince to Christianity.

The Prince drew off his men, vowing that never in his lifetime would the island suffer invasion from his countrymen. England was saved—by a holy hermit—and the people would not rest until he had been elected Archbishop of Canterbury.

The country grew prosperous, for while the King of Norway (the one-time Prince) lived, there was nothing to fear from invasion. But the good king died, and in his place another ruled who saw no need to honour an ancient pledge. In A.D. 1041 the Norsemen returned; they attacked Canterbury, burning the cathedral, murdering priests and laymen alike. Alphege they took prisoner and bore him off to Greenwich with the idea of holding him up to ransom.

The saintly Archbishop would have none of it; stoutly forbidding his flock to contribute one halfpenny towards any kind of fund—and meanwhile busily converting to the faith half the heathen soldiers in the camp.

How it would have ended if Alphege had lived is the historian's business, but he did not, for he was killed by some of the very pagan soldiers he had come to look upon with something like affection. His courage in trying to prevent their drunken brawl turning into something more deadly resulted in his own end. First to St. Paul's they took his body, and then in A.D. 1033 to Canterbury, where for centuries the people of England showed how well they remembered what he had done for them by venerating his shrine.

The Holy Land, as we have said, is the place to which Christians chiefly wished in ancient days to go on pilgrimages. Where Jesus lived and taught and died,

Death of Thomas Becket

Photo Mansell

his followers longed to go. They do so still.

St. Ignatius of Loyola desired at first to spend all his life there, preaching to the Moslems. But there have been great difficulties down the centuries about visiting the Holy Land; the Crusades began because of such difficulties raised up by the followers of Mohammed against Christian pilgrims. So there is a special interest about the shrine of Loreto. Since the Christians could not go to the Little House at Nazareth, the little house was brought to them. This happened at the end of the thirteenth century, just about two hundred years after the model of the Holy House was built at Walsingham.

Loreto is in Italy, close to the Adriatic coast. How the Little House of the Holy Family came to rest there is a story

which makes us think of magic carpets and Arabian Nights, and all the more so, because for the first twelve hundred years the House of Our Lady was preserved at Nazareth.

Then came the first of its two great journeys, conducted by God's own messengers, the angels; for at the end of the thirteenth century the Little Holy House disappeared from Nazareth—to reappear at Tersatto in Dalmatia.

The shepherds who discovered it in their fields consulted their parish priest, who confirmed, having been warned in a dream of its arrival, that it was indeed the House from Nazareth.

What the holy parish priest knew by divine inspiration, the faithful learned to know and accept by simple material proof, for it was shown later on that the

Little House was of the exact size, and identical substance as the House of Nazareth.

The faithful of Tersatto rejoiced to have such a wonderful shrine in their midst, but grief followed soon enough, for just over three years later the Holy House once again took wing—it came to rest at Loreto, and from 1294 onwards pilgrims crowded the roads that led to the home of the Holy Family.

A long line of popes and saints (among them Francis Xavier, Charles Borromeo, Stanislaus Kostka, Francis de Sales) have worshipped at this shrine, which has become the greatest in the Christian world in honour of Our Lady, linked as it is in the hearts of the faithful with England's Walsingham.

Our Lady spent the last part of her life near Ephesus. In recent years pilgrimages have been resumed to the little house at Panaya Kapula, where she lived. It is very consoling to know that not only Christians, but Turkish Moslems too, now go there on pilgrimage, for the Turkish Moslems greatly reverence Mary, Hazret Meryem Ana, as they call her.

These are places where Our Lady lived. There is, of course, no shrine at any place where she was buried, because she was assumed into heaven. But there are countless shrines dedicated to her, and many of these are in places where she has shown herself in apparitions; others are places where there are famous pictures or statues of her, which have been the instruments of miraculous help given to men.

Most of the great shrines of Christendom are shrines of Mary, because it is Mary who comes to recall us to her Son. There are places made holy by apparitions of the Lord himself, and of these Paray-le-Monial, where he made the revelations of the Sacred Heart is one of the greatest. There are shrines made

sacred by the bodies of saints that rest there, such as St. Peter's in Rome, but we can tell here only about a few, and we will choose from among the many dedicated to Our Lady.

One of them takes us back to the Age of Discovery, the finding of the New World. It is Guadalupe in Mexico.

Our Lady of Guadalupe

The story of Our Lady of Guadalupe, Patroness of the Americas, concerns a poor Aztec Indian called Juan Diego, who lived nearly five hundred years ago in the Mexican village of Cauautitlan.

Before the Spaniards conquered Mexico, the Indians had never seen cows or sheep or horses; they lived primitive, hard lives toiling in their fields for long hours. Their conquerors taught them a new way of life—not altogether welcomed by the Indians who grew to fear their proud Spanish overlords. That is why the missionary fathers, following in the wake of the conquering army, found it difficult to win the trust of the peasants.

Juan Diego had witnessed the destruction of the ancient Aztec temples; had known that the Spanish rulers were often cruel and grasping, but there was no bitterness in his heart against the holy fathers themselves and after listening to them, he and his good wife, Maria Lucia, desired to become Christians. They were among the first, and as there was no church in his village Juan walked fifteen miles each morning by way of a hill called Tepeyac to hear Mass at the Franciscan convent.

The years passed; Maria died. Juan began to find his early morning trek increasingly hard. One morning, it was a Saturday, December 9, 1531, he set out as usual. It was cold and he wrapped his tilma, the Indian's apron-like cloak, more closely round him as the bleak Tepeyac came in sight, but

Our Lady of Guadalupe

scarcely had he set foot on the hill than he was surrounded by an intensely bright light. Dazzled, but unafraid, Juan followed the voice which then spoke his name and seemed to be beckoning him up the slope.

When he reached the top, he saw a lady, whose garments were "shining like the sun," and who told him that she was the Holy Mary, Ever Virgin Mother of the True God. . . .

The short conversation which took place between Juan, the Mexican Indian, and Our Lady Mother of God, who chose to appear before him as an Indian maiden, was tenderly human and matter of fact. For after enquiring where he was going, and being told, Our Lady said: "I want you to do something for me. I wish to have a church built here; it shall be named in my honour and be under my protection. It is my wish to show myself a mother to you and to your people; but you must take my message to the Bishop. Tell him it is I that have spoken. . . ."

Juan's interview with the Bishop, whose palace was in Mexico City, was the most terrifying experience of his life; for one thing he was overawed by the magnificence of his surroundings, and for another he was conscious of the scepticism of the high-born Spaniards surrounding the prelate. But the Bishop himself was kindly tolerant, treating him as a child who believes in a fairy story.

Defeated and humiliated Juan returned to the hill certain that he would find the Lady, and find her he did, standing above the bare rocks, more wondrously radiant than he even remembered.

He told her of his interview with the Bishop and concluded by begging that she send someone of more importance than his poor self with her message. Our Lady's answer gave Juan no choice; he must return again to the Bishop, and so the next day he set out for Mexico City, first hearing Mass. This time his reception was even less favourable, but he went on insisting that a temple must be built on Tepeyac, and at last the Bishop said that next time he came he must bring with him some sign from the Queen of Heaven.

The Bishop's servants trailed the Indian as far as the hill, then unaccountably lost him. Meanwhile Juan was telling the Lady about his latest interview, and listening to her assurance that if he returned in the morning he should have his sign.

But Juan did not return to the summit the next morning; at home he found his uncle seriously ill and the next day was spent in caring for him. The day after he set out to bring the priest, fearing his relative was on the point of death, and in order to avoid a meeting with the Lady, he took the long way round the base of the hill . . . and met the Lady on the lower path! Poor Diego!

But she did not reproach him; she told him that he would find his sign on the summit; that he must pick the flowers he would see growing there among the rocks and take them to the Bishop.

Roses in December and growing in a barren rocky spot at that! Diego filled his tilma with them scarcely knowing what to think. And when at last he was once again in the Bishop's presence, the miracle of the showering, scented flowers which dropped from his tilma was all at once forgotten when the watching prelate and his dignitaries saw that dyed into the coarse material of his cloak was the wonderful, radiant figure of the Queen of Heaven—just as Juan had described her.

In less than three months the chapel was built and the Picture enshrined. Down the centuries millions of pilgrims have shown their devotion to Our Lady of Guadalupe, and today the Picture rests in a magnificent basilica, as freshly beautiful as it was four hundred years ago.

We are all so familiar with the story of little Bernadette Soubirous through the medium of the written word and the screen that it is unnecessary to recount in detail the miracle of Lourdes. The Queen of Heaven in singling out Bernadette for her royal commands astonished the world. No less surprising was her choice of the three small children of Fatima, Lucy, the eldest, being only ten; Francis and Jacinta Mario, her cousins, were nine and seven respectively.

The Miracle at Fatima

Our Lady appeared to them on Sunday, May 13, 1917, while they were watching their sheep. They saw her among the branches of a little evergreen oak, surrounded by light and dressed in a white robe and veil which was beautifully worked in gold. A rosary, the beads of which appeared to be composed of light, hung from her right hand. It was the first of a series of monthly meetings which Our Lady asked the children to keep, and this they did, despite threats and beatings, even imprisonment.

On October 13, the children learned who the beautiful Lady really was: "I am Our Lady of the Rosary," she told them. "I want a chapel built here in my honour where the Rosary must be recited every day. . . ." And then in the presence of a crowd of fifty thousand the sun seemed to spin, not once but three times. Men and women fell to their knees in terror as the sun appeared to be falling out of the sky.

The miracle at Fatima happened in the lifetime of our parents. Our Lady's revelations to the children resulted in the consecration of Portugal, on May 13, 1931, to the Immaculate Heart of Mary, and in a revival of devotion to the Rosary, Our Lady's own prayer.

Both at Lourdes and Fatima, the Queen of Heaven chose to give her royal commands to children. At Beauraing, a village in Belgium, on November 29, 1932, five school-children, one boy and four girls, saw Our Lady for the first time.

Our Lady of Beauraing

Belgian children know the story by heart. Albert Voisin, they will tell you, was eleven, and he had two sisters, Fernande and Gilberte. Fernande was fifteen and Gilberte was thirteen.

Gilberte went to a convent school. She could see the trains—for the classroom windows looked on to a railway. The nuns didn't like the railway or embankment, and were glad that their Lourdes grotto in the garden hid some of its ugliness.

Every day Fernande and Albert went to convent to meet Gilberte; they had to walk under the stone viaduct. This day, it was November 29, 1932, they had with them two friends, Andrée Degeimbre and her sister. She was called Gilberte too, but was only nine.

They were going to do something very naughty on their way home; they were going to pull people's bells and run away. But they didn't after all, because Albert suddenly saw a bright light moving up and down by the viaduct.

Gilbert came out of school and saw it too, so did the others, and as they all stared at it, all at once they knew it was Our Lady. They saw her, you know, very plainly. She was dressed in a long robe of pure white, and far more beautiful than any of their statues.

Of course, nobody believed their story. The next night they saw her again, this time close to the grotto, and she was wearing a golden crown.

How angry their parents were, when they came rushing home with the same story. They said that all the village would be laughing at them; that they were fools and liars. And so angry was

Our Lady of Fatima

Andrée's mother, that she grasped a big stick and took it with her to the grotto. The children saw Our Lady clearly, but Madame Degeimbre did not, and she struck at the bushes with her stick. Then M. Voisin came with a torch and searched all round for evidence, but he could find none.

The children themselves could only repeat over and over again what they had seen, and at last a few grown-ups began to wonder if they were perhaps after all speaking true words.

Did the Lady speak, you ask? Not to begin with, but later when Albert asked her: "Are you the Immaculate Virgin?" the Lady smiled and nodded, and then when he asked: "What do you want?" she said: "Always be good."

The children were good, no ringing of door-bells any more. And they

DESSIN AUTHENTIQUE DE LA GROTTE   DE NOTRE DAME DE LOURDES

Apparition de la Sainte Vierge   à la jeune Bernadette (11 Février 1858)

Photo Mansell

*This is an old engraving which claims to give an authentic picture of the Grotto at Lourdes when
Our Lady appeared to St. Bernadette*

"Universe"

as it looks today

suffered, because people tried to frighten them and make them change their story.

The Lady told them to be certain to come to the garden on the day of the Immaculate Conception. This they did, and their parents came too, and doctors and men who study the diseases of the mind. And the children saw Our Lady, and she was so wonderfully beautiful, that little Gilberte wept, then grew very still. She did not answer when the doctor spoke to her. And so it happened with the others. It was as if they had fallen into a deep sleep, and even though some of the doctors slapped them and pricked them, they did not come to life—until the huge crowd which had gathered to watch finished saying the Rosary.

The children saw the Blessed Virgin many times, thirty-three times in all. Then on January 3, 1933, she said "good-bye" to them. To each she gave a different message, and to each she entrusted a secret which we may not be told.

Many, many pilgrims come to the Shrine of Our Lady of Beauraing. They know her as Our Lady of the Golden Heart, and there have been miracles.

And the children? They are grown up now. Albert is a missionary; the girls married. They are very happy and very good. . . .

We have said that most of the great Shrines of Christendom are shrines of Our Lady. There are few countries which you could name which have not at one time or another had a manifestation of the Virgin Mother. And if we study the history of such shrines we find that frequently Our Lady appeared to her children in order to strengthen them to face some great national crisis, or to comfort them in times of war and persecution.

Our Lady of Hope of Pontmain

The Franco-Prussian war in 1870 tore the heart out of France. Paris had fallen to the Germans. The faithful beseeched Our Lady to avert the next attack. The German army was massed against Laval. Pontmain's turn would come next . . . so thought Cesar Barbadette, the local farmer, as he stoically prepared his animals' feed. Helping him in the barn were his two young sons, Eugène and Joseph.

Eugène saw the beautiful Lady smiling down at him when he crossed to the open door. She seemed to be poised between sky and rooftops and she was surrounded by a triangle of brilliant stars. Excitedly, he described her to his father as wearing a blue dress covered with stars and wearing blue shoes with gold buckles; but the farmer was annoyed with his foolish talk and even when little Joseph announced that he too could see the beautiful Lady, their father remained unconvinced.

Not so their mother; she smacked them first, and then because she had never known them to tell lies, accompanied them into the barn where they prayed together.

Two more children, very much younger, saw the beautiful Lady, and now Eugène cried that there was a red cross on her dress. The grown-ups admitted they could see the triangle of brilliant stars, but that was all.

Then the Curé and the nuns from the convent school arrived, and the crowd grew bigger. Presently, led by their parish priest, they began to recite the Rosary.

Meanwhile, the Queen of Heaven uttered no words; her message was written on a long streamer which slowly unfolded across the sky. There were three messages for her awestruck children: the first in simple French read, "But pray, my children"; the second: "God will soon answer your prayers," which could only mean one thing, that Pontmain would be saved from the

Our Lady of Hope of Pontmain

Prussians, and the third: "My Son allows himself to be moved in compassion." When the third message appeared, the children saw that she was no longer smiling, and that in her hand she clasped a blood-red crucifix.

The grown-ups as well as the children saw the white cloud which then descended and slowly enveloped her.

The events which followed almost within hours convinced all France that the Blessed Mother had indeed intervened to save her children. The Prussians withdrew from Laval; Pontmain was not attacked. Eleven days later the armistice was signed.

Joseph and Eugène eventually became priests, Joseph joining the Oblates of Mary Immaculate whose Congregation were responsible for the beautiful church at Pontmain, consecrated in 1900, and now ranking as a basilica. To it come hundreds of thousands of pilgrims each year, among them soldiers of all ranks, to offer their devotion to Our Lady of Hope of Pontmain.

The Miraculous Medal

But Our Lady does not always choose to manifest herself to children. Below the altar of Our Lady of the Globe in the convent of the Rue du Bac lies enshrined the body of St. Catherine Labouré.

Catherine Labouré joined the Sisters of Charity and began her novitiate in 1830 at their Paris House, 140 Rue du Bac. It was there she had her mystical experiences, and received warning from Our Lady of the Revolution and the sufferings in store for Catholic France. It was there too that she was told to make a medal after the vision which Our Lady revealed to her, and which we now know as The Miraculous Medal.

Our Lady of Salette

In Catherine's own lifetime, but far away from the city's crowded streets, two children were acting as cowherds. They had driven their herd from La Salette, a little French village set among the mountains, to a cool shaded spot where the beasts could drink from a running stream.

Maximin did not know the district well, but Mèlanie, who was fifteen and four years older, had lived all her life at La Salette. Mèlanie saw the Lady first, seated on a rock on the floor of the dried-up river-bed, where they had rested before eating their lunch.

Then Maximin saw her emerging, it seemed, from a great ball of light which dazzled their eyes. They were terribly frightened, although Maximin took courage when he saw that his dog had settled at her feet.

The message which the Mother of God gave to the children on that hot September afternoon in 1846 was one of terrible warning to France and to the world. If the people would not repent and honour her Son, they would suffer. She spoke to them at length, and then she told them each a secret, which both the children during all the interviews and questionings which followed carefully guarded until the Holy Father (Pope Pius IX) asked that they should reveal their secrets to him.

On their return to the farm, Mèlanie and Maximin obeyed Our Lady by trying to make people believe their story. Over and over again, they repeated the warning she had asked to be given to the world. But no one would listen. They were beaten and threatened with terrible punishments, even imprisonment, if they persisted. When that failed, they were offered large bribes to admit they had made it all up. But Our Lady had chosen her messengers well. The children remained faithful to their vision, and then a miracle occurred at the dried-up river-bed; water began to flow freely, and a small blind child received her sight after her eyes had been bathed.

In 1851, after the Holy Father had learned the nature of the secrets en-trusted to the children, the Apparition of Our Lady of Salette was approved by the Holy See.

Our Lady of Salette has warned her children . . . and those who make a pilgrimage to her shrine among the mountains take with them the grave words of Pius IX: "These are the secrets of La Salette; unless the world repent it shall perish."

Our Lady of Czestochowa

There are many great and magnificent shrines of Our Lady to be found all over the world, but perhaps the one with the most interesting history is to be found in south-western Poland on the Hill of Light at Czestochowa.

A Polish Prince in 1382 invited a group of Hungarian monks to come to Poland. They built their monastery on a low hill called the Hill of Light, and the Prince gave into their keeping a wonderful picture of Our Lady and the Child Jesus painted on cypress wood. Legend said that the Picture was the work of St. Luke, the Apostle, but even if it were not quite so ancient, it was certain that it had been venerated by the very early Christians.

So the monks became guardians of the Picture and of many other national treasures, and pilgrims soon found their way to Czestochowa when miracles began to happen at the Shrine.

The monks knew that their monastery was always in danger of being attacked by invaders, and so gradually they fortified it and trained themselves to defend it. And in 1655 it was attacked—by an army of Lutheran Swedes. The Prior heroically defended his monastery and held off the invaders. Then, on Christmas Day, the brave monks, after months of hardship, walked round the ramparts in a procession of the Blessed Sacrament. This so impressed the Swedish general that he called off the siege. How could

Photo *Planet News*

The procession to Our Lady's Shrine at Czestochowa

he hope to break the spirit of such brave men?

On April 1, 1656, just a year after the historic siege, King John Casimir dedicated his country and his people to Our Lady as Queen of the Polish Crown.

Through all the years of war and occupation, pilgrimages to Our Lady's Shrine at Czestochowa have never ceased. Many of the pilgrims walk in groups behind roughly-fashioned Crosses covering hundreds of miles, and on important Feast Days, like the Feast of the Assumption, hundreds of thousands come to Czestochowa to hear Mass, receive Communion and visit the ancient chapel where the Picture is exposed for veneration twice a day.

No wonder then that it was a national event in Poland when the Bishops decided to proclaim a Marian year from April 1, 1956, to May 3, 1957, the Feast of Our Lady Queen of Poland.

A million people gathered round the old monastery-fortress on that great day. The dark chapel was ablaze with lights and candles shining on the walls covered with votive offerings. They shone on the gold frame of the Picture, on the gold screen which covers it when closed, on the jewelled crowns given by Pope Pius X.

The Picture is exposed by the slow raising of the golden screen. Our Lady and Child are visible, the pilgrims crowd forward into the little sanctuary, trumpets and kettle-drums sound from the choir, and there is an indescribable feeling of joy. When the screen slowly descends again, the pilgrims are conscious of sadness, and many of the women sob.

The people of Poland have suffered and died for their faith. Their devotion to Our Lady of Czestochowa on the Hill of Light is something which no anti-Catholic Power can understand or destroy.

Photo Chauffourier

Statue of St Peter in the Basilica of St Peter's, Rome

EPILOGUE

So we close our Book of the Kingdom. It is the end of the Book, but it is not the end of the story. This story will never end, for of this Kingdom there shall be no end. It begins in this world but it will last for ever in heaven.

The Kingdom is the Kingdom of God. We pray for its coming when we say the Our Father. It is given by our heavenly Father to Jesus Christ his Son. To reign in it and be its King Jesus has to win it back, because the people who make up the kingdom had rebelled against his Father and himself. When we pray "thy kingdom come" we are doing our share in the winning back.

That is why the story of the kingdom in this world is the story of the crucifixion. It was through being crucified that Jesus won back his own. That is why the story is of a great battle, a war that is still going on.

The Kingdom of God is not a country or a land. It is a union of men and women. But it is not just a union of people such as makes a nation or an empire. It is a much closer union than that. There is a life that lives in every man and woman in the Kingdom, and that life makes all together into one living whole. Jesus is the life. He lives in each, by his grace, and the living whole of which he is the life, or the Head, is called his Body. It is the Church.

The Church, which is the Kingdom of God, is the most wonderful thing in God's creation. All the marvellous universe which surrounds us, the sun and the moon, the myriad stars, the hills and seas and forests, the flowers and fish and birds and animals, all are made as a setting for this jewel that God holds so dear. For it is more than a jewel; it is a dwelling-place, and more than a dwelling-place. God lives in it, as our souls live in our bodies; and as our bodies are our own, and we think of them as being ourselves, so Jesus speaks of his Body the Church as being himself. "Saul, Saul, why persecutest thou me?" he said, when Saul was persecuting his disciples.

The Church is the Kingdom of God; it is the Heavenly City Jerusalem, "coming down out of heaven from God as a bride adorned for her husband," as St. John the Evangelist wrote in his great vision, the Apocalypse. But the Church is also the union of men and women in Christ in this life, upon the earth.

While it is upon the earth, it is the One, Holy, Catholic and Apostolic Church; it is Roman because the Pope lives in Rome, and the Pope is the viceroy of Christ the King. It is an organised Society of men and women, with laws and government like any other society or nation. It is made up of all the people who have been taken into it by baptism.

Although only a part of the men and women on the earth have been taken into the Church by baptism, yet in another way all men and women belong to the Church. They belong to it because God meant his Church to be made up of all the human race. Jesus died "to gather into one the children of God who were dispersed." We are living through a part of the story of the Kingdom, and that part is the gathering together again.

In the midst of the battle, with the air

all round us thick with smoke, we cannot see all that is going on. It even looks as if Christ the King were being defeated; but God, looking down from the peace of eternity, knows that the victory is won. "Have confidence," said Jesus to his Apostles, "for I have overcome the world."

He has overcome it by love, and though it takes time for the full effect to show, the triumph is assured. The Son will bring back to the divine Majesty "the kingdom of truth and life, the kingdom of holiness and grace, the kingdom of justice and love and peace."

Thus sings the Church in the Holy Mass, in the Preface for the feast of Christ the King. We are watching the unfolding of a vast design. "We are the sons of God," wrote St. John, "and it hath not yet appeared what we shall be." This is "the mystery which hath been hidden from eternity in God who created all things." This is the Kingdom of which our Book, like a stammering child, tells a halting story. None but God can tell the whole.

INDEX

A

AARON, **I**, 355
ABBEYS, **II**, 416
    Cluny, **II**, 310
    Douai, **III**, 298
    Downside, **III**, 307
    Fountains, **II**, 320
    St. Albans, **II**, 312
    Westminster, **II**, 425
ABBOTS, **III**, 206
ABDENAGO, **I**, 91
ABRAHAM, **I**, 5
    founder of Hebrew Nation, **I**, 7
    his Sacrifice of Isaac, **I**, 142, 354
    his Vision, **I**, 42
ACACIA, **I**, 220, 370
ACHAB, King of Israel, **I**, 69
ACHAZ, **I**, 87
ADAM AND EVE, **I**, 35
ADVENT, **I**, 155–160
AFRICA, under Romans, **I**, 186
AGAR, **I**, 44
AGATHA, St., **II**, 213
AGNES, St., **II**, 221
AGNUS DEI, **III**, 262
AGONY, **I**, 382
AKKAD, **I**, 11
ALARIC, **II**, 205
ALB, **III**, 285
ALBAN, St., **II**, 230
ALEXANDER THE GREAT, **I**, 121, 172
    and the High Priest, **I**, 203
ALEXANDRIA, **I**, 172, **II**, 155
ALOYSIUS, St., **III**, 165
ALPHEGE, St., **III**, 352
ALTAR,
    of Incense, **I**, 28
    of Repose, **I**, 267
AMBROSE, St., **II**, 296
AMICE, **III**, 284
AMPÈRE, André, **III**, 177
ANDERTON, Blessed Robert, **III**, 94
ANDREW, St., **I**, 366; **II**, 43–45
ANGELICO, Fra. Beato, **II**, 179, 473
ANGELS, **I**, 141
    and Balaam's Ass, **I**, 146
    and Tobias, **I**, 148
    appear to Abraham, **I**, 42, 143
    at the Tomb, **II**, 16
    Gabriel, **I**, 133, 136, 142
    in Jacob's dream, **I**, 144
    Michael, **I**, 142; **II**, 144
    Raphael, **I**, 142, 154
ANIMALS OF THE BIBLE, **I**, 269
ANNUNCIATION, **I**, 136; **II**, 475
ANTIOCH, **II**, 118, 121, 293–5
ANTONY AND CLEOPATRA, **I**, 181; **II**, 119
ANTONY, St., **II**, 259
APOSTLES, **II**, 31–54, 89–92, 144

APPARITIONS OF OUR LADY,
    at Beauraing, **III**, 357
    at Czestochowa, **III**, 362
    at Fatima, **III**, 356, Story in pictures following p. 162
    at Guadalupe, **III**, 354, Story in pictures following p. 162
    at Pontmain, **III**, 360
    at Salette, **III**, 361
AQUINAS, Thomas, St., **II**, 413, 443–50
ARAMAIC, **I**, 238
ARCHBISHOP, **III**, 205, 219
ARCHITECTURE,
    Gothic, **II**, 419–31
    Romanesque, **II**, 416–18
    modern (Illus.), **III**, following p. 290
ARIUS, **II**, 249, 288
ARK
    of the Covenant, **I**, 28, 200, 208, 220
    Noah's, **I**, 36, 218
ART
    Byzantine, **II**, 265–76
    Gothic, **II**, 428
    from Duccio to Masaccio, **II**, 463–77
    from Mantegna to Rubens, **III**, 17–34
    great Italian, **III**, 23
    modern, (Illus.) **III**, following p. 218
ASCENSION, **II**, 27–30, 92
    symbols, for **I**, 321, **II**, 30
ASH WEDNESDAY, **III**, 257
ASHES FOR REPENTANCE, **I**, 264
ASPERGES, **III**, 260
ASSOCIATIONS, Pious, **III**, 324
ASSUMPTION, **II**, 143–6
ASSYRIANS, **I**, 16
ASTROLOGERS,
    ancient, **I**, 105
    of Nabuchodonosor, **I**, 92
ASTRONOMERS, **III**, 175
ASTRONOMY, **I**, 105; **III**, 8
ATHANASIUS, St., **II**, 288
ATHENS, **I**, 26; **II**, 118, 127
ATONEMENT, Day of, **I**, 30
AUGUSTINE, St., **II**, 297
AUGUSTUS CAESAR, **I**, 125, 181
AZARIAS, **I**, 149

B

BAAL, **I**, 70
BABEL, Tower of, **I**, 41
BABYLON, **I**, 15
    conquered by Cyrus, **I**, 120
    hanging gardens, of, **I**, 17
    kings of, **I**, 15, 90
BACON, Friar Roger, **III**, 1
BADAGES, **III**, 126
BALAAM AND HIS ASS, **I**, 146
BALL, Frances, **III**, 302

371

LIST OF MAPS